Save Our Sons

Save Our Sons

Women, Dissent and Conscription during the Vietnam War

Carolyn Collins

MONASH
UNIVERSITY
PUBLISHING

Save Our Sons: Women, Dissent and Conscription during the Vietnam War
© Copyright 2021 Carolyn Collins
All rights reserved. Apart from any uses permitted by Australia's Copyright Act 1968, no part of this book may be reproduced by any process without prior written permission from the copyright owners. Inquiries should be directed to the publisher.

Monash University Publishing
Matheson Library Annexe
40 Exhibition Walk
Monash University
Clayton, Victoria 3800, Australia
https://publishing.monash.edu/

Monash University Publishing brings to the world publications which advance the best traditions of humane and enlightened thought.

Monash University Publishing titles pass through a rigorous process of independent peer review.

ISBN: 9781925835960 (paperback)
ISBN: 9781925835977 (pdf)
ISBN: 9781925835984 (epub)

Design: Les Thomas
Typesetting: Jo Mullins

Cover image: Sydney SOS protest c.1966.
Mitchell Library, State Library of New South Wales and courtesy SEARCH Foundation.

A catalogue record for this book is available from the National Library of Australia.

CONTENTS

List of Abbreviations vi
Prologue viii
Introduction: 'A Distress Call' xi

    Chapter 1 Dress Rehearsal 1

PART 1: ROLL CALL 19
    Chapter 2   Rebels with a Cause 21
    Chapter 3   The 'Founding Mothers' 45
    Chapter 4   'Mothers Are on the March' 75

PART 2: TAKING IT TO THE STREETS, 1960S 129
    Chapter 5   'Heads Bowed, Hands Clasped', 1965–66 131
    Chapter 6   Gloves Off, 1967–69 158
    Chapter 7   On the World Stage 190
    Chapter 8   'Fan Mail' 199

PART 3: KEEPING UP APPEARANCES, 1970S 217
    Chapter 9   Moratoriums, Chain Gangs and 'Falsies' ... 219
    Chapter 10   The Fairlea Five and the 'Underground' ... 234
    Chapter 11   The Final Push 249
    Chapter 12   Rolling up the Banners 257

Notes 279
Select Bibliography 316
Index 328
Acknowledgements 336
About the Author 338

LIST OF ABBREVIATIONS

ABC	Australian Broadcasting Corporation
ACC	Abolish Conscription Campaign
AICD	Association for International Co-operation and Disarmament
ALP	Australian Labor Party
ASIO	Australian Security Intelligence Organisation
CICD	Campaign for International Co-operation and Disarmament
CND	Campaign for Nuclear Disarmament
CO	Conscientious Objector
CPA	Communist Party of Australia
DLP	Democratic Labor Party
DRM	Draft Resisters' Movement
DRU	Draft Resisters' Union
DRV	Democratic Republic of (North) Vietnam
EYL	Eureka Youth League
FPC	Federal Pacifist Council
NAA	National Archives of Australia
NLA	National Library of Australia
NCC	National Civic Council
NLF	National Front for the Liberation of South Vietnam
QPC	Queensland Peace Committee
RSL	The Returned and Services League
RVN	Republic of (South) Vietnam
SCCAC	South Coast Citizens Against Conscription

List of Abbreviations

SDS	Students for a Democratic Society
SIP	Sisterhood of International Peace
SOS	Save Our Sons
UAW	Union of Australian Women
VAC	Vietnam Action Committee
VMC	Vietnam Moratorium Campaign
WCTU	Woman's Christian Temperance Union
WEL	Women's Electoral Lobby
WIDF	Women's International Democratic Federation
WILPF	Women's International League for Peace and Freedom
WPA	Women's Peace Army
WSP	Women Strike for Peace
YCAC	Youth Campaign Against Conscription

PROLOGUE

> What sort of mothers do they think we are that
> we should put up with this treatment from this
> Government and say nothing?
>
> *Helen Christofides*[1]

On a crisp Canberra afternoon on 11 June 1970, 12 neatly dressed Wollongong housewives strode through King's Hall of Parliament House and entered the public gallery of the House of Representatives. Inside, they worked quickly, pulling chains and padlocks from their bulging shopping bags, attaching themselves to the gallery's railings. Among the group was Helen Christofides, a cafeteria worker whose 21-year-old son Louis was currently serving 52 days in Sydney's Long Bay Gaol for refusing to register for national service. She led the women in a noisy chorus of protest demanding her son's release. The disturbance forced the Speaker, Sir William Aston, to take unprecedented action, suspending parliamentary business and clearing the public and press galleries while the Serjeant-At-Arms and a police constable attempted to free the women.[2] This took some time. While officers searched for a heavy set of steel cutters to break the chains, a doctor was summoned to examine one heavily pregnant protester to ensure that she was not 'adversely affected by the strain and the excitement'.[3] Ballet teacher Edna Gudgeon, who had joined the Wollongong Save Our Sons (SOS) group to support her own draft resister son, later described the protest as an act of desperation 'because I cannot seem to reach this Government in any other way'.[4]

Prologue

The 'chain gang protest' capped off a traumatic day in parliament. Earlier there had been an emotional grievance motion concerning the death of a young South Australian conscript, Stanley Gordon Larsson. The 23-year-old fitter and turner had been sent to Vietnam earlier that year despite being so short-sighted that, according to his parents, he 'could not see a hand held four feet away'. They had appealed to the Minister for the Army, Andrew Peacock, to excuse their son from active service. Instead, an army 'investigation' found Private Larsson was 'fully fit for service everywhere'. He was subsequently issued with two pairs of spectacles 'in accordance with the normal army practice' and instructed to 'to keep them clean' – an impossible task, his father noted, given 'the torrid humidity of Vietnam'. Private Larsson was killed in a mine explosion on 6 June 1970, an accident his parents had no doubt was a direct result of his poor vision and 'of the cowardice of men too proud to admit to a horrible, tragic error'. In a letter addressed to the prime minister, John Gorton, and written shortly after being informed of his son's death, Stan Larsson senior told of his 'depthless horror and sorrow of grief' and of the questions he had no answers for: 'He went, Mr Prime Minister, because you told him it was right and honourable. Was it, Mr Prime Minister? Why? For Whom? A thousand questions flood my mind. How do I answer his young widow, or my children?'[5]

The letter, read to parliament that June day by the Larssons' local member of parliament (MP), Labor's Norm Foster, was a sobering reminder to those gathered of the cost of a war that seemed no closer to being won than it had been four years earlier when Australian troops had first been committed to Vietnam. After initially garnering widespread support, opposition to Australia's involvement in the war had since grown exponentially. A month earlier, hundreds of thousands of Australians had joined moratorium protests in cities across the nation, and draft resisters were currently playing a public cat and mouse game with authorities. Meanwhile, groups like Save Our Sons that had appeared five years earlier as a peaceful, law-abiding protest against conscription had become more militant, as members, like Edna Gudgeon, despaired each time another group of young men was dispatched to Vietnam, and the dead and injured were brought home. By its conclusion, the war would account for the deaths of 521 Australian soldiers and more than 3000 wounded.[6]

While it was entirely coincidental that the Wollongong women chose that day to stage their protest, it is perhaps not surprising, given the reading of Stan Larsson's letter, that the Speaker decided to be lenient with them. Ignoring his colleagues' demands to arrest the women and make an example of them, Sir William instead ordered that, once freed, they be taken to a nearby parliamentary office where they were served cups of tea before being politely escorted out of the building. The women were not placated. Nor did they stop protesting. 'I will not sit idly by while young men are being gaoled because they refuse to kill', Wollongong SOS president Flo Garber declared. 'I will defy the law as long as it conflicts with my conscience.'[7] The following year, that vow would land her in a Sydney jail, while in Melbourne, five SOS women would spend Easter of 1971 interred in Fairlea women's prison, away from their families. For, as Garber and her SOS colleagues were soon to learn, not everyone in authority was prepared to be as lenient as Sir William.

INTRODUCTION

'A Distress Call'

> Yesterday they appeared again ...
> that somewhat mysterious group of women
> who call themselves the SOS ...[1]

In May 1965, the *Australian* newspaper reported that Joyce Golgerth, an apparently ordinary housewife from the Upper North Shore Sydney suburb of Pennant Hills, had taken the extraordinary step of founding a group of mothers to oppose conscription for the Vietnam War. Golgerth, whose previous public activities had been limited to tuckshop duty at her children's school, had been horrified to learn that her 20-year-old son Michael had won the Menzies government's 'lottery' to join the first batch of conscripts destined for duty in Vietnam. Determined to bring the government to its senses, she joined other concerned mothers in forming a new protest group whose single aim was identified by its name: 'Save Our Sons'. In their first press release, the women denounced conscription as 'morally wrong', issuing 'a distress call – SOS – to mothers everywhere'.[2]

Though deemed worthy of just four short paragraphs in the national daily, the women's clarion call was heard and spread by others across the country who were inspired in turn to form Save Our Sons (SOS) groups of their own. Of varying ages, backgrounds, religious and political persuasions, they were united in their outrage over the Menzies government's conscription of young men – still too young to vote – to fight in an undeclared foreign war (although their reasons for this sometimes differed). Their anger was compounded by the random and 'ghoulish' method of selection: birthdays chosen by balls pulled from a wire bingo barrel, a so-called 'lottery of death'.[3] Within a few months SOS groups had formed in Melbourne, Brisbane and Newcastle. A year later, the movement was 'truly Commonwealth-wide', with 'branches' operating in Townsville, Wollongong, the Blue Mountains, Perth and Adelaide, and another planned in Tasmania.[4] Exactly how many people were involved in SOS overall is difficult to discern, although at their height both the Sydney and Melbourne groups boasted mailing lists in excess of 500 supporters. While they remained autonomous, all the groups adopted the Sydney group's statement of aims, vowing to campaign against conscription until the *National Services Act* was repealed.[5] In 1965, nobody envisaged this would take eight long years, or that some would be arrested and jailed in the process.

Between 1965 and 1973, SOS groups were a highly visible part of the anti-war movement in Australia, in part because they did not look – or dress – like the stereotypical long haired, scruffily dressed student protestor of the era. Turned out in their respectable best – hats, long white gloves and handbags teamed with sensibly heeled shoes and blue and white SOS sashes – they were among the first to unfurl their banners in 1965 after the Menzies government announced conscripts would be sent to Vietnam – and among the last to pack up when conscription was finally abolished by the incoming Whitlam Labor government in 1973. In the intervening years, SOS groups maintained a heavy schedule, so much so that in Sydney, the *Sun* newspaper joked that these 'mysterious ... women with banners' had become a 'moveable city landmark', seemingly present on every street corner.[6] They held public meetings; organised petitions, demonstrations and vigils;

staged sit-ins at Commonwealth offices; picketed train stations; lobbied politicians in their home cities and in Canberra; produced and distributed reams of anti-conscription literature (and music); tirelessly fundraised; attended court cases; and counselled and supported, both financially and morally, young men who decided to disobey call up notices. Their efforts were not always welcomed. In Sydney and Melbourne, SOS members were present at every intake of conscripts where they frequently encountered hostile reactions from the families of those they were trying to 'save'.

Their early forays were tentative, relying on peaceful, lawful and well established means of protests, including their signature 'silent vigil'. But as war and conscription dragged on, and the death and injury toll in Vietnam rose, many abandoned their genteel tactics and became more radical: scandalising Melbourne Cup goers in their scanty anti-war fashions; hijacking a Billy Graham evangelical rally; holding and publicising parties to fill in false conscription papers; refusing to pay their taxes; threatening to go on hunger strikes; padlocking themselves to Canberra's Parliament House; and actively assisting young men to break the law. In the 1970s, they joined other protest groups to organise the moratorium activities and helped conscientious objectors and draft resisters avoid the authorities, moving them between a network of 'safe houses' they helped to establish. While police were initially reluctant to act against them, increasingly there were consequences. The jailing of five SOS 'mums' at Easter in 1971 led to nationwide outrage protests and strikes and was hailed by activist leader and Labor MP Jim Cairns as a turning point in the anti-war campaign.

The history of Save Our Sons, and of those who answered its 'distress call', is the focus of this book. Interestingly, it is a project that the founding mums mooted in the organisation's first year but soon pushed to one side as they concentrated on more pressing concerns than their own place in history. In the intervening five decades, much of what has been remembered and written about the anti-war campaign has tended to come from younger members of the protest movement, many of whom were draft resisters or part of the student movement that rallied against the war and conscription on university campuses across the nation. SOS's contribution, while not forgotten, has tended to be relegated largely to the sidelines of any broader historical analysis, noted as an interesting and novel sideshow but very much secondary to the efforts of the larger, noisier, mostly student-led protest groups in Sydney and Melbourne, many of which only formed much later in the campaign. Many of these texts have been authored by participants of these groups, some produced even as the history they were describing was being made.[7] In these accounts SOS women are largely invisible. Notable exceptions include works by Ann Curthoys, Ann-Mari Jordens and Siobhan McHugh, who have all examined the role of SOS women in wider works about the anti-war movement published in the 1990s, while Pauline Armstrong, whose son was a draft resister, focused on the Victorian SOS in her 1991 Masters thesis.[8] The Victorian group was also the subject of an insightful 1997 documentary by Rebecca McLean, daughter of one of the Victoria SOS leaders.[9] This is the first attempt, however, to fulfil the original intention of the founding mums to produce a national history of their organisation, one of the earliest and longest surviving anti-conscription groups of the Vietnam period.

* * *

SOS's campaign was fought against a backdrop of percolating change in Australian society. In the seventies this would see the emergence,

INTRODUCTION

in parallel to the anti-war movement, of many new social movements seeking women's rights, Aboriginal land rights, gay and lesbian rights, and environmental safeguards. Much of this pressure for change, however, was only ramping up as SOS's campaign wound down. Indeed, when SOS formed in the mid-sixties, Australia was still riding the wave of postwar prosperity, Cold War fears of a communist invasion via Asia were still real, and traditional gender roles confining women to their familial duties and domestic spheres still prevailed. Opinion polls at this time showed that most Australians supported conscription and their government's intervention in Vietnam, putting SOS firmly out of step with their fellow countrymen and women. Even the right to protest in the streets was still contested and, in some places, such as Melbourne and Brisbane, actively repressed. As such, SOS events could be intimidating and frightening experiences, especially for women who were entering the public sphere for the first time. As a schoolboy, Maurie Mulheron tagged along with his mum to many of the early SOS protests in Sydney, witnessing firsthand the hostility the women faced. In 2012 he reflected:

> It was one thing to join 40,000 or 70,000 people marching in the moratoriums in 1970 but it was much more difficult to go to an induction at Marrickville army barracks in 1966 with six or seven other women and stand there and have young men get off the buses laughing and shouting at you, police pushing you, threatening you and to just stand your ground.[10]

The backlash was inevitable, and often laced with gendered subtexts. SOS women were not only routinely accused (as all protesters during this period were) of being 'reds under the bed' but denounced as bad mothers and neglectful wives, told by members of the public, in no uncertain terms, to get back to their kitchens and families.

Many women were under tremendous personal strain but continued to protest anyway. Their children were bullied at school (by teachers as well as classmates); one-time friends abandoned them on the advice of their parish priests or crossed the street to avoid them; they faced hostility in the workplace (one woman's workmates poured boiling tea water over her), and sometimes within their own families; and they received foul, threatening hate mail. They were subjected to surveillance and intimidation by police and the Australian Security Intelligence Organisation (ASIO), as well as 'red-baiting' and ridicule by politicians and the media. Many chose to view this kind of reaction as a 'badge of honour', proof that their campaign was rattling the right cages. But for others, like Brisbane SOS leader Vilma Ward, who went from insisting on a strict hat and glove dress code for her members to later facing a prison sentence for civil disobedience, it was 'a rude awakening' to life beyond the domestic sphere.[11]

The image of respectable, well-behaved middle-class housewives, which the SOS women nurtured in their early years, was extremely potent, making it difficult for their opponents to dismiss them, although ASIO still diligently tracked their activities, convinced they were part of a sinister communist agenda. But while their political allegiances may have been questioned, their sincerity could never be denied, forcing even their staunchest opponents to pause and think. 'These ladies weren't loudmouth sluts from the backstreet from some slum suburb', recalled one former Commonwealth policeman tasked with keeping the Victoria SOS leaders under surveillance. 'These were mothers who were showing grave concern for the lives of their sons.'[12] The involvement of these so-called 'respectable women' helped to widen the appeal of the anti-war movement and made public dissent more acceptable to a broader audience, particularly women.

Introduction

But appearances could be deceiving, sometimes deliberately so, as the first part of this book examines. SOS was made up of a diverse bunch of women from different walks of life whose motivations reflected nuanced attitudes to conscription and the Vietnam War that were shaped and complicated by family histories, personalities and individual experiences. At the same time, it must be said, there was little ethnic diversity. The vast majority were white women, either Australian born or from other Anglo-Saxon backgrounds. Most were not university educated and did not have paid employment outside the home, although there were notable exceptions. Contrary to popular belief, however, not all were mothers of conscription-age sons; some had no children at all. Nor was SOS strictly a 'women's only' movement. Indeed, in some parts of the country a small number of men marched under the SOS banner too, while in Perth and Adelaide they held positions on committees. But while SOS never actively excluded men, it primarily attracted women. This book focuses on SOS's female constituency, guided by the fact that the two largest groups, Melbourne and Sydney, along with those in Townsville, Newcastle, Brisbane and Wollongong were all founded by and run by women. SOS groups were also widely regarded, and often referred to, as mothers' groups.

Politically, SOS members represented a multitude of views. While many of the founding women had links with the left side of politics, a large number who subsequently joined SOS were, or had been, long-time supporters of the then Prime Minister Robert Menzies. Groups initially only opposed conscription, not the Vietnam War itself, in deference to some members who feared the latter would be viewed as too political. They were also overwhelmingly optimistic, if naïvely so, that law-abiding, peaceful tactics would be enough to bring Menzies and his government to its senses. Over time, many members opted for a more radical approach. These changes in tactics and attitudes, explored in the second half of this book, can be traced over three distinct periods of the Vietnam War, each concluding with a federal election: 1966 and 1969, in which the conservative government was re-elected, and, finally, 1972, when the Whitlam Labor government swept to power promising to end conscription and bring home the troops. But these new tactics also threatened to undermine SOS's carefully crafted public image and sometimes led to conflict within its supporter base, as Perth member Joan Davies discovered in 1966 after she threw her shoes at Prime Minister Harold Holt at Perth Airport. The Perth group aside, however, SOS groups were notably free of the bitter internal politics, and the blatant sexism experienced by many younger women, that caused considerable tensions in other anti-war groups during this period.

Nonetheless, hopes of a quick outcome soon gave way to increasing despair; over the years of the campaign, there were many setbacks, disappointments and challenges. Supporters came and went, some groups folded, but a core of stalwarts persevered until the end. Indeed, unlike most grassroots movements then or since, SOS was successful in achieving its major aim: in 1973, it was with relief, and much satisfaction, that those left standing toasted the end of conscription of Australian sons for the Vietnam War.

* * *

Over the years, SOS women and their families have voiced disappointment that their role has been overlooked or underplayed. 'Quite a few of the men wrote their books and never mentioned us', Victoria SOS secretary Jean McLean told me in a 2014 interview. 'Even when you worked every bloody day with them, they didn't mention the women and, in fact, some of them were draft resisters who I spent all my time with.'[13] Labor MP Jim Cairns, who chaired the Victorian Vietnam Moratorium Committee, later expressed regret at failing to credit any women for their role in the moratorium movement in his 1970 book, *Silence Kills*, a curious omission given McLean was one of his deputies and marched alongside him.[14] Rather than revealing a sinister intention, however, his explanation points to a broader tendency during this period not to 'see' women. 'In a way we took women too much for granted', Cairns said. '[In] *Silence Kills* there isn't mention of women per se. I had to do that quickly and I just took the protest movement as a whole … we just took [the women's involvement] as a matter of course but it wasn't a matter of course, it was something quite unusual and it had an unusual significance.'[15]

SOS women are also missing from histories of social change during this period, particularly the rise of second wave feminism in Australia which occurred in parallel with the anti-Vietnam protests. This is more curious given the SOS women were living the slogan 'the personal is political' long before it was adopted by the women's liberation movement which was gaining momentum just as SOS was winding down. Their reliance on traditional maternal rhetoric, which even during their own time was considered by many to be outdated, means SOS women do not fit neatly into narratives about the changing role of women in Australia during this period. But their sidelining ignores the long history of women's activism in Australia during the 20th century. Indeed, the movement grew out of a long history of maternal peace activism that can be traced back to World War I when Australians refused to endorse two plebiscites that would have allowed conscripts to serve overseas in that conflict. Having recently been granted the vote, women took an active part in the debate, and were specifically targeted by emotional appeals from both sides of the campaign. Likewise, women's peace groups that formed in the early 20th century, such as the Sisterhood of International Peace (rebadged after World War I as the Women's International League for Peace and Freedom – WILPF), the Women's Peace Army (WPA), and, later, the Union of Australian Women (UAW), shared common philosophies and protest tactics that were later taken up by SOS women. These were based on traditional maternal politics: a belief in the universality of motherhood and the sacred role of mothers to nurture children and human life everywhere by opposing war and promoting peace.

Some of the original SOS women were also members of the Union of Australian Women (UAW), a national organisation formed in 1950 along the lines of similar women's unions in Europe to represent the interests of working-class women. Along with better pay and work conditions for women, the UAW also campaigned strongly for peace. Its campaigns, particularly against nuclear weapons, also relied on maternal rhetoric, focusing on the effect war had on children while promoting the image of 'peaceful motherhood'. This was in line with language used by other women's groups around the world in the 1950s and '60s, including the powerful Women Strike for Peace (WSP) movement in the United States. In November 1961, WSP came to the world's attention by staging a one-day national peace protest in which an estimated 50,000 mainly white, middle-class women in communities across America 'came out of their kitchens and off their jobs' to demand that President John F. Kennedy 'End the Arms Race – Not the Human Race'.[16] In the 1960s and '70s, the WSP expanded its campaign to protest against the Vietnam War. It maintained strong links with women's peace groups worldwide, including the UAW, and later with the Sydney SOS group. SOS also exchanged correspondence with other women's protest groups in the US, Asia and Europe during this period. Hence, the emergence of SOS needs to be seen in the context of a worldwide movement of women who had been fighting for peace throughout the 20th century.

But by the early 1970s, maternal rhetoric (and anyone who used it) was considered both old fashioned and somewhat embarrassing by those embracing the emerging women's movement. The uneasiness flowed both ways. While some SOS women later became involved in the movement, others spoke of their discomfort with the more radical tactics, language and attitudes of younger women, particularly towards men. This undoubtedly reflected not only differences in ages (many of the SOS women were the same age as the mothers of those in the women's movement), but also differing experiences of the protest movement. Younger women in student protest groups often complained of having been relegated to auxiliary roles, often menial ones, while the men took the leading roles. This was not the experience of those who joined SOS groups. In the 1990s, Curthoys, herself a former student protestor, interviewed several women who were involved with different elements of the peace movement in Sydney, including SOS members. She found that women in mixed peace groups had markedly different experiences from those in separate women's groups. Women in SOS, for example, 'did not have to fight for a hearing ... as they so often did in the student and youth organisations'. She concluded that younger women tended to feel marginalised within the anti-war movement and this led many of them 'to value collective female action and build a new movement for the liberation of women'. In contrast, many of the older women, who had a positive experience as part of an all-women's group like SOS, often found the women's liberation movement to be 'uncongenial'.[17]

Yet there is no denying that there was a distinctly gendered element to the attacks on SOS women and these strong reactions to the group undoubtedly reflected the changing times in Australian society, and an underlying unease with women engaging in public life. Even seasoned campaigners were shocked and dismayed to find themselves branded as bad mothers and depicted by cartoonists as old trolls and ugly hags. The witch metaphor immediately comes to mind here. Interestingly, while the 'Holy Mother and wife' may have been out of the kitchen, as author Michael Caulfield has noted, it was not only men who found this transgression 'unseemly and threatening'.[18] Some of the most vitriolic criticism emanated from other women, one of whom denounced SOS as 'a disgrace to womanhood'.[19] Like World War I, the debate during the Vietnam era was complicated by differing concepts of maternal duty and what it meant to be a woman, a mother and a patriotic Australian in times of war. As we will see, one of SOS's most high-profile critics was Nancy Wake, the Australian World War II heroine who saved thousands of Allied lives while working for the French resistance.

Clearly, the SOS experience was not representative of all women during this period. But it did have strong appeal to a certain group of women for whom it provided a safe vehicle by which they could become involved in the political sphere for the first time. Many were drawn in by the very traditional maternal rhetoric that younger women were rejecting and evolved with the organisation as they were exposed to new ways of thinking and campaigning. Some women discovered their vocation and went on to become trailblazers in their own fields.

* * *

Introduction

While it has become fashionable for authors to cite their own personal connections to their subject, I have no familial link with anyone who fought in that conflict. Nor am I aware of any relative who protested. While I have vague memories of the Vietnam War as a black and white blur on the nightly news, I have none of the protest movement, other than those imposed by one university lecturer, a former student protestor, who regularly deplored the political disinterest of my generation. With the Grim Reaper always on TV, and looming over every rock concert, perhaps we had other things to worry about. If one of the ageing Cold War leaders did not push the button ensuring nuclear obliteration, then AIDS would surely finish us.

It was not until much later that I came across SOS while researching a completely different subject and time period. At the time, I was a mother of a teenage son myself and it was not hard to imagine how conscription might jolt even the most politically disengaged woman into action. As I write this book, my son is now a towering 20-year-old, the age that young men during the Vietnam era faced an anxious wait to see if their number came up. As I scanned the results of the conscription lottery, it was sobering to note that my son's birthday came up multiple times over the years. Imagine what it must have been like for mothers of twins? It seemed important to know more. Who were these women, what were their backgrounds, what had motivated them, especially those who had no sons of their own, to join the protest movement at this time? What did they do? How did they do it? And, importantly, how did they fare?

For this book I have drawn on a wide range of primary sources such as official records maintained by a couple of the SOS groups (minutes, annual reports, press statements, correspondence and newsletters), personal correspondence, autobiographies, police and intelligence reports, newspaper articles and oral histories. This diversity of sources partly reflects the difficulties inherent in researching any small grassroots movement where written records are not always kept. In the case of the SOS movement the task was made more difficult by the different structures of the various groups; some kept strict minutes and held elections and annual general meetings thus generating copious amounts of records, while others operated informally, bypassing the need for constitutions, official titles or even formal membership. In some cases, records simply 'disappeared' after the groups were disbanded, perhaps destroyed or forgotten in a corner of someone's shed. I was extremely grateful, therefore, to the last Sydney committee members who, before turning out the lights in 1973, decided to deposit their records in the National Library of Australia, in Canberra, albeit with a proviso that researchers seek permission before viewing the files. Maurie Mulheron, son of the group's last secretary Nora Mulheron, who has held the virtual 'key' to this collection since his mother's death, explained that at the time members were fearful that the contents might be used against them by their right-wing critics.[20] This act alone provided me with an insight into the workings and mindset of committee members who during their campaign came under intense pressure and scrutiny.

ASIO files proved to be a major source of new information for this book, many of which had previously not been opened. Convinced from the outset that SOS was a communist 'front', the organisation kept detailed dossiers on all SOS groups as well as key individuals, many of whom were already on file due to their involvement with other 'suspect' groups, like the UAW.[21] The Townsville group, for example, never kept written records, deeming them a waste of valuable time, so ASIO's file, which included attendance records, reports of meetings and telephone conversations along with newspaper clippings, was particularly helpful. Members told me they thought they were under surveillance and, clearly, they were not being paranoid. Townsville SOS founder Margaret Reynolds recounted how years later after giving a lecture in Cairns, she had been approached by a mature-age university student who revealed that as a young ASIO officer he had been sent to Townsville to monitor the activities of SOS and had followed her on several occasions.[22] It is also clear from the files that by July 1965, less than two months after SOS's inaugural meeting, ASIO had an informant inside the Sydney group who provided detailed descriptions of meetings and conversations conducted between members. Presumably a woman, the identity of this 'mole' was never discovered. ASIO apparently had less success infiltrating the Melbourne group, however, with most of its early reports drawn from newspaper clippings, intercepted phone calls with Communist Party of Australia (CPA) members and reports from public meetings. Perhaps the biggest 'treasure' I uncovered was a complete set of handwritten minutes for the Perth group in a file of a Western Australian member. How they came to be there, we can only imagine.

Given the paranoid nature of the times, ASIO files must be used cautiously. Many of the people the agency identified and held under surveillance were not communists and agents were sometimes quick to jump to conclusions about organisations to fulfil the preconceived ideas of their superiors. A former ASIO agent related in 2014 how agents would 'gild the lily just to make themselves interesting and feel that they're fulfilling what their handlers required'.[23] One son of an SOS supporter, for example, was astounded when I told him his grandmother who resided in a remote north Queensland town had been described in one ASIO report as 'a red terror'.[24] The woman's only apparent 'crime' had been to attend a few gatherings of her local UAW group. After obtaining her ASIO file, Victoria SOS founder Jean McLean also disputed several 'facts' including that she had ever been a member of the communist youth group, the Eureka Youth League.[25] Even information filtered by such slanted preconceptions, however, is useful in providing a window into the mindset of authorities during this period and their view not only of SOS but of individual women. It also enabled me to ascertain links with other groups. As much as possible, I have sought to corroborate information or have otherwise made clear that it originated from a security file.

Oral histories brought a wider range of voices to the SOS story and were useful in fleshing out the backgrounds and experiences of those involved, as well as providing insight into how those experiences influenced what participants did after the campaign was over. Researcher Pauline Armstrong's collection in the National Library of Australia (NLA) yielded a series of interviews with Victorian anti-war identities, still on their original cassette tapes, that library staff kindly allowed me to transcribe. I also conducted 30 interviews of my own. Most of the older SOS women had passed away but family members were often able to fill in some of the gaps with memories of their own. I was too late to speak to Joyce Golgerth, for example, of whom very little archivally is known but her children, including her son Michael, generously shared their memories of their mother and her time in SOS. An unexpected bonus was speaking to family members who had participated in the anti-war movement themselves either as younger children accompanying their mothers or as student protestors. Many women I interviewed were self-deprecating about their efforts; to them their experience in SOS was a brief interlude of little importance in the wider performance of their lives. Family members, on the other hand were often astounded by their mothers' bravery given the times. Mindful that memories can become skewed with the benefit of hindsight, either consciously or unconsciously, I have not relied exclusively on oral testimony but used it in conjunction with archival sources, including first-person contemporary accounts, to illustrate points throughout the narrative.

SOS groups were all different; the movement was not a homogenous anti-conscription 'franchise' reproduced in strategic locations across Australia. While they shared a common name and purpose, SOS groups differed markedly in terms of their structure, constituencies, tactics, degree of radicalisation and longevity. In the past, the lack of information on these smaller groups has led to studies with a broader focus on Australia's involvement in the Vietnam War to concentrate on the activities of the larger Sydney and Melbourne groups. This has resulted in a more uniform image of SOS than in fact existed. A national focus allows for a more nuanced examination and comparison of these differences, albeit within practical limits. When examining their formation, I considered each group as an individual entity. However, when it came to reconstructing SOS's contribution to the anti-war movement, decisions had to be made about what to include and omit. While I have endeavoured to maintain a national perspective throughout this book, during the latter years of the campaign the focus inevitably tends to be on the more active and radical actions of the larger groups. One way of countering this Sydney and Melbourne 'bias' has been to follow the involvement of individual women from different groups. Understanding the women involved helps us understand the organisation itself. Some of these women, such as Melbourne's secretary Jean McLean had high profiles, generating plenty of archival sources including written accounts of their own;

others preferred to work quietly in the background, leaving behind little more than their name on an attendance list. In considering the effect of their activism, I have not discounted any on the basis of how active they were or how long they were involved. In the case of some women, even a relatively short experience with SOS had a long-lasting effect on their lives.

SOS's legacy and contribution to the anti-conscription campaign continues to be difficult to assess, not least because the subject of the Vietnam War and the protest movement still evokes raw responses among some segments of the population. Collective memory for this period is still very much a work in progress. With this in mind, I relied on different parameters to assess the legacy and influence of SOS, finding that, in their own way, and as volunteers, SOS members made a significant contribution to the anti-war movement. Behind the scenes, mostly away from the glare of the television cameras and newspaper reporting, they provided practical assistance and moral support to conscientious objectors and draft resisters and brought important organisational skills and fundraising abilities to the moratorium movement. Moreover, the involvement of these so-called 'respectable women' helped to widen the appeal of the anti-war movement and made public dissent more acceptable to a broader audience. Their experiences left important personal legacies too. After they rolled up their SOS banners, some returned to their domestic lives, others joined new causes in the emerging environmental and women's movements, or continued to work for peace with other groups. A few, as we will see, went on to break down new barriers, forging successful public careers.

* * *

INTRODUCTION

In December 1965, Sydney's *Sun* newspaper dismissed SOS as a group of 'eccentrics' who nobody took seriously.[26] But campaigning against conscription was always serious business for SOS members. They stood their ground, and they achieved their aims. While the organisation may have been just one chip 'in the huge mosaic of the anti-Vietnam War movement in Australia', without all the pieces, our overall picture and understanding of the Vietnam protest era remains incomplete.[27] To that end, this book seeks to reinstate the narrative of SOS into the broader history of the anti-conscription/anti-war movement during the Vietnam era, just as the story of the women who opposed conscription during World War I has been preserved as part of the broader history of that period. The importance of this task was underlined by former draft resister Louis Christofides, whose mother Helen was among the Wollongong SOS members who chained themselves to Parliament House in 1970. He lamented in the early 1990s that the contribution of many of the women involved in SOS had already been forgotten, including that of Wollongong SOS leader Flo Garber. 'People say, "Who's Flo Garber?" Well, she's not just a name. She was one of many who played a significant role … she is dead … and she is forgotten. That's a tragedy', he said.[28] Agreed.

This, then, is the story of Flo Garber, and of Joyce Golgerth, Nora Mulheron, Helen Christofides, Joan Davies, Edna Gudgeon and all those other forgotten women who during the Vietnam War dared to defy their government, stepping out of their familial comfort zones into what was often a vicious public sphere, to stand united under the banner of Save Our Sons.

Chapter 1

DRESS REHEARSAL

> There'd be no war today,
> If mothers all would say,
> I didn't raise my boy to be a soldier.
>
> *American anti-war song, 1915*[1]

On 23 November 1964, two weeks after he announced the reintroduction of conscription to a largely disinterested Australian public, Prime Minister Robert Menzies gave a speech at a political rally in Sydney's northern suburbs.[2] As expected, the gathering of party faithful gave their leader a rockstar welcome. But as he began to extol the virtues of national service, a large group of well-dressed women sitting quietly among the audience dramatically rose as one, covering their heads with black veils. Heads bowed, they stood silently for several minutes as the room around them erupted into jeers and boos, before filing slowly out of the room, handing out anti-conscription leaflets as they left. Forced to temporarily abandon his speech, and struggling to be heard above the uproar, Menzies quipped, 'You can see from these little activities that there is a bit of controversy on this issue'.[3] While headlines the next day claimed Menzies had taken the protest in his stride, Margaret Holmes, who helped organise the protest, recalled it differently. 'It stopped him in his tracks', she said.[4] The Hornsby protest, organised by the Women's International League of Peace and

Freedom (WILPF), was the first recorded public opposition by women to conscription during the Vietnam era – and just the beginning of 'the controversy' for Menzies and his government, inspiring those who went on to form the Save Our Sons movement the following April after it was confirmed that 20-year-old conscripts would be sent to fight alongside regular troops in Vietnam.

Save Our Sons' (SOS) story began amid the sub-zero temperatures of a global Cold War, when most Australians supported Menzies' Vietnam policy as a means of thwarting the spread of communism in the region – and had little patience with those who took a contrary view. In a sense, however, the history of SOS began much earlier. The Vietnam era was not, after all, the first time in Australian history that women had opposed conscription. Indeed, the movement grew out of a long history of maternal peace activism that can be traced back to World War I when Australians refused to endorse two plebiscites that would have allowed conscripts to serve overseas in that conflict. Having recently been granted the vote, women took an active part in the debate. The maternal arguments and tactics that SOS women employed during the Vietnam era were, in many cases, remarkably similar to those used by women who protested against conscription during this earlier time. To fully understand the emergence of SOS, and the form it took, the organisation must be placed within the context of this broader history. For while SOS hailed a new era in women's activism history in Australia, providing a foothold for women tentatively testing their place in the public sphere, the movement also owed a great debt to the past.

Conscription was first introduced in Australia in 1911 as a form of national service for young men aged between 12 and 26 years. Overall, this so-called 'Boy Conscription' aroused little opposition which came from predictable quarters, notably Quakers who, in 1912, founded the Australian Freedom League in Adelaide. A group of 25 ministers of religion also signed a manifesto opposing it.[5] Among women's groups, the Woman's Christian Temperance Union (WCTU) expressed concern 'about the harm that might be done to the morals of the boys and about the morality of the war'.[6] Those who supported the scheme, on the other hand, saw it as a way of instilling discipline and a work ethic in wayward youth of the day. This was supported by police who in 1914 credited national service for a marked decline in 'juvenile cigarette smoking' and 'larrikinism' among boys of conscription age.[7] However, it was another matter when it was proposed that conscripts should serve overseas. Indeed, opinion polls taken from 1942 until 1964 consistently suggested that while a majority of Australians supported some form of national service for home defence, they objected to conscripts being sent abroad.[8]

World War I

Not even the onset of World War I could convince Australians otherwise. When Labor Prime Minister Billy Hughes argued that conscription was necessary in order to boost the dwindling number of recruits prepared to fight in the Australian Imperial Force, the majority of Australians disagreed, voting 'no' in two plebiscites held in 1916 and 1917, albeit by a narrow majority.[9] Hughes had previously stated his strong opposition to sending conscripts overseas but changed his mind after a trip to England in 1916 where conscription had recently been introduced. He opted to put the issue before the people because he lacked the majority in the Senate necessary to amend the *Commonwealth Defence Act* of 1903 which stated that no Australian soldier – regular or conscript – could be forced to serve overseas.[10] The ensuing debate split not only the country but Hughes' own party, eventually forcing his resignation.

Women played a leading role in this debate with groups such as the Sisterhood of International Peace (SIP) and the Women's Peace Army (WPA) actively campaigning against conscription.[11] However, as in the Vietnam era, women did not universally oppose the scheme. Other women played forceful roles in pushing the pro-conscription viewpoint, organising campaigns designed to 'out' eligible young men who were not willing to do their duty, handing them white feathers symbolising cowardice.[12] The debate was heavily influenced by the women's suffrage movement that encouraged women to enter the political sphere. While it is impossible to know how many women ultimately voted against conscription, much of the propaganda generated by both sides of the debate was targeted at them suggesting the female vote was considered influential. Certainly, pro-conscriptionist Sir William Irvine was sufficiently worried on the eve of the second vote to declare that 'on an issue such as this, it should not be left to the sentiment of a very large section of the population – the women'.[13]

Sisterhood of International Peace

The World War I debate over conscription was also significant because it led to the emergence of women's peace groups as separate entities. Previous to this, women had participated in mixed peace groups, like the London Peace Society, which established a branch in Melbourne in 1905.[14] In March 1915, the Sisterhood of International Peace (SIP) was formed in Melbourne 'to promote mutual knowledge of each other by the women of different nations, goodwill and friendship to study the causes – economic and moral – of war' and 'to bring the humanising influence of women to bear on the abolition of war, and the substitution of international justice and arbitration for irrational methods of violence'.[15] The group was the idea of Australian Church founder, Dr Charles Strong, a veteran peace campaigner who 'believed that this was a matter wherein women could and should exercise great influence'.[16] SIP sought to educate other women about their stance on war and tended to appeal to middle-aged, middle-class women. Most of the women who joined had previous organisational experience, having belonged to church societies or other bodies for 'furthering social welfare'. However, 'it was another matter to come out publicly in opposition to the declared policy of a nation and an Empire'.[17] According to the group's secretary Eleanor Moore, the group initially 'hesitated' to campaign against conscription, concerned that its constitution prevented it from pronouncing on questions 'directly connected with the waging of the war'. Inevitably, however, the most active members joined the anti-conscription movement.[18] Moore, an 'uncompromising Pacifist', was a constant presence at public meetings during this period and also became an executive-member of the Australian Peace Alliance, a composite group comprised of delegates from many societies that campaigned for negotiated peace and against conscription. But her public stand came at a cost; she was later expelled from the National Council of Women of Victoria for her anti-conscription activities.[19]

Women's Peace Army

The more radical Women's Peace Army (WPA) was formed in Melbourne during July 1915, with branches in Sydney and Brisbane established later the same year. While its objectives were almost identical to those of SIP, the groups did not join forces but worked separately for the same cause. This was due to what Moore politely referred to as 'a difference in tone'.[20] WPA's leaders had all been active in the suffragist movement and their more radical approach reflected their experience – and personalities. President Vida Goldstein, a long-time campaigner for women's rights, was founder and president of the Women's Political Association, editor of *The Woman Voter*, and was the first Australian woman to stand as a candidate for federal parliament.[21] She was joined by two dynamic English suffragettes: Adela Pankhurst, the daughter of the famous British suffragette leader Emmeline Pankhurst, and Cecilia John. The group promptly declared 'We war against war', apparently seeing no irony in the combative style they adopted in order to push their anti-militaristic agenda.[22] They even had their own flag. On one occasion, John turned a firehose on soldiers who were trying to remove the flag from the top of the Guild Hall in Melbourne.[23] John knew the value of a spectacle. A report of a procession through the city during this period noted it was led by 'the striking figure of Miss Cecilia John on horseback' accompanied by a large banner that read 'Gentle maiden, trust him not!'[24]

The WPA women went on interstate speaking tours and held militant street demonstrations and open-air meetings, not shying from acts of civil disobedience. Reaction to the women was frequently hostile and it was not uncommon for meetings to turn violent. In the course of their campaign, WPA members were heckled, assaulted, pelted with eggs, and imprisoned for their anti-conscription behaviour while the office of *The Woman Voter* was threatened with closure unless it ceased printing anti-war literature.[25] Pankhurst and John were also banned under the *War Precautions Act* of 1915 from performing their popular rendition of the American anti-war folk song *I Didn't Raise My Boy To Be A Soldier*.[26] Perhaps the WPA's greatest opposition, however, came from other women loyal to the imperialist cause. In Queensland, the WPA's secretary Margaret Thorp, a 25-year-old Quaker pacifist, was attempting to address a public meeting called by loyalist women when she was knocked to the ground by several women, 'punched and scratched, rolled on the floor and kicked and punched and scratched again'.[27] A few weeks earlier, Thorp's home had been raided by military police searching for printed copies of the banned song.[28] In Melbourne, there was trouble when opposing groups of women on either side of the conscription debate attempted to hold marches at the same time. One elderly woman campaigning for the 'No vote' was reportedly attacked by a soldier with her own umbrella but refused to be bowed, stoically completing the march.[29]

In 1916, Goldstein used the pages of her newspaper to issue 'a special appeal to women from women'. She argued women had a far greater responsibility on the issue of conscription than men, urging: 'Be true to your motherhood by voting no'.

> As the Mothers of the Race, it is your privilege to conserve life, and love, and beauty, all of which are destroyed by war. Without them the world is a desert. You, who give life, cannot, if you think deeply and without bias, vote to send any mother's son to kill, against his will, some other mother's son.[30]

These sentiments were also a central theme of SOS literature produced during the Vietnam era.

Conscription Referenda 1916–17

Propagandists on both sides of the 1916–17 debate targeted women, particularly mothers. The pro-conscription campaign played on traditional fears of invasion, depicting women as the likely victims of any imminent enemy attack. As Carmel Shute noted, it also sought to elevate maternity to 'the realm of heroism', whereby the value of a woman was seen to be determined by the number of sons she 'was willing to abandon to the imperialist cause'.[31] There were frequent references to the patriotism of classical women who sent their sons off to war with one pro-conscription petition reminding women that 'Sparta stands not alone in the heroism of its women'.[32] Closely linked to appeals to patriotism were campaigns that played on feelings of shame. The National Council of Women called on women to refuse to play sports with men eligible to serve, while a massive demonstration against male race patrons in Brisbane saw 'one thousand women, wearing black arm bands' lining the entrance to the local race course to shame young men who would rather go to the races than fight.[33] A letter to Brisbane's local paper summed up the view of loyalist women proclaiming that 'any right-minded woman would rather be the mother and sister of a dead hero than a living shirker'.[34] Both sides of the campaign also evoked deep-seeded fears of widowhood, which in those days could condemn a woman to a lifetime of poverty. One 1917 pro-conscription leaflet, that claimed married men would only be exempt if conscription was supported, depicted a young boy imploring his mother to 'Vote Yes Mum or else they'll take Dad'.[35]

The anti-conscription campaign also sought to evoke passionate reactions among women, appealing to them as nurturers who could harness male aggression while also inciting fears of losing loved ones. 'Women of Australia, Beware! Lest you make your Country a Land of Mourning', thundered one leaflet. 'Do you want the furnace of war to consume all your fathers, husbands and brothers?'[36] Another powerful anti-conscription image from the period entitled 'The Mothers' depicted the Grim Reaper standing over a woman as she contemplated her ballot paper. An angelic young son in a cradle was a visual reminder of the high stakes involved in supporting conscription. The accompanying poem emphasised maternal rights over the state, suggesting women should not give up the sons they had brought up 'to believe in life as a sacred thing' when 'every jingo screams'. Rather, it urged women to act like a tiger mother 'shielding its suckling offspring against the warring world'.[37]

One of the most powerful pieces of anti-conscription propaganda was a leaflet entitled 'The Blood Vote' which showed a woman pausing as she placed her 'yes' vote in the ballot box or 'blood box':

> "Why is your face so white, Mother?
> Why do you choke for breath?"
> "O I have dreamt in the night, my son
> That I doomed a man to death"[38]

Anti-conscriptionist E. J. Holloway, trade unionist and later a minister in the Curtin Labor government, described 'The Blood Vote' as 'the most effective single piece of propaganda for our side, which decided the votes of perhaps tens of thousands of women'.[39] 'Women in mourning' was a powerful motif that was also employed by SOS throughout its Vietnam campaign. SOS literature and newsletters frequently included poetry that also emphasised themes of motherhood and the assumed moral superiority of mothers when it came to issues of peace.

While the WPA wound up at the end of the war in 1919, its beliefs in the universality of motherhood and that no mother should ever be forced to deliver up their sons for sacrifice in wars lived on through other women's groups, including the Union of Australian Women and, later, SOS. Many of Goldstein's statements were reproduced in newsletters and anti-conscription literature produced by these groups during the Vietnam era. Initially, however, SOS women shied away from acts of civil disobedience. In that respect, at least at first, women's groups during the Vietnam War were more in line with the actions of

SIP than the WPA. Also missing from the anti-Vietnam campaign was publicly organised opposition from pro-conscription women's groups, though many individual women did make their support for Menzies' scheme felt through letters, newspapers, and by joining the few mixed pro-war groups that emerged from time to time.

Women's International League for Peace and Freedom

SIP continued in another form. In 1920, it was 'rebadged' as the Australian section of the Women's International League for Peace and Freedom (WILPF). The League was founded in The Hague in 1915 by two American women, Jane Addams and Emily Greene Balch, who had been prominent in the suffragist movement. Its aims were: 'To achieve through peaceful means world disarmament, full rights for women, racial and economic justice, an end to all forms of violence, and to establish those political, social, and psychological conditions which can assure peace, freedom, and justice for all'.[40] The organisation's Australian arm, which still exists today, actively opposed conscription and the Vietnam War, providing a direct link to the World War I conscription debate. It was the WILPF that organised the first protest by women against conscription during the Vietnam era, and many WILPF women actively supported or joined SOS. Eleanor Moore served as the WILPF's Australian secretary from 1928 until her death in 1949.[41] An inspiration to generations of peace activists, Moore's words were frequently quoted in literature produced by the WILPF and other anti-conscription/anti-war groups, including SOS, during the Vietnam era. One anti-war leaflet, 'I AM A WOMAN', which somehow escaped the censor's pen during the 1916 anti-conscription campaign, was a perennial favourite that still struck a chord in the late 1960s:

I can only be loyal in a woman's way ... I have an obligation to men at the front, but I know I cannot relieve them by swelling the numbers of sufferers ... I know that as long as war continues such suffering cannot be prevented or mitigated. For this reason I will not sanction the war system by forcing any man to be a soldier.[42]

This notion that women brought a different viewpoint to peace and war continued to be echoed by the WILPF and groups like SOS during the Vietnam campaign.

World War II

Australia's first universal national training scheme was abolished in 1922 but the outbreak of World War II saw the issue back on the political table. In November 1939, six months after Australia entered the war, the Menzies government reintroduced compulsory military training requiring unmarried men turning 21 to undertake three months training with the militia. At the time the Prime Minster stated categorically that 'there is no question of conscription for overseas service'.[43] While in Opposition, Labor leader John Curtin also stated his party's irrevocable and unequivocal opposition to conscription of any description.[44] As a wartime prime minister, however, Curtin changed his mind. In January 1943, after a bitter debate, parliament passed an amendment to the *Defence Act* to provide for the limited use of Australian conscripts in the South Western Pacific Zone during the period of the war.[45] While there was some public criticism, including by the WILPF, there was no repeat of the bitter public debate of 1916–17 – and no referendum. The majority of Australians accepted that conscription was necessary, particularly in light of the Japanese bombings of Townsville and Darwin. Indeed, the strict adherence to absolute pacifism by the WILPF's Australian members put them out of step with their overseas affiliates during World War II when many European women, faced with the threat of fascism, were forced to qualify their anti-war stance.[46] The Chifley Labor government abolished conscription following the surrender of Japan in 1945.

In 1951, in response to the Cold War in Europe and fears of communism spreading through South-East Asia, the re-elected Menzies government moved to introduce a new National Service Scheme. This scheme operated until 1959 and required 18-year-old men to undergo six months of compulsory service training and to remain on the Reserve of the Commonwealth Military Forces for five years. There was no provision for overseas service. During this time, more than 500,000 men registered and about 227,000 took part in actual training.[47] There was widespread compliance and opinion polls indicated broad community support.[48] Women were among those who publicly supported the scheme in letters to the government and newspapers. There was strong opposition, however, from the armed services who argued it took up too much of their resources 'to produce partially trained men under no obligation to serve overseas'.[49] With fear of another world war receding, the scheme was abolished in 1960.

Cold War

The advent of the nuclear age and the Cold War provided plenty of opportunities for women after 1945 to hone their protest skills. While the WPA folded, women continued to be involved in peace activities through the WILPF, church groups, mixed peace groups, trade union groups, the Communist Party of Australia (CPA), and in women's organisations such as the Women's Service Guild, the Woman's Christian Temperance Union, and the New Housewives Association, which in 1950 reinvented itself as the Union of Australian

Women (UAW). In 1942, the WILPF also joined other pacifist groups – the Australian Peace Pledge Union, the Christian Pacifist Movement and the Religious Society of Friends (Quakers) – to form a national body, the Federal Pacifist Council (FPC), which played a leading role in the anti-war movement during the Vietnam era.[50]

The development and testing of atomic weapons, the Cuban missile crisis, increasing tension in South-East Asia, and the establishment of US military bases were the focus of the peace movement's concerns during this period. In response to Prime Minister Menzies' announcement in February 1952 that Britain would test atomic weapons in Australia, for example, the WILPF called a public meeting in Melbourne to condemn the move.[51] The WILPF's international networks proved particularly important in providing members with an alternative source of news and information, much of which never made its way into the Australian media. Members held study meetings aimed at educating themselves about world issues, travelled overseas to countries behind 'the Iron Curtain', and produced papers and pamphlets on international issues that were distributed to politicians and other influential members of society. After World War II, the WILPF had branches in Western Australia, South Australia, Victoria and regional NSW.

In 1960, the WILPF underwent a 'revival' after a Sydney branch was formed in the Mosman home of Margaret Holmes.[52] Holmes, a long-time pacifist, doctor's wife, and mother of six grown children, was inspired to start the branch after attending the WILPF's conference in Stockholm as part of a 'six month worldwide journey of peace' following her 50th birthday.[53] Holmes became one of the most regular demonstrators against the Vietnam War, and, while she never formally joined, was immensely supportive of SOS. Like its other Australian branches, the WILPF in NSW appealed to 'well educated, well-travelled middle-class women', with membership records showing many indeed hailed from 'genteel' Liberal voting north shore suburbs.[54] Members were encouraged to read widely and critically. At least one member subscribed to French newspaper *Le Monde*, which was anti-war and pro-independence for Vietnam, and this provided an alternative viewpoint on these issues.

Union of Australian Women

The Union of Australian Women (UAW) was also concerned with peace issues. Formed in August 1950 and inspired by similar women's 'unions' in Italy and France, it aimed to represent the interests of both working-class mothers and workers.[55] Branches soon spread to Victoria, South Australia, Western Australia and Tasmania, with representatives from state groups forming a national executive in 1956. Established as a 'non-party political organisation', it had a diverse constituency, with ALP supporters, communists, Christian activists, and members of the New Housewives' Association among its founders. Many could not see past the involvement of communist women, however, and as a result it was frequently tagged as a 'communist front'.[56] In 1954, in response to a UAW petition calling for a ban on atomic weapons, federal Minister for Labour and National Service Harold Holt sent back each slip to its signatory, accusing the UAW of being 'completely under the control of the Communist Party of Australia'.[57]

The UAW campaigned on issues such as equal pay for women, Indigenous rights, environmental causes, maternity allowances and child endowment, as well as world peace. The group is also credited with reviving the International Women's Day march during the 1950s. Many of its peace campaigns focused on the effect war had on children and the image of 'peaceful motherhood'.[58] In 1954, the

UAW encouraged women to attend the Australian Peace Council's Convention on Peace and War by relying on many of the same arguments used to appeal to women during World War I. 'Mothers do not want war, with its attendant separation, and interference with young children's education, happiness and highest welfare', argued an article in *Our Women*.[59] This template continued to be used throughout the Vietnam campaign by both the UAW and SOS.

The UAW also devised innovative protest methods to circumvent strict by-laws that existed in all states. In Melbourne, for example, peace campaigner Margaret Frazer recalled 'you were not allowed to stand still; you had to walk around the block in single file, six feet apart and keep moving'.[60] Unauthorised signs and placards were also illegal. The UAW countered by walking in groups of twos or threes, pinning anti-war messages on aprons and scarves, and carrying paper shopping bags with peace slogans inscribed on them.[61] After Australia committed advisors to Vietnam in 1962, the UAW staged a series of demonstrations in Australian capital cities employing these methods.[62] In WA, five UAW women were arrested and fined for walking through the streets of Perth wearing scarves and aprons emblazoned with peace messages over their clothes. A subsequent appeal against their convictions was upheld in the Supreme Court, much to the satisfaction of UAW members across Australia. These same methods of protest were adopted by SOS women, many of whom were also members of the UAW.

Vietnam

Vietnam first came to the peace movement's attention in 1959 during an international peace congress held in Melbourne. One of the guest speakers was Isabel Bloom, a female socialist member of the Belgian

Government who spoke about Vietnam. According to Margaret Frazer, while it was not evident at that stage what effect Vietnam would have on Australia 'as the 1960s went on, it became apparent that it would be very big indeed'. When Australia committed troops in 1962, 'we knew it was the thin edge of the wedge'.[63]

The WILPF was focused on Vietnam from the early 1960s and objected when Australia sent a small contingent of advisers there to work with American forces in 1962. The WILPF considered the war in Vietnam to be a civil war which could only be solved by the Vietnamese after the withdrawal of foreign troops, but the situation was of little interest to the majority of Australians who probably struggled at the time to find Vietnam on a map. To counter this, the WILPF formed a Vietnam-subcommittee to publish and distribute pamphlets, and organise street demonstrations and seminars to discuss the war.[64] Information about the situation in Vietnam was also sent to federal MPs and other influential Australians. In August and September 1964, the WILPF placed advertisements in the *Australian* and the *Sydney Morning Herald* headlined 'Is there a Current Alternative to Force in Asia?' The public notice argued that a political settlement 'can and must be found' and asked readers to cut out the advertisement and send it to the Minister for External Affairs, Mr Hasluck.[65] More than 200 of the WILPF's advertisement were sent to Mr Hasluck who responded by ordering that every signatory be sent a letter, signed by him, stating the government's policy.[66] Three weeks later, Menzies announced the reintroduction of conscription.

The National Service Scheme that Menzies introduced during the Vietnam era was fundamentally different to previous schemes because it allowed for conscripts to be sent overseas at a time when Australia was not officially at war and introduced a perceived randomness in its selection process. Under the scheme, all British subjects resident in Australia who turned 20 after 1 January 1965 were required to register for national service. As the number of 20-year-olds in the community in any one year exceeded the army's need, a ballot was held. Menzies' initial announcement, which made no mention of conscripts serving overseas, did not unduly upset the Australian public.[67] A poll taken the same month showed that 71 per cent supported conscription, with only 25 per cent opposed to it.[68] The WILPF immediately responded to Menzies' announcement on conscription by writing to all federal MPs condemning the action and accusing the government of having 'sidestepped the democratic rights of people to consider this important proposal'.[69] A couple of weeks later, the group organised the protest at the Liberal rally in Hornsby where the prime minister was speaking.[70] On 29 April 1965, Menzies informed the House of Representatives that Australia would commit troops, including conscripts, to Vietnam following a request from the South Vietnamese government. Between 1964 and 1972, 804,286 young men registered for national service, with 63,735 serving in the army.[71]

* * *

Opposition to conscription clearly was not unique to the Vietnam era. Nor was it the first time women had voiced their collective dissent to the concept of conscripts serving overseas. In World War I, women, who had gained the right to vote in federal elections only 14 years earlier, argued passionately, and sometimes violently, on both sides of this bitter and divisive debate. Their votes were targeted by emotive propaganda that emphasised maternal rights and incited deep-seeded fears of losing children and loved ones, echoes of which can be found in SOS literature.[72] Women continued to take up the peace mantle after World War I. Indeed, SOS emerged from a long history of peace activism involving Australian women in the 20th century. Hence, by the mid-1960s there were already organised groups of women across Australia whose members were not only experienced peace campaigners but well-informed about the situation in Vietnam. Many of these women were also well-travelled, having had unique access to countries behind the Iron Curtain and in Asia. Their descriptions of what they had seen raised questions about the official version of events being spread by the Australian Government. While they protested using traditional methods that echoed those used by women's groups and pacifists since 1916, they also were not afraid to push the boundaries and test existing 'rules'. Groups like the WILPF and UAW became important role models for the establishment of SOS, with their members generously providing organisational guidance and access to existing networks. Hence, while SOS is often credited with creating opportunities for 'new' women to enter the public sphere, it should not be overlooked that the movement also represented a significant degree of continuity with the past.

Part 1

Roll Call

Chapter 2

REBELS WITH A CAUSE

> We mothers know that wars don't solve problems; wars kill. If men and governments cannot, or will not, save our sons, then we mothers must.
>
> J. Harrison[1]

One of the earliest images of the Save Our Sons (SOS) movement shows a line of women standing along a Sydney street, conservatively dressed in sensible shoes, gloves and hats, their handbags politely placed on the dirty pavement in front of them. Pinned to their clothes are pieces of cardboard bearing a single word that, read together, spell out an anti-conscription slogan. The image all but screams middle-class respectability. But there are other images from this time. Black and white snapshots show mothers pushing infants in strollers, young women in fashionably short miniskirts and long boots, and elderly women in their Sunday best, all protesting alongside each other. This visual evidence alone hints at the diversity of women who were moved to protest during the Vietnam era. Individual stories support this observation. Ballet teacher, child-care worker, Blitz-survivor, war widow, Greek migrant, housewife, Quaker, communist, folk singer, union organiser, Liberal voter, Outback poet and television star – these were just some of the women who supported the SOS movement. Located across the nation, in capital cities, country towns and on isolated rural properties, they varied widely in age, socio-economic backgrounds, and in their political and religious views.

Their reasons for protesting were equally diverse, and often deeply personal. There were grandmothers, mothers, wives, sisters and girlfriends of young men who because of the fall of a marble now faced being shipped off to fight a foreign war. Some had connections to the peace movement; others had no prior political experience at all. Many had lived through previous wars and were determined to avoid another; others protested on religious grounds; some were lifelong pacifists. Contrary to popular belief at the time, not all were mothers with sons eligible for conscription; some had very young infants, older offspring or no children at all. And while all SOS members opposed the use of conscription in the Vietnam War, their views on national service were nuanced and complex. Some women actually supported the principle of conscription, believing that citizens bore an obligation towards the state or that it would help 'make boys into men'. 'I do not object to the idea of National Service even if it is only to correct the self-admitted shortcomings of some parents who seem unable to bring up their sons properly', explained one SOS recruit in a 1965 letter to the *Armidale Express*. 'I do object, however, to the using of these conscriptees, without their consent, in a war of very doubtful moral justification.'[2]

Tracing some of the pathways that led women to join SOS reveals the group's diversity. Piecing together those stories has not been easy. While some were well-known, generating multiple sources upon which to draw, others worked behind the scenes, leaving behind few traces other than a name on an attendance list or a note in an ASIO file. What becomes abundantly clear, however, is that contrary to popular belief, there was no typical SOS supporter.

Attitudes to Conscription

In the early 1960s, conscription evoked mixed feelings. Many women, including those who later dissented, actually supported the principle of national service, viewing it as a panacea for the ills of society. But Menzies' scheme differed from previous national service schemes in that the government could require recruits to serve overseas at a time when Australia was not officially at war. This rankled with many women. 'Let armies for abroad be purely voluntary and let our young men (professional or conscripts) defend their own shoreline', argued one Sydney SOS woman in her local paper.[3] This was not an uncommon reaction. A gallup poll published in January 1966 found most Australians were against sending national servicemen to Vietnam. Interestingly, while men were evenly divided on the question, women were notably two-to-one against.[4]

Menzies' scheme also introduced an element of random selectivity; as the number of 20-year-olds in the community in any one year exceeded the army's need, a ballot was held.[5] This struck many as inherently unfair. 'We believe that if our country is facing an emergency and our Government finds it necessary to enforce conscription, all the facilities of Australia should be mobilised by the conscription of labour, all the national resources and all the wealth of our country, with each and every citizen sharing equally the burden of responsibility, not just a minority of 20-year-olds', argued Edna Cullen, who joined Newcastle SOS. 'We believe it a grave injustice to force some 20-year-olds to fight in Vietnam while others live to the full in an affluent society, and business goes on as usual not making any sacrifice whatsoever.'[6] From country NSW, a 'horrified' Jean Bonner, mother of two sons, wrote: 'It seems so undemocratic that it should be declared by ballot, more like the tribute to Minos than Australia 1965'.[7]

Some also expressed concern at the length of time (two years) that young men would be required to serve. Others complained that migrants, who were initially exempt, would 'steal' the jobs of Australian boys 'doing their duty'.[8] One South Australian woman who had lost her only son in World War II declared herself in favour of conscription but argued that 'all young men from eighteen years' should be called up for national service 'irrespective of colour, race or occupation' for a period of six to nine months so as not to adversely affect career prospects. 'There is a hard-core of bad behaviour even among University Students and a term of military discipline would prove invaluable to them and to other young irresponsibles', she wrote.[9] Peggy Rose, of Mangerton, NSW, opposed conscription on many levels but also expressed concern that 'a hapless youth, born in the wrong month' could be carried off to military camp 'while his contemporaries amuse themselves, further their careers or travel'.[10]

Others questioned the government's rationale that the war in Vietnam presented a real threat to Australia's national security and argued that conscription should only be used to defend the country's borders. The mother of one teenage son wrote to the prime minister to object to conscripts being sent off to wars 'with which Australia is not directly concerned'. She wrote: 'It is a disgusting thing to think about sending 18-year-old boys, mere children, to foreign parts to engage in war'.[11] Clearly, views on conscription among women were not straightforward. They were further complicated by personal backgrounds, religious beliefs and experiences of past wars.

The War Weary

Many women in the 1960s were all too familiar with the effects of war. Depending on their age, many had lived through one or even both world wars and had close male relatives who had been killed or wounded in them. For women with fathers, brothers or husbands left psychologically as well as physically scarred by their battlefield experiences, war was not some distant, foreign event but part of everyday life. Yet, some women in this situation strongly supported conscription and believed their sons ought to do their patriotic duty as their fathers and grandfathers had before them. Elizabeth Deakin, from Hornsby, for example, was 'the wife of a retired Indian Army officer who managed to survive three wars, the daughter of a one-time soldier, the sister of a RAF officer and an AIF sergeant, both killed in World War II, and the sister-in-law of a Spitfire pilot who survived the Battle of Britain'. She was also 'the mother of a National Serviceman who, I am proud to say, takes it for granted that he should be trained to help the country he is lucky enough to live in'.[12] However, others who had rebuilt their lives and given birth to postwar babies found it inconceivable that their government could ask women to once again sacrifice their sons. In Newcastle, Isobel McArthur had two sons, aged 18 and 17, and was terrified by the 'heartbreaking thought of what lies ahead of us'. 'I know it is heartbreaking as I know what my own mother went through in the last war when her two sons aged 21 and 25 were killed … within 6 weeks of one another', she wrote in 1965. 'My father had a breakdown and passed away before the year was up and my mother slipped away from us in 1953 at the age of 59. I know what war can do to a family – there is only a brother and myself [left] out of a family of six.'[13]

Brisbane SOS supporter Hazel Dean saw her husband die slowly from his war injuries and vowed to go to jail rather than see her 19-year-old son David, a builder's labourer, sent to Vietnam. 'I saw what happened to my husband and as long as there is breath in me, the same thing is not going to happen to David', Hazel, then aged 44, told her local newspaper in 1965.[14] David's father, Mervyn Dean, had enlisted in both wars. He was gassed in France in World War I and seriously wounded in the Middle East during World War II, losing the sight of an eye. He died in 1961, aged 54, leaving his widow with three children. 'He may have been a volunteer in both wars, but it cost him years of sickness and eventually his life', his wife said.[15]

Women with personal links to previous wars also grappled with what it meant to be patriotic in the face of accusations that they were traitors, communists or, worse, 'un-Australian' for opposing conscription. The concept of a 'loyal opposition' whereby citizens could be loyal to their country while opposing government policy was still difficult for many Australians to accept in the postwar period. While many ex-servicemen, publicly and privately, opposed conscription and the Vietnam War, the most vehement support for the government's policy – and disdain for those who dissented – often came from within the ranks of the Returned and Services League (RSL). From Armidale, Mrs Ebere wrote passionately that she was 'not a coward, neither do I come from a race of cowards'.

> My father was killed in France in 1916, fighting with the Canadians, my stepfather still has the scar on his neck from a bullet he collected on the beaches at Gallipoli. My four brothers and my husband all served with the Australian forces in World War II and my cousin was a paratrooper at Arnhem. Should our beloved Australia be attacked I personally would push at least one invader into the sea. Until that time comes, I will resist to the utmost the belief that our sons should add to the misery of unhappy Vietnam.[16]

Defending her decision to join SOS, she wrote 'there are a few women amongst us who are sick and tired of creating life at the cost of suffering and years of careful nurturing only to see it wantonly destroyed every twenty-five years or so'.[17] In country Victoria, Judith Harrison concurred. 'Two generations of mothers have already lost beautiful, well-grown sons because their paternal governments have sent boys to war. I speak not only of Australian mothers but English, European, Japanese, American and Russian mothers', she wrote. 'We mothers know that wars don't solve problems; wars kill. If men and governments cannot, or will not, save our sons, then we mothers must'.[18] In a similar vein, Mrs C. Atkins, of Balwyn, Victoria, observed:

> Once again ageing politicians and military brass are making decisions on behalf of the voteless youth of this country to take part in military adventures overseas. Once again mothers live in fear – watching, without joy, their teenage sons reaching military age. The authorities are to strike a medal for those who serve in Vietnam. What will we give to the widows and sorrowing mothers?[19]

In Melbourne, Gwen opposed conscription because she did not want to go through what her own mother and grandmother had experienced. Three generations of her family had fought in wars: her grandfather in the Boer War, her father in the Great War, and her husband in World War II. Her mother had lost three brothers in World War I, another returning 'with half a right arm', while a close cousin had perished as a prisoner of war working on the infamous Burmese railroad. When Menzies committed Australian troops to Vietnam, Gwen was working as a trainee buyer at an upmarket Melbourne department store, her oldest son was studying law, and her youngest was 'wrapped up in football' in which he was considered to have 'a future'. That future was never realised when he was called up as a 20-year-old to fight in Vietnam. While he went willingly, according to his mother he was a different person when he returned and 'never forgave the army'. Talking about her experiences three decades later, Gwen said she still vividly recalled 'the feeling of panic I had during our dreadful time of sending our young men to the Vietnam War! The government of the day was very high-handed in the way they sent these beautiful young men off to fight someone's dirty war'.[20]

Not all the women who joined SOS were Australian born. English immigrant Irene Miller experienced the effects of war firsthand as an ambulance driver in London during the Blitz. One of her enduring nightmares involved taking her eldest child to a shelter as bombs rained down on the city. She immigrated in 1948 because 'Australia seemed such a large peaceful country' and was horrified when Australia subsequently became involved in Vietnam, which she felt was 'a totally immoral war'.[21] By this time, her family had expanded. 'In the '60s, I was just an average housewife. I had 10 children ... I didn't want to see other cities destroyed like London', she said.[22]

In Wollongong, German-born Lydia Post became a vocal supporter of the anti-war movement because World War II had taught her that 'silence can also be a crime'. Her husband, a local steelworker who became vice-president of the Wollongong Moratorium Committee, had served with the SS and deeply regretted 'keeping his mouth closed and failing to oppose Hitler'. Post told the local newspaper that the Vietnam War had violated her conscience and she and her husband did 'not want to be called fellow travellers again, closing our eyes and not seeing anything'. 'Twenty years ago we kept quiet', she said. 'Never again.'[23]

Peace Movement Veterans

In the early stages of the Vietnam protests, women from non-political backgrounds tended to see conscription and the war as two separate issues. Over time – and as women became more familiar with the situation in Vietnam – the two issues became entwined. There were some women, however, who opposed the war on moral, political and humanitarian grounds even before conscription was announced. These tended to be women who were already active in the peace movement, either through religious groups or organisations such as the Union of Australian Women (UAW) and the Women's International League for Peace and Freedom (WILPF). During the Vietnam era, some continued to protest from within these groups while others, like UAW members Noreen Hewett, Babs O'Sullivan and Nora Mulheron in Sydney, Marion Henderson in Western Australia, Vilma Ward in Brisbane and Loma Thompson in Townsville, helped to set up SOS branches in their states. Some held dual memberships or supported other groups as well as their own. These 'veterans' of the peace movement were generous in sharing their expertise and networks with newcomers.

Some of these women, like Dorothy Gibson in Melbourne and Vivienne Abraham in Sydney, had no children of their own. Their objection to conscription and the war went beyond any obvious personal links to the issue. Gibson, a former teacher, confirmed pacifist, and communist, was quite elderly by the time the Vietnam War began. She had still been at school when the conscription debate flared in World War I and recalled that while her female teacher had been 'tremendously patriotic about the war and had us knitting every spare moment', her father had been totally opposed and determined that her older brother should not enlist. She witnessed one anti-conscription meeting in her usually genteel street where 'women were screaming at each other'.

Experiences like these helped mould her political views: 'It seemed such a terrible thing. I couldn't see a procession of soldiers without crying. "Going away to die" was all I thought'.[24] Gibson had been a stalwart in the peace movement since the 1930s through her involvement in several organisations, many of them communist-linked. She had been an executive member of the Victorian Council Against War and Fascism, a member of the International Peace Campaign, and during the Cold War served as an executive member and full-time organiser of the two main communist-backed peace organisations, the Australian Peace Council, and its successor, the Congress for International Cooperation and Disarmament (CICD).[25] The Vietnam War and the new debate over conscription affected her deeply and she was an early member of the Victorian SOS. Her husband Ralph recalled that Dorothy 'felt for the Vietnamese people very intensely' and found reading about their plight 'almost unbearable'. She became 'convinced that the struggle in Vietnam was linked with our struggle for liberty at home, and thus it had decisive importance for the future'.[26] Despite ill-health, Dorothy attended all SOS meetings and took part in the early morning demonstrations during intakes of conscripts at the Swan Street army barracks. Ralph Gibson recalled that his wife suffered terribly from arthritis, so this was 'a severe test ... especially in winter, and certainly contrary to medical advice, but she never hesitated about going'.[27]

Another veteran peace advocate was Vivienne Abraham, who, while never an official member lent her considerable support to SOS and was present at the first and last SOS meetings in Sydney.[28] Though she had no children of her own, as a Quaker, Abraham was 'determined not to support any kind of war and to strive for the removal of all causes of war'.[29] Born in Melbourne in 1920, Vivienne had already spent a lifetime fighting for peace and social justice issues by the time Australia committed troops to Vietnam. She had been active in the Melbourne Jewish Youth Council during World War II and with the Victorian Branch of the Peace Pledge Union in the 1940s and 1950s.[30] She was also a long-time member of the WILPF and an active campaigner for social reforms for Indigenous people. In the early 1960s, she briefly lived in Israel and joined friend and fellow pacifist G. A. Bishop in representing the Federal Pacifist Council of Australia (FPC) at a peace conference in Lebanon. During the Vietnam War she was honorary secretary of the FPC and also edited the pacifist newspaper, the *Peacemaker*, with her sister Shirley as co-editor for some of this time. The paper was a major source of alternative news on the Vietnam War and provided practical information for draft resisters and conscientious objectors. A copy was included in a special pack given out to young men who sought draft-counselling. Armed with a law degree from Melbourne University, Abraham also travelled throughout Australia, counselling potential conscientious objectors, organising their legal representation, helping with the preparation of their court cases and testifying on their behalf.[31] 'I've got no time to be domestic', she declared in 1969, explaining that she spent most of her time fighting for the rights of conscientious objectors.[32] Draft resister Mac Gudgeon remembered meeting Abraham at an anti-war rally in Sydney and being impressed by her 'fierce intellect'. At that time she was also involved in hiding and moving draft resisters between 'safe houses'. 'She had a very strong intellectual basis as Quakers do for their peace campaign so it was another part of my education, talking to her and reading *Peacemaker*', Gudgeon recalled. 'I remember many long nights and cups of coffee arguing about campaigns and tactics … She had her fingers in a lot of pies but when people write the history, she seems to be someone that not many people know about.'[33]

For some veteran activists, the Vietnam War was both political and personal. In Sydney, Nora Mulheron was already an experienced peace activist, having campaigned for nuclear disarmament during the 1950s and early 1960s as a member of the UAW and the Association for International Co-operation and Disarmament (AICD). She also had three sons – two of whom became eligible for conscription during the Vietnam War. Born in Liverpool and brought up in a strong Irish Catholic family, she had deep working-class roots. She was 12 years old when her family moved to Australia, just in time for the Great Depression during which her parents and older siblings all experienced long-term unemployment. After 'surviving a Catholic education' and leaving school at 13, Nora held a variety of jobs and became involved with the Unemployed Workers Movement. Like many of her peers, she was greatly affected by the Spanish Civil War and volunteered to work for the International Brigades as a nurse but could not obtain a visa. According to her youngest son Maurie, the Spanish War became a touchstone that she referred to continuously throughout her life. When she was about 20, Nora joined the Communist Party of Australia (CPA), a membership she never relinquished. She was working in the party's bookshop towards the end of the war when she met her husband, an activist in the Railways Union, and later ran her own home-based child-care centre. Nora was one of the many women who did not fit the 'middle-class' image that became closely associated with SOS during the course of the Vietnam War.

Mums of 'Ratbags'

Many women became involved with SOS, at least initially, to support their own sons who had decided to make stands as conscientious objectors or draft resisters. Some of these women were already veterans of the peace movement, like Noreen Hewett in Sydney whose son Rex became a high-profile conscientious objector. Others were new to activism, like Helen Christofides and Edna Gudgeon in Wollongong who dipped their toes into activism for the first time when their sons announced they would not register for conscription. This abrupt transition from the private to the political sphere could be fraught. In an unusually prominent letter to the *Australian* in 1969, Elizabeth Jones outlined in vivid terms her own political 'coming of age' when her son Mike was jailed for his stand against conscription.

> When my son was gaoled, I felt numb then despairing. This was followed by a blinding, almost overpowering anger and hatred for the people responsible for his suffering. Now I understood how the Vietnamese people feel towards the oppressors of their country. This passed, and I experienced physical pain, then a mental anguish so intense I begged on my knees for help and guidance. At last the pain eased and I knew that what my son was fighting for was right and I knew that whatever the Government did to him and despite the suffering that this would bring about, I could never try to turn him away from the stand he is taking against the crime this Government is committing against the Vietnamese people.[34]

Some women initially struggled with their sons' decisions. When Dorothy Dalton's son Tony announced he was becoming a draft resister, she tried to talk him out of it. 'I [said] "why can't you become a conscientious objector, do it legally", and of course he pointed out, "no, that's saying I'm not going to go but it's okay for someone else to go" so I was very wrong there but of course I was worried about his future', she recalled.[35] Dorothy and her husband Les, who had been members of the CPA in their younger years, had been hesitant to join the anti-war movement but were given a push by their two sons who challenged them to put their words into action. Dorothy recalled that 'from the time our kids could talk we had always discussed world affairs at the dinner table and in the end they would say to us, "well why do you always talk and never do anything?"'[36] From then on Dorothy became a committed campaigner against conscription.

In Wollongong, where she worked at the chip counter of the local Coles cafeteria, Helen Christofides was confounded by the Australian Government's policy. Born in Cyprus, she had moved to Australia to join her husband in 1950. When he returned overseas ten years later, she was left with five children to raise on her own in a strange country. She first became aware of conscription when her 19-year-old son Louis announced his intention to become a draft resister.[37] Non-Australian residents were initially exempt from national service but the legislation was later amended after a vocal lobby argued that migrants would steal the jobs of Australian lads sent away to fight. All Helen knew was that the Australian Government wanted to take her son and she was at a loss to understand why. 'I was born in Cyprus and am told that if I don't give my sons up to support American aggression in Vietnam they will go to gaol for refusing to kill. What sort of mothers do they think we are that we should put up with this treatment from this Government and say nothing?' she asked.[38] Her son Louis described his mother as a working-class migrant woman who always voted Labor, and who was not afraid to stand up for what she believed in. 'Being Greek, she had this fire in her belly', he added.[39]

Edna Gudgeon had been running a popular ballet school in Wollongong when her son announced he was not going to register for conscription. Born in Sydney she had grown up in a poor, working-class family, and joined a travelling vaudeville dance troop before settling down in Wollongong with her pharmacist husband where they were both respected members of the local community. Their children had subsequently grown up in a middle-class environment with their son, Mac, attending Sydney's prestigious King's School before enrolling in an Arts/Law degree at the University of Sydney. At university, he became politically active, opposing the Vietnam War on the grounds that it was a civil conflict, and conscription because he believed all armies should be comprised only of volunteers.[40] Given his father was an ex-serviceman, it was 'with some trepidation' that Mac finally told his parents that he did not intend to register for the draft. Under the *National Services Act*, this meant he would forgo his chance of his birthday *not* coming up in the lottery and would be automatically conscripted or jailed if he refused to comply. He recalled: 'Once I'd explained my reasons, I wouldn't say they were at first too excited about the prospect but they respected my decision and then they began to educate themselves about the war'.[41] Edna immediately joined the local SOS group, becoming an office-bearer and one of its most vocal members. 'My son will never register', she told the local press. 'I am proud he will never kill mothers and children in Vietnam.'[42]

Political Beliefs

There was a diverse range of political views and affiliations among women who joined SOS. Many of the more experienced campaigners were drawn from groups like the UAW or women's auxiliaries in the trade unions were communists, socialists or Australian Labor Party (ALP) supporters. Some groups, like SOS in Victoria, had strong links to the ALP from the beginning. One of its earliest supporters, Nola Barber, an ALP member, had been the first female councillor and mayor of her local council. She later stood unsuccessfully for election for federal parliament.[43] As the war dragged on, many women who had been apolitical before their involvement in the protest movement found themselves drawn to the ALP in the hope that a change of government would bring about a speedy end to conscription. Most women, however, were motivated to protest not by party politics but by their humanitarian views and their personal connections. In Townsville, for example, political activism was in Loma Thompson's blood. A member of the CPA and later the ALP, she was married to Fred Thompson, a high-profile union organiser with the Australian Manufacturing Workers' Union (AMWU). A former nursing sister from Melbourne who had hitchhiked to Townsville in the 1950s, Loma had supported her husband's efforts during the drawn out 1964 strike at the Mount Isa mines. She also had years of volunteer experience in the UAW and women's trade union auxiliaries, working for peace, Aboriginal rights and other social justice issues.[44] But she insists politics played little part in her decision to protest against conscription. As a mother of a teenage son she said SOS 'was just one of those things you *had* to get involved in'.[45]

While less obvious, many conservative women also took issue with conscription. Some, like Val Reid in Outback NSW, changed their politics over their opposition to the Vietnam War. Years earlier, Reid had campaigned for the Liberal party against a communist candidate in a local election but during the Vietnam War she actively campaigned against the government, cautioning that a vote for conservative parties would be akin to signing 'your sons' death warrant'.[46] Another 'staunch Liberal supporter', Mrs D. J. Simes, of Keiraville, NSW, wrote to the prime minister warning him that 'whilst I don't want a Labor government in power, I am sorely tempted, for purely selfish reasons, to vote for one'.[47] Those 'selfish reasons' were five teenage sons. While stressing that her boys did not 'come from a family of shirkers' (both grandfathers having served as volunteers in World War II), Simes wanted reassurance from the Prime Minister that if one son was conscripted, the others would be 'automatically exempted'.[48] Liberal voter Margaret Boddy, of Daylesford, Victoria, similarly found herself faced with a conundrum when it came to deciding who to vote for at the 1966 election. In a letter to Prime Minister Harold Holt she wrote: 'We prize our British heritage, value the support of the United States ... but I am totally against conscription ... I do not wish to vote Liberal but cannot bring myself to vote Labor. What can one do?'[49] Being married to a State Country Party MP did not stop Perth's Mollie Cornell from opposing conscription. Molly had four sons and was 'very distressed and disgusted' by conscription, particularly the random method of selection.[50] After researching the issue, she produced a paper that argued forcefully against the *National Service Act*, circulating it to contacts across Australia. 'My husband knows what I am doing – and if he disapproves, he has certainly not shown it', she wrote.[51]

Religious Beliefs

Quakers, Catholics, Methodists, agnostics and atheists all joined forces to oppose conscription, some against the express wishes of their clergy. Mrs Ebere spoke for many Christian women when she declared, 'I am at a loss to understand how a Christian can condone the violation of another country accompanied by the brutal destruction and terrorising of helpless children'.[52] Quakers were strong opponents of the Vietnam War and conscription. Jean Richards, described in one press report as 'a housewife and a Quaker', was president of the Federal Pacifist Council (FPC). She told a 1964 rally that as a woman she opposed conscription because it 'put allegiance to the state above allegiance to God', and because she could never believe it was right for any man to be trained compulsorily to kill.[53] However, the Vietnam War created deep divisions in both Protestant and Catholic churches. While many church leaders were outspoken opponents of the war and conscription, others strongly supported it. As a result women often found themselves out of step with their spiritual leaders. In Sydney, Margaret Holmes was a devout Anglican but that did not stop her from publicly opposing church leaders who supported the government's policies, once picketing the airport to protest against the visit to Vietnam by the Anglican Primate of Australia, Archbishop Hugh Gough.[54] On another occasion she wrote a public letter to the Archbishop arguing against the church's approval of Australia's involvement in the war. She also helped organise a meeting of about 80 Christians of different denominations who opposed the war.[55] A Catholic woman in SOS, Noreen McDonald, also organised a delegation to see a Catholic bishop who supported the war and later helped establish Christian Women Concerned, a broad group comprising women from various denominations.[56]

Val Reid also struggled to reconcile her Christian beliefs with her politics. From her home on an isolated station in Outback NSW where she home-schooled four primary-school-aged children, she waged a one-woman campaign against conscription, writing letters and poems, taking out full-page advertisements, and producing a cassette tape entitled 'A History of Vietnam Documented by Christian Conscience' which she sought to distribute to a 'pro Christian audience'.[57] In an open letter to her neighbours she explained, 'I protest against conscription. I protest against the war in Vietnam and I protest against the destruction of Christianity and democracy'.[58] Sensitive to suggestions she was disloyal to her country, she pointed out that her family had had Australian Army representatives at Queen Victoria's Diamond

Jubilee and volunteers 'at every war since that time'.[59] 'I was 11 years old when my father volunteered for the Second World War. He would never have permitted young 20-year-olds to be conscripted to fight for his family', she wrote.[60]

In Townsville, Esme Hardy was a devout Catholic but opposition to the war put her at odds with her local priest and her fellow parishioners. Raised in northern NSW, Hardy later moved between Melbourne and Brisbane after joining the Women's Army Service where she worked in the typist pool. One of her jobs was to type the telegrams that were sent to the families of soldiers killed or wounded in action in WWII. After the war she moved to north Queensland where she met Henry Hardy, who skippered the boat that operated between Dunk Island and the mainland. The couple married and settled in Townsville where Henry worked as an engine driver in the powerhouse and became involved in the local union, while Esme was fully occupied bringing up seven children, six of them boys.[61] Esme and Henry were heavily involved in their local parish, where the politics of ardent anti-communist B. A. Santamaria and his National Civic Council were regularly preached from the pulpit. As strong Labor supporters and 'blue collar Catholics', they frequently found themselves at cross purposes with their fellow parishioners, most of them 'upper crust conservative Catholics'. According to their son, Tom, these existing tensions were exacerbated by the Vietnam War when both Esme and Henry became involved in the local peace movement.

'New' Women

While the Vietnam War protests were a continuation of a life of activism for some women, they also radicalised a new constituency of women who had never been involved in politics before. These women were drawn from many areas of life. Some of these women have already been discussed: the good Catholic Esme Hardy; and Wollongong's ballet teacher, Edna Gudgeon. In Sydney, Alma Scaysbrook and Ella Outhred were also motivated by their concerns about conscription to protest for the first time. Scaysbrook, who had five children, went on to become a president of the group, delivering a stirring address at the first moratorium in Sydney. In a leaflet widely distributed by SOS during the 1970s, she explained her reasons for becoming involved: 'I oppose conscription because it denies a person the right to choose the cause for which he must sacrifice his life if need be'.[62]

Many of the women who became involved were stay-at-home housewives and mothers but this job title frequently obscured a wealth of life experiences and concerns that contributed to their stand against conscription. Ella Outhred, for example, a suburban housewife in her fifties, was one of the first to join Sydney SOS. To the casual observer, her motivation seemed clear. With three sons at university, two of whom became eligible for conscription, the most obvious trigger for her involvement in SOS was the personal threat to her family unit. However, her sons believe her commitment to the cause had more to do with a deep social conscience that had been stirred from an early age and nurtured in places as diverse as Ipswich, Kalgoorlie and Wollongong. Denied the chance to study medicine by a father who did not believe in women doctors, Ella instead became a nurse, later marrying Ken, a doctor who maintained a special interest in the health of coal miners throughout his life. His work took the family first to Queensland and then to Kalgoorlie where Ella developed friendships among the local Aboriginal community and a life-long interest in Indigenous rights. Some of her son's earliest memories involved picnics in the bush and the local Aboriginal people who used 'to call by our house because they were welcome there'.⁶³ The experience affected the entire family, with son Alan becoming one of the original 'freedom riders' with Aboriginal activist Charlie Perkins in the early 1960s. The family later moved to Wollongong where Ken took up a position as Medical Officer with the Commonwealth-State Coal Board before relocating again to Sydney. Hugh Outhred said both his parents had a strong interest in equity issues and while Ken had been constrained by his job as a Commonwealth public servant, he also opposed the war. He believed his mother would have become involved even if there had not been a threat to her family. 'For her the broader issue was the question, "What the heck was a rich country like Australia doing beating up a poor country like Vietnam?"', he said.⁶⁴

Other 'new women' included popular Australian Broadcasting Corporation (ABC) TV presenter Corinne Kerby and folk singer Glen Tomasetti. Again, appearances could be deceiving. In 1962, the *Australian Women's Weekly* heralded Corinne Kerby as 'TV's Clever Career Mother' photographing her hanging curtains and marvelling at her ability to juggle a career, two young children, and the housework.⁶⁵ The 'vivacious personality' who hosted several national programs on Channel 2 was considered 'the first lady of Australian television' but she was also the daughter of an outspoken union leader who had lost his job with the Melbourne tramways after visiting Russia in the 1940s. Kerby's infant son was in no danger of being conscripted but she was deeply disturbed by the effect of the war on Vietnamese children and lent her considerable celebrity to the anti-conscription movement through SOS, much to the unease of her employer. 'I was terribly emotional about it', she recalled. 'I [was] very aware of the Vietnamese children and thinking this could so easily be my own son.'⁶⁶ Born and raised in Melbourne, Kerby joined the Women's

Auxiliary Air Force (WAAF) towards the end of World War II, later working at the ABC as a typist/stenographer before successfully auditioning as a radio announcer and switching to the new medium of television. Declared 'a natural', she read the news, interviewed the rich and famous, and hosted her own programs.[67] In 1962 she became the compere of Channel 2's first national women's program *Mainly for Women* but was reportedly unhappy with the concept that included a segment on household tips, believing that women did not need their own special program.[68] She eventually succeeded in convincing her TV bosses to change the name and the format to include politics and current affairs.[69]

Kerby was a considerable drawcard at SOS events, addressing demonstrations and public meetings. She was also a talented poet, publishing two books. Several of her poems about the Vietnam War were used by the anti-war movement.[70] At one public meeting, she took on opponents who branded anti-war protesters as 'communists, tools or dupes'.[71] 'We must see through this trick in this hour of the Vietnam War, when we have grown familiar with pictures of lines of prisoners fastened together with wire through their hands or cheeks and of children with faces melted by napalm', she told the gathering.[72] After her death in 2003, the *Age* noted that while during her early career Kerby had struggled to be taken seriously by the media, through her activism she had become 'a role model for women hitherto inhibited from joining what were, at the time, anti-Establishment causes'.[73]

Melbourne folk singer Glenys (Glen) Tomasetti was also a vehement opponent of the Vietnam War. She wrote and recorded anti-war songs and was a popular performer at anti-war rallies. In 1966, her song *The Ballad of Bill White*, which told the story of Sydney school teacher and conscientious objector William White, became the anthem of anti-war protests across the country. Born in Melbourne, Tomasetti attended the University of Melbourne on a Commonwealth Scholarship, graduating with an honours degree in English and History, where she was a student of Manning Clark with whom she had a life-long friendship. She married and had two children but comfortable domesticity and the role of a suburban housewife did not suit her. To counter domestic boredom, she formed the 'Making Balwyn Bearable Society' where members 'enjoyed jazz and wild dancing'.[74] After her second marriage failed, Tomasetti taught herself to play the guitar and started writing songs and singing them. During the 1960s, she wrote and performed political songs on a weekly television current affairs program, released 11 albums and wrote scripts for ABC radio. She also travelled widely, including a trip to China in the late 1950s with a troupe of folk singers. She later said that her travels had been 'crucial' in forming her anti-war beliefs.[75] Like many women in the 1960s, Tomasetti was involved in multiple causes that often overlapped with the anti-war movement. In 1969, she became 'a hero of the feminist movement' after changing the words of a popular shearer's ballad, to 'Don't be too Polite, Girls' in support of the case for equal pay.[76] The *Age*'s obituary remembered Tomasetti as an 'author, poet, folk singer, biographer, political activist, and a steadfast feminist'.[77] In 1965, she was also one of the original members of Victoria SOS, her background further underlining the diversity among women who joined the organisation.

* * *

While photographs and reports that appeared in the media tended to reinforce the general impression of SOS as a group of middle-aged, middle-class mothers protesting to save their sons from conscription, there was, in fact, no 'typical' SOS supporter. Women who protested during the Vietnam era were a mixed group: individuals with their own unique stories united by their mutual objection to conscription and/or the Vietnam War. Their reasons for objecting to conscription were not straightforward but influenced by their own personal situations and experiences. Inevitably, however, they were drawn to like-minded souls, both in women-only and mixed anti-war groups, including SOS. As founding member Noreen Hewett later observed, SOS attracted women 'some with children, some without, from across the political spectrum and from all walks of life including Quakers, Catholics, Methodists, agnostics, atheists, Labor, communists, even Liberal and non-party women'.[78] The fact that such a diverse group of women was able to unite behind a single cause was a feat that did not go unnoticed. 'It is a lesson in tolerance', Wollongong SOS supporter Gillian Wilding observed in 1970, 'when a group of mothers belonging to different churches, political parties and organisations can sit down, forget differences, and say, we have two things in common: we are mothers [and] we are opposed to conscription and the war in Vietnam'.[79]

Chapter 3

THE 'FOUNDING MOTHERS'

> Mothers resist all sorts of pressures to bring up their children as useful citizens, to look forward to useful careers and to be of service to the community. Then, suddenly, their lives are disrupted ...
>
> *Joyce Golgerth*[1]

In late 1964, Joyce Golgerth took a phone call that would change the course of her life. On the line was her sister-in-law Ruby 'Babs' O'Sullivan, a former dancer, wife of one of Australia's most successful jockeys, and a discreet, card-carrying communist. O'Sullivan wanted to know if Golgerth had heard Menzies' announcement about national service and if she realised what it would mean for her own son. Golgerth was horrified. Her youngest daughter, Candy, vividly recalls her mother sitting in the hallway of their neat Pennant Hills home talking to O'Sullivan. 'I remember my aunt called my mother and said, "Have you heard of Vietnam? Michael will be going to war", and my mother hadn't, and she didn't know anything about it and very quickly she had to learn and understand what it was all about. To her it was absolutely horrific.'[2]

Golgerth was galvanised into action. In May 1965, the *Australian* reported that she had founded Save Our Sons (SOS), a group of like-minded mothers who opposed conscription.³ A week later, four carloads of SOS women travelled to Canberra to take part in a protest outside Parliament House in Canberra, where Golgerth led a delegation of mothers to see the Minister for the Army, Dr Jim Forbes.⁴ A Union of Australian Women (UAW) bulletin produced at this time praised the effort reporting that 'Mrs Golgerth and her friends emerged triumphant from the interview. They had expressed their feelings in no uncertain terms to Dr Forbes and left him bereft of argument in answer to their point of view'.⁵ By the end of May, SOS had collected an impressive 1000 signatures for a petition condemning conscription.⁶ The following month, SOS held an all-day vigil outside the Marrickville Army Depot during the first intake of conscripts.⁷ (The group held protests at every intake of conscripts thereafter.) In August, SOS produced and distributed 20,000 leaflets opposing conscription.

As news of SOS spread, it looked like Golgerth was set to become the leader of a national movement.⁸ Four months after Sydney SOS was founded, satellite groups had been established in Brisbane, Melbourne and Newcastle.⁹ Within a year, there were also groups in Wollongong, Townsville, Adelaide and Perth.¹⁰ At the group's first annual general meeting, members paid tribute to Golgerth 'whose inspiration it was to get mothers together to discuss what could be done to oppose the Government's conscription law'.¹¹ But some – principally within government, police and intelligence circles – were not convinced that Golgerth had acted alone in founding the group. Scrambling to learn all they could about the 44-year-old, Australian Security Intelligence Organisation (ASIO) officers were disappointed when they were unable to find anything in her past that even remotely linked her with the

Communist Party of Australia (CPA) or its various 'fronts'.[12] She was, for all intents and purposes, exactly what she purported to be: 'just a housewife and a mother' who was deeply concerned about conscription and what it would mean for Australia's sons.[13] Convinced, nonetheless, that SOS itself was a front, ASIO still decided that a personal file on Golgerth was warranted.[14]

This story of how an ordinary suburban housewife mobilised a band of like-minded Australian mums to save their sons from conscription and the Vietnam War has a certain universal myth-like appeal and, not surprisingly, this version of SOS's foundation attracted media interest. Accounts crediting Golgerth as the sole founder have also been preserved in the historical literature documenting the anti-war protest movement as a whole.[15] But the origins of the SOS movement are not as straightforward or as spontaneous as they first seem; there was a deliberate move by the founding mothers of SOS to carefully manage the public image of the movement in order to create an acceptable face of dissent during this period. This reflects a degree of political savvy that runs counter to the popular view that SOS was a band of political neophytes who were literally stepping out of the kitchen and onto the political stage for the first time. In fact, of the nine founding Sydney women, this label could be applied to just one, Golgerth.

When conscription was introduced, Golgerth had four children: a son and three daughters. She had grown up in Melbourne as an only child and had been a talented violinist and an accomplished horsewoman, going on to study commercial art and music. While working as a commercial artist, she had met her future husband, a draftsman in the same office.[16] After the birth of their son, Michael, they moved to Sydney, to take advantage of job opportunities in the booming postwar building industry there. While her husband worked in various jobs, building housing commission homes, selling real estate and cars, Joyce stayed at home bringing up their children. Her sister-in-law encouraged her to volunteer at the RSPCA where she eventually became an honorary inspector. According to her family, Golgerth's politics were always more closely aligned with the left, although these never came to the fore until the Vietnam War.

When conscription was announced, Golgerth's eldest daughter had recently married, leaving Michael and two younger daughters still living at home. Candy, the youngest, was only 10 years old and frequently accompanied her mother to SOS meetings and events. Having a son in the first batch of conscripts made the political situation personal, adding urgency to Golgerth's response. But her daughter Sue Foster believes that while the threat to her own son was undoubtedly the trigger, the circumstances of the Vietnam War also tapped into a deeply held belief that the war itself was wrong.[17] 'She thought they were going to take Michael and she thought, like most mums do, "I didn't have my son and raise my son and look after and nurture him all his life to have him kill or be killed"', Foster recalled. 'But she also thought that the whole killing of other human beings was ghastly and the Vietnam War was something that should never have happened [and] that we should never have been there.' Golgerth suffered from debilitating migraines but Foster said she was 'a very, very strong woman' who commanded authority. 'She never had to raise her voice, she never used to swear but she just had a way where she could say a couple of words and you would say, "Yes, I'd better do it".'[18]

Golgerth was the ideal public figurehead for SOS, but whether she or someone else 'created' SOS remains a matter of conjecture. On the one hand, Golgerth's children have never had any reason to doubt that their mother was the sole founder. This is reinforced in official SOS press releases, newsletters and correspondence. On the other hand, Golgerth's lack of experience in setting up a grassroots protest group, or, for that matter, significant involvement in any group prior to this time, does raise questions particularly when considered alongside SOS's busy agenda in its first months and how well-organised, connected and politically astute the group appeared to be. The origins of the group have never fully been explained. The official press release announcing the group's formation provides no details of how the women came together. It mentions only that Golgerth, who had 'a son in the first batch of conscripts' was the convenor.[19] This was the version carried by the *Australian* and other newspapers in May 1965. A slightly different version appeared in the *Sun*, which quoted another founding SOS member, Margaret Lee, claiming that the group had been formed after a chance meeting between Golgerth and the group's first secretary, Pat Ashcroft, in a Pennant Hills butcher shop. The two had apparently 'fallen into conversation and discovered that they both opposed conscription'.[20] The best explanation from the time was offered by Golgerth herself. In a strident letter to the *Bulletin* published in April 1966, Golgerth stated that she wished 'to make it very clear to all concerned' that SOS was 'not the direct product of the Union of Australian Women' or any other supposed 'communist front', but 'was instigated by myself and other mothers of 20-year-olds who were strongly opposed' to conscription.

> In October 1964, when this legislation was about to be implemented, I started contacting other mothers of boys eligible for conscription. From then until May last year it was my main thought that there must be other women who felt as I did and gradually I came into contact with some … By May last year

> I had contacted a number of mothers in a similar position to myself. We met on May 13 to discuss what could be done. All were enthusiastic to form a mother's organisation and the name Save Our Sons was chosen.[21]

Golgerth concluded by stating categorically that SOS had spread to almost all States and to country centres 'without the aid, influence or motivating force of the Communist Party of Australia or any other organisation'.

On the surface, this seems to settle the matter of SOS's origins. However, Golgerth's purpose in writing this letter – to respond to an article that had accused SOS of being a communist 'front' – has to be taken into account, especially if the group was deliberately seeking to downplay its CPA and UAW connections. Golgerth's letter is certainly a spirited defence of the organisation against suggestions that it had been set up by the UAW and was under the influence of the CPA, highlighting the sensitivity of SOS to these accusations. It is also noteworthy that Golgerth does not suggest that there are no CPA or UAW women within the organisation or attempt to defend their involvement.

Years after the group wound up, a different narrative emerged with another member, Noreen Hewett, being credited with establishing the group. Hewett had a very different upbringing from Golgerth. Her father had fought in World War I and suffered with post-traumatic stress disorder. He committed suicide when she was just 14. Hewett joined the CPA when she was 21 after a door-knocker persuaded her to buy a copy of the party's newspaper. For a little more money, she was told, she could also join the party. While she had not known much about the CPA, she had 'relished the fact that it was illegal' so handed over the extra coins. At the time she was a member of the Australian

Labor Party (ALP) where she had been campaign manager for left-wing politician playwright and journalist Les Haylen, who was said to have been one of the Opposition Leader Arthur Calwell's 'closest confidants'.[22] Hewett later resigned from the ALP and worked for the CPA as 'a low paid functionary' in one of its district offices and was involved in a number of CPA campaigns for better working conditions for women, including the provision of child care. In 1944, she married fellow communist and boilermaker Syd Hewett, a widower 15 years her senior with a teenage son. Her own son Rex was born the following year. After World War II she worked as a journalist, helping to edit the Miners' Federation's journal, *Common Cause*, and reporting on the coal miners' strike of 1949.[23] Convinced that the coal miners' wives needed a voice, she reinvigorated the Miners' Women's Auxiliaries, which supported the campaigns of miners and became a political force in their own right pushing women's policies.[24] She accompanied auxiliary women on two trips to Canberra to protest against miners' low wages, on one occasion 'forcefully' presenting the women's case to Harold Holt, then Minister for Labour. The Deputy Leader of the Labor Party, Dr H. V. Evatt, who was present at the meeting, is said to have told Hewett as she left the room, 'You were brilliant'.[25]

When the UAW formed in 1950, Hewett was an inaugural member, becoming its first NSW president and later national secretary and president. Among the causes she championed at the UAW were adequate child care, increased child endowment and price control of basic foods.[26] She was also a strong advocate for Aboriginal Rights, working closely with Aboriginal UAW members Pearl Gibbs, Faith Bandler and Oodgeroo Noonuccal.[27] In 1959, Hewett was one of 10 women representing 10 countries invited through the Women's International

Democratic Federation (WIDF) to attend China's 10th anniversary celebrations of the Chinese Revolution where she met leaders of the Chinese Women's Movement.[28] A year later she returned to China for an eight month CPA study tour during which she represented the UAW at the WIDF conference in Warsaw and visited Moscow, forging links with many foreign women leaders.[29] Conscription was both a personal and political issue with her son Rex and his cousin Les both eligible for the first ballot. On the eve of the formation of SOS, Hewett – unlike Golgerth – was already an experienced political campaigner and her skills proved invaluable in establishing the new movement.

In 2001, Hewett was invited to address a conference organised by the Sydney Branch of the Australian Society for the Study of Labour History where she spoke about the establishment of SOS and of meeting Golgerth for the first time. Interestingly, in the subsequent book which published the conference papers Hewett was listed as 'co-convenor of the Save Our Sons in Sydney and national SOS coordinator, 1960s'.[30] Whether this title was provided by Hewett or bestowed by one of the conference organisers is unknown but, according to SOS archives, it is certainly not a title she held during the group's existence. Indeed, according to accounts of early meetings, she actively refused to hold any office higher than assistant secretary, and only accepted this role with great reluctance.[31] Hewett died in early 2012, leaving behind apparently contradictory versions of SOS's origins. Her obituary in the *Sydney Morning Herald*, recorded that she had founded SOS with Golgerth.[32] It was also impossible to clarify the situation with Golgerth who, at the time of researching this book, was in advanced stages of dementia and unable to be interviewed. She died in early 2015. According to her family, she rarely spoke about her time with

SOS and did not keep in touch with the other women.[33] Nor has she left any personal recollections in the form of diaries, letters or minutes that might help to clarify the situation. However, an alternative, more nuanced, version of SOS's origins can be gleaned by comparing and piecing together evidence from personal interviews and various archival documents, including ASIO files, as well as researching the backgrounds of the original membership.

What is certain is that by May 1965, Hewett was already a seasoned grassroots protester while Golgerth was not. Moreover, Hewett was already leading the UAW's protest against conscription. In November 1964, under the UAW banner, she organised an anti-conscription demonstration in the gallery of federal parliament in Canberra where a large group of women had silently stood, holding up printed cards opposing conscription.[34] Their 'relatively mild action' resulted in the women being evicted from the gallery.[35] Hewett told the 2001 conference that it was at this protest that Golgerth 'approached me as another mother of a conscript to cooperate in forming a movement of women focussed on opposition to conscription for Vietnam'.[36] This version of events is also included in Siobhan McHugh's 1993 book, *Minefields and Miniskirts*. McHugh interviewed Hewett and recorded that it was Golgerth who had suggested to Hewett that 'they form an independent pressure group to fight conscription'.[37] It is not known how Golgerth came to be at the Canberra protest but she may have been invited by her sister-in-law Babs O'Sullivan who, as a member of the UAW and CPA, moved in Hewett's circle. It is also probable that it was O'Sullivan who introduced Golgerth to Hewett. The introduction also may have come via Pat Ashcroft, who was active in both the CPA and UAW. Either way, Hewett clearly seems to be suggesting that it was Golgerth who came up with the idea for the group. However, in Dorothy Cora's 2010 biography, Hewett provided more information about that first meeting that put a different slant on events:

> Amongst the demonstrators was a non-UAW woman, Joyce Golgerth, the mother of a son of conscription age. Joyce was reluctant to be associated with UAW's dissent because of its perceived links to communism, so *I suggested* that we form a new organisation and call it Save Our Sons.[38]

In this extract Hewett seems to be taking responsibility for initiating SOS. In view of her experience, Hewett certainly had the contacts to organise the venue for the first SOS meeting and to encourage fellow UAW women to join. She also had the experience necessary to organise SOS's first demonstration in Canberra just a week later. Golgerth had none of these contacts or political experience and it seems unlikely she could have achieved any of this without considerable assistance.

But if Hewett was the founder, or at least the co-founder, why was she not recognised as such in SOS literature? In Cora's biography, Hewett offered the explanation that her role was downplayed because of fears that her political links would 'taint' the new organisation even before it got off the ground.

> From previous experience I knew that if I were the public face of this new organisation, the media would discount it on the basis of my links with the Communist Party, so I asked Joyce if she would be willing to be the convenor of Save Our Sons and also be the media spokeswoman. She agreed.[39]

Not without misgivings, apparently. Minutes of an early meeting preserved in ASIO files show Golgerth refused to lead the group unless the more experienced Hewett agreed to be her co-secretary.[40] On 2 September 1965, when Golgerth was elected Organising Secretary, an ASIO insider also made a special note of a conversation between Golgerth and Hewett:

> After Golgerth had been elected Organising Secretary, she requested Hewett to assist her and become Joint Organising Secretary. Hewett replied that she would not do this. Golgerth said "You began this Movement and contacted me and got me the contacts and helped me to organise it". Hewett eventually agreed to assist in emergencies and was elected Joint Organising Secretary.[41]

This account would seem to support Hewett's later statement that she had been the one to initiate the group, enlisting Golgerth as its 'front woman', though it would also suit ASIO's narrative that SOS was a UAW front. At a subsequent meeting later that month, there was another disagreement during which 'Mrs Hewett firmly stated that she did not wish to be Joint Organising Secretary with Ms Golgerth as was discussed at the last meeting but would help when really necessary'.[42] In June 1966, Golgerth was elected president and Hewett assistant secretary. The ASIO informant present noted that prior to the vote Hewett again refused nomination to become secretary and only after some reluctance agreed to accept any position.[43]

No reason was ever recorded to explain Hewett's apparent reluctance to hold a senior leadership position. It is likely, however, that in addition to her concerns about 'tainting' the group, Hewett just had too many other responsibilities and felt that she could not devote the time necessary to establishing the new group. As well as holding down a job, she already had a huge commitment with the UAW leadership, including editing the group's magazine *Our Women*. Within a year of SOS forming, however, she resigned from this post, explaining that her SOS duties had become all-consuming.[44] But there were others within the founding membership who were also much more experienced than Golgerth and who could have taken over the leadership.

*　*　*

SOS Sydney's first annual report lists its foundation members as Pat Ashcroft, Dorothy Bendick, Joy Decker, Winifred Garland, Joyce Golgerth, Ann Gregory, Noreen Hewett, Margaret Lee and Babs O'Sullivan.[45] All nine attended the first meeting on 13 May 1965.

With the exception of Golgerth, all had direct links or loose affiliations with left-wing groups, along with varying degrees of experience as activists. At least four were involved with the CPA. Two had strong links to the ALP and at least four were also involved with the UAW. They were not all homegrown, however. Three founding members were foreign nationals. Nor, contrary to their first press report, were they all mothers of potential conscripts. At least one had no children of her own; others had sons who were too old or too young to be conscripted.

A committed peace activist, Patricia (Pat) Ashcroft became SOS's first secretary. Known to ASIO since 1962, she was an active member of the UAW and, with her husband, also supported the CPA, attending meetings and functions, although there is some doubt over whether they were actual members.[46] Ashcroft was also active in local peace committees and the Association for International Co-operation and Disarmament (AICD).[47] NSW election rolls show Ashcroft had previously been a shop assistant but by the 1960s was a full-time 'home-maker'. Her husband, John, a former grocer, is listed as a 'taxi proprietor'. A background check by ASIO in 1962 also revealed the Ashcrofts had been born in the United Kingdom.[48]

In 1965, when SOS started, Ashcroft was in her early fifties and had two sons nearing 'military age'. The family lived in Pennant Hills, not far from Golgerth, and it is possible the women may have known each other before SOS was formed. Ashcroft knew Hewett from the UAW, attending state and national meetings.[49] In March 1965, she had also taken part in an AICD 'peace delegation' to Canberra with another founding member, Dorothy Bendick.[50] In an 1966 interview about SOS published in the UAW's journal *Our Women*, Ashcroft was described as 'a mother of two grown up sons' who felt 'strongly that she has not reared and educated them to fight in an undeclared war on foreign soil against a country, Vietnam, that has never shown any hostility to Australia'.[51]

Dorothy Bendick was an American 'visitor' who arrived in Sydney in 1961.[52] Her peace activities with the UAW, AICD, and the Women's International League for Peace and Freedom (WILPF) soon aroused the interest of the NSW Special Branch and ASIO who recorded that she had been born in Pennsylvania in 1921, had one son, and worked as a 'freelance journalist'.[53] She and her husband were also recorded attending CPA events, with one ASIO agent unflatteringly referring to her as 'the American woman with the gaunt face and highly magnified horn-rimmed glasses'.[54] In April 1965, her seven-year-old son fell off a train at Chatswood Station and was saved by a 'wonderful Australian hero' who held him until the train could be stopped. In a letter published in the *Tribune*, Bendick thanked her son's saviour but also took the opportunity to highlight her concerns about the Vietnam War. 'After this close brush with death I weep for the mothers of Vietnam whose children are being burned and blown to bits by American bombs', she wrote. 'I implore my adopted country men: be as great nationally as you are individually. Compel your government to use its good offices as mediator to end the slaughter in Vietnam now.'[55] In another article in the *Peacemaker* she was described as 'a veteran of the inter-racial movement in the US'. ASIO noted that she was an associate of Australian civil rights activist Faith Bandler.[56] After a radio interview, in which she condemned America's involvement in Vietnam, an ASIO agent recorded: 'Dorothy Bendick is very anti-American about everything. She once said that her son will be eight on 4th July 1965 and added "I used to be patriotic in those days"'.[57]

In 1965, Bendick was elected to the UAW's NSW management committee and was heavily involved in its 'No War Toys' campaign in the lead-up to Christmas that year.[58] In fact, the slogan had been her suggestion and was inscribed on balloons that UAW members carried when they visited store managers in the city and suburban shopping malls to demand they withdraw window displays and television commercial advertising 'war toys' like guns and GI Joe dolls. SOS groups also embraced this campaign. Through Bendick, the UAW linked up with a like-minded group based in Los Angeles called 'No War Toys'.[59] In April 1966, Bendick arranged for the group's mascot, a life-sized rag doll known as 'Peaceful Pete', to be brought to Australia to assist with the UAW campaign. She was also a conduit for news from America, warning the UAW in October 1965 that the US planned to make Australia a war base in the Pacific.[60]

In August 1965, ASIO reported that Bendick and her family were preparing to return to America because they were 'not happy with the future of Australia' in light of the Vietnam War. She apparently also predicted that the country would become 'the last bastion of white supremacy as far as the Far East is concerned'.[61] ASIO noted concern among the local CPA branch that the Bendicks could be 'picked up' on their return by the Un-American Activities Committee and forced to disclose the names and addresses of party members and supporters connected with the Australian peace movement.[62] Bendick was apparently nonplussed. Before she left, she took part in a UAW/SOS protest in Canberra against the visit of US Vice President Hubert Humphrey. She was sadly missed by her UAW and SOS colleagues when she finally departed Australia in mid-1966.[63]

According to the 1968 NSW electoral roll, Joy Decker was a housewife living in Engadine, in Sydney's south. Born in Victoria during the Depression, she had worked as a stenographer and met her husband, Harold, a builder, during the war.[64] Both were long-time ALP members and active in the Building Workers Industrial Union. In 1968, she was elected as an ALP candidate for the Sutherland Shire Council, serving as a councillor until September 1971 when she was the victim of a messy pre-selection battle in her local party branch.[65] That same year she courted controversy when she represented the Australia–China Society on a three-week 'goodwill trip' to China that included a two-hour interview with the Chinese Premier Chou En-lai.[66] Quizzed on claims that the Society had communist links, she told the local paper it was strictly non-political and non-sectarian, adding: 'I'm not frightened of the Red bogey'.[67] On her return, she appeared in the same paper dressed 'in a typical Chinese dress for women'.[68] Conscription was also a personal issue for Decker who had three children, two sons and a daughter. Her eldest son, Philip was eligible for conscription in the first call-up but received an indefinite deferment. His younger brother was eligible for the last call-up, but his number never came up.[69] Philip Decker, who was involved with Youth Campaign Against Conscription (YCAC), believes his mother was also involved with the UAW and knew some of the other SOS women through that group and the union movement.[70]

Winifred Garland was a 'homemaker' from the eastern suburb of Waverley, according to NSW electoral rolls from the 1960s. She had three sons, all of whom became eligible for conscription during the course of the war.[71] Earlier rolls indicate she had previously been a 'tobacco worker'. She had strong links to the trade union movement through her husband John, a toolmaker, who served as a shop steward, district official and national secretary of the Amalgamated Engineering Union (later the Amalgamated Metal Workers Union). They were active members in their local branch of the ALP. John Garland went on to hold numerous offices in the party including a nine-year stint as State vice-president.[72] In 1981, he was elected to the NSW Legislative Council, retiring in 1990. It is not known if Winifred Garland was a member of the UAW. In the 1960s, ALP members risked being expelled from the party if they joined the UAW, although this did not deter some.[73]

Ann Gregory had been subject to ASIO's attention since 1960 when she immigrated to Australia from England where she had been active in the communist party and the peace movement.[74] She took part in the first Aldermaston march held in 1958 to protest against nuclear war.[75] ASIO apparently raised a security objection about her proposed immigration but a bureaucratic bungle meant the Chief Migration Officer in Australia's High Commission in London had not become aware of the objection until just before Gregory was about to leave England. A blunt memo to ASIO from Australia House stated that for 'an objection to have been raised at that stage would have caused considerable embarrassment'.[76] It noted that only 'a small percentage' of persons immigrating to Australia from the UK were being vetted at this time, including teachers. While Gregory had been a teacher before her marriage, she had listed her occupation as housewife, a category that was not vetted. Nevertheless, Australia House wanted it on the record that the Chief Migration Officer had stated that 'in sending Mrs Gregory to Australia he was acting against his better judgment' and that the High Commission would, as a result, be pushing for a review of the vetting categories in the United Kingdom.[77]

Once settled in the inner western Sydney suburb of Balmain, Gregory fulfilled Australia House's worst fears by joining her local branch of the CPA and becoming active in the Australia–China Society, the AICD and, along with her children, in the CPA's youth organisation, the Eureka Youth League (EYL). Gregory also was a frequent correspondent to the CPA's newspaper, the *Tribune*, and in 1964 was a guest speaker at a Marxist conference in Sydney where she spoke about intellectuals and the working class.[78] Her son Mark was one of the founding members of Sydney University's campaign for nuclear disarmament.[79] In April 1965, shortly before the formation of SOS, the Gregorys hosted a CPA meeting at their home where the guest speaker, the then foreign editor of the *Tribune*, warned 'the situation in Vietnam was deteriorating rapidly'.[80] At the same meeting there had been discussion about CPA campaigning on anti-conscription at the upcoming NSW state elections and on encouraging young people to register as conscientious objectors.

As a result, Ann Gregory was well-versed on both the situation in Vietnam and the politics of anti-conscription before SOS formed. University-educated, politically experienced, and a talented speaker, she was a valuable asset for the movement in its early stages. It was a far cry from her upbringing on a small farm in England where she had originally trained to be a professional milkmaid. Her son Mark recalled that his grandfather had thought it was a good career for a woman with poor eyesight. 'I'm not sure where the logic was for that but she was very good at milking cows; she certainly won prizes for milking', he said.⁸¹ But it was not to be her career. She was enrolled in university until World War II intervened and later completed a degree part-time at the University of Sydney. By 1965, she had six children aged between 11 and 24, including one 20-year-old son eligible for conscription. As well as studying, she also worked part-time at the local hospital. 'She was very forthright in her beliefs, very fair, incredibly generous and very quick to correct people who thought women should remain in their place, so to speak', Mark Gregory recalled.⁸² She was part of SOS's first delegation to Canberra in May 1965 where she told the Minister for the Army, Dr Forbes, that one of her reasons for moving to Australia was her 'belief that Australia would not be involving herself in other people's quarrels'.⁸³

While effective, Gregory's time with SOS was brief after she became disillusioned with the government's refusal to abolish conscription. At SOS's second annual meeting in June 1967, Gregory announced that she was returning to England because she did not intend to have her sons fighting in Vietnam. She apparently told the group: 'Don't worry you'll always find me outside Australia House if any of you come over to England'.⁸⁴ ASIO was not sorry to see her leave, adding the following postscript to Gregory's SOS career: 'Looking back over the history of SOS Ann Gregory was what might be called the manipulator or organiser of [the] SOS movement behind Mrs Golgerth'.⁸⁵

Electoral records show that Margaret Lee was a homemaker who resided in the lower north shore suburb of Greenwich. Her ASIO file notes she was Scottish-born and a widow. She was in her early sixties when she attended SOS's first meeting, making her one of its older members, but was a constant presence at demonstrations throughout the movement's existence.⁸⁶ She attracted ASIO's attention as an active member of the peace movement, attending meetings of the AICD and UAW. She was also a member of the Australia–China Society. In 1965, she had a 20-year-old son who was eligible for conscription.

Golgerth's sister-in-law Ruby 'Babs' O'Sullivan was a foundation member and later treasurer of SOS. Blonde and always 'immaculately dressed', according to ASIO reports, O'Sullivan had performed overseas as a dancer before incurring a career-ending back injury.[87] Born in Melbourne, she first became a 'security interest' in the early 1950s; her ASIO file describes her as 'a dedicated communist of long-standing'.[88] She was also a member of AICD, and various other peace groups in Sydney, including Women For Peace. In 1959, she was listed in the records of the Australian Assembly for Peace as someone 'who can be relied upon to take an active and prominent part in the organisation of the assembly'.[89] During her time with SOS, she was also treasurer of her local branch of the CPA. In the 1960s, she was well known among racing circles; her second husband Jack was one of Sydney's leading trainers, and as a jockey had ridden the winning horse in the 1933 Melbourne Cup. The whip he had used in the race was proudly displayed in their home. The couple had no children, but O'Sullivan shared Golgerth's moral outrage over conscription and the Vietnam War. According to her niece, however, O'Sullivan was careful to downplay her strident political views around her husband's more conservative circle of friends.[90]

Given the backgrounds and experience of these founding members, it is not surprising that SOS was able to quickly organise and become an effective voice of dissent. Or, given their left-wing links, that they were keen to let Golgerth be the public face of the organisation. All except Garland, Bendick and Decker took on committee roles in the first two years. Pat Ashcroft presided over early meetings and was an active and effective secretary, answering letters from supporters all over

Australia until ill health forced her to reduce her load. O'Sullivan was variously treasurer, social organiser and vice-president. Hewett was assistant secretary. Lee was appointed convenor of the liaison committee with responsibility for 'contact for women and peace groups', and Gregory was a 'roving ambassador' and general committee member.

* * *

In addition to the nine 'founding mothers', there were three guests at the inaugural meeting: Vivienne Abraham (law graduate and editor of the Federal Pacifist Council of Australia's journal, the *Peacemaker*); Barry Robinson (YCAC secretary); and Bill Leslie (then assistant secretary of the Teachers Federation). These guests were invited to advise the group on 'how to proceed', and their input was valuable. Abraham assisted Hewett in the preparation of an early letter to federal members of parliament and worked closely with members involved with counselling of conscientious objectors and draft resisters.[91] Robinson, a young ALP member and draft resister, also worked closely with SOS and occasionally addressed its meetings. Many of SOS women's sons were also involved with YCAC. Robinson's co-founder in YCAC was another young ALP member, Wayne Haylen, the son of left-wing Labor MP Les Haylen. Haylen's mother later joined SOS.

The presence of Bill Leslie, then a rising star in the Teachers Federation, was indicative of the close links members in this group had within the union movement. He was also an incredible resource when it came to dealing with the media and the group's public image. Indeed, as his 2013 obituary in the *Sydney Morning Herald* noted, 'working with media was one of Leslie's strengths'.[92] In 1964 during a by-election campaign, he directed and produced what was thought to be 'the world's first union-made television ads'. A union ad created four years later won a 1970 Cannes Film Festival award in the social commentary category.[93] The presence of these three 'outsiders' at the first SOS meeting is indicative of the influential ties and connections the group would be able to draw upon throughout its existence. They were also people with whom someone of Golgerth's background is unlikely to have previously crossed paths.

ASIO soon had an insider in the Sydney SOS group, presumably a woman who was well-known to the other members and most likely also a member of the UAW, who tried valiantly to pin down the group's origins. An early ASIO report stated that Golgerth was 'induced to act as a "front" for the organisation, she having no apparent political affiliations and having a son in the call up'.[94] This information, contained in a report prepared by J. W. Clowes of ASIO's counter-terrorism branch was apparently supplied by 'a reliable source'. It is clear from this report that nothing was ever going to convince ASIO that SOS had not been formed for ulterior motives. In June 1965 – a month after SOS's formation – ASIO's Deputy Director General in NSW stated categorically: 'It will be seen that SOS can rightly be described as a "front" for the CPA "front", [for the] Union of Australian Women'.[95] Interestingly, this initial damning assessment progressively became more nuanced as the Vietnam War continued. In September, in response to 'urgent' requests for information on SOS by the Minister for Defence and the prime minister's office, ASIO replied that 'although a number of persons with widely different political views are associated with the movement, the driving force is the communist front organisation, the Union of Australian Women'.[96] Reports in later years actually came to the opposite conclusion, noting the involvement of a number of CPA and UAW women but determining that there was no proof that SOS itself was a front.[97]

***

It was not ASIO, however, that the original SOS women were trying to influence. It was recruitment that the founding mothers were concerned about in those early days. They understood that in order to be an effective voice of dissent, SOS needed to grow. To do this, it needed to recruit other women, particularly those from middle-class backgrounds. Early SOS members who were also part of the UAW knew from firsthand experience that many of these women might have been deterred from joining an organisation seen as a communist front. Even, if the women themselves had not been personally concerned, they knew some husbands would be, perhaps even preventing their spouses from becoming involved. To mobilise this new constituency, SOS needed to nurture a 'respectable', non-political image. Indeed, concerns about public image serve to underline the political climate in which SOS was formed and operated. In the mid-1960s, fears about 'reds under the beds' were still very real and anyone associated with a peace group was automatically dismissed as having communist sympathies. UAW women were most certainly conscious of the paranoid nature of the times and so it is understandable that those involved with SOS's formation would have been cautious about drawing attention to their other political associations. Earlier in 1965, for example, the UAW's national president Freda Brown had bemoaned the fact that her group's membership numbers were in decline and that further expansion was being hampered by it being constantly labelled 'communist'.[98] This was exemplified by a letter to the editor printed in the *Sydney Morning Herald* that accused Brown of 'providing an excellent example of a communist at work in a "front" organisation'. The disgruntled correspondent was commenting on an earlier letter to the editor about the UAW which Brown had apparently signed, not unreasonably, in her capacity as the group's national leader. Her failure to also mention her CPA links, however, had G. H. Yates, of Sydney, fuming: 'There can be little doubt that Mrs Brown and her fellow communists regard the UAW as a vehicle of communist indoctrination and an instrument of furthering communist policies'.[99]

Hewett, for one, had no doubt that SOS would have been singled out for similar treatment if she had become its public face. As it was, her involvement did not go unnoticed for long: 'Buzz Kennedy, a radio commentator who covered the first SOS demonstration at Marrickville army barracks, spotted me as a communist and then suggested on radio that SOS was a communist front.'[100] ASIO already had copious file notes on Hewett, dating back to 1952, and was also quick to note her involvement and to come to the same conclusion. Golgerth was also aware of Hewett's CPA links and had expressed concerns about the group's public image to her daughter. Candy Cole remembers her mother telling her that Hewett was a communist: 'I don't know how many were in the group but I know she had to be very careful of that because of the fact that she didn't want the reason for their real existence to be lost'. Cole had never heard Hewett's version of events but believed her mother never really wanted to lead SOS. 'While she was very, very strong in her beliefs as to why she had formed the group, I don't think she really necessarily wanted to be the leader through any sort of ambition', she said. 'It was more that it was just such an important cause and she was prepared to take up the cause and go with it.'[101]

As Hewett hoped, Golgerth's role as the early figurehead did help to negate claims of communist influence in the media which, in the main, tended to accept her leadership and SOS on face value without delving into the backgrounds of other members. Importantly, it helped to attract other women who, like Golgerth, had not previously ventured out of their domestic sphere and who would have been reluctant to associate themselves with a UAW-led group, let alone one allegedly under the influence of the CPA. Golgerth represented exactly the constituency that SOS was seeking to mobilise – middle-class, non-political women, ordinary Australian housewives and mums. It was this 'type' of woman who came to be recognised as the public face of SOS, a notion that has been largely preserved in subsequent historical accounts. By the time Golgerth relinquished the leadership in 1968, SOS was well-established and the communist 'tag' was being used less frequently and, importantly, less effectively to dismiss not only SOS but peace groups in general. As the group grew, 'most of the women', Hewett noted, 'were new to political action' and from a wide variety of backgrounds.[102]

While ASIO files concentrated on identifying women who had links with the CPA, it also noted the broad range of backgrounds. An ASIO informer sent to a Sydney meeting in 1965, duly reported that 17 people had attended the meeting but that attempts to ascertain the backgrounds of the women present had been thwarted.

> It was a little difficult to really get the truth from any of the women present for they all agreed that they knew that other members' politics and religion etc. were different to their own. Because of this nobody appeared to be quite sure whether they were saying the right or the wrong thing when attacking different people.[103]

However, the agent said Hewett, Ashcroft, Mulheron and Gregory 'showed their true colours' (presumably red) in a later discussion when they complained about rough treatment from the NSW Special Branch.[104]

In October 1965, ASIO 'acquired' a list of Sydney SOS members and set about comparing the names and addresses with its own files, electoral rolls, and the results of a series of 'habitation checks'.[105] The list was apparently compiled from 'a handwritten alphabetical list that had recently been in the possession of Pat Ashcroft'.[106] ASIO does not say how it happened to come by Ashcroft's notes. Not all those on the list, however, were 'members' of SOS. Freda Brown and Vivienne Abraham appear on the list, though they were never members. Even allowing for a sizeable margin of error of this type, the results did not reinforce ASIO's underlying belief that SOS was a 'communist front'. Of the 83 'members' listed (including the above women), only 28 of the women are indicated, either by reference numbers or other annotations, to have been previously recorded by ASIO. A further three women, while not recorded themselves, had husbands who had previously been recorded by ASIO. Fifty-two women had never come to ASIO's attention before their involvement with SOS, suggesting they were not existing members of the UAW, the CPA or other suspected 'front' groups. This supports the hypothesis that, as Hewett and her fellow founding mothers had hoped, a new constituency of previously non-political women, with no attachment to the traditional peace movement, was indeed being tapped by SOS.

* * *

Babs O'Sullivan is credited with having moved the motion at the first meeting to adopt Save Our Sons as the group's name.[107] It is not known, however, who came up with the idea, whether any alternatives were discussed or why it was finally chosen. It certainly had strong appeal, neatly summing up the group and its aims. In its literature, the group played on the metaphor by stating that it was issuing a distress call to other mothers.[108] Maurie Mulheron still has the group's original blue-and-white banner printed by his mother's nephew-in-law, an American World War II veteran who met his future wife while on leave in Australia. Mulheron believes the choice of name was extremely effective not only in attracting media attention but in striking a chord with other women. 'The name was just one of those little strokes of genius. S.O.S. – Save Our Sons – it just captured people's imagination', he said.[109] At times, however, the name also worked against them, leaving the women vulnerable to criticism that they were motivated by selfish concerns and that their sons were less than real men, still tied to their mothers' apron strings. In a scribbled note across one of the group's petitions in 1966, University of Sydney anthropologist Ian Hogbin wrote:

> Much as I disapprove of sending conscripts to Vietnam I would be horrified to have my name associated with any movement called "Save Our Sons". Our sons can, I hope, think for themselves. If not, they ought to be able to do so and not [be] dependent on silly parents.[110]

Hewett later expressed some regrets about the choice: 'In hindsight, Save Our Sons may not have been the most appropriate title for the movement. While we explained that the "sons" referred to were not only young Australians, but also young Vietnamese, there were often accusations that the SOS movement was comprised of women who were narrowly concerned about their own sons'.[111] In its statement of aims, SOS tried to make it clear that this was not the case:

> SOS speaks not only for our sons but also for those boys possibly less able to speak for themselves who are being forced into the army against their wishes. We act, in fact, in the interests of

all humanity, convinced that the experience of generations has shown that war is ineffectual as a means of settling international differences.[112]

Overall, however, the name was an effective recruitment and marketing tool, clearly identifying its constituency and goals.

The founding members of SOS were also very clear about the group's mandate, issuing a statement of aims soon after its formation. Adopted by the other SOS branches, it did not oppose conscription per se but rejected conscription for overseas service. It did not, however, specifically oppose the war in Vietnam. That came later. In an early letter to a supporter Pat Ashcroft noted: 'We strongly oppose conscription for overseas service but are strictly non-political, non-sectarian. When we have to, we oppose our government's policy on Vietnam'.[113] In addition to overseas service, the group was also concerned about the length of time a conscript was expected to serve (two years) and the severe penalties that came with refusing to register (jail time). In its September 1965 newsletter to members, the group stated that its aims were, first, 'to oppose conscription of youth into the armed services for service overseas, especially in the present conflict in Vietnam'; and, second, 'to seek the amendment or repeal of the National Service Act with regard to objectionable clauses providing for long periods of compulsory service, engagement in military action abroad and severe penalties for infringements'.[114]

But the women believed they were not only fighting for their sons' rights but their own as parents. Conscription, according to Joyce Golgerth was nothing less than 'an infringement of parental rights', arguing 'such boys must have their parents' consent to marry, to buy a car or a house, to go to sea in the Merchant Navy, to obtain a passport or travel overseas. Yet the Government is taking minors without any possibility of parental consent or refusal'.[115] The sense of moral outrage over this loss of parental, specifically maternal, rights is palpable in the group's first statement:

> Mothers resist all sorts of pressure to bring up their children as useful citizens, to look forward to useful careers and to be of service to the community. Then suddenly their lives are disrupted. Their good citizenship merely makes them more likely to be selected for the army whereas others with a criminal record are excluded.[116]

It concludes with direct appeal to mothers:

> Thousands of Australia's best young citizens have sacrificed their lives in past wars. The boys conscripted now are the cream of our youth. The mothers who have joined SOS refuse to give them up so easily. We hope that this initial action will spread to other mothers throughout Australia. We appeal to all those mothers who agree with us to come forward now and take their stand before it is too late.[117]

As the war dragged on and SOS members became more aware of what was happening in Vietnam, they also joined other groups in opposing the war. But SOS never wavered from its initial stand against conscription. Joyce Golgerth would express concern in later years that the group was sometimes portrayed as not having had a clear mandate. Her daughter Candy recalled:

> She was concerned that some of the information read as if they were just a flippant group of females who didn't have anything to do and didn't know what to do with themselves so they just took this up. She wanted to make it very clear that the group had a very strong mandate. They knew exactly what they were doing and why they were doing it. They were concerned about the rights of these young men being taken away, their democratic rights.[118]

Unlike some of the other SOS groups, Sydney SOS was structured along traditional lines like those of the UAW, with regular elections, a constitution and annual general meetings. A monthly newsletter was produced from May 1966. The meetings themselves were relatively formal. Reflecting the times in which they operated, honorific titles were commonly used to address members as well as in official correspondence. It took an exchange of several letters over a course of some weeks, for example, before Pat Ashcroft informed one correspondent that 'it was quite common these days for women to address each other by their Christian names'.[119] Candy Cole, who attended several meetings with her mother, remembered the formality: 'A lot of things were done to make it very formal and structured. It was all quite official'.[120] Meetings were held both in the evenings and daytime to accommodate working women like Hewett, pointing to a constituency that extended beyond housewives. Membership was not limited to women but in reality the Sydney SOS group was, for all intents and purposes, an all-women's group. Men, usually husbands, tended to play supportive roles, called upon for access to their contacts in the workplace and unions, and to provide transport, security and general 'grunt' work. A letter written by Pat Ashcroft in October 1965 advised: 'Our members are not all mothers, relatives have joined and now fathers want to take part. We will find a way to use them'.[121]

* * *

By downplaying its links to other suspected 'fronts' and projecting a respectable, politically neutral image, Sydney SOS managed to do what the UAW was struggling to do during this period: tap into a new constituency of middle-class women. The Sydney women were the inspiration for SOS groups that formed in other parts of Australia and in the early days, there were hopes that SOS would become a close-knit national coalition. This never happened. While they adopted the name and SOS's aims, as we will see, the groups elsewhere differed, often markedly, from the 'parent' body.

Chapter 4

'MOTHERS ARE ON THE MARCH'

> "To save your son, mother, your weeping is not enough" … Join with mothers all over Australia in the Save Our Sons movement.
>
> *SOS Recruitment leaflet, 1965*[1]

In late June 1965, inspired by newspaper reports about the activities of Sydney Save Our Sons (SOS), a group of Melbourne women decided to stage a protest at the first intake of Victorian conscripts. On arrival at the Richmond Barracks, Vilma Ames, attending her very first demonstration, decided not to wait for the others, unfurling her banner and bravely protesting on her own:

> I stood in silent protest outside the Engineers' Depot at Swan St, Richmond, as our first recruits arrived for enrolment. It was a very sad and moving sight as sweethearts said their goodbyes. I acted in response to the Save Our Sons Sydney group and I carried a banner which stated our opposition to conscription …[2]

Ames was later joined by several other women and they continued to protest until the last busload of recruits left the barracks. 'It was an unforgettable experience', Ames recalled. '[The recruits'] greetings and calls of "good on you!" encouraged us to continue our work.'[3]

Ames was not the only woman inspired to act after reading about Sydney SOS. Women from around Australia wrote to the organisation praising its efforts and seeking information about setting up their own groups. The response was overwhelming but extremely gratifying, according to secretary Pat Ashcroft, who was tasked with replying to them all. Among the correspondence was a letter from a young Melbourne mother, Jean McLean, writing on behalf of 'approximately fifty Melbourne people' who were interested in forming a local branch. 'As we have no previous experience to guide us, we would value your suggestions on the best way to start', she wrote.[4] From Brisbane, Vilma Ward wrote that she had been organising weekly lunch-hour vigils in the city's Anzac Square and was interested in joining forces with Sydney.[5] Isobel McArthur, from Newcastle, was so impressed that she decided to take the train to meet the Sydney women and join one of their vigils.[6] Rose Fitzgerald, of Portland, NSW, hoped the movement would be 'the basis of something tremendous'[7] while from Adelaide there came the 'exciting news' that five women there had staged an airport protest under the SOS banner.[8]

Sydney SOS women did not just field letters, they wrote them by the dozens, urging women's organisations in other states, particularly their Union of Australian Women (UAW) contacts, to set up their own SOS groups. 'Mothers are on the March', declared an SOS recruitment leaflet from this time and to the Sydney women it seemed that indeed they were.[9] Within four months, enthusiastic groups of women had formed SOS 'branches' in Brisbane, Melbourne and Newcastle.[10] By the end of the first year, others had been established in Townsville, Wollongong, Adelaide and Perth. The Sydney women were also confident that a group would shortly be formed in Tasmania.[11] Everything seemed on track for SOS to become a truly national movement, a dream the Sydney founders articulated in May 1965 when they issued a clarion call to the women of Australia 'to come forward now and take their stand before it is too late'.[12]

Hopes of a nationwide movement were never realised. There was never a group in the Northern Territory and attempts to form a permanent group in Tasmania floundered. And while they shared a common name and aims, the satellite SOS groups retained their independence, and some evolved very differently. There were solid, practical reasons for this. While there were a few successful joint activities involving women from Brisbane, Wollongong, Newcastle, Sydney and Melbourne in the early years, the distances were too great, and the communication and travel costs too high, for these to be held on a regular basis. For supporters in Perth, Townsville and Adelaide, attending these events in Canberra was simply out of the question. Moreover, the Sydney women had neither the time nor the resources to establish a separate national committee along the lines of the UAW. In any case, SOS was always considered a 'temporary' movement. Formed in response to an urgent problem, its founders fully expected it would fold just as quickly once enough Australians had been convinced that conscription was wrong, and the federal government had been forced to abandon its policy. The urgency of the situation did not allow SOS founders the luxury of long-term planning.

There were other reasons a cohesive, national movement did not emerge. The groups that followed Sydney SOS's lead did not necessarily replicate its structure or attract the same types of supporters. While the Sydney group provided inspiration, a guiding hand, and an initial template for the other groups, most only had the movement's name in common. Individual groups were moulded as much by the personalities of their leaders as they were by the backgrounds, age and experience of the supporters they attracted. The close proximity meant there were always more natural links between Sydney, Newcastle and Wollongong. In the early days, some women also knew interstate colleagues from other organisations with which they were involved. But the younger 'more Bohemian group' in Melbourne ultimately had little in common with the Sydney founders.[13]

Those groups that were dominated by women from traditionally structured groups like the UAW also tended to likewise establish constitutions, have elections and hold annual general meetings. However, the founders in Melbourne and Townsville, who had no prior political experience, eschewed any formal structure on the grounds that it was too time-consuming and rigid. This inevitably affected the way these groups operated and meant Melbourne, in particular, was more responsive to quickly changing circumstances.

Supporters in different groups also came from varying socio-economic backgrounds. Some had supporter bases that were predominantly working class; others attracted supporters from more middle-class backgrounds. Again, this was influenced not only by the background of the founders but also the city or town where the group was based. There was no set policy on male members; however, most became 'women's only groups' by default. Of all the groups, WA SOS, it could be argued, with its male leadership and stated opposition to the Vietnam War from the start, had the least in common with the Sydney group. It was also the shortest-lived. While this does not necessarily imply a correlation, the Perth group certainly encountered a degree of dissent within its ranks that was not evident in other groups.

* * *

Two very different SOS groups emerged in Queensland, at opposite ends of the state, in Brisbane and Townsville.

Brisbane

In June 1965, a SOS group appeared in Brisbane. As in Sydney, women there had also been exploring ways to voice their protest against conscription. To this end, about 30 women – including wives of union officials, Quakers, members of the UAW and the Women's International League for Peace and Freedom (WILPF) – had been holding regular silent vigils in the city centre during the Friday lunch hour. These were organised by the UAW's Balmoral branch but after reading about SOS in the *Australian* some of the women decided to form a new group and adopt the SOS name. 'We have organised six (vigils) so far and each has proved better than the last so if we could do something up here to correspond with you down there it might have a better effect', wrote Vilma Ward, a UAW member who became Brisbane SOS's secretary.[14] She did not wait for a reply. 'You will be happy to hear that I have been instrumental in forming a Brisbane "Save Our Sons" committee', Ward subsequently informed Sydney SOS in July 1965. 'Several women have approached me, and after a lot of thought, I have decided it would be a very good idea, I thought that you would not object, and this way we can do a lot more and perhaps other states will catch on now we have formed one.'[15]

The Brisbane group grew quickly. It adopted Sydney's statement of aims and a formal structure similar to the UAW. By mid-July, a committee of eight had been established, comprising a president, vice-president, secretary, treasurer and four executive members, and SOS letterhead had been ordered.[16] Those wishing to join were asked to pay a 10 shilling subscription fee, in contrast to the Sydney group which only much later started requesting a small payment towards the production and distribution of its newsletter.[17] But while the Brisbane group kept in close contact with Sydney during its early months, it remained autonomous, forming its own rules for demonstrations with 'particular attention given to strict discipline among women demonstrators', and sometimes even offering Sydney advice.[18] Extremely proactive, it organised forums and public meetings addressed by 'expert' guest speakers, collected signatures for petitions, lobbied politicians and counselled conscientious objectors. Ward held fortnightly 'classes' at her home for would-be conscientious objectors and legal aid was offered to those young men who found themselves before the courts.[19] SOS also protested at intakes of conscripts and continued to hold well-publicised weekly vigils in the city centre where women would line up with a single word pinned to their dresses, spelling out anti-conscription slogans. They were forced to 'wear' their anti-conscription messages because holding placards was illegal in Queensland at that time. In its first six months, SOS held 30 silent vigils, an indication of how busy its members were.[20]

The UAW strongly supported SOS in Brisbane but continued to hold its own protests and anti-war activities.[21] With many SOS women straddling both organisations, it was sometimes difficult for outsiders to distinguish who had organised which event. In the early period, the Queensland Peace Committee (QPC), run by secretary Norma Chalmers, usually took the lead in organising Brisbane's anti-war activities and worked closely, for a time, with Ward and SOS. The relationship was not always an easy one. After listening to a series of intercepted phone calls between the two women, one Australian Security Intelligence Organisation (ASIO) agent noted, 'it becomes evident that Norma Chalmers is guide and mentor for Vilma Ward, and although there might not be any great love lost between them, Vilma accepts Norma's "suggestions" on all important decisions.'[22] This was of particular import to ASIO as Chalmers was a well-known member of the Communist Party of Australia (CPA) and her liaison added weight to its belief that SOS was a 'front'. Indeed, it was not long before Ward had to deal with public suggestions that her group had communist links. In July 1965, she described how a high-profile local television reporter had thrown her 'some curly questions' about her members' political affiliations.[23] 'My interview with Ron Brady was on these lines: "Are you a communist?" I said, "no – I am ALP". "Are the women who will be joining SOS communists?" My reply, "I don't know. It is open to all who are concerned about 20-year-old sons being conscripted" and so on.' The 'funny part', Ward confided later, was that of the women who had already joined, five were from the Society of Friends (Quakers), three were Australian Labor Party (ALP) members, and one had 'no political policy' at all. 'But I have no doubt there are ladies who belong to the Communist Party who will want to join and, as you say, security will be after you. I have no doubt they will be after me too. I will have to at all times exercise caution.'[24] ASIO did not find it amusing, however, identifying three women shown in the television interview as CPA members.[25]

SOS in Brisbane had strong working-class roots and links to the ALP and trade unions. Ward's husband Len was an organiser for the Queensland Transport Workers' Union while Ward herself was elected to the UAW's national committee. This enabled her to meet other SOS women at UAW national conferences. She was also secretary of her local branch of the ALP. In 1967, the *Australian Women's Weekly* chose to overlook her political affiliations, describing her as 'a jolly Brisbane housewife with not a sign of a whinge about her'.[26] When she started SOS, Ward was 36 years old and the mother of three teenage daughters. While she had no personal link to conscription, its introduction outraged her and she was determined 'that our boys should not be conscripted to murder or be murdered'.[27]

Other ALP supporters among the group included Molly Macdonald, a UAW member and former nurse whose husband Alex was secretary of the Queensland Trades and Labour Council. The couple had two daughters who also took part in SOS and other anti-war demonstrations. Another supporter, Margaret Baxendell, was a humanist, a life member of the ALP, and a member of both the UAW and the WILPF. A former Congregational Sunday School teacher, she had two sons and four daughters.[28] Her husband Cedric was also involved in the peace movement.

Another founding member and office holder, Shirley Jamieson, grew up in an experimental village set up by a group of Quakers on the outskirts of Brisbane known as Paxton (or village of peace).[29] At 16 she began work in her father's inner Brisbane poultry shop and became 'a licensed chicken sexer' after passing an exam that involved determining the sex of 100 day-old chicks in 20 minutes with a 96 per cent accuracy rate, an achievement remembered with much pride by her husband.[30] As Quakers, her family practised absolute pacifism; her two brothers were conscientious objectors during World War II. So there was some initial unease when she began dating a returned serviceman, Gordon Jamieson, who served with the 2/26th Australian Infantry Battalion in Malaya and Singapore before being taken prisoner and forced to work on the infamous Burmese Railway. While never an absolute pacifist like his wife, in a 2013 interview Jamieson said he came to share her family's 'logic' on matters of war.[31] He also supported SOS before the couple relocated to the Gold Coast. 'We played an active part within the organisation, attending public meetings, street marches, and vigils', he recalled.[32] It was a family affair. The couple's son and a nephew were both of conscription age and subsequently became involved in the anti-war movement. Shirley's mother was also a founding member of SOS in Brisbane. In September 1965, Shirley Jamieson accompanied Ward to a national SOS Canberra protest where they met interstate members.[33] In a heartfelt letter to the editor after the death of the first conscript in Vietnam, Shirley noted that prime ministers Menzies and Holt had both avoided military service themselves. 'These old gentlemen of our tribe stay home and enjoy the privileges of our society while the young bucks are sent out to slaughter ragged peasants or themselves be slaughtered', she wrote.[34]

Publicity for the group was tightly controlled with only Vilma Ward permitted to speak to the media. Indeed, at times SOS appeared to be a one-woman show. Ward took care to nurture key contacts within the local media. In one intercepted phone call, ASIO noted, she repeatedly referred to 'her friend Bruce' of the *Courier-Mail* and her 'little boy' in the ABC.[35] Sydney members were impressed with Brisbane's hale and hearty leader, noting that on the first day Queensland conscripts left for camp 'this enthusiastic woman had recruited 56 women to stand for an hour in Anzac Square'.[36] The Baxendells' daughter, Joan Ross, who used to attend meetings for conscientious objectors at Ward's home, remembered the SOS leader as big-hearted but also a 'moth to the flame, someone who enjoyed the public attention the position afforded her'.[37] This did not always win her friends. On occasions there was tension with members of the QPC, frustrated by what they saw as Ward's tendency to run her own campaign. In 1966, Chalmers was recorded telling a colleague, that there had been a falling-out with Ward who had subsequently 'divorced' SOS from a QPC demonstration and 'even disassociated herself from Save Our Sons in other states'.[38]

Ward soon made it clear that she was not taking orders from Sydney SOS either, though initially she was keen to emphasise the national links. The Sydney group even paid her fare to attend a national delegation in Canberra. On her return there was a new sense of camaraderie in the letters between Sydney's secretary Pat Ashcroft and Ward, who addressed each other by their first names, in contrast to the formal titles used to address secretaries in other states at this time. When several weeks passed without correspondence from Ward, Ashcroft expressed her relief at finally receiving a letter: 'Was darned glad to hear from you at long last, had begun to think you were sick'.[39] Ward explained her SOS work had been put on the backburner because her children had been on school holidays. 'It is a bit difficult to try and do anything with children around', she wrote.[40] Later, however, there was a falling out over a misunderstanding concerning payment for an advertisement that left Brisbane footing the bill.[41] Until then, letters between the two groups had been frequent and familiar but after this incident, they slowed to a trickle. The tone of a couple penned by the new Sydney secretary verged on frosty and there was a return to honorific titles.[42] Relations seemed to return to a more level tone in 1967 when Ward was facing imprisonment for failure to pay a fine resulting from a SOS protest, with Sydney SOS sending a much appreciated telegram of support.[43]

In the end, however, Ward apparently decided against martyring herself. In October 1967, the day before she was due to face court, she announced her 'retirement' from public life (including SOS and the UAW) in the local newspaper. The *Sunday Truth* reported the news with some surprise, and a little regret, that 'Queensland's No.1 trouble-shooter' had decided to become 'just an ordinary housewife':

> Mrs Ward's stubbornness and determination to fight anything she regarded as an injustice has involved her over the years in brushes with the Prime Minister Mr Holt, the Queensland Governor, the American Consul, Brisbane's Lord Mayor, the Police Commissioner, Mr Bischof, court officials and anyone else who happened to be around.[44]

Officially, Ward explained she wanted to spend more time with her teenage family but hinted there were other reasons, 'some of which I can't tell because they are hurtful'. 'I've taken a long hard look at myself', she told the paper. 'I suppose you could call it the rude awakening of Vilma Ward.'[45]

There had been signs, however, of friction between Ward and other SOS members in the months prior to her surprise announcement. Earlier in the year, she had written a cryptic letter to Sydney describing the situation in Brisbane as 'one hell of a mess up here'.[46] Explaining it was 'too long and complicated to tell you in a letter', Ward outlined a recent dispute within the group regarding representation in the QPC that had led to her own committee trying to bring a vote of no-confidence against her. 'I do not think it will succeed', she told Sydney. 'Will let you know further. This must be kept strictly in the organisation down there. Do not write formally to me (SOS) but as an individual.' She ended with a plea: 'Could anyone come up for a day or so, must have a long discussion'.[47] Secretary Adele Pert replied that SOS members in Sydney were 'a bit in the dark about the situation in Brisbane' and could not be 'of much assistance without knowing more'. There was no possibility of travelling to Brisbane but Pert mooted a possible interstate conference of SOS members in the future. 'I am wondering if you have a constitution for SOS. Maybe you should have another look at that; something there might need revising to make for smoother functioning of your organisation ... for goodness sake, don't do anything without giving it some thought', she implored.[48] There appears to have been no further 'official' correspondence on the matter and there was never any mention of Ward's 'resignation' in Sydney's newsletters.

What happened to the Brisbane SOS after Ward's departure is unclear. In late 1967, a QPC meeting was told SOS was 'practically on the rocks' after Ward's defection. According to an ASIO agent's account, a QPC delegate noted that SOS had not met 'for ages, and now that Vilma Ward has pulled out, it will probably die a natural death'.[49] According to Gordon Jamieson, Brisbane SOS did continue but became less relevant as student groups took a leading role in the anti-war movement and protests in Brisbane became increasingly violent.[50] However, ASIO did not add to its Brisbane SOS files beyond 1968, nor is there any record of further correspondence with Sydney SOS in that group's archives.

Townsville

Margaret Reynolds was a 25-year-old school teacher with a toddler and another baby on the way when she put an advertisement in the local paper in early 1966 seeking interest from other Townsville women in setting up a local branch of SOS. While her own son was not in any imminent danger of being conscripted, she was astounded and outraged that any government could so easily introduce a policy that selected young men at random to be sent to a war zone.[51] When she read about the activities of the southern SOS groups, she felt compelled, for the first time, to take a political stand herself. 'I myself have only a two-year-old but I feel all women should be vitally concerned with this question of conscription, regardless of personal relations', she said at the time.[52]

Unlike many of the early SOS leaders, Reynolds had not served any apprenticeship in other women's groups, nor did she have any established community networks. She was not even a local. Born and educated in Tasmania, she and husband Henry, a university lecturer, had arrived in Townsville just the previous year after two years spent living and working in London. As a working mother who expected her husband to pitch in at home, Reynolds was regarded as a bit of an oddity by the close-knit university social circle.[53] She quickly discovered that like most Australian women during this era, she was expected to lay aside her own career and 'just support Henry's new career and manage an efficient household'.[54] Having grown up with a working mother, this did not gel with Reynolds' own expectations. She was, by her own account, politically naïve, having little interest or knowledge of world affairs or party politics. Nor did she have any familiarity with Cold War rhetoric, remaining blissful unaware of the 'red peril' that the Australian Government insisted lay on her doorstep. When she was later accused of being a communist, Margaret had to ask her husband to explain what that meant.[55]

Henry Reynolds was involved in the local branch of the ALP and it was at a party fundraiser in honour of then federal opposition leader Arthur Calwell that Margaret Reynolds first heard about Vietnam. In her memoirs she recalls: 'Suddenly this old man was talking about the Vietnam War and strongly arguing against the conscription of young Australians. I became focused on this speech, listening intently'.[56] With Henry, she began attending meetings of the Townsville Peace Committee but soon started thinking about setting up a group of her own. 'I used to go along to meetings and all these blokes would be pontificating and I probably thought "Oh dear, here they go again, I'll set something up on my own"', she said.[57]

Townsville, and north Queensland, was 'a complicated place' in the 1960s,[58] intensely conservative and pro-military, but with a streak of radicalism forged through its strong history of unionism.[59] The region had deep military roots. An important staging post for the Pacific campaign during World War II, in the 1960s Townsville remained a strategic military centre with a RAAF base and a new army base that were important contributors to the local economy. In the 1930s and 1940s, however, north Queensland had also been the strongest base of the CPA, electing Fred Paterson, the only communist ever to serve as a member of an Australian Parliament.[60] In the 1960s, the local CPA branch remained strong and many union organisers and their wives were members. A 'remarkably strong and independent' women's movement had also developed in Townsville during the late 1930s and 1940s, both within and independent of the CPA and union auxiliaries.[61] One long-term resident recalled that Townsville in the late 1960s was something of a paradox: above all a union town but with a conservative community whose residents, despite their geographic proximity to Asia, were not as worried about 'reds under the beds' as their southern counterparts.[62] Reynolds was not aware of any of this when she arrived expecting to find 'Tasmania in the tropics'.[63] Instead, she found a hot, dusty 'frontier town' with a main street 'reminiscent of a set from a western movie', full of 'masculine bravado'.[64] It was within this contrasting political and social landscape that Townsville SOS was formed.

Reynolds' initial advertisement attracted considerable media attention.[65] The *Townsville Daily Bulletin* hailed her as a part-time housewife and school teacher who had 'decided to do something to fight what she considers abhorrent'.[66] Despite this, only a handful of women responded to Reynolds' advertisement, perhaps indicative of the level of concern or knowledge about conscription in Townsville at that time.

The first meeting, attended by eight women, was held at Reynolds' home. All, except one older woman, were known, to some degree, to Reynolds.[67] Townsville adopted Sydney's statement of aims but, like Melbourne, there was never a formal constitution, or even a formal form of membership. This meant the group could concentrate on action, rather than being 'bogged down' with meeting procedures – a strategy Reynolds still advocates today to grassroots' community action groups.[68] There was a core of between five to eight women with other supporters attending activities, meetings or lending support at different times. In May 1966, Reynolds reported to Sydney that the group had 'not been idle', having already held two meetings and formed an 'active committee of eight'.[69] After the initial meetings, the group met once a month.

The group was supported and encouraged by the Townsville Peace Committee, which at the time was comprised almost entirely of older, male unionists and members of the ALP and CPA. Perhaps not surprisingly then – Reynolds' lack of political allegiances at the time notwithstanding – most of the women who initially joined SOS were the wives of unionists, or were themselves involved in left-wing political parties. They were also, on average, 20 years older than Reynolds, mostly in their forties, many with teenage sons, some of whom were eligible for conscription.[70] Prominent among them was Loma Thompson, an active member of the UAW and the CPA.[71] When SOS was formed, she was 44 years old with three children, including two school-aged boys.[72] Loma's sister, Nancy Phillips, who was visiting from Melbourne, also attended SOS meetings. She had previously been involved in the peace movement in Victoria.[73] Another regular was Esme Hardy, a working-class Catholic mother with seven children, including six boys.[74] As a new arrival, Reynolds had 'no knowledge of the local scene' and was grateful for the advice of Thompson and Hardy who became 'important mentors', teaching her how to 'be effective' in organising a local community organisation.[75] 'They taught me a lot about politics, they knew how to organise things', Reynolds recalled. 'I didn't have the networks that Loma had in the union movement and Esme had through the [Catholic] church.'[76]

Other supporters/members included: Hazel Jack, mother of five, including a son eligible for conscription; Jan Doyle, a single woman who was friendly with Reynolds; local radio broadcaster Shirley (Gilliver) Webb, who taught Reynolds 'how to write press releases and condense information for radio and television interviews'; and Eleanor Timms and Joan Hill, who knew Thompson through the CPA.[77] Ethnee Brunker, a 40-year-old mother with a son eligible for conscription, was another strong supporter.[78] According to ASIO, which had files on both her parents, Mrs Brunker had been an active member of the UAW in Collinsville while her second husband was 'a suspected communist'.[79] Mrs Brunker's mother, ASIO further noted, had been widely known as a 'red terror' in the Collinsville area.[80] This was news to her grandson, Vince Prasser, who described his grandmother, with whom he lived for a time, as 'one of the most wonderful women you had ever come across in your life and definitely not an activist type of person'.[81] He believed she had probably come to ASIO's attention for her support of the miners' strike. 'My grandmother and grandfather were all fairly generally speaking anti-war. I wouldn't say they were pacifists, with the Second World War we realised we didn't have much of a choice but they, and I had the same opinion, believed Vietnam was a civil war.'[82] Prasser said his mother shared the family's anti-war beliefs but probably only joined SOS because her son was eligible for conscription. Sheila Keeffe, wife of Senator Jim Keeffe, then National

President of the ALP, was also a supporter. A secretary who later served as an alderman on the city council, she had two daughters and a son.[83] Reynolds reported to Sydney that there were other women 'who support us, but for various reasons, cannot become active', some because of the positions they or their husbands held or because their spouses opposed their involvement.[84]

Like SOS in other states, the Townsville branch included a strong element of self-education. At meetings, members took turns in reviewing literature relating to the Vietnam War. One of the first books to be reviewed was Gerald Stone's *War Without Honour*, which analysed the background of the war and discussed Australia's role in it.[85] The group conducted surveys and held silent vigils in the city centre, an experience many found daunting given hostility from local police, business owners and the public. Reynolds said she also regularly fielded calls and written enquiries from women throughout north Queensland.[86]

However, 'active' membership remained low throughout the group's existence. Reynolds complained to her Sydney colleagues that 'the main problem up here is that people are not really aware nor do they wish to be enlightened and hence involved'.[87] Lack of funds was always an issue, although the group did receive some financial support from individual unions, the Townsville Trades and Labor Council, the CPA, the ALP and the Townsville Peace Committee (TPC).[88] The TPC was particularly encouraging, recognising that the women's group, if initially only for its novelty value, was able to generate publicity its group could not.

While the Townsville group corresponded with Sydney, received their newsletters, collected signatures for the national petition and distributed their pamphlets, it remained an autonomous group. Unlike their counterparts in Brisbane, for example, no Townsville member ever attended SOS events in Canberra. Nor did the Townsville group ever have any association with the Brisbane group, despite encouragement from Sydney.[89] Sydney also suggested, at one stage, that Reynolds contact Glen Tomasetti in Melbourne, to see if the Melbourne group could help with commercials for TV and radio.[90] But according to Reynolds, distance was a major obstacle to closer relationships with the other SOS groups. The cost of long-distance telephone calls was prohibitive, rendering even the closest group in Brisbane, 1360km to the south, 'another world away'.[91] Sydney members apparently had no concept of the vast distances involved. After Reynolds passed on a request for 200 pamphlets to be sent directly to a woman in Collinsville (a 277km drive from Townsville), Sydney's secretary instead posted them to Reynolds asking if she could deliver them.[92]

According to ASIO, the TPC and SOS decided to amalgamate in 1967.[93] Reynolds disputes any formal amalgamation but estimates that SOS was only active for between 12 and 18 months after which it continued to exist as 'an outreach group', holding occasional meetings and activities but not with the same level of intensity as during 1966. While many of the women continued to be part of the general peace movement in Townsville and to be concerned about conscription and the direction of the war, their attention became more focused on pressing local concerns. 'It wasn't so much a dropping off; it was more sort of moving much more into local media issues', Reynolds explained.[94]

* * *

Beyond Sydney, there were two other groups in NSW, in Newcastle and Wollongong. These groups had the closest links with the founding group.

Newcastle

Sydney SOS's activities were also being closely monitored by women in Newcastle. 'Over the past few weeks I have been reading of the wonderful work SOS is doing, and I admire the women very much as it takes a lot of courage to do the good work you are doing', wrote Isobel McArthur in June 1965.[95] A housewife with two sons in their late teens, McArthur had lost two uncles in World War II and was horrified at the thought of her own sons going to war. 'I have to do something', she determined.[96] McArthur travelled by train to meet the Sydney women who encouraged her to set up a local branch. Her first attempt was unsuccessful but McArthur persisted, contacting other women who had sons who were eligible for conscription. On 2 August 1965, nine women attended the first meeting of the Newcastle SOS held in a meeting room at the Town Hall. McArthur was elected secretary with the group's co-founder, Edna Cullen, who also had a teenage son, serving as president. Both women were members of the Newcastle branch of the UAW. Cullen was also an active member of her local branch of the ALP and both came from working-class backgrounds. McArthur's husband was listed in electoral rolls as a 'cleaner and greaser' and later as 'a marine engineer' while Cullen's husband was a labourer. Both listed their own occupations as 'home duties'.

The group quickly grew, thanks to good publicity courtesy of 'a young chap' from the local television station who wandered into the hall before the first meeting. 'We feel that gave us a wonderful start', McArthur told Pat Ashcroft.[97] Most of the original members were mothers of young men who were, or soon would be, eligible for military call-up. According to McArthur, they 'were very keen'. The following weekend, the group had its public 'coming out', taking part in the Hiroshima Day march down the main street of Newcastle.

The women wore SOS badges and marched under their own banner, which was obtained at short notice courtesy of 'a "digger" friend of ours'.[98] McArthur and Cullen planned to carry the banner but in the end it was so windy that it took six women to keep it from flying away. Members announced the group's formation in a flurry of letters to local unions, ministers of religion, politicians and the media, and were soon in demand as speakers by local community groups.

Newcastle accepted Sydney's statement of aims and of all SOS groups probably had the closest ongoing links with the original group. The proximity of the two made it possible for Newcastle members to travel to Sydney for events while Sydney committee members made the reverse train trip to attend Newcastle's annual general meetings. However, in other ways Newcastle developed very differently from the other groups. While it did not have male members, it admitted men as 'sponsors' and proudly advertised the support of local clergymen, businessmen, community leaders, trade unionists and even the local member of parliament. These names were listed in a separate column to women members on advertisements that appeared in the local press and on literature produced by the group. At a time when dissent by women was considered outside 'the norm', the Newcastle women relied on their male sponsors to validate their own credentials and lend gravitas to their cause. This is underlined in a letter to the local paper from Edna Cullen:

> We are a group of sincere, honest mothers who oppose conscription into the armed services for undeclared wars such as Vietnam, on humanitarian, religious and pacifist grounds. We have highly esteemed men sponsoring our movement – ministers of various denominations, a Member of Parliament, business men, professional men and trade unionists.[99]

The Newcastle group also had strong support from local Anglican and Methodist ministers, who preached against the war from the pulpit and were popular guest speakers at SOS functions. A leaflet produced by SOS in 1966 included the names of seven clergymen and 11 other male sponsors in addition to the names of 32 SOS women.[100] The ALP's Albert 'Bert' James, a former policeman who was the federal member for Hunter from 1960 until his retirement in 1980, was among the sponsors. He frequently addressed anti-war demonstrations and SOS meetings in Newcastle. The women also received influential early backing from community stalwart Roy Hobson, who was extremely generous financially. Hobson had served in the RAAF during World War II as a bomb aimer, rising to the rank of Flight-Sergeant. After the war he took up teaching, became a school principal, and served as a member of the local Cardiff Urban Committee for 16 years, including seven stints as chairman. Well-known in the community, he had three sons (all over conscription age) and a daughter. Two of his sons were local soccer stars and Hobson had been president of the local soccer club.[101] His unsolicited support of SOS was considered highly influential and he regularly corresponded with both Newcastle and Sydney members. After meeting McArthur and Cullen in August 1965, he wrote to the Sydney group 'paying tribute to their courage in essaying forth on such a noble and difficult task, to the honesty and sincerity of their motives and to the very good image they have given the movement':

> It is heartening to know that opposition to the obnoxious conscription legislation passed in Federal Parliament last year is slowly emerging and organising; and I trust it will grow in strength and power throughout the length and breadth of the nation.[102]

In closing, Hobson promised to try and donate one pound a week 'to help defray the political costs of your activities'.

Support also came from unexpected quarters. An ex-serviceman, E. Warburton, wrote to SOS explaining how he had volunteered for both world wars, been wounded and now relied on a war pension. He sent the women $2 towards their legal challenge against conscription. 'We as soldiers twice defeated a referendum for conscription. This should be respected as expressing the highest law in any land', he wrote. 'These lads should be given the same opportunity as ourselves and not forced or pressed into service for foreign investments.'[103]

The Newcastle women also enjoyed strong support from local unions and from other peace groups in the region. They held silent vigils, demonstrations and public meetings of their own, as well as participating in events organised by other groups. The group was active through the 1960s but from 1970 its members became increasingly involved in the moratorium movement. ASIO noted that Edna Cullen announced at a local moratorium committee meeting in July 1970 that the Newcastle SOS had disbanded, its executive deciding to split the $240 left in its kitty between the Association for International Co-operation and Disarmament (AICD) and the moratorium committee.[104] It was not until February 1971, however, that Cullen officially advised Sydney SOS of the Newcastle group's demise apparently due to unexplained 'political differences'. Sydney secretary Adele Pert was reportedly 'extremely upset' about 'political strife' interfering with SOS and urged members to 'keep politics out of the group' as was set down in the constitution.[105] There was no mention of Newcastle's demise in the Sydney newsletter.

Wollongong

The last group to form was in Wollongong. Women in this heavily working-class, industrial centre on the south coast of New South Wales had also been following the activities of SOS but it took a small push from Sydney SOS before they set up their own group. This did not mean women in Wollongong were slow to protest against the Vietnam War. There were several existing groups already protesting against conscription and the war, including the UAW and the Waterside Workers' Women's Committee. In June 1965, a group of UAW women wearing black sashes inscribed with anti-Vietnam war messages caused a stir when they held a silent protest outside the Wollongong Cenotaph. The women used the occasion to collect signatures for SOS's national petition against conscription. Local members of the Returned and Services League (RSL) sent a written complaint to the police, accusing the women of 'desecrating' the monument.[106]

However, efforts by the UAW to form a separate SOS group were evidently unsuccessful. In March 1966, Sydney secretary Pat Ashcroft wrote a letter to four Wollongong contacts, suggesting the women organise a meeting of mothers in the area to which Sydney promised to send a speaker.[107] The response was prompt. On 31 March, the *Illawarra Mercury* reported that Sydney SOS representative Noreen Hewett was in town 'to discuss with women the formation of a Wollongong branch of SOS'.[108] The newspaper noted that two women had agreed to act as convenors, identifying one as Mrs Nancy Davenport. ASIO subsequently did a background check and reported that Davenport was employed at the Wollongong Workers' Club and was the de facto wife of a wharf labourer 'who recently won a large prize in the State Lottery'.[109] She had five children, including a son of conscription age but, ASIO concluded, had 'never been known to express any sympathy to the Communist Party of Australia'.¹¹⁰ The other convenor was later identified as Audrey Kelly, who also had not previously come to ASIO's attention.¹¹¹ Shortly after Hewett's visit, Davenport wrote to inform Sydney that the group had 'secured a promise of the Workers' Club Committee Room' for its first meeting while one of the 'watersiders' had printed a sign for it.¹¹² Another founding member, Norma Thomas, who on a 1967 anti-war advertisement gave her occupation as 'cleaner', wrote to inform Sydney that this inaugural meeting had been 'a great success' and thanked the parent group for sending down some of its sashes.¹¹³

Backed by individual unions and three members of the local clergy, SOS quickly became active. On 21 April 1966, SOS women protested at the entrance to the Wollongong Railway Station where local conscripts were departing. The *South Coast Times* reported that the women stood 'in an orderly line … supporting banners' that read 'No Conscripts for Vietnam' and 'No Guns for Our Sons'.¹¹⁴ The following week, delegates from Wollongong SOS joined a national SOS deputation in Canberra where they 'interviewed' their local member, Labor's Rex Connors.¹¹⁵ SOS supported activities organised by other groups, including weekly vigils, but one of their first individual acts was to start an appeal for a local conscientious objector, Richard Pettett, who was sacked by his employer after he went public with his views.¹¹⁶

The Wollongong group never attracted large numbers but had a strong core of active women who formed its committee. In March 1969, the secretary reported that membership had reached 17, noting, 'we consider this good, considering the past'.¹¹⁷ The group mainly comprised working-class women with strong links to the trade union movement. Many of the SOS women were married to miners, waterside workers, carpenters, labourers, boilermakers or trade union officials.¹¹⁸ Some of the women were also involved in trade union auxiliaries. One of Wollongong SOS's most energetic members, Flo Garber, for example, was also publicity officer for South Coast Waterside Workers' Women's Committee and included SOS news in the monthly newsletters that she edited.[119] In May 1967, she wrote 'our committee is very impressed (with SOS) and realising the importance of such a movement, unanimously carried a resolution to become a sponsor of SOS'.[120]

Garber's husband, a maritime worker and a member of the Waterside Workers Union, was also active in the anti-war movement, helping form the South Coast Citizens Against Conscription (SCCAC) in January 1969 in support of two local draft resisters.[121] Garber's son Carl was its secretary. Many of the husbands of SOS members joined this committee and these close familial links led to the groups coordinating many joint activities. Local chemist, Mac Gudgeon, was another SCCAC leader while his wife Edna, who with Garber later took part in the Parliament House 'chain gang', became a mainstay of SOS. Their draft resister son, Mac, recalled while both his parents were traditionally Labor party voters, neither had been involved in any political lobbying groups prior to their involvement in the anti-conscription movement.[122] Ballet teacher Edna Gudgeon was one of the few Wollongong SOS women who might have qualified as 'middle class'.

SOS's membership also included women from the UAW and CPA. The highest profile CPA member was Sally Bowen, who by 1966 was already a veteran peace activist. Born in 1918, she had joined the CPA during the 1949 coal strike, helped organise activities for miners' children, and later joined the Miners' Women's Auxiliary.[123] In 1964, she led a CPA women's delegation to the USSR to look at how women were integrated into communist society. A committed peace campaigner, she was also an active member of the AICD.[124] Gillian

Wilding also had links to the communist party through her husband who was secretary of the South Coast Communist Party.[125] Another supporter, Mary Smale, was active in the UAW and was a regular attendee of its national meetings. Her husband was the president of the Miners' Federation.

Wollongong SOS did not escape the accusations that it was a 'communist front'. In a letter to the local paper, Garber took issue with another woman correspondent who had made this allegation, playing up the middle-class membership of the group: 'SOS has a large membership throughout Australia and many are wives of prominent people such as pharmacists, lawyers, doctors and professors'.[126] Garber concluded by inviting the 'misguided' woman to an SOS luncheon 'to meet some of these very fine women'. There is no record that the invitation was accepted.

Although it received initial support and encouragement from Sydney, Wollongong, like the other satellite groups, was an autonomous body. However, its proximity to Sydney did enable closer links. Correspondence between the two groups continued throughout the Vietnam War. Many of the women knew each other from other organisations and occasionally joined in each other's activities, including protests in Canberra. In 1969, Flo Garber wrote to Sydney asking for their support when she and Edna Gudgeon were facing charges relating to a protest at the local railway station.[127] Sydney sent Nora Mulheron whose presence in the court room was greatly appreciated.[128] Victoria's Jean McLean also visited Wollongong twice to address local groups. In 1970, she returned home with wigs donated by the Gudgeons that were used to disguise draft resisters in the Victorian 'underground'.[129]

While they may have been last to form, Wollongong SOS were a feisty bunch who made a valuable contribution to the local anti-war movement. 'They were a quite a fearsome bunch of women', Gudgeon's son, Mac, recalled. 'They were pretty determined. Whatever they put their mind to they'd make sure that it would happen.'[130]

South Australia

The South Australian SOS group officially formed in August 1965 but efforts to organise it began in late June with UAW women playing a key role. On 29 June 1965, two women sent out a general letter headed 'Save Our Sons' inviting women to demonstrate against conscription at Adelaide Airport the following Thursday when local conscripts were due to depart for military training camp in Victoria. The letter also advertised a public meeting to be held on 12 July 1965 'in order to extend the activities of SOS here'.[131] While the UAW was not mentioned, ASIO quickly made the link, noting one of the signatories, Hazel Hoare, was a UAW member while the other, Clair Hoare, was a member of the South Australian Peace Committee who had once 'addressed a UAW luncheon on the subject of peace'. She was also believed to be president of the SA section of the WILPF. Furthermore, ASIO noted, the recipient of the letter was a UAW member 'who would be unlikely to receive it from any other quarter, unless the UAW membership list was obtained to provide names and addresses to which to circulate material'.[132]

Five women subsequently took part in the protest at Adelaide Airport, standing silently in front of the building housing the Vickers Vimy aircraft flown by brothers Ross and Keith Smith on their epic flight from England to Australia in 1919. A report in Adelaide's afternoon daily newspaper was accompanied by a photo showing the women wearing aprons over their winter coats. Handwritten messages on the aprons read: 'Youth Raw Deal', 'No Fighting Career for Our

Sons', 'No Overseas Conscription' and 'Kindness not Killing'.[133] One of the women, Audrey Potticary, later remembered the trepidation the women felt in staging that first protest:

> It was a freezing cold winter's day ... the photograph shows us all rugged-up against the bitterly cold weather. The protest took the form of a silent vigil, and we expected to be arrested, but instead our photo was taken for the paper and we were interviewed by the *News* and invited to appear on Channel Nine's "A Current Affair".[134]

Three of the women (Dot Edwards, Clair Hoare and Audrey 'Potter') allowed their names and addresses to be published in the newspaper. The other two declined 'because they had sons who could be called up'.[135] One woman said her son had been called up in the first intake but his training had been deferred because he was a student. 'My son's views may not agree with mine, in fact he doesn't even know I am here today', she told the newspaper.[136]

ASIO had two informants at the airport to report on the protest. They identified the fourth woman as Maureen Cook and corrected the spelling of Potticary.[137] Cook had two sons eligible for conscription. ASIO was unable to identify the fifth woman but noted that the other four women all had existing files due to their links to the UAW. According to the UAW's former state secretary, Beryl Miller, all four were indeed members of the UAW, though not office bearers, who went on to play 'a leading role' in the establishment of SOS in South Australia.[138] 'They were a mixture of women whose husbands worked in blue and white collar jobs but did not work themselves at the time', Miller recalled. 'They were very much opposed to the war on the basis that their sons looked like being conscripted. Of course, that made them very angry. They wouldn't just sit back and take it.'[139]

Many UAW members, like Valerie Howe, saw SOS as an extension of the UAW's work:

> The UAW had a strong commitment to world peace ... We strongly opposed the Vietnam War, and again took to the streets. Many of us joined Save Our Sons. I felt particularly strongly as I had two sons eligible for the deadly conscription draft.[140]

A SA delegate later reported to the UAW's national body that the airport protest had been 'initiated by individual UAW members', rather than the local UAW, and had garnered 'some good results' in terms of publicity.[141] One of the women had subsequently received a phone call from a woman who passed on the names and addresses of seven other women 'who wanted to do something'. It noted that women had also performed admirably when interviewed on television:

> The girls shaped up really well, particularly as most of them have never done anything like this before and despite opposition from their families they are still determined to go ahead ... all in all it has been a wonderful experience for these women and they are bubbling over with joy at the results so far achieved.[142]

A report of the airport protest in the *Australian* also reached SOS in Sydney which sent its congratulations to the new group: 'We are very encouraged to hear of such an effort.'[143] Potticary, who took over as secretary in 1967, recalled that 'hectic days followed [the airport protest] as we humble housewives were caught up in the huge groundswell of opposition that gradually developed against the Vietnam War'.[144] She also recognised the importance of assistance from UAW members:

> I found it hard-going at times as I had no experience of being a South Australian secretary of an Australia-wide movement that was SOS. But with the help and support of the wonderful

women of the UAW and other organisations, we felt we made a difference in the successful opposition to the war.[145]

The SA group adopted Sydney's statement of aims but opted for a chairperson instead of a president. It also permitted men as members with men holding leadership positions at different times. The first president was May Wharton, mother of three sons, one of whom was conscripted. A Menzies supporter until conscription was introduced, she was not part of the UAW but was a member of the Woman's Christian Temperance Union (WCTU).[146] Hazel Hoare became the group's first secretary. The group held formal meetings, took minutes, and held elections and annual general meetings, along the lines of 'traditional' groups like the UAW. Highlighting the difficulty many groups experienced in communicating with their members during this period, a telephone chain was established so members could efficiently relay information to each other. (At one stage Potticary tried to resign as secretary because she did not have a telephone at home but was convinced to stay on after it was pointed out members could call her next-door neighbour if the issue was urgent.)[147]

In the early days, the group went 'all out in publicity campaigns'.[148] They held public meetings and organised guest speakers who spoke about conscientious objection and the war in general; collected signatures for the national SOS petition; took part in protest marches under their own striking blue and white banner; and held silent vigils at each intake of conscripts. They also conducted letter-writing campaigns, lobbying members on both sides of politics; provided financial and moral support for conscientious objectors; and were a constant fixture at court cases in which young men were trying to avoid conscription. Like the Sydney SOS, the SA group also suffered from negative publicity about its so-called 'communist links'. The accusation was particularly galling to Mrs Wharton, described in a 1966 newspaper article as 'a 57-year-old grandmother who has been a Liberal supporter all her life'.[149] 'I have carried placards in some marches and I have been called a malicious communist', she complained.[150]

The SA group strongly identified Sydney as its 'parent' group and corresponded regularly with members there. It also closely followed the activities of other SOS groups, sending a letter of support when Brisbane's secretary faced court, and inviting Melbourne's secretary to address a protest rally.[151] However, limited finances ruled out attending 'national' activities in the eastern states. In 1965, Hoare wrote to Sydney apologising for not sending a delegate to a joint protest in Canberra: 'We are a very small movement here with low membership and very low finances'.[152] Ashcroft was sympathetic: 'We were once a small group in Sydney but as you see we have spread to many states, so keep on trying and you will grow'.[153]

Aside from the heady days that followed the 1965 airport protest, the group constantly struggled to recruit new members. This was due in large part to the competition from the plethora of other anti-war and conscription groups that formed in Adelaide during the same period. Many women also preferred to protest as part of groups of which they were already members, including the UAW and the WILPF, both of which were very active in SA.[154] At a meeting in early 1966, Wharton revealed she had approached several women about joining SOS but all had declined. By July 1966, there were about 30 'members' on the group's mailing list.[155] This was probably the group's peak. At this stage, there was some discussion regarding 'the effectiveness of our name' and whether it should be changed. But 'after some consideration it was decided that as the name is Australia-wide and had such a good image in the other states, it would not be wise to change it now'.[156] In

May 1967, there was no going back after the group placed an order for 20 SOS badges from Sydney.[157] According to Eulalie Tapp, there was a mainstay of about 17 men and women throughout the group's existence while 'many others came for a few meetings and left to join other peace groups'.[158] However, at protests and marches, SOS banner 'always attracted scores of people'.[159]

Nevertheless, by 1968, there was 'quite vehement argument on what, if anything, the local SOS was achieving'.[160] It was decided to seek Sydney's advice on how to gain new members and how best to help conscientious objectors. Sydney replied that it was experiencing similar difficulties which gave the Adelaide women heart. 'It helped us a lot to realise that we all come up against much the same problems in our work in SOS. I think we were becoming rather depressed about the lack of response and contact and things move at a much slower pace here', Potticary reported.[161]

In 1969, Potticary expressed further frustration about efforts to recruit parents of young men eligible for conscription: 'Recently we sent out invitations to attend our meetings to 53 sets of parents and not one turned up, although some got in touch with us and expressed support for our aims'.[162] At another point, she suggested that the group change its meetings to the daytime in order to attract more mothers, highlighting the difficulties of catering to a mixed constituency. 'As we are aiming at drawing mothers in, I feel sure meeting in the day time will suit more women', she wrote in a memo to members. 'This will mean curtailing our men members perhaps but we could hold meetings on a Saturday or Sunday afternoon as they do in Sydney as this would suit fathers.'[163] SOS was not alone in finding it difficult to recruit new members in SA during this period. In 1968, the chairman of the high-profile South Australian anti-war group, Campaign for

Peace in Vietnam (CPV), also expressed concern about the group's apparent inability to attract active members and the fact that it had 'so far achieved very little'.[164]

In her June 1969 annual report, however, Potticary remained upbeat: 'All in all I think our organisation stands up well, both here and in the other states, but of course we will, I am sure, do bigger and better things in the coming year'.[165] However, by June 1970, membership had seriously declined; so few attended the annual general meeting that it could not go ahead. Subsequent discussions centred on whether SOS should become an auxiliary to CPV or the Conscientious Objectors' Advisory Group.[166] Ultimately, members decided to continue as a separate group, actively supporting the organisation of the moratorium marches. However, recruitment problems continued, and many of the more active members found themselves increasingly splitting their time between SOS and other anti-war groups. An ageing membership was also an issue. The secretary's annual report for 1970/71 noted while the group had gained three new members, two had been 'lost through death'.[167] By early 1972, it was clear the group could not continue to operate given its ongoing membership and financial issues. A letter was duly distributed asking members to vote on whether to continue, disband or place the group into 'caretaker mode'. As a result, in March 1972, SOS went into 'indefinite recess', just eight months before Gough Whitlam's election heralded the end of Australia's involvement in Vietnam.[168]

Western Australia

The SOS group that formed in Perth on 29 March 1966 also had a mixed membership with male leadership but the UAW still played a key role in its formation with many of its members – and their husbands – joining the new group. Initially, however, the local UAW women were reluctant to get involved. Already juggling a full agenda that included its own Vietnam protests, and faced with a declining membership and finances, the UAW's management committee did not want to set up another group that would inevitably drain its already limited resources. After repeated approaches for assistance, state UAW president Roma Gilchrist sent an apologetic letter to Sydney SOS, expressing disappointment that a local group had not been formed but pointing out that 'with a much smaller population it is a problem as the active people are all very busy'.[169]

As in other states, there were also concerns that a new group would be dismissed as a CPA front if the UAW was seen to be too closely involved. While happy to circulate SOS petitions and make financial contributions when it was able, the UAW's executive committee felt that a SOS group would be better 'fostered by some leading citizen'.[170] To this end, individual UAW members approached local identities in 1965 but the response only reinforced their concerns. One minister of religion 'became quite nasty and he gave (the UAW member) an anti-communist blast', another 'identity' approached said he and his wife could not be involved 'because of her job'. A local councillor and his wife, who had been overheard at church saying they would go to jail before their sons were sent to Vietnam, expressed some interest but only if the new group was entirely independent of the UAW.[171]

Despite the response, a few UAW women remained convinced that a local SOS group was needed. Marion Henderson, a UAW executive member, recorded that WA SOS was finally formed after several parents of Perth boys wrote to local newspapers to protest against conscription: 'One (UAW) woman wrote to all these people and within a few weeks it led to the formation of a Western Australian branch of the

Save Our Sons Movement'.[172] Among those who responded favourably was printer Terence Lockwood, who had staged a one-man public protest in the city centre, and Shirley McGuinness, who had written to the *West Australian* newspaper protesting the call-up of her son.[173] Buoyed by the response to their letters, the UAW women arranged a 'citizens' meeting' for 29 March 1966 to discuss a proposal to officially form the SOS group. The minutes recorded that 54 people attended but not all were keen on the proposed name of the new group. While UAW women (including Henderson, Mary Thorp, Beryl Boardman and Mary Woodhams) spoke for it, school teacher Jim Kane felt that the name was 'too narrow in outlook', suggesting instead that it be named the Vietnam Action Committee.[174] However, the majority voted for SOS and to affiliate with the movement in Sydney.[175]

Among those who attended the first meeting were leading peace activists, academics and members of the clergy. ASIO also noted the attendance of prominent communists including Harold Clements and Mary Thorp's husband, Albert. Later the same night, Clements was overheard enthusiastically reporting the group's formation to his local CPA branch.[176] Among those who could not be 'classified' were: Ray Collie, a railways worker and union organiser, who became the group's first secretary; his wife Elsie, who joined the committee (the couple had two sons of conscription age); and William Clarke, a high school history teacher who chaired the first meeting.[177] A nine-member 'temporary' committee was appointed at this meeting comprising the Collies, Terry Lockwood, Shirley McGuinness, Marion Henderson, Jim Kane, Albert Thorp, Edward Keady and Kathleen Wearne. Enthusiasm at the first meeting was reflected in the collection plate with an impressive $45 raised to pay for an advertisement publicising an upcoming public meeting. According to Henderson that was 'the beginning of a combined activity which brought hope for those who had feared they were alone and without support'.[178]

Unlike most of the other groups, WA SOS was never considered a 'women's group' and the positions of chairman and secretary were always held by men. If the Sydney committee found this curious, it never commented on it in correspondence between the two groups. There was some initial confusion, however, when the Sydney secretary, responding to the first letter from Perth's new secretary Ray Collie, inadvertently addressed her reply to 'Mrs Collie'. In a handwritten note at the end of the letter, Pat Ashcroft apologised for her mistake.[179] She was delighted by the 'heartening' news that Perth has finally formed 'a definite SOS group'. 'Now we only need Nth Territory to come forward, then we are truly Commonwealth wide', she wrote. 'I know Sydney members are going to be tickled to death when they hear of your group.'[180]

The new committee lost no time in organising a march for the following Saturday 'to show by numbers and slogans that there was a voice of protest'.[181] To abide by local by-laws, marchers walked in pairs around a city block, finishing on the steps of the GPO where they were addressed by Ray Collie who used his hands as a megaphone.[182] According to one newspaper's account, about 50 protesters, including men, women and children, marched silently, carrying banners inscribed with anti-war messages that decried 'Holt's Marbles of Death'.[183] Another newspaper estimated the number involved to be closer to 100 and carried a photograph of women carrying placards and banners.[184] ASIO officers in attendance noted that while only a few of the regular communists took part in the actual march there were 'quite a few congregated' along the route.[185] It was also recorded that the 2000 leaflets advertising an upcoming public meeting distributed during the march had been stencilled and printed in the UAW's rooms, leaving ASIO in no doubt as to who was really behind the new group.[186] The newly pledged SOS members were pleasantly surprised by the success of their first outing. Henderson, who led the march, later reported to Sydney that the event had been 'well-received' by the general public and had 'won wide publicity' on TV, radio and in the newspapers.[187] In contrast, a WA Special Branch constable in attendance reported that 'public interest in the demonstration was very slight'.[188]

A better gauge of public interest came two days later when close to 200 people attended SOS's first public meeting in the Unity Theatre at Trades Hall. Among them were the parents of the first West Australian conscript, Sapper McIlroy. His father told the *Daily News*: 'It's too late to stop him going, but my wife and I intend to keep fighting this whole Vietnam business by going to meetings such as Save Our Sons'.[189] The meeting was addressed by Reverend Peter Hodge, hospital worker John Wearne (identified by ASIO as a communist) and Irene Greenwood, a well-known local radio announcer and a member of the WILPF who had recently returned from the UK where she had represented a number of women's organisations at peace events. The meeting passed a resolution to write to Prime Minister Holt deploring his government's actions and calling on him to end the policy of conscripting young men for overseas service. The resolution went further than Sydney SOS's aims, which at that time were limited to conscription, by calling for the withdrawal of Australian forces from Vietnam and demanding the government work to negotiate peace in line with the 1954 Geneva Agreement on Vietnam. Before closing the meeting, an ASIO agent noted that Mr Clarke warned all present that they would probably be labelled communists but said this should not deter the effort. Clarke said as far as he knew no communists were present at the first meeting which had represented 'a good cross section of the public of Perth'.[190] ASIO, nonetheless, still managed to compile a lengthy list of communist members and sympathisers among those present.[191]

The group adopted the Sydney SOS group's statement of aims but also produced a constitution of its own. There was considerable debate over this document, particularly over two points that declared the group's opposition to 'long periods of compulsory service' and 'Australian support of the American intervention in Vietnam' with some members concerned that this was not the domain of SOS and would only serve to 'get the backs of the public up'.[192] A letter to the editor from a SOS member that appeared in the *West Australian* declared that SOS was not against national service per se but did object to overseas service for conscripts 'especially using a lottery barrel'.[193] The group corresponded regularly with Sydney, ordering leaflets and exchanging news. The prohibitive cost of travel ruled out any closer links, although Marion Henderson may have taken part in one Sydney SOS protest when she was there for a national UAW conference where she reported on the activities of the WA SOS.[194] Certainly, she would have known UAW women from the Sydney SOS. Apart from one early letter from Merle James on behalf of Victoria SOS, there is no evidence that Perth communicated with any other SOS group.[195]

Membership of WA SOS was dominated by parents of young men eligible for conscription. Like their interstate counterparts, however, local ASIO agents believed the group had an underlying motive. A December 1966 report by the intelligence agency categorically stated that 'it is clear that the establishment of SOS in WA was instigated by the CPA and its front the UAW'.[196] While some members did indeed belong to the CPA and the UAW and, not surprisingly, featured frequently in ASIO's surveillance of the group, there is no independent evidence to support this claim and plenty to suggest that it was indeed a group of like-minded souls concerned with saving young Australian men from being conscripted to fight in Vietnam. While it speculated that Ray Collie was the same 'Mr Collie' who had once written to the Minister for the Army seeking the discharge of his son on the grounds his father was opposed to the government action in Vietnam, it could find nothing to link him to the CPA.[197] However, ASIO did identify four executive members – Albert Thorp, Marion Henderson, John Wearne and Dolores Wilson – through whom, it believed, the CPA had 'ample scope for influencing and directing the activities and policies of the Association'.[198] Dolores Wilson, while not a CPA member herself, was apparently a risk because her husband was a communist, while Marion Henderson, who had three sons, was singled out because of her membership with the UAW (this is despite her security files suggesting that ASIO knew full well that neither she nor her husband were members of the CPA). The third member identified, John Wearne, had joined SOS with his wife Kathleen. Both were indeed CPA members but ASIO failed to highlight that they also had two sons nearing conscription age. According to their son Stuart, the family had long been involved in the local peace movement, with his father serving for a time as secretary of the WA Peace Council. 'At our first march there were about 15 people and five of them were Wearnes', he recalled. 'Marches were novel in Perth in the 1960s.'[199] Likewise, treasurer Albert Thorp was a CPA member, but he and his wife Mary also had a son of conscription age.

Other SOS members also came under scrutiny. Vice president Jim Kane was listed as 'left wing socialist' while assistant secretary Beryl Boardman, a UAW member, was identified as 'the wife of communist sympathiser'.²⁰⁰ ASIO neglected to mention that she had three sons and thus could be reasonably presumed to have felt a personal stake in the conscription issue. Joan Davies was identified as a lapsed CPA member but her husband Lloyd, a well-known lawyer, was described as 'a rabid member'.²⁰¹ Another SOS woman, a high school teacher, came to ASIO's attention after her brother in the RAAF sought a higher security clearance. It was eventually decided that her involvement in SOS was of a minor nature and should not affect her brother's advancement.²⁰² The security report also noted the woman's husband was 'anti her activities' in SOS so presumably this counted in her favour. Nonetheless, ASIO maintained a strict watch on the activities of WA SOS, convinced that 'it is currently penetrated and influenced by the CPA and it would only require a small increase in party penetration to be regarded as a communist frontal organisation'.²⁰³

During its relatively short existence the Perth group staged a number of successful public meetings and demonstrations on its own and in concert with other anti-war groups. It also produced several pamphlets and leaflets. It worked particularly closely with the Youth Campaign Against Conscription (YCAC). Husbands and wives frequently joined or attended SOS events together and several had sons and daughters who were active members of YCAC, who also supported SOS demonstrations.

However, it did not take long for cracks to begin to show in the group's leadership. The first came as early as a month after its formation when it was revealed the inaugural chairman Bill Clarke was also part of the Vietnam Action Committee (VAC) that had been created the same month as SOS. Clarke then approached the UAW's executive for financial assistance to fund the VAC's stationery. A well-placed ASIO source in the UAW's executive meeting reported that Molly Thorp and Marion Henderson vehemently opposed the request. Thorp accused Clarke of 'splitting SOS' and of being 'a dangerous element', urging the UAW not to have anything to do with him or his friends.[204] At the following UAW executive meeting, Henderson reported that SOS meetings were being poorly attended and that there was a lot of internal friction.[205] By mid-year, Clarke had been replaced as president by Terry Lockwood but the group was dealt another blow early in 1967 when hardworking secretary Ray Collie announced that he was resigning due to an imminent move to the country.[206] Internal friction continued. There were complaints by members about the increasingly radical nature of its leaflets and about the behaviour of individual members at protests; frustration over the failure to make an impact; and concerns that the group's focus on conscription was too limiting.

Like other SOS groups, the WA group was subject to ongoing smear campaigns by its opponents and was forced to defend itself in the press.[207] However, the group continued to have a high profile, particularly in the lead up to the 1966 election. Morale dipped when the government was returned but there was worse to come. In early 1967, the group found itself in serious debt, unable to pay the costs of advertisements, leaflets and posters produced for the election campaign. A meeting in February was dominated by this financial crisis with various solutions suggested including social fundraising evenings, approaching the unions for assistance (this was rejected), finding cheaper meeting rooms and placing a levy on members.[208] The group eventually found a new meeting place in the UAW's rooms, paying 50 cents per night rent, and held social functions to help reduce the debt.[209]

However, internal rumblings of discontent continued. In June 1967, a special meeting was called to discuss a proposal to amalgamate with VAC. The discussion was reportedly 'lively'.[210] Jim Kane, who had argued against the SOS name at the inaugural citizens meeting, spoke strongly in favour of amalgamation, noting many present were already members of both organisations and that the proposal would stop duplication.[211] Another speaker argued that SOS's aims were too narrow and that the issue was now the war itself, not whether conscripts should be sent to Vietnam. But there was also vehement opposition. One speaker argued that both groups appealed to different constituencies, with SOS thought to be especially appealing to mothers. Some opposition was more fundamental, one woman voicing her concern that the VAC was a 'communist inspired organisation'. In the end supporters of the status quo were outvoted at the general meeting, 13 to 7.[212]

The amalgamation formally took place the following week at a combined meeting of SOS and VAC chaired by Bill Clarke (who declared himself 'impartial') where it was agreed that the new group would be called the Vietnam Action Committee.[213] At a subsequent meeting it was decided to rename the group the Vietnam Objectors' Campaign (VOC).[214] In hindsight, it is difficult to understand why SOS allowed this to happen given that at the time of the amalgamation it was claiming 200 members while the VAC had less than 40.[215] SOS was also by this time free of debt with its treasurer signing over funds of $62.22 to the new group, compared to just $11.45 contributed by the VAC.[216] It is also worth noting that after SOS handed its records over to the new group, its minutes (many handwritten) subsequently appeared in full in ASIO's records.[217] If anybody benefitted from the amalgamation, it clearly was not SOS.

Some SOS members went on to serve in a much smaller executive of the new group. SOS founding members Terry Lockwood and Jim Kane were elected vice chairmen of the new committee while Lavina Holmgren was appointed its first secretary (but resigned shortly after citing personal reasons). Other SOS members declined to join the new organisation or fell away soon after the amalgamation. John Wearne had already lost faith that conscription would ever be overturned, moving his family to the relative safety of Canada. 'I was at uni, getting into all sorts of fights over Vietnam, I was close to the age of conscription but in the end my family moved to Canada, in part to avoid the draft', Stuart Wearne recalled. 'I had just told my parents cheerfully not to worry that I would go to jail but they said, "I don't think you know anything about military jails" which they were in those days.'[218] Other SOS members, including Marion Henderson, whose son later became a conscientious objector, continued on in the new group.[219] Henderson also went on to join Perth's Vietnam Moratorium Campaign, along with other UAW women.

It was symptomatic of the relationship between Perth and Sydney that the latter did not know of the amalgamation for almost six months. In late 1967, Henderson wrote to the Sydney group requesting SOS Christmas cards and advising that following the amalgamation the group was now known as the VOC.[220] Despite talk of the need for more 'direct action' during the amalgamation talks, in reality little was achieved in the VOC's first year, a fact that was bemoaned at its first general meeting in April 1968 when it was revealed that the group had been unofficially 'in recess' for some months.[221] In any event, the new group by now bore little resemblance in its aims or constitution to SOS and there was no further communication with the Sydney group.

Victoria

At the same time as the Sydney women were getting together, women in Victoria were also seeking ways of making their objections to conscription known. After seeing reports of SOS's activities in newspapers in May 1965, several wrote as individuals to Sydney for advice on how to set up a similar group.[222] Nance Walsh wrote that as a mother of two boys, aged 18 and 19, she had 'always felt very strongly against war … and would like to start something in my area'.[223] She was in possession of an 'excellent' SOS pamphlet, obtained from the local branch of the WILPF, which was reprinting and distributing SOS literature in Melbourne at this time.[224] Dorothy Gibson, a well-known local peace activist and long-time member of the CPA, was also advocating on SOS's behalf, writing to friends about the group's actions and plans. 'The Sydney women are very anxious to be strengthened by an extension of the movement to all states. They are planning another demonstration and would like to make it national', she wrote, adding:

> I feel this could be an enormously powerful movement. It provides an opportunity for actions for those mothers worried to death about the possibility of their sons being sent to fight in a war that they abhor.[225]

Gibson noted that some women had already begun to act in Box Hill-Blackburn, Malvern and Oakleigh, conducting a public opinion poll amongst women, circulating the Sydney SOS petition, and holding a meeting in Box Hill attended by about 90 people.[226]

It was also during this period that Jean McLean, a young housewife from the seaside middle-class suburb of Beaumaris, encountered some friends at her local shopping centre. McLean's two-year-old son was not in any imminent danger of conscription, but her friends were mothers of young teenage boys and were very concerned about how conscription might affect them. McLean, who at the time was pregnant with her second child, had always had an interest in foreign affairs and had been following the war in Vietnam with mounting concern so she suggested they do something about it. 'I said, "Well there's not much point in us standing around complaining about it, if we want to change the situation we should get people together and do something"', she recalled.[227] Shortly after, McLean convened a meeting at her home, inviting 'everyone I knew who shared my concern'.[228] Among those who attended were Dr Moss Cass, a member of the Central Executive of the ALP and his wife Shirley, who later joined SOS. He brought along a copy of the article in the *Australian* reporting the formation of the Sydney SOS and it was subsequently decided by those in attendance that the Melbourne group should adopt the same name.[229]

The Save Our Sons Movement of Victoria (Victoria SOS) group first came to the media's attention at the 30 June protest attended by Vilma Ames. The WILPF's Anna Vroland, a former headmistress who was once dismissed from a prestigious private girls' school because of her progressive teaching methods, recalled in a subsequent newsletter how the protest came about:

> When we heard of Sydney's proposed demonstration as young conscripts were assembling, a few Melbourne women decided to follow suit. At very short notice, Mrs Vilma Ames made a courageous stand – alone at first. And she had never participated in a demonstration before! Soon she was joined by Cr Nola Barber. Doubtless it was the courage of these two women that attracted reporters.[230]

McLean referred to this protest when she wrote to Sydney a week later, lamenting that due to short notice it had only been 'moderately effective'.[231] While numbers may have been low, the resulting publicity succeeded in attracting new recruits. On 7 July, about 30 women staged an 'impressive demonstration' outside Watsonia Army Camp where conscripts were arriving. Aileen Walker reported that some of the women had prepared a leaflet 'based on the original SOS leaflet' and this had been distributed to the media.[232] On 2 August, the ALP's women's committee also held a public lunchtime meeting on conscription in the Lower Melbourne Town Hall. It was addressed by six women, including 'well-known TV personality' Corinne Kerby.[233] Most in the audience were supportive, except for 'about 30 or 40 women who made an attempt at breaking up the meeting, unsuccessfully'.[234] They were asked to leave but did not go quietly, calling out 'Keep sending our boys to Vietnam to kill the Commos, Blast the Commos to bits or else we'll be blasted to bits'.[235] Miriam Mason, who had also been corresponding with the Sydney SOS group, was in the audience. Appalled by 'such ignorance and fascism', she felt compelled to take a stand: 'When I told these women they were servants of Bob Santamaria they went very quiet', she told Sydney SOS later.[236] Mason vowed she would 'support any move which will bring a united action against this most brutal war in Vietnam'. Following this meeting, McLean again wrote to Sydney advising that a meeting was planned for 18 August at the Assembly Hall in Melbourne 'to form an SOS group here in Melbourne'.[237] The day after she reported to Sydney that 50 women had attended: 'We are now officially organised, enthusiasm was general and many good suggestions were put forward'.[238]

Jean McLean became the group's secretary, a position she held throughout its existence. Much younger than her interstate counterparts, she was 30 when SOS formed and lived in a bespoke beachside home that she and her builder husband had designed together.[239]

But her background was anything but conventional. Her mother, a Russian Jew, had come to Australia with her family in 1936 where her grandmother, who spoke little English, established a shop that was frequently targeted by vandals who painted its walls with swastikas and racist insults. 'At a very early age I became fairly politically aware, and aware of prejudice and racism', McLean later recalled.[240] By contrast, her English-born father was an atheist who had been brought up as a Presbyterian. During the 1940s, both her parents were members of the CPA but left in 1947, 'more for personal than ideological reasons'.[241] Her father became a 'committed socialist' who, according to McLean, 'practised what he preached'.[242] 'He had a factory and all his workers were shareholders ... We learned a lot about how we should treat each other and that war was bad and one should do everything against it. I suppose that's why I got involved in conscription.'[243] Growing up in this 'politically aware atmosphere' with her two sisters, McLean also became interested in international politics, which she absorbed from reading magazines like *Time* and *Newsweek*. 'What was happening to our north, in Indo-China, the Asian scene, always interested me. I was aware of the so-called 'secret' war in Laos in 1961 and the history of Ho Chi Minh and the Vietnamese people's struggle for independence for Vietnam from foreign rule', she said. 'Then when Menzies introduced conscription, I knew that this was the beginning of Australia sending troops to Vietnam.'[244]

While there were no records preserved of the inaugural Sydney meeting, detailed minutes of the first Melbourne meeting provide an insight into the passion behind its formation. After reading Sydney's Statement of Aims, which was later adopted, Ames urged those present to join together to fight conscription. 'Women do possess power, let us go on a CRUSADE for PEACE', she enthused.[245] Nola Barber, one of two guest speakers, followed in a similar vein, evoking the maternal duty of women to nurture and protect life:

> As women we have a moral obligation to stand together and fight the conscription issue. It is our clear duty to exercise our right to voice our opinion. We should call the government to account.[246]

The second guest speaker, Dr Alan Roberts, a physicist from Monash University, welcomed the formation of SOS, and speculated that if Australian people really supported the war, 'conscription would not be necessary'.[247] His comments reflected a belief among those present that their campaign would be short-lived once the general public had been educated about the issue.[248] Glen Tomasetti then sang a song she had composed herself that again evoked maternal duty:

> I didn't bear him to carry a gun,
> I didn't feed him to carry a gun
> I didn't teach him to carry a gun
> To kill somebody else's son.[249]

McLean later suggested making it the group's 'theme song'. Initially, there was a general sense of camaraderie with SOS women in other states. Several women indicated their eagerness to join their interstate colleagues at a national SOS delegation planned in Canberra the following month. Plans for an official SOS sash, like those worn by Sydney, were also discussed.[250]

Pauline Armstrong, the mother of a draft resister who later wrote her master's thesis on the Victorian SOS, noted that the group was heavily represented by middle-class women from Melbourne's 'sand-belt claret suburbs'.[251] Joan Coxsedge, who joined the committee in 1967, agreed there had been a high proportion of 'fairly well-heeled' women and lamented that more was not done to engage women in working-class suburbs.[252] McLean, however, said that this was largely due to the fact that most of the early members were friends or acquaintances who lived in the same suburb of Beaumaris as she did. 'They came from there because they were the people I talked to. If I had lived in any other suburb they would have come from there', she said.[253] McLean described the group as comprising mainly lower middle-class women, with the exception of a couple who came from very wealthy Melbourne families.[254] Nevertheless, the high proportion of middle-class involvement did set the Victorian SOS apart from other SOS groups. The group held monthly public meetings with the committee meeting more frequently, usually at someone's home, and produced a monthly newsletter. While not, by design, a women's only group, in reality, as the meetings were held during the daytime, it was only women at home who were able to attend. According to Coxsedge, the group's name also tended to attract women more than men. She believed many women were more comfortable in a women's group, having traditionally found it difficult to have a voice heard in more male-dominated groups.[255]

Many of the Melbourne women were also very well connected to the local arts community and were able to raise impressive amounts of money from social functions, auctions, concerts and theatrical events. One raffle, for example, offered a Clifton Pugh painting as its prize. Coxsedge, an artist, whose husband was a banker 'on lousy pay', said she did not always feel entirely comfortable at these events. 'They were some very nice women but a lot of them were very middle class. They were able to kick in quite a deal of money for fundraisers. You ended up going to dinners, luncheons', she recalled. 'I wouldn't say it was exactly my bag but I went along and did it because you needed the money.'[256] Money raised was used to fund hall hire fees, posters and leaflets, and later to help defray the costs of bail money, court costs and fines incurred by its own members, draft resisters and other protesters.

The Victorian SOS also differed from Sydney SOS in that it never embraced a formal structure. Its committee decided early on to forgo the distractions of annual elections and constitutions in order to get on with the task at hand. For this reason, McLean remains adamant that SOS in Victoria should be referred to as a 'movement' not an 'organisation'. 'You acted according to need. You got on with it', she recalled.[257] There were only ever a couple of elections in the group's history. If anyone expressed an interest or the time to become involved on the committee, they were immediately 'co-opted'. McLean said she became secretary because she was the only person willing to put her name on the campaign literature. 'At the time people were scared of getting stones through their window or it affecting their husband's jobs', she said. 'I didn't hold these fears so I put my name there and that is how I became secretary and I stayed there the entire time because nobody challenged it and everyone was happy with the way it ran.'[258]

According to McLean, while a couple of women had initially pushed for more 'formality', there had never been any power struggles or attempts to unseat the committee. Other SOS committee members concurred with this view, remembering an air of consensus that they had not experienced before or since in other groups. Coxsedge believed that part of SOS's success was due to women being able to participate at a level where they felt comfortable. While there was a core group of 30 to 40 'active' members, dozens of others contributed to the group in various ways.

> It's like, if you threw a stone in a pond you'd get ripples, these layers, and you'd have some women close in the middle and then

people who would come to certain things ... or they would put on functions and raise money. Nobody pushed them into doing anything more than what they wanted to do and if all they wanted to do was to shove leaflets into envelopes, fine. That is how it was, it was always voluntary.[259]

Despite the lack of structure, Coxsedge noted there was a clear hierarchy within the group, with McLean at the helm. However, decisions were always unanimous. This made it very different from other anti-war groups at the time, many of which were wracked by internal politics. According to Coxsedge, 'there was a feeling that we had to pull together because of the importance of the issue which was profound. It was such a shocking war and we felt it was very, very important to work together'.[260]

At its peak there were about 10 women on the committee. The original members included Ames, McLean, McLean's sister Alice Hammerly, Tomasetti, Joan Anderson, Mary Sticklan and Walsh. They were later joined by Coxsedge, Chris Cathie, Mary McCutcheon, Shirley Cass, Irene Miller and Jo Maclaine-Cross. Dorothy Gibson also played an important role in the group's early years but declined to join the committee fearing her communist links would taint the new organisation. Nevertheless, her presence did cause some uneasiness among a couple of the other women, including Tomasetti. 'Some of our people tried to suggest that somehow or another we could be being infiltrated', McLean recalled. 'I was not hung up about having communists on the committee or not but Dorothy thought it could harm the committee and she did not want to do that. She was a brilliant woman ... just terribly helpful on things like raising funds, she never tried to interfere with the political decisions we were taking ... she was perfectly happy to play a background role.'[261]

Most of the women who joined Victoria SOS had never been politically active. Among them were women who had voted Liberal all their lives but changed their political views after conscription came in. A few, like Vilma Ames and Shirley Cass, were already ALP members. Some subsequently joined the party. After it was suggested that SOS might have a stronger voice if its members joined the ALP, a group of about 16 descended on their local branch meeting one evening to sign up. Expecting to be welcomed into the fold, they were instead suspected of being part of a hostile takeover.[262] While the Victorian SOS women did work closely with elements of the ALP during the course of the anti-conscription campaign, as will be seen, they certainly did not feel duty-bound to follow party directions.

Like their Sydney counterparts, the Victorian women initially wore sashes, printed literature and protested outside army barracks during intakes of conscripts, handing out leaflets that informed the young men of their rights to be conscientious objectors. By the end of its first year, McLean estimated they had 500 members, about the same number that Sydney SOS was claiming.[263] Connections between the two groups, however, were already waning, despite Melbourne's impressive contribution of 17,000 signatures to the national petition and several of its members taking part in the Canberra delegation in September 1965. The groups continued to swap newsletters and occasional letters but operated autonomously. There were practical reasons for this, according to McLean; both groups found themselves increasingly preoccupied with affairs in their own states and joint ventures, like the Canberra delegation, were expensive. Even the cost of telephone communication during this period was prohibitive. There were other reasons. According to McLean, the Sydney women were 'mainly UAW women' and generally of an older age group so there were not many natural connections. 'To us they were people doing the same thing, if we had a few draft resisters we would tell them and send our newsletters but mainly it was just too difficult', she said.[264]

* * *

While the Sydney SOS founders sincerely hoped that a strong national movement would emerge from the satellite groups that formed across the nation, this never eventuated. Each SOS group was shaped not only by the personalities that formed them but also by the places in which they were located. Distance and the cost of keeping in contact, further complicated matters. Despite their initial enthusiasm for a 'truly Commonwealth wide movement', the founding mothers in Sydney soon recognised their limitations in overseeing the interstate groups. The only expectation placed on new groups who wished to use the SOS name was that they would adopt Sydney's Statement of Aims.[265] But even this document was 'fine-tuned' as time went by, reflecting evolving opinions among the different groups not only concerning conscription but also the Vietnam War. One thing all the groups did share was the constant pressure to raise funds and recruit new members. This left them with very little time to worry how their colleagues in other SOS groups were faring. Subsequently, while Sydney SOS members always maintained a maternal interest in the other groups, by 1970 only a couple of these groups were still in regular contact with them.

Part 2

Taking It to the Streets, 1960s

Chapter 5

'HEADS BOWED, HANDS CLASPED', 1965–66

> Jean always used to say 'hats and gloves ladies',
> we looked most respectable, we didn't look
> a bit radical.
>
> *Irene Miller, Victoria SOS*[1]

Before their weekly lunch-hour protests in palm tree-lined Anzac Square, Brisbane Save Our Sons' (SOS) impeccably turned-out secretary Vilma Ward would remind those gathered of the 'vigil rules': stand silently and act 'dignified and ladylike', no matter what the provocation. 'I tell my ladies before each vigil "no talking at all and ignore all wise cracks"', she wrote in 1965. 'Sometimes it is very hard, but for the sake of our movement we obey our ideals first … we must not provoke the police at all because we are sincere people who are concerned about their sons.'[2]

The founding mothers established SOS as a peaceful, law-abiding protest movement, believing sincerely, if naïvely, that once the wider public was educated about the reality of conscription, common sense would prevail, and the government would be forced to reverse its policy.[3] During this initial period of establishment, from 1965 until the 1966 election, SOS groups relied almost solely on traditional means of protest, embracing 'all the accepted ways of protest open to "law abiding" citizens', including silent vigils, petitions, letter-writing campaigns, lobbying politicians, public speaking engagements, anti-conscription literature, marches and demonstrations.[4] These tried and tested tactics reinforced the movement's respectable, law-abiding image, and reflected the connections many of the participants had with the existing peace movement.

As its profile grew, SOS also became a natural 'first point of call' for worried conscripts and their parents. Subsequently, its activities expanded into the provision of legal aid and counselling where members sometimes walked a fine legal line between offering support and inciting young men to defy the law. During this period, SOS groups were represented at major protests and peace marches in every mainland state and worked closely with other like-minded groups, such as the UAW. At times SOS members found themselves on the fringes of violent demonstrations and did not hesitate to support other protesters who broke or 'bent' the law. The movement's leaders were rigorous during this period, however, in ensuring that their own protests did not contravene local, state or federal laws.

In its early days, SOS also did not oppose the Vietnam War per se, only conscription for overseas service. 'The reason for this was that there were some people who joined SOS who didn't want to get involved in questioning the particular war', Victoria's Jean McLean explained.[5] 'They were against conscription overseas generally but wouldn't buy into whether or not they were against the war in Vietnam.' Opinions changed or evolved, however, as members became more aware of the situation in Vietnam and realised the war could not be divorced from conscription. McLean explained:

> In the beginning of Save Our Sons we accepted not mentioning Vietnam because we felt that people wouldn't understand it enough but they were all against conscription so we picked that one issue that everyone agreed on and we said, 'we are not going to involve you in other things before you are ready for it'. I believe we did the right thing in moving people in that direction rather than hitting them over the head.[6]

Later, when SOS's agenda expanded, there were a few members who disapproved and dropped out. 'Most people accepted it', McLean recalled. 'There were a couple who were a bit edgy, but they were free to go. We had women from Brighton and places who were a bit worried about their husbands but who ended up saying, "you are right and so I'll stay with you"'.[7]

In its first two years, however, the focus was on conscription and respectability as leaders concentrated on recruiting members, expanding nationally, gaining publicity and raising funds.

* * *

The silent vigil was SOS's signature event and was used throughout its evolving campaign. This was a traditional method of protest long favoured by women in the peace movement and was also employed by other women's groups during the Vietnam War, sometimes in conjunction with SOS.[8] Vigils were sombre, dignified occasions during which groups of well-dressed women would silently protest against conscription. These early images, carried by television and newspapers, introduced the movement to the wider community and served as a respectable counterpoint to protests by younger people. Leaders were careful to preserve this image, praising members for their good behaviour. 'We feel that we are creating a good image in the minds of the public when our vigils are described as "quiet", "silent", "orderly"', Victoria SOS's leadership wrote after an early protest. 'We commend every woman who remained silent when she longed to express her feelings vocally.'[9]

However, Sydney's first organised action on 30 June 1965 – a vigil outside the Marrickville Army Barracks followed by a demonstration at Central Railway Station during the first intake of conscripts – did not go completely to plan. There was a tussle with supporters after police tried to confiscate the SOS banner at the railway station.[10] It was also reported that one SOS woman had 'tried to lead a group of mothers to lie in front of the train'.[11] The Sydney group subsequently formed a committee tasked with ensuring its members acted with 'dignity and restraint' at all times.[12] Other groups adopted similar policies: WA SOS vowed to 'press its aims by legal, democratic means';[13] Brisbane members were subject to a strict written code of 'vigil discipline';[14] while the Melbourne group advocated a 'heads bowed, hands clasped' approach.[15] 'Jean [McLean] always used to say "hats and gloves ladies", we looked most respectable, we didn't look at bit radical', recalled Irene Miller, who would often push a stroller carrying the youngest of her 10 children.[16]

Organising a vigil, however, was not always straightforward. SOS groups had to negotiate various local regulations which varied from state to state. These were subject to revisions and were more rigorously enforced in some places than others. In the Sydney CBD, SOS had to keep moving or risk being charged with obstructing traffic. As secretary Pat Ashcroft explained, this could be physically demanding: 'Our main vigil was a walk up and down Martin Place where the War Memorial stands … we walked for two hours'.[17] The Melbourne women had to walk in single file on the footpath '100 yards apart so as not to obstruct other pedestrians'.[18] In Brisbane, the women could stand still during vigils in the city's Anzac Square but were not allowed to hold placards. Instead they pinned single words to their clothes and stood together to spell out protest messages.[19]

SOS groups in Sydney and Melbourne held vigils outside army barracks during every intake of conscripts. Brisbane women held a weekly vigil in the CBD while the Wollongong group held vigils at the railway station when conscripts were leaving. Intakes were frequently 'morbid, frightening and depressing' affairs.[20] In Melbourne, Irene Miller was horrified to see families setting up tables with white tablecloths and having champagne and chicken breakfasts to send off their sons. 'There would be mothers and fathers and sisters and brothers having a great old time to send their sons off to war', she said. 'I used to think that was terrible, I really couldn't believe it.'[21] The women would hand out leaflets that explained alternatives to conscription to young men entering the barracks. Some took them politely, others screwed them up and threw them away.[22]

SOS was also represented at major protests and traditional peace parades during this period, members marching behind their banners in Hiroshima Day, May Day and International Women's Day parades across the country. In May 1966, the Australian Security Intelligence Organisation (ASIO) reported that SOS in Brisbane had entered a colourful float in the city's May Day parade which consisted of seven people posing as '[South Vietnam Premier] Marshal Ky and his wife, a Coolie, several dead soldiers and Mrs Ward'.[23] In 1965, Melbourne women risked the ire of the Returned and Services League (RSL) by holding a vigil during the official Remembrance Day ceremony. The *Herald* reported that 15 SOS women wearing sashes held posies with cards attached that read 'honor the dead, with peace'.[24]

The death of the first conscript, Private Errol Noack, on 24 May 1966, was a sobering reminder of the urgency of SOS's mission. In Melbourne, SOS women held a vigil outside the town hall in the pouring rain while the Sydney women laid a wreath on the Cenotaph in Martin Place 'on behalf of all mothers' and sent a letter of condolence to Noack's family.[25] After distributing leaflets blaming politicians for his death, they were accused by a member of the public of 'politicising' the tragic incident.[26] In Brisbane, 26 members of SOS held prayers and a vigil in Anzac Square where they stood silently for an hour, each holding a copy of the previous day's *Brisbane Telegraph* showing the headline announcing Noack's death and wearing a card with the word 'Why?' pinned to their chests.[27]

In October 1966, during US President Lyndon Johnson's visit to Australia, SOS members, some wearing black veils, joined noisy protests in Sydney, Canberra, Melbourne and Brisbane. Adelaide was left off the president's itinerary but the local SOS group still protested against LBJ's Vietnam policy on the steps of Parliament House.[28] The Sydney women invited the First Lady to meet mothers of conscripts during her visit only to be informed that Ladybird Johnson's schedule was regrettably full.[29] During this period, it was not unusual for SOS members to be involved in protest activities or meetings several times a week. In mid-1966, Sydney's newsletter observed that SOS had surely established something of a record, attending demonstrations almost every day for more than a week.[30] Noreen Hewett recalled that after following SOS women to three events in one day, one senior security officer had complained: 'Don't you women ever get tired?'[31]

SOS also joined the UAW in taking a strong stand against 'war toys'. Founding SOS 'mum' and UAW member Dorothy Bendick was one of the instigators of this campaign. During the Vietnam War, production, sale and promotion of toys like GI Joes, toy tanks and guns increased markedly, with some toy stores said to resemble munitions dumps.[32] Protest letters were sent to the makers, retailers and media organisations that aired advertisements for the toys during broadcasts aimed at children. In Brisbane, SOS took up a petition calling on the State government 'to take immediate steps to legislate to control the manufacture and/or sale of "War Type Toys" in the interests of Education and Humanity'.[33] Vilma Ward claimed 'a great victory' after she contacted the manager of the local McWhirters department store and threatened to picket the store unless he removed a full window display of war toys, which he duly did.[34] By early 1968, retailers were reporting a dramatic decline in the sale of war toys that were now rarely displayed. A spokesman for Foys department store in Melbourne blamed the decline on a sustained 'campaign waged by the Save Our Sons organisation'.[35] Getting rid of the war toys, however, proved easier than ending conscription.

* * *

While SOS leaders had their own strict rules on behaviour, they could not control that of other groups and individuals when they took part in joint events. During this period, SOS women frequently witnessed the arrest of fellow protesters, although police at this stage seemed reluctant to single out SOS members. On several occasions, SOS complained about the behaviour of officers and offered to provide witness statements on behalf of those arrested. Sydney SOS also took issue with authorities after its members were photographed during a vigil by plain-clothed men they suspected of being attached to the

NSW Special Branch or ASIO.³⁶ During LBJ's visit, SOS women in Melbourne and Sydney found themselves on the edges of clashes between police and protesters and later signed a statement alleging police brutality. Witnessing the unfair treatment of other protesters undoubtedly contributed to the radicalisation process of SOS and the broadening of their agenda.

But, while SOS groups during this period were determined to stay on the right side of the law themselves, members had no hesitation in supporting the more radical, illegal actions of other protesters. While they advised young men during this period to comply with the law by registering for conscription and then applying for status as a conscientious objector, they also fully supported those who burned their registration papers, refused to register or attend medical examinations. Not only did they show moral support by attending court cases and holding demonstrations, they also provided financial aid. In 1966, in a sign of the formality of the times, a polite letter was received from Barry Robinson representing Youth Campaign Against Conscription (YCAC) seeking SOS's opinion on 'draft card burning'. The issue was discussed at an early SOS meeting but 'general opinion expressed no disapproval of its action'.³⁷ SOS later publicly praised draft card burners Robinson and Wayne Haylen who pursued and tackled the man responsible for an attempted assassination of the then Opposition Leader, Arthur Calwell, pointing out that the two were not without significant courage even if they objected to fighting in Vietnam.³⁸ Sydney SOS also produced a highly emotive leaflet in support of the draft card burners, demanding 'which is the greater crime – burning draft cards or burning children?'³⁹ The leaflet explained that SOS supported the rights of young men to refuse to take part in an immoral war because the government was conscripting 20-year-olds 'without voice or choice' for an undeclared war in which women and children were being 'burned, gassed and tortured'.[40]

More controversial was Sydney SOS's support for Nadine Jensen. In June 1966, the young secretary, acting independently, threw red paint at soldiers taking part in a welcome home parade. Jensen was not a member of SOS but after the incident Adele Pert wrote on behalf of the movement, congratulating her on the courage she had shown. 'It is very good to know that someone feels as strongly as you do about the iniquitous and cruel war and we commend you for your courage', she wrote.[41] Jensen subsequently thanked the group for its support.[42] While SOS members would not have dreamed of taking such action themselves, it seemed they were happy to support the radical tactics of others.

There was little sympathy, however, for SOS supporters who broke the 'rules', as WA member Joan Davies discovered. Davies was arrested after she 'became very emotionally upset' and threw her shoes at Prime Minister Harold Holt during an SOS vigil at Perth Airport in April 1966 'much to the surprise of those present'.[43] (Both missed their target but the second hit one of Holt's bodyguards.) Charged with creating a disturbance, she was represented in court by her lawyer husband, given a suspended sentence and fined $20, which SOS quietly paid.[44] Davies' five-year-old adopted half-Malaysian daughter, Shelley, accompanied her mother to the airport that day and almost 50 years later still remembered it clearly as the first time she had ever heard her mother swear. She recalled:

> She got carted off in a paddy wagon and I was sent in a taxi to my Auntie Margaret's ... I don't think she actually planned it, my impression was that she was just so angry ... some things made her angry but (conscription and the Vietnam War) just incensed her.[45]

Joan Davies was a long-time peace activist but her reaction to the Vietnam War and conscription was deeply personal.[46] According to her daughter, she was particularly distressed by reports of Vietnamese children being harmed. Wendy Kendrick – who was a member of the UAW with Davies – believed the shoe incident was Davies' 'own personal expression of objection to the Vietnam War' stemming from her adoption of Shelley. She recalled the incident as 'more amusing than serious'.[47] However, at the time fellow members of the WA SOS took it very seriously indeed.[48] Fearful the incident would harm the group's reputation, secretary Ray Collie promptly moved to distance it from Davies and to reassure the public that SOS did not support violent demonstrations.[49] Joan Davies, however, was unrepentant. Two years later she made the news again when she vowed that she would keep her then nine-year-old son 'thin, pale and under-sized' in order to avoid any future national service. 'That's how David is now and that's how he'll be until he fails his army medical', she told reporters. 'After that we'll build him up into a useful citizen capable of doing a constructive job for humanity.'[50] As for the offending brown leather brogues, after being tendered as evidence in court they were reclaimed and proudly displayed in the Davies' living room. Shelley Davies still has them, a precious reminder of her family's radical history.

* * *

SOS women were also frequent visitors to Canberra in the early years, where MPs who encountered them soon realised they were not as demure as they appeared. In May 1965, several Sydney women took part in a Bishop's Vigil in Canberra after which they had an animated audience with the Minister for the Army, Dr Forbes.[51] They also delivered a petition to the Prime Minister's Department, signed by about 1200 women, pointing out that Menzies had 'exercised' his right to refuse to fight in World War II and demanding that he extend the same 'right' to other young men.[52] Two national delegations in Canberra were also organised during this period. During these visits, the women would seek to meet as many MPs and ministers as possible, but their requests were frequently rebuffed by government members. Those who did meet them were often hostile and sometimes downright offensive, reactions that were duly reported back to the SOS membership. A 'Contact Your Members Week', instigated by the Melbourne group, was also held in December 1965, during which supporters were encouraged to lobby their local MPs.[53]

In September 1965, 16 women representing Queensland, Victoria, Sydney and Newcastle attended a three-day national delegation in Canberra. It was the first time the women had met their interstate colleagues. During the three days, the women interviewed 'dozens' of parliamentarians, staged two demonstrations, addressed a students' meeting at the Australian National University and held 'interstate discussions about the rapidly growing SOS movement'.[54] They also presented the second stage of their first petition totalling 800 signatures, in addition to the 1200 signatures presented during the May visit. The delegation attracted widespread publicity after the women were banned from entering King's Hall in Parliament House, apparently under a 'new rule' that had been issued at noon on the day of their arrival. 'King's Hall is the traditional venue for lobbying of parliamentarians and the refusal shocked us', Pat Ashcroft told reporters.[55] Undeterred, the women lobbied politicians on the steps of Parliament House until officials, perhaps alarmed by the publicity the women were attracting, ushered them into a small waiting room. This became their 'office' from where they organised 'non-stop deputations' and received visiting MPs. The ban was subsequently lifted after the intervention of Opposition MPs but as Ashcroft noted: 'We think this ban harmed the Government more than it did the delegation. Through it we got extra publicity in newspapers, radio and TV'.[56] The women also secured themselves a prime position outside Parliament House when hundreds of reporters and visitors gathered for the arrival of the new Governor-General, Lord Casey, for his investiture ceremony. For more than an hour, the women stood silently, heads bowed, with pieces of card pinned to their frocks spelling out an anti-conscription message. 'This was the highlight of our visit', reported Ashcroft later. 'It was described by MPs as a most inspiring sight. Others praised it for its dignity and sincerity.'[57]

Many of the women were lobbying for the first time and were 'astounded' by the attitude of some government members, Ashcroft recalled. 'When Mr Turner, MHR, told one member of our delegation she was a "communist stooge" she quickly retorted that up to now she had been a "Liberal stooge" but would not be any more.'[58] Victorian delegates also told MPs that many in their organisation had, until conscription, been 'Liberal in outlook'.[59] Ashcroft later noted: 'Perhaps the greatest impression we made at Canberra was to convince some [MPs] that Government policy had lost votes even among their own supporters'.[60]

Limiting their discussions to conscription, however, proved difficult, with the women frequently drawn into wider discussions concerning the war in Vietnam. As Ashcroft explained: 'We went to argue against conscription for overseas. We found ourselves forced, by the Government Members' attitude, to debate also the issue of Vietnam'.[61] Menzies declined to meet the women, much to the disgust of Rose Fitzgerald in Portland, who, unable to attend, had sent him a telegram on behalf of the SOS delegation requesting an interview.[62] Thanking Fitzgerald for her efforts, Ashcroft noted: 'I still think we dented his (Menzies') armour. We heard through Labor members, who at all times were very helpful, that Liberal members had commented on our apparent sincerity and dignity. It would have been easier for them if we had behaved badly'.[63] In a letter to a Wollongong SOS member, she observed: '[Liberal members] realised we were a force to be considered, we were not the "yelling ratbags" they had expected and planned to dispose of easily'.[64]

In April 1966, the Victoria SOS group organised a second national delegation to deliver its petition to Canberra where Labor MP Dr Jim Cairns had agreed to present it to parliament. The petition was visually impressive, its 17,000 signatures creating a tower more than a foot high. 'I think we put the fear of God into the government, it was so big', recalled Jo Maclaine-Cross, who was one of four women charged with transporting 'the tome' from Melbourne. They almost did not make it. Maclaine-Cross recalled:

> The road to Canberra was 50 per cent dirt in those days and we encountered trucks going 20mph, flocks of sheep and other endless delays ... nevertheless we swept into the front of Parliament House, as you could in those days, backed in with a flourish, knocking over the 'no parking sign' and rushed up to Jim Cairns with the bells ringing inside just in time to present 'IT'.[65]

The Victorian women were joined in Canberra by six others from Sydney and two from Wollongong. Again, they sought to press their case with as many MPs as possible. Requests to meet several government ministers were denied but they did have a lively debate with the acting Attorney-General, Gordon Freeth, over whether Australia was breaching the *United Nations Act* by its intervention in Vietnam. Unable to convince the group that Australia was in the right, Freeth switched tactics, accusing SOS of being a communist front. Jean McLean argued vigorously to the contrary. They did, however, receive a warm reception from the Opposition Leader, Arthur Calwell, who urged them to 'keep up the good work'. In terms of publicity, the deputation was deemed a success with the petition receiving national coverage in newspapers, on radio and television. 'Above all, the presentation of the impressive stack of petitions gives fresh encouragement for continuing this method of impressing upon the Government the widespread public opposition to their policy of conscription for overseas', the Sydney delegates reported.[66] In October 1966, two Sydney women delivered the 'second edition' of this petition to Canberra where it was presented to parliament by sympathetic NSW Labor MP Les Johnson.[67]

While Townsville SOS members never made it to Canberra, they did manage to present their petition directly to Prime Minister Harold Holt during his brief visit to the north Queensland town. After discovering where his entourage was staying, Margaret Reynolds, pregnant with her second child, dressed in her best outfit and set off to the hotel accompanied by a member of the local Peace Committee. At the motel's reception, she asked the person behind the desk for Mr Holt's room number and was 'amazed' when they duly told her. Outside his door, however, she lost her nerve and decided to wake one of the PM's staff members instead. 'He knocked on the (Prime Minister's) door and Harold Holt came out', Reynolds recalled. 'I can still see his dressing gown; it was one of those plaid affairs.'[68] Surprisingly affable despite having been woken at 'the crack of dawn', Holt shook his visitors' hands and accepted their petition. The impromptu meeting was not noted in either the local press or the prime minister's official papers. As for the petition, Reynolds suspects it was filed in the hotel bin.

'HEADS BOWED, HANDS CLASPED', 1965–66

* * *

By early 1966, SOS's initial novelty had worn off and members were finding it difficult to gain publicity for its activities. 'Unless we do something sensational, the news men tell us we are no longer news value', Pat Ashcroft complained to her Adelaide colleagues, adding cryptically 'well we are contemplating something that will be news'.[69] In March, newspapers across Australia carried the story that SOS was launching a High Court challenge to the federal government's constitutional powers to send 20-year-old conscripts overseas.[70] The move coincided with Holt's announcement on 8 March that the number of troops in Vietnam would be increased to 4500. In a series of advertisements placed in newspapers around Australia, SOS promised free legal advice to any parents who wished to be part of the test case. An appeal was also launched to meet the costs of the challenge with the *Australian* reporting that one generous Sydney citizen had already donated $1000.[71]

Ashcroft informed other SOS groups that 'legal men' from Queensland, Melbourne and Sydney, including a Queen's Counsel, 'all sympathetic to our cause', had held a meeting in Sydney and believed there were good grounds for a High Court case. Sydney SOS agreed to support the move and, 'as a truly parent body', to act as the contact between parents and the lawyers.[72] Other SOS groups were asked to urgently wire their response to Sydney. Telegrams were duly received from Melbourne, Adelaide and Newcastle in support of the proposal but Brisbane protested strongly against it, warning that 'publicity could endanger SOS cause'.[73] In a follow up letter, Ward explained that Brisbane's committee feared that SOS would be 'violating a section of the *National Service Act* if we influenced a boy in any way to take action which he would not necessarily otherwise have taken'.[74] In response, Sydney claimed that Queensland had misunderstood what was being proposed 'and thought we intended advertising for a 20-year-old conscript to come forward to take advantage of the legal aid we offer'. This would have indeed contravened the *National Service Act*, but Sydney was actually making the offer to parents of conscripts, 'and in this we are fully within the law'.[75] Reassured by its 'panel of legal men', Sydney SOS sent two members to Brisbane to meet Ward's committee and its legal adviser. The Brisbane committee reluctantly agreed to support the planned challenge but continued to express concerns about 'the wisdom of placing advertisements in SOS's name'.[76]

SOS did manage to recruit a family willing to be involved in a test case but it never proceeded after a rethink by the lawyers, who advised that it was unlikely such a case would have succeeded at that time. 'The view has been expressed that if we lose the case, the Government would use it to say the High Court upheld the validity of their action', Sydney's Ella Outhred reported. 'With this in mind, plus the upsurge of public opinion against conscription for Vietnam which may lead to the same result anyway, we now consider it inadvisable to take a risk on the outcome of a test case.'[77] Instead SOS decided to examine other ways of helping those conscripts who objected to going Vietnam, including providing legal assistance to any conscript already in the army who wished to apply to be registered as a conscientious objector. Outhred observed sadly that now they knew they were going to be sent to Vietnam, some of the conscripts had changed their views. 'We are very disappointed at not being able to prevent them sending the conscripts but at least we hope they will not be there for long', she wrote.[78]

Each SOS group subsequently set up its own legal aid fund that was used to support young men who objected to being conscripted.

Anti-conscription float during May Day procession, Brisbane 1967.
Grahame Garner Collection, Fryer Library, University of Queensland. F3400, Folder 11, Item 8.

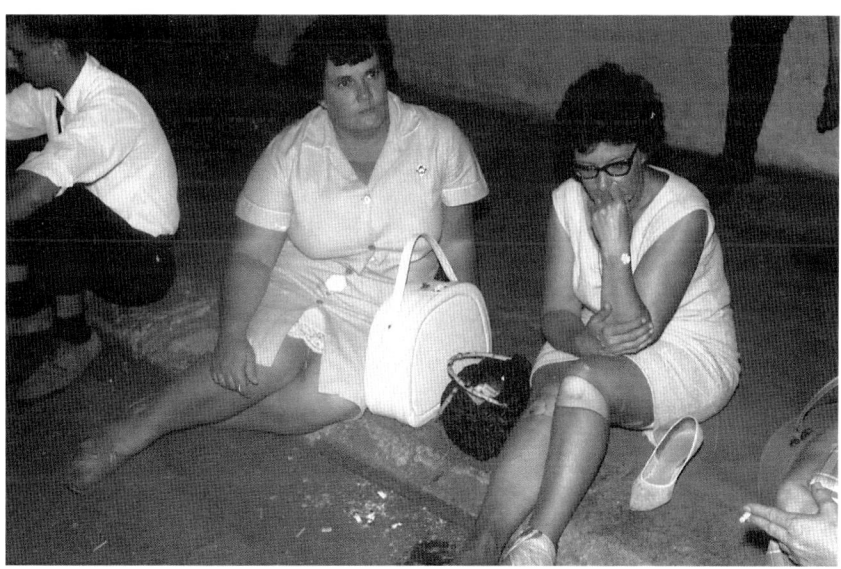

Queensland SOS secretary Vilma Ward (L) and Normal Chalmers
during Ky protest in Brisbane.
Grahame Garner Collection, Fryer Library, University of Queensland, F3400, Folder 5, Item 148.

Save Our Sons members demonstrate outside the front steps of Brisbane City Hall, c1963.
Fryer Library, University of Queensland, F193, Box 17, Folder 1.

SOS Women protest in Sydney against conscription, 1 October 1965.
The Sydney Morning Herald / Fairfax Syndication. Courtesy of Fairfax Archives.

SOS protest at Adelaide Airport.
State Library of South Australia, SRG 781/60/10.

SOS flag at Vietnam Moratorium March in Adelaide.
State Library of South Australia, PRG 156/14/F17/3.

Jean McLean (holding child), Jo Maclaine-Cross and Joan Coxsedge being welcomed by union leader George Crawford at a rally to celebrate their release from Fairlea Prison, April 1971.

University of Melbourne Archives, Communist Party of Australia, Victorian State Committee collection, 1991.0152.00047. Reproduced with permission of SEARCH Foundation.

A Save Our Sons demonstration at Marrickville Army Barracks, NSW. Noreen Hewett is second from left.

University of Melbourne Archives, Communist Party of Australia, Victorian State Committee, 1991.0152. Reproduced with permission of SEARCH Foundation.

The 'Fairlea Five', Joan Coxsedge, Jean McLean, Chris Cathie, Irene Miller and Jo Maclaine-Cross, at the Anti-Vietnam War Moratorium 20th anniversary, 11 May 1990.
University of Melbourne Archives, John Ellis Collection, 1999.0081.00955.

Protest against Vietnam War in Perth, 10 June 1966.
State Library of Western Australia, slwa_b3807794_4:380167PD.

Facing page

Top:
Anti-Vietnam War moratorium march in Melbourne on 8 May 1970.
Jean McLean is second from right.
Arthur de la Rue, *The Age* / Fairfax Syndication. Courtesy of Fairfax Archives.

Middle:
SOS women holding a silent vigil outside Parliament House in Canberra in September 1965.
The Canberra Times / Fairfax Syndication. Courtesy of Fairfax Archives.

Bottom:
Woman holding sign 'death lottery' at Sydney SOS protest, 29 September 1965.
Courtesy of News Ltd / Newspix.

Women protest in Melbourne, 5 July 1965.
Courtesy of News Ltd / Newspix.

Front page of *The Canberra Times*, 12 June 1970, showing women who chained themselves inside Parliament House, including Edna Gudgeon and Flo Garber.
The Canberra Times / Fairfax Syndication. Courtesy of Fairfax Archives.

Women protest in Sydney c1966.
Mitchell Library, State Library of New South Wales. Courtesy SEARCH Foundation.

In Sydney, three trustees were appointed to oversee the fund: two male supporters and Ella Outhred. First to benefit were Wayne Haylen and Robin Melrose who were arrested after burning their registration papers. SOS paid their solicitor's fees.[79] A roster also was established so that SOS could be represented at all conscientious objector court cases. Outhred was convinced such shows of support could make a difference. 'It is my personal view that demonstrations, vigils, displaying of placards etc. on their belief is the best protection for a CO [Conscientious Objector]', she said. 'The army can do practically anything they like to these lads who are in detention camps … and no one knows about it unless their case and treatment is publicised.'[80] In 1965, the Brisbane SOS assisted two men who were later granted conscientious objector status. The mother of one man had approached SOS members for help during a lunchtime vigil. 'It is heartening to have these two lads exempted from service', Vilma Ward told reporters. 'Others are objecting, and SOS will assist all who ask our aid.'[81]

In Sydney, Outhred also conducted a regular discussion group for young men considering registering a conscientious objection, but denied they were being 'coached' to give evidence. The aim of the group, she argued, was 'to help young men clarify their thoughts and develop ideas and knowledge of the war in Vietnam, pacifism, non-violence etc.' although she conceded that 'the more articulate a CO is the better chance he has of convincing the magistrate of his conscientious beliefs'.[82] In Brisbane, Ward also held fortnightly meetings at her house to counsel young men and their supporters. According to ASIO, these included mock court cases where the young men were coached on how to give evidence. Joan Ross, whose mother was a member of SOS, attended some of these as a teenager and remembered them as fun, social occasions and a chance to meet 'interesting people'.[83] In

Melbourne, SOS committee members were regularly contacted by parents and conscripts or potential conscripts who were contemplating legal action. They were directed to legal advisers and invited to seek financial aid from SOS if they needed it.[84]

Education was a major plank of SOS's activities. Public meetings were organised by all groups with 'expert' speakers invited to help raise awareness about conscription. In Melbourne, SOS also held US-style 'teach-ins', usually at a member's home, to which speakers on both sides of the debate were invited to argue their view. Federal Liberal MP Don Chipp, who went on to form the Australian Democrats, was one of the few government members who accepted the invitation. He attended a 'teach-in' at McLean's Beaumaris home in 1965 where he heatedly argued the pro-war position alongside Jack Little, of the Democratic Labor Party (DLP). Monash University politics lecturer Max Teichmann and Australian Labor Party (ALP) federal MP Gordon Bryant argued the anti-war position. There was no meeting of minds. 'When we asked vaguely intelligent questions [Chipp] replied, "Beaumaris is full of communist cells"', McLean recalled.[85]

SOS women also actively sought out public speaking engagements, addressing community organisations and public meetings at every opportunity. Nora Mulheron was a regular speaker throughout SOS's eight-year campaign even though she dreaded it to the point where she would be physically ill before taking the floor.[86] Public speaking was vital, SOS leaders believed, to 'help spread our message and correct much of the inaccurate information about SOS which has appeared occasionally in the daily press'.[87]

SOS groups produced several leaflets during this period which members 'letterboxed' in their neighbourhoods and handed out at public events. These included 60,000 copies of a leaflet 'Conscription is Wrong', which was widely distributed in NSW, Townsville and Adelaide.[88] Leaflets were designed to be emotive and elicit a response, often including a reply slip for those seeking more information. A 1965 Christmas leaflet, for example, demanded: 'Will you think of the thousands of young men being brutalised in Vietnam? Will you think of the Vietnamese families being slaughtered for no fault of their own?'[89]

Politicians and media outlets were also targeted in letter-writing campaigns, but all groups reported difficulty in getting letters published in newspapers. In June 1966, the WA SOS group wrote letters to the British media warning that intending migrants could find their sons being conscripted to fight in Vietnam. 'As soon as they step ashore, these young men are liable to be conscripted and sent off to fight and perhaps die in the jungles of Vietnam – and all in the interests of American power politics', the letter warned. 'Our advice to intending migrants in this category: Don't come.'[90] It is not known if the government responded to this letter. Other SOS groups paid for advertisements and 'open letters' to the prime minister in their local newspapers.[91] The Townsville group also conducted a street survey on attitudes to conscription, the results of which were published in the local paper.[92] While SOS at the time claimed the results were an indication of the level of local opposition to conscription, ASIO and Special Branch officers were not convinced the results were strictly 'scientific' or independently counted.[93] Recalling the informality of the 'count' decades later, Margaret Reynolds conceded they were probably right.

From her property outside Albury, prolific letter writer Val Reid was involved in a long-running stoush with the editor of her local newspaper who at one point imposed a one-month ban in the letters' pages of any mention of conscription and Vietnam. Reid was outraged. 'I appreciate "that the interminable discussion on any one subject becomes intolerable to a majority of readers" but the death of young Australian men and Australia's participation in the genocide of Vietnam is also intolerable', she informed the paper's chief-of-staff. 'For the sake of my children (4), I shall continue to write and oppose the Government's policy on Vietnam – even if the subject bores other Australians.'[94] After subsequent letters continued to be 'spiked', Reid paid for a full page 'In Sympathy' notice in which she apologised 'to the people of Vietnam, on behalf of fellow Australians and Christians, for the wanton genocide of your people and destruction of your country'.[95]

* * *

Throughout their campaign, SOS women also expressed their objections to conscription and the war through poetry and songs. Again, this was a traditional expression of dissent long employed by women in the peace movement. Poems by members were regularly published in Sydney's newsletters, used in leaflets and included in Christmas cards. At the start of the campaign these tended to focus on the effect of conscription on Australian sons and their families. A poem in an early recruitment leaflet produced by Newcastle SOS, for example, aimed straight at the heartstrings of mothers. It read in part:

> We nurtured him through childhood
> Joined his laughter, shared his tears,
> Whilst visions of great things to do,
> Inspired those twenty years
>
> Then came the dreadful edict
> Don uniform and kill
> Suffer and die on foreign soil
> My Son! Why lie so still?[96]

This poem was widely used by other SOS groups. However, as SOS's campaign broadened, poems were published expressing horror at the war itself, particularly the use of napalm bombs on Vietnamese women and children. A Mother's Day leaflet produced by Wollongong SOS in 1970 included an uncredited poem that read in part:

> Think of a Vietnam baby
> Napalm burned
> Or shot while cradled
> To his Mother's breast –
> Then stand with her in agony.[97]

In Melbourne, ABC personality, poet and SOS member Corinne Kerby recited, and later published, a series of anti-Vietnam poems. 'Writing this poetry I felt it very deeply, it was terrible, very emotional', she recalled.[98] One, titled 'Lines Written on the Picture of a Vietnamese Child Burned by Napalm', reflected her reaction to seeing photos of dead and injured Vietnamese children. It began:

> Child,
> Look not at me,
> Look somewhere else
> Eyes, above your twist of flesh
> Are quiet now ...[99]

Poems by other SOS members focused on peace. Asked to write a verse for the 1967 Christmas card, regular contributor Val Reid, in Albury-Wodonga, offered the following:

> "Write of peace"
> But how can I
> When children die?
> What can I say
> This Christmas day
> When men make war?[100]

Others, like Lorna Fisher, in Maroochydore, composed songs that they subsequently offered to SOS to use in its 'struggle against conscription'.[101] Sydney SOS forwarded a number of these to Glen Tomasetti in Melbourne who at one stage expressed interest in producing a compilation of anti-conscription songs. It never eventuated; however, Tomasetti wrote, performed and recorded a number of anti-conscription and anti-war songs herself during this period. A 1966 composition titled *No!* began, 'No we don't want to be conscripted to kill' and included the 'SOS anthem' as its middle verse.

> We didn't bear them to carry guns
> We didn't feed them to carry guns
> We can never tell them it's fine to carry guns
> To kill somebody else's sons.[102]

The lyrics were adapted from the controversial 1915 American folk song that was sung by Australian women fighting conscription during World War I. In a similar vein, Tomasetti's song *The Army's Appeal to Mothers* urged women not to bring up their sons to be sensitive or kind or 'to believe that a man can use his heart and mind' because:

> When it comes to twisting a bayonet,
> Or sticking in a boot,
> He'll find it so much easier
> If you bring him up as a brute.[103]

The lyrics and music for this song were included in *The Vietnam Songbook*, a compilation of more than 100 songs from the American and international protest movements, along with 'fighting songs of the Vietnamese People', edited and published by US folk singer Barbara Dane and music journalist Irwin Silber in 1969. Tomasetti performed at many events organised by SOS and other anti-war groups during the 1960s. She also helped to organise a Peace Concert at the Myer

Music Bowl.[104] A lunchtime folk concert organised by Tomasetti in 1965 raised £31 for SOS while sales of her record before the 1966 election raised $500.[105]

* * *

As the 1966 federal election campaign loomed, SOS members remained confident that bad policies like conscription – and maybe even a government – could be changed through legal, democratic means. Buoyed by growing membership numbers, interstate expansion and apparent public support, they saw the poll as a de facto referendum on conscription in which they were sure that the anti-conscription movement would prevail. But such confidence flew in the face of opinion polls that continued to indicate broad public support for conscription ahead of the election.[106]

Gearing up for the election, Victoria SOS produced a two-page flyer which declared, in capital letters:

> 'THIS IS THE ELECTION FOR FREEDOM OR CONSCRIPTION. THIS IS THE ELECTION FOR PEACE OR WAR'.[107]

It also announced an ambitious plan to raise $12,500 for a series of television and radio ads. In Sydney, Adele Pert announced 'an all-out program of activities', telling supporters that the election would be 'more fateful for our country than any since the Second World War':

> We only need to persuade 10 per cent of Liberal and Country voters, especially women that their vote means life or death to hundreds of young men and the present conscription for overseas policy of the present Government will be defeated.[108]

SOS targeted swinging voters in marginal seats across the country. In New South Wales, newspaper advertisements and 100,000 copies of a special election leaflet were distributed in marginal electorates. The object, according to Sydney's October newsletter, was not to support any one party but to 'give facts to voters about conscription and the Vietnam War to enable them to make up their minds about these important issues'.[109] While the group publicly maintained its non-party, non-political stance, many SOS members canvassed for particular anti-conscription candidates, mostly from the ALP. They also publicly supported conscientious objector 21-year-old Brian King who contested the seat of the Minister for Labour and National Service, Leslie Bury. As a 10-year-old, Maurie Mulheron helped his mother distribute leaflets in Sydney's suburbs. 'Night after night, Dad would drop us off somewhere and go to work and we would leaflet for hours', he recalled. Years later, his mother, somewhat guiltily, used to relate how when her youngest son wanted to sit down for a rest, she would not allow it, urging 'one more street, we'll just do one more street'.[110] Not everyone appreciated their efforts. One woman wrote to SOS objecting to 'having your subversive literature thrust on me per my letter box' and accusing SOS of being 'organised by frightened women who are overprotective of their offspring'.[111]

Unlike Sydney, the Victoria SOS group had no qualms about advising its members to support ALP and Liberal Reform Group candidates. Noting that some had suggested SOS was departing from its non-party political position, the editor of Melbourne's October newsletter responded: 'Not so. In opposing conscription for overseas service, it is logical to support the ALP in this election'.[112] Members handed out 'how to vote' cards, leaflets and doorknocked in their areas. They were also urged to organise 'stick-ups' in their local areas (to ensure

'Melbourne is ... covered with the "vote no" campaign poster') and to put anti-conscription stickers on as many cars as possible.[113]

The lead up to the election was dominated by the high-profile case of Bill White, a young Sydney school teacher who was called up in July 1965 but sought exemption as a conscientious objector on the grounds that war and killing were wrong. A clean cut, sincere, 'good' Australian lad, he became the poster boy for the anti-conscription movement in the lead up to the 26 November election. SOS closely followed the case from the outset. While White declined SOS's offer of financial aid, members gave him 'every moral and practical support', attending all his court cases, holding demonstrations, writing letters to the federal government, seeking support from other organisations and reproducing 5000 copies of White's statement in which he explained his stand.[114] In Melbourne, Tomasetti wrote and recorded *The Ballad of Bill White*, described by one critic as 'moving and persuasive'.[115]

SOS members across Australia followed White's case as it played out in the national media. After being refused complete exemption and losing a subsequent appeal, White was ordered in July 1966 to report to the army. Instead he notified the Department of National Service that he would not serve, prompting the Department of Education to order him from his classroom.[116] A highly public stand-off ensued with White waiting at home for several days before police finally moved in and arrested him, dragging him from his home as SOS members and other supporters waved placards around him.[117] In Melbourne, SOS held a vigil outside Harold Holt's home, holding a banner proclaiming 'White is Right', which some passing school boys misinterpreted as being racist.[118] White was jailed but eventually succeeded in winning objector status – after the 1966 election. Grateful for SOS's support,

White's mother, Isobel, became a member until her premature death just a few months after her son's release.[119] Bill White also later expressed his gratitude for SOS's support. 'My family gave me total support and SOS were very good', he said.[120]

* * *

The 1966 election result came as a 'complete shock' to SOS members, returning the Holt government with the largest parliamentary majority in 65 years.[121] In hindsight, this should not have come as any great surprise. According to a gallup poll taken a week before the election, domestic issues were more important in voters' minds than either Vietnam or conscription.[122] Nevertheless, it was a huge defeat for the anti-conscription movement – and the ALP, whose leader Arthur Calwell had campaigned on an anti-conscription ticket. Some anti-war groups, including the Australia-wide Youth Campaign Against Conscription movement, quickly folded.[123] Irene Miller, meanwhile, was so disheartened that she contacted the Canadian High Commission to enquire about emigrating. In the end, the family decided to stay but, for safe measure, sent both sons eligible for conscription back to England to live with their grandmother.[124] 'It was devastating for the women', Maurie Mulheron recalled. 'They really did fall into despair.'[125] According to McLean, the women had been 'lulled' into a false sense of hope. 'We had so much support of anyone we had time to talk to. We had the impression that many more people than really were, were like-minded', she said. 'We fondly believed if we could just get people to realise that conscription had been snuck in for the purpose of involving us in the war in Vietnam then they'd automatically understand, as we did, how wrong it was.'[126]

Victoria's post-election newsletter was reflective but defiant. SOS women may have been 'naïve', it conceded, but the fact 'that people did not take this opportunity to change the Government shows how much they need movements such as ours'.[127] Sydney SOS echoed this mood and noted while the extensive publicity campaign may have failed to sway the election result, it had brought in many more members and generous donations:

> Undoubtedly the Australian electorate was confused by the mass of misinformation on the important questions of genuine defence of Australia, the Vietnam War and conscription. But facts are facts, whether they are understood at this moment or not ... as women, as mothers we will not give up in our determination to make the facts known and to change the present wrong policies.[128]

In Adelaide, morale was also low. 'Naturally we are very disappointed at the outcome of the recent elections and feel like sitting down and "licking our wounds"', Mrs Wharton told her Sydney colleagues. 'However, we realise we must redouble our efforts.'[129]

Spirits dented but not broken, SOS members took a break for Christmas. However, some supporters privately wondered how, and if, the movement would be able to recapture its momentum.

Chapter 6

GLOVES OFF, 1967–69

> We were pretty ladylike at first, but we found
> that didn't work, you had to get out and
> do something more to get attention.
>
> *Irene Miller*[1]

After the disappointment of the 1966 elections, Save Our Sons (SOS) regrouped but did not immediately change its tactics. 'As it has always been, our role is to educate', Victoria's post-election newsletter declared. 'We will persist in the aims for which SOS Victoria was formed and we must not be deflected from our methods which have been essentially rational and peaceful.'[2] However, events between 1967 and the 1969 election, both overseas and at home, forced SOS into a new direction, initially in response to what members saw as a threat to their civil liberties. Ironically, it was the group with the strictest code of behaviour, Brisbane, which took this path first. Closer links with more militant student groups and a 'crack-down' by authorities on demonstrations also convinced the Victoria SOS group that civil disobedience had its place. During this period SOS members openly defied federal, state and local laws, staging sit-ins, refusing to pay fines and taxes, even threatening to conduct hunger strikes. Many were arrested. SOS continued to assist and counsel young men who opposed conscription but went further, publicly advocating non-compliance in open defiance of the federal *Crimes Act*, and actively assisting non-compliers to evade the law. This period also witnessed a broadening of SOS's agenda beyond its strict focus on conscription.

* * *

After the 1966 election, SOS leaders were left wondering how to rally their dispirited members. In January 1967, the federal government provided the lightning rod, welcoming South Vietnam's controversial premier Air Vice Marshall Ky to Australia. The visit was disrupted by protests in Canberra, Sydney, Brisbane and Melbourne; SOS was represented at all of these.[3] Perth members were also galvanised, sending telegrams of protest to federal politicians and distributing leaflets describing Ky as a 'Little Hitler' and the self-appointed head of 'a corrupt and fiercely oppressive' government. 'Our sons are compelled to fight to keep this little dictator in power', they protested.[4] In Canberra, a large contingent of SOS women from Newcastle, Sydney and Wollongong took part in a demonstration led by the Opposition Leader, Arthur Calwell, staying overnight to meet Mrs Calwell and visiting British MPs. The following day SOS held a 'special demonstration' outside The Lodge where Madame Ky was lunching with Mrs Holt. 'The women stood in grim silence thinking about Vietnam's baby napalm victims as Madame Ky left to visit a Canberra Baby Health Centre', Sydney's newsletter noted. 'No one responded to her blithe wave from the car (in contradiction to a highly imaginative report in the *Daily Telegraph* which claimed a SOS member could not help waving back).'[5] At a protest at the Hotel Canberra, SOS women witnessed 'an appalling display of police brutality', and subsequently made an official complaint, claiming police had thrown punches and moved into the crowd of demonstrators 'without provocation' to make arrests.[6] In the *Newcastle Morning Herald*, local SOS president Betty Harris pointed out that 'a good percentage' of the 800 who took part in the Canberra protests were women who never had any other intention than to conduct an orderly demonstration. 'We regarded police intervention and consequent arrests as provocation because we were too orderly', she wrote.[7]

Brisbane was the scene of some particularly nasty incidents. A photograph taken after an anti-Ky demonstration shows a dishevelled SOS secretary Vilma Ward sitting on the street kerb next to Norma Chalmers, of the Queensland Peace Committee, who has her foot bandaged and stockings torn at the knees.[8] 'Boy, we gave him a reception but we have scars as a result (worth it!)', Ward informed her Sydney colleagues.[9] Chalmers later alleged that she had been attempting to deliver a letter to Ky when she was thrown to the ground and dragged along the road by two plain-clothed policemen. 'One policeman in the second group forced my head to the ground with a throat-lock while others kicked and stamped on my arms and legs. In the course of which the bone in my left heel was fractured.'[10] Ward complained that another police officer had snatched pamphlets from her hands:

> He whistled arrogantly. I said "Excuse me, what did you do that for?" He replied, "I don't have to tell you what I did it for, I just did it." As he walked away whistling, the security officers present and a sub-inspector pretended as if nothing had happened.[11]

Ward said she had witnessed police using wooden structures as 'battering rams' to disperse people, leaving the street looking 'as though a tornado had hit it'.[12] Later, at the city watch house, she had helped 'bail out' demonstrators until 2.30am. Sydney SOS subsequently protested to the Queensland Police Commissioner and called for a public inquiry, alleging 'police brutality and breaches of civil liberties'.[13]

Yet newspapers along the tour route tended to view events differently, concentrating on the enthusiasm shown for Ky and his young wife and dismissing protests as small and ineffectual. In his 2008 book, Paul Ham also concluded that the anti-war agitators had failed to make a mark, noting 'their every action seemed to fall like snowflakes on the sunburned land, sizzle and melt away'.[14] In SOS's case, however, the Ky demonstrations helped overcome the post-election malaise, strengthen its resolve and reinvigorate its campaign. Melbourne and Sydney SOS newsletters became more forthright and militant in tone, while in Brisbane, incensed SOS members resolved to take a stand alongside students against new rules designed to limit demonstrations – even if it meant going to jail.

* * *

The Ky protests were not the first in which police had clashed with protesters in Brisbane. In late 1966, 140 people were arrested after 4000 students and staff marched from the University of Queensland into the city. According to Pam Young, after the Nicklin government's invoked the *Traffic Act* requiring organisers to apply and pay for permits to hold marches, distribute leaflets and hold placards, 'the fight for civil liberties became linked with the anti-war campaign'. Permits were frequently denied and as a result 'the right to free speech, assembly, and to march became an obvious part of the protest movement'.[15] SOS members in Brisbane played their part in this campaign, refusing to pay the $1 required for permits to carry placards in demonstrations. During one march in February 1967, SOS women 'deliberately walked for some time carrying only blank placards and were left unmolested by police'.[16] However, when they swapped these for posters with slogans on them, their leader Vilma Ward was 'booked' under the *Traffic Act* and fined $12.[17] Ward refused to pay the fine, telling the Sydney SOS that despite 'anonymous phone calls threatening harm to her children' she was determined to go to jail rather than pay. 'I have decided to defend myself because I intend to let all hell loose in court about the stupid law and how it is applied to certain sections of the community, and, who knows, I could end up with more than seven days jail', Ward wrote.[18] Supporters were on standby, she confided, to hold a non-stop vigil outside the prison during her sentence. Ward's stand was 'unanimously supported by Sydney's annual general meeting' where members deplored the use of the *Traffic Act* to 'stifle demonstrations'. Letters of complaint were again sent to both the Queensland Premier and the Queensland Police Commissioner. 'It appears that the *Traffic Act* is being deliberately used for political reasons, in particular to discriminate against people who are carrying out activities which are quite legal in other States of Australia', Pert wrote. 'In NSW, for instance, there is no law which requires the payment of money for permission to carry placards.'[19] Other SOS groups also wrote to Ward, applauding the Brisbane group's 'courageous challenge'.[20]

Ward's actions attracted plenty of media attention. At one point she protested 'violently' in court when prosecutors sought to delay the case.[21] 'I argued back and forth with the magistrate, [and] won my point', she told the Sydney group. 'He agreed with me that it was very wrong for a person to come to have a court case heard and they had not any intention of hearing it.' Ward was confident that she would not end up in jail: 'Security said to me that "we will not let you go to jail, you will cause too much trouble"'. As the wife of a trade union organiser, it was apparently feared that her jailing would have 'unions in an uproar'.[22] In the end, Ward did not go to jail; she paid the fine and her subsequent 'retirement' from public life for reasons not altogether clear, effectively ended the case.[23]

It was not the end of the Brisbane SOS's involvement in the civil rights campaign, however. In 1967, SOS groups around the nation deplored the treatment of another Brisbane supporter, Elsie Pettigrew, who was arrested under the *Traffic Act* for impeding movement during a demonstration against conscription on the steps of Brisbane's City Hall, even though, on this occasion, SOS had been granted a permit to demonstrate there. 'The City Hall steps at the time were wide enough to ride a chariot up', Pettigrew recalled. 'I always felt the police down in Albert St – there was a big crowd of them – were the ones impeding traffic'. In court, Pettigrew disputed the evidence of a young policeman who claimed she had answered in the affirmative when asked if she knew she was breaking the law. 'I suggested that I had said no such thing', she said. 'I wouldn't have said "yes" because I knew we had a permit for the right to demonstrate.' Pettigrew was still convicted but her fine was reduced from $10 to $2 with costs. 'At the time it was a common occurrence – women being arrested for demonstrating', she said. 'It showed us how much we needed to learn in Queensland to prepare ourselves for the undemocratic bans against street marches when many were arrested and harassed by police.'[24]

* * *

Victoria SOS's conversion to civil disobedience was more gradual than Brisbane's. In May 1967, its newsletter was still espousing the power of the pen, urging its supporters to write to politicians. 'It really does do good', it reassured. 'It has been reported that before Menzies resigned he was greatly disturbed by the number of letters he received criticising his policies – and in the House actually thumped his hand on the table with a highly emotional outburst: "These letters must stop".[25] By February 1968, however, the committee was frustrated by what it saw as a lack of progress and apathy on the part of the Australian public. That month's newsletter urged members to 'redouble our efforts in this year of crisis' and to 'keep reminding the Government that there is a strong opposition'.[26] While SOS was already signalling a stronger approach, it was an attempt to quash and limit protests that effectively pushed the movement over the line.

The first indications that police were moving to limit SOS demonstrations came in October 1967 when SOS women were told they could only demonstrate on the opposite side of the road from the barracks. Previously, they had been allowed to demonstrate closer to the gates as long as they kept moving. Some took this as a positive indication that such protests were starting to have an effect on deterring conscripts.[27] At the February 1968 intake, SOS women were joined by a large crowd of students and other anti-war protesters, who sat down on the street, obstructing the entrance of the Swan St barracks. Some members of the newly formed Draft Resistance Movement (comprising members of the Young Labor Association, University Labor Clubs, the Young Socialist League and former members of the Youth Campaign Against Conscription) chained themselves to the gates. SOS women decided to join in, as the March SOS newsletter reported:

> Save Our Sons members, supporting this effort, sat down in the drive way and pavement. When they were requested to move by the police, they remained seated with arms linked. There was no violence and the police were polite. If we did not move, we were carried carefully away to the nearby grass, only to return through the nearest gap in the crowd and sit down again.[28]

Following the demonstration, Max Teichmann, a lecturer in politics at Monash University, gave a roadside speech in which he praised the 'courage of the women who were prepared to execute acts of civil disobedience to bring public notice to the growing opposition to the war'.[29] SOS women, however, noted that 'in spite of all our efforts, the police only arrested the young demonstrators'. Nonetheless, the sit-down was a turning point for the Victoria SOS group, according to the newsletter:

> We felt we had made our first step to move active and insistant [sic] protest against conscription. We feel that the situation is so desperate, that civil disobedience is our only course. If it is well organised and peaceful, it can be a most effective means of protest.[30]

However, the women soon realised that it was not always within their power to ensure acts of civil disobedience remained peaceful and orderly. A violent protest outside the US Consulate in Melbourne on 4 July 1968, where mounted police charged into a crowd of demonstrators, had some SOS supporters questioning this change of direction.[31] Melbourne's July newsletter argued that 'most of the demonstrators were peaceful and all were genuine, and that the police used too much force too soon'. However, there was also a note of caution: 'We do not rule out the use of civil disobedience, but feel that it has to be planned in such a way, as to protect the participants and public alike from violence'.[32] There was further outrage the following month when a police inspector giving evidence at a hearing for some of the arrested protesters denied knowing that SOS had been present outside the US consulate. The SOS committee thought it 'more than odd' that the inspector could not recall seeing the SOS flag at the protest, much less his conversation with Jean McLean earlier in the evening. For the committee the implications of this were 'rather disturbing', the July newsletter observing:

> Quite obviously, the message being put across is that it is the student body alone who disagrees with our country's continued involvement in Vietnam – and students, as the press tells us incessantly, are by definition, immature thoughtless ratbags. This is a gross insult to all of us to start with, to the students and to any thinking citizen who disagrees with government policy.[33]

At the next intake vigil at Victoria Barracks, the newsletter reported that a group of about 30 SOS women and student supporters were outnumbered by 150 uniformed police, 50 security police, horses and paddy wagons. SOS was informed that members were free to demonstrate if they went to the other side of the road, did not approach or interfere with conscripts or parents and did not distribute pamphlets. 'On consideration, however, we decided to stay on the Barracks' side and walk up and down in single file to hand out literature', the August newsletter explained. 'It seems more important to us to break the law than to be stifled and we are now pursuing a policy of civil disobedience in this respect.'[34]

The law the women were defying was an 'archaic' Melbourne City Council by-law that made it illegal to hand out pamphlets in the street. Originally intended to prevent littering, Melbourne City Council By-law 418 Clause 24 (1) stated: 'No person shall upon any street, road or footway or other public place give out or distribute to bystanders or passers by any handbills, placards, notices, advertisements, books, pamphlets or papers'.[35] According to McLean, the by-law had been on the statute books for a hundred years but nobody had been arrested under it before July 1968 when she and fellow committee member Jo Maclaine-Cross were 'booked' by traffic officers at an SOS demonstration for handing out leaflets.[36] The women's cases were heard separately. McLean's case was dismissed on a technicality, but Maclaine-Cross was convicted and fined $5.[37] Inexplicably, a student protester who was convicted with her was fined $20. However, the mother-of-six gained widespread publicity by telling reporters she would go to jail rather than pay the fine.[38] McLean was booked again on 11 December for distributing handbills on Collins Street and again the following month at the national service intake, along with another SOS woman. After pleading guilty in court, an unrepentant McLean advised reporters that more of the handbills would be given out at the GPO the following Saturday.[39]

It was soon clear to SOS that authorities were intent on using the by-law 'as a political tool' to crack down on anti-conscription and anti-war protests.[40] Even the *Age*, while careful not to condone the protesters' actions, noted 'a taint of selectivity'.[41] In early 1969, 35 students were arrested on 65 charges in just two weeks. Like the Brisbane SOS group, the Melbourne women found themselves drawn into a wider civil liberties campaign that they saw as being inextricably linked to the conscription debate. 'We believe it is most necessary at this time to continue to hand out literature in the city streets as the most direct way to reach the unconverted public', its February newsletter explained.[42]

The women continued to defiantly hand out leaflets at all their protests. They also took part in weekly mass hand-outs where students, trade unionists and other groups would gather each weekend on the steps of the Melbourne GPO to distribute literature. The GPO was chosen because it was believed the council could not enforce its by-law on Commonwealth property. Dozens were arrested all the same. Some SOS women, like McLean and Maclaine-Cross, were repeatedly 'booked', but the committee made it clear members did not have to go that far:

> Anyone not wishing to face or not able for professional reasons to face prosecution, may, after the initial warning by the City Council Officers, just stop handing out leaflets. Those who are able and willing to make a stand against this undemocratic law may do so giving only their name and address when approached for the second time.[43]

By April 1969, seven SOS women (some more than once) had been fined or had cases waiting to be heard. McLean was arrested seventeen times for breaking the by-law. Generally, however, it was student protesters who were arrested while the women were ignored; a fact no longer ignored by the trailing media corps. At a demonstration outside the Melbourne GPO on 17 February, the *Age* reported that 25 people had been 'booked', however, 'inspectors and police ignored the secretary of the Save Our Sons Movement, blonde Mrs Jeannie McLean, who stood on the footpath handing out leaflets'.[44] The *Herald* photographed the 'militant women' from SOS on the streets again the following weekend, handing out leaflets unimpeded by authorities.[45] In one of these leaflets, SOS informed the public 'you will not be fined for reading this but the person who distributed it could be jailed under the Melbourne City Council By-law 418'. The leaflet, endorsed by McLean, explained that SOS women were acting in defiance of the by-law because they believed they should have 'the right to speak on behalf of suffering humanity and to persuade others to do likewise'.[46]

At an April demonstration organised by SOS, several 'big names' were recruited to help hand out pamphlets. Jim Cairns, ABC presenter (and SOS supporter) Corinne Kerby, actor Terry Norris, Edward McCormick (Victorian president of the Waterside Workers Federation) and Methodist minister Reverend Terry Lane were among 12 people, including McLean and Joan Coxsedge, subsequently arrested for breaking By-law 418.⁴⁷ 'We were all arrested, but they ran out of police wagons to hold us', McLean recalled. 'A group of us were shoved into a green Parks and Gardens van on a stinking hot day and kept there until they eventually drove us to Russell Street.'⁴⁸ Corinne Kerby recalled later that the police on duty had been reluctant to arrest a TV star. 'We did it deliberately, we were where we shouldn't have been and we had to force the police to take me', she said. 'I said (to one police officer): "Please take me. You are the one who has to oppress me"'.⁴⁹

A few days later, under immense pressure, the Melbourne City Council repealed the by-law and dropped all charges against those arrested. In a letter to the *Herald*, Reverend A. J. Lloyd, general secretary of the Campaign for International Co-operation and Disarmament (CICD), declared it 'a victory for democracy and freedom of speech', congratulating 'the Save Our Sons and university students who have conducted an unwavering campaign at some considerable cost and sacrifice'.⁵⁰ The SOS committee was triumphant but there were rumblings among some supporters that the by-law campaign had been a distraction from the movement's real aims. Such concerns were directly addressed in the March 1969 newsletter. 'You may wonder if, with so much attention to the City By-laws we have forgotten the fight against conscription', it stated. 'On the contrary, the distribution of leaflets is a vital link in the line of communication between us and the public – we do not have the radio and TV on our side so the written word is still a most effective weapon.'⁵¹

Publicity from the By-law 418 campaign certainly lifted SOS's profile during this period as well as strengthening links with student and trade union groups. Importantly, it also marked a change of tactics. 'This was a campaign that we stuck to, refusing to budge on and we won it', McLean said. 'And that had a terrific morale-building effect amongst our movement'.[52] From here onwards, acts of civil disobedience were regarded as a legitimate course of protest. These took different forms. Irene Miller recalled going out at night with 'two or three middle-class mums' to plaster anti-war posters around Melbourne. One would drive and keep watch, one would 'paste up' in the back of a Holden station wagon and the other would use a long-handed broom to 'plonk' the poster on the wall. Sometimes they went with student protesters. Miller recalled these outings as extremely frightening but exhilarating: 'I used to think, "Oh this is a terribly naughty thing to do" when I first did it'. These nocturnal adventures usually passed unnoticed but one night their luck ran out. 'The women just got let go – [the police] didn't want to know us – but they took [one of the students] in', Miller recalled.[53]

SOS had not only been on the frontline of the By-law 418 campaign. Behind the scenes, supporters worked tirelessly to raise funds urgently needed to pay legal costs, fines and bail, not just for SOS women but also for other protesters arrested. This was a vital, if largely unrecognised, role played by SOS throughout the anti-conscription campaign. Indeed, in many ways, SOS women 'bankrolled' the protest movement in Melbourne in its later years, proving remarkably talented at raising large amounts of money at short notice in order to bailout and pay the fines of non-compliers and fellow protesters. Sometimes this meant securing short-term loans from unions, which the women would later repay from money raised at fundraising events.[54]

Many of the Victorian SOS women, including McLean, had good connections to the arts community and were able to organise successful fundraising events. These ranged from concerts, film screenings, art exhibitions, auctions, jumble sales and bumper stickers to casual barbecues and 'expensive dinners where we charged people heaps of money'.⁵⁵ Painter Clifton Pugh was a regular supporter, and donated paintings for raffles and auctions.⁵⁶ Corinne Kerby was also a big drawcard at SOS functions and demonstrations.⁵⁷ Collections were taken at public meetings and functions addressed by SOS women. With the cooperation of unions, they also went to worksites and spoke to workers at lunchtimes, and a collection would be taken afterwards. 'We had auctions of good paintings, we had concerts with interesting people and when we had meetings we'd take the hat around', McLean said.⁵⁸ Many women who could not, or did not want to, demonstrate helped to fundraise as their contribution to the cause. Ceci Cairns described Victoria SOS's approach to fundraising as 'innovative'. 'We got people in. We didn't just sit there and think "how can we make money?" We rang up and we got people who had ideas, we got artists and musicians in, we used the creativity of people and they wanted to be used.'⁵⁹ By contrast, other SOS groups constantly struggled to raise funds.

* * *

In New South Wales, SOS continued to hold vigils at intakes of conscripts. While the women were frequently subjected to heckling from the public, the vigils were orderly and police mostly left them alone. At other demonstrations, however, women were harassed, pushed and 'bundled out of the way' by police. Maurie Mulheron recalled that his mother would always wear her best underwear to protests (which she called her 'demo drawers') after seeing one woman dragged away by the police with her second-best knickers showing.⁶⁰ At a demonstration outside the 1967 Easter Show, where SOS displayed graphic posters of injured Vietnamese children, the women were warned by police and subsequently sought advice from the Civil Liberties Council about their 'rights' to hold placards and distribute pamphlets.[61] However, as SOS women themselves recognised, NSW police were, on the whole, seen to be more tolerant than their counterparts in Queensland and Victoria.[62] As a result, there was no similar 'campaign for the streets' in Sydney that resulted in any hastening along the path to civil disobedience.

Nevertheless, like their interstate counterparts, NSW women came to realise that more direct action was needed during this period. This, in part, reflected a broader change in the way young men were also responding to the prospect of national service. Instead of taking their chances as conscientious objectors in the courts, more were choosing outright defiance of conscription laws, becoming 'non-compliers'. Some of these young men were sons of SOS members. There was no question of not supporting these men, but it meant crossing a legal line – and potentially breaching the federal *Crimes Act* – if SOS encouraged them to take this action. In its June 1968 newsletter, Sydney SOS observed that recent events indicated that 'non-violent civil disobedience and support for young men who refuse to serve because they have a moral objection' would increase in future campaigns as a 'method of defeating conscription and the use of conscripts in the Vietnam War'.[63] Sydney SOS subsequently drew up a 'declaration of conscience' for women to sign in support of young men who resisted conscription. Along the lines of a similar resolution from the US, it read in part:

> We believe that support for those who resist the war and conscription is both morally and legally justified. We believe that it is not we who are committing crimes but those who send young men who have a moral objection to kill and be killed. We do, however, recognise that there may be legal risks involved – but because we believe that these young men are courageous and morally justified in rejecting the war regardless of consequences, we can do no less. We urge all women to stand with us.[64]

This was printed as a leaflet and widely distributed. As elsewhere, the emphasis in NSW was on 'peaceful' civil disobedience. Newsletters subtly educated the broader membership, pointing to the changing political environment and suggesting such tactics were inevitable. One featured an article from the ANU student newspaper that argued 'non-violent civil disobedience and direct action' was 'more appropriate' than constitutional dissent.[65] In August 1968, Sydney also directed its members' attention to a 'hard-hitting' leaflet produced by their counterparts in Melbourne that declared support for draft resisters. 'Every single Australian must bear responsibility for the savage allied assault on a largely helpless rural population in Vietnam', the leaflet stated, noting it was 'the young' who were being left to carry this burden. Calling on others to join SOS in its campaign of resistance, the leaflet declared: 'There is only one moral response that we can make to the courageous few who have conscientiously refused to go. THEY MUST NOT STAND ALONE'.[66]

By October 1968, it was reported that a new group of 'unconscriptables' had appeared – young men who refused absolutely to comply with any aspect of the *National Service Act*. Those who refused to register or attend the medical faced terms of imprisonment for refusal to comply with the Act. Several were jailed during this period. Sydney SOS's newsletter urged its members to 'stand ready' to give the men support 'on every occasion action is taken against them', declaring 'the courage and determination of such a group deserves the support of all anti-conscriptionists'.[67]

In March 1969, SOS held all-night vigils outside Long Bay Gaol where three young men – Stephen Townsend, Michael Jones and Jeremy Gilling – were serving sentences for non-payment of fines for failing to register. SOS groups openly defied the *Crimes Act* by handing out leaflets titled 'Why register for National Service?' that set out alternatives to conscription. SOS women were also constant fixtures at court cases involving non-compliers and conscientious objectors, and many objectors and their relatives expressed their appreciation for the support. 'This is one way in which the adult section of the community can show their identification with the motives of the brave young resisters', Sydney's newsletter noted.[68]

* * *

Wollongong SOS was also actively supporting three non-compliers in its city – Mac Gudgeon, Chris Gerrard and Louis Christofides. Two were sons of members. The group held vigils at the railway station every time a group of conscripts left. These were usually peaceful affairs but in August 1968 Flo Garber and Edna Gudgeon were arrested for allegedly throwing anti-conscription leaflets onto the train tracks during their regular vigil. A visiting magistrate subsequently dismissed the charges but was unimpressed by the women's 'excitable' conduct in court. 'It may well be that the ladies were so emotionally involved in the events on the day that they lost the control they normally would have had', he concluded.[69]

Earlier, in March 1968, SOS women, some pushing strollers, had taken part in a major peace demonstration at Port Kembla to protest against the arrival of an American destroyer. In a letter to Sydney SOS, one member described the scene 'as the first time anything like this has happened on the coast. We got very good publicity, and ... we got our point across so well that the local mayor took the hint and postponed the civic dinner he had prepared for the captain and officers'.[70]

In 1969, Edna Gudgeon threatened to go on a hunger strike if her son was put in jail.[71] The local paper noted her threat had 'no precedent in the stormy history of conscription' and anticipated such action could be a 'trump card to play against the federal government' in an election year.[72] Gudgeon never had to carry out her threat; her son managed to successfully evade authorities.[73] During one 'quiet SOS vigil' at the Wollongong Railway Station, however, another 'SOS son', Louis Christofides, decided it needed a bit of 'livening up'. He jumped the fence and sat in front of the train that was transporting the latest batch of conscripts until he was dragged off by police. 'That made reasonably big news', he recalled.[74]

SOS and the South Coast Citizens Against Conscription (SCCAC) worked in tandem during this period, holding joint demonstrations and activities. Many women were members of both groups, and their husbands and sons were frequently members of the latter, so protests were often 'family events'. The two groups held a noisy demonstration inside and outside the court where Christofides was subsequently fined $10 and placed on a $100 good behaviour bond.[75] SOS women, including Flo Garber and Edna Gudgeon, were also among demonstrators who staged a 'sit-in' at the national service offices in Wollongong in May 1969. Police carried the women from the building one by one but a 'violent struggle' broke out when they attempted to do the same to male demonstrators, according to the local paper. Five men were subsequently arrested.[76] Wollongong Police later reported to the Special Branch in Sydney that the demonstration had been organised by the members of the SCCAC and SOS.[77]

Literature produced by SOS during this period became more strident and even more emotive, reflecting the move towards direct action. Topics covered not only conscription but broader issues about the Vietnam War. The use of napalm was a source of outrage that led to some graphic posters and leaflets. One produced by the Newcastle group included a photo of a severely burnt Vietnamese girl and declared: 'All Children Have the Right to Live'.

> A million children have been killed, wounded or burnt in this war in Vietnam. Torn flesh, splintered bones and screaming agony are bad enough, but the most heartrending of all are the little bodies scorched and seared by fire. We are confused and indignant. We ask "what can we do?" As mothers we must beseech our Government to negotiate an end to this needless war.[78]

Recruitment leaflets continued to target mothers. One distributed by SOS in Melbourne in 1968 urged women to move out of their private realm and into the public arena: 'Your decision will become MORE MEANINGFUL as a collective, rather than an individual one, as a public rather than a private one, as an active rather than a passive one'.[79]

* * *

SOS continued to offer support and legal aid to all young men who objected to national service during these years. In Sydney, the women printed and distributed 10,000 leaflets in support of a young railway employee, Tony McFarland, after his application for conscientious objection was rejected. SOS committee members also spoke on his behalf at railway workshop meetings. The leaflet stated explicitly that SOS 'supports Tony McFarland and others like him who resist the Government's conscription and Vietnam policies'.[80]

Ella Outhred continued to oversee the legal aid fund and to conduct counselling sessions. During this period, three sons of committee members lodged conscientious objections: Noreen Hewett's son Rex (an electrical fitter), Outhred's son Hugh (an electrical engineering student), and geologist Bernard Kirkpatrick, son of SOS vice-president

Daisy Kirkpatrick.[81] Other members reported that their sons had been 'balloted out' or failed medicals at this time. While some women supported their sons' decisions to publicly disobey the *National Service Act*, others saw this as too risky. Nora Mulheron chose passive resistance. 'She made the political decision that she would fight at the time of her sons' conscription rather than allow them to become conscientious objectors', Maurie Mulheron recalled.[82] Hence, when her eldest son became eligible for conscription in 1967, his mother sat the entire family around the dinner table and had them take turns at using a medical dictionary to find diseases and ailments that could prevent him being called-up. 'Mum left strict instructions that it had to be a disease that a male could have, not a female', Maurie recalled. 'She typed up four or five pages of all these fictitious diseases he was meant to have and sent them in … it was her way of saying "don't think you are going to be able to conscript my son"'. His eldest brother almost immediately won a deferment. While technically still able to be called-up at some time in the future, he never heard from the army again. The same exercise was repeated when Maurie's second brother became eligible for conscription in 1970. His call-up was also deferred. Both brothers were involved in the anti-war protests. Maurie recalled one demonstration where his brother was arrested: 'Mum found out and went around to all the paddy wagons calling "Dennis are you in there?" and of course all the kids were yelling out "Yes, Mum, I'm here" … it was a bit like the [Monty Python] *Life of Brian* skit'.[83]

In Victoria, SOS set up a sub-committee with a group of supportive lawyers, called Conscientious Objectors Non Pacifists. The group counselled prospective conscious objectors on a case-by-case basis and advised them of the best way to fight their case. The lawyers provided their services for free, except where the client could afford to pay.

McLean estimated, on average, that 10 to 12 conscientious objectors a week sought SOS's help.[84] SOS always advised the young men to have legal representation as this was looked upon more favourably in court. McLean said that for a long time Victorian magistrates accepted that the law, which stated 'against any war', meant any particular war, so conscientious objectors in that state could argue they were against the Vietnam War but did not have to prove they were against all wars. However, this changed after the lawyer for John Zarb, a young Victorian postman who was a conscientious objector, decided to challenge what was covered by 'all wars' in the High Court. The court subsequently ruled that it meant 'all wars and not one in particular', and an appeal to the Privy Court was 'thrown out in one minute'.[85] From then on, it became extremely difficult to prove conscientious objection cases. Other SOS groups also supported Zarb, contributing several hundred dollars to his legal campaign. In March 1969, six Melbourne women who took part in a national cavalcade to Canberra related how 'at one stage an army truck took off into the depths of the Hume Highway with a large "Free Zarb" sticker firmly attached to its tailbag'.[86] Deeply appreciative of SOS's support, Zarb's mother Irene subsequently joined the movement.

* * *

Like all minority grassroots groups, SOS needed to maintain a strong public profile to ensure its message had an audience. In November 1967, SOS women showed their creative side when they managed to grab the spotlight at the nation's premier sporting event, the Melbourne Cup.[87] Taking their cue from model Jean Shrimpton, who, two years earlier, had caused a stir by turning up in a miniskirt, the Melbourne women held a sewing bee to produce two identical, even shorter, miniskirts, with matching bonnets and capes for McLean and Ceci Cairns to wear to the track. The women hoped their attire would catch the eye of the organisers of the Fashion on the Field parade at which they planned to dramatically flip their capes to reveal anti-conscription slogans and 'get a bit of publicity'.[88] Ceci Cairns recalled she had never worn a skirt so short – or indeed panty hose, which were only sold in a few places in those days. 'What we didn't bank on was that we had the shortest skirts in the whole of the Cup, and we had all these men lying down on the grounds in circles around us to photograph the short skirts', she said. 'We realised we couldn't wait … we had to turn our capes around while all these photographs were being taken, we couldn't miss our opportunity.' The messages revealed read: 'Gamble on Horses Not with Lives' and 'Stop the War in Vietnam'. According to Cairns, the stunt was 'an incredible success' with photos of the women appearing in newspapers around the nation, and as far away as Los Angeles and the Soviet Union.[89]

Another protest that created national headlines was the November 1967 court appearance by Glen Tomasetti. The Melbourne folk singer and SOS founder had refused to pay one-sixth of her tax bill ($40) on the grounds that this was the proportion of the federal budget used to finance the Vietnam War.[90] Tomasetti's tax protest was not an entirely novel idea. In April 1964, American folk singer Joan Baez had refused to pay 60 per cent of her 1963 income taxes due to the Vietnam War.[91] Tomasetti argued that to pay the outstanding tax would be contrary to the charter of the United Nations. She told the court that apart from conflicts with opposing forces in Vietnam, Australian soldiers had been engaged in the destruction of villages, farms and local industries. She also referred to a picture of a middle-aged woman with a soldier's rifle pressed against her head that had appeared in the *Age* earlier that month. 'I believe that the practices shown violate the United Nations Charter and the Australian Act approving the Charter', she told the court. 'In accordance with all these laws, I owe nothing to the Taxation Department or to the Government of Australia which could in any way be used for such practices'.[92] The court did not agree.

SOS women staged another high-profile protest in March 1969 during a rally by visiting US evangelist Billy Graham at the Myer Music Bowl. Graham had publicly supported US President Johnson's Vietnam policy, much to the disgust of SOS members in Adelaide who sent telegrams of protest to Graham and rally organisers.[93] In Melbourne, about a dozen SOS women managed to smuggle banners and placards under their coats into the rally. When Graham was well into his sermon, the women silently walked down the main aisle in single file and assembled in a semicircle behind him holding up their placards. 'Preacher G didn't miss a beat and nor did his flock', recalled Coxsedge:

> Not a soul moved. The silence was awesome. People had their heads bowed and eyes closed, but quick little looks darted at us from all directions ... After more prayers and without a single word acknowledging our presence, we walked off the platform and stood in a line at the rear with our placards, waiting for the proceedings to end. As the faithful hurried past to catch trains and trams home, some stopped to ask why and to argue, while others did a Billy and pretended we weren't there.[94]

Irene Miller said the size of the crowd and the silence made the demonstration 'really scary'.[95] After talking to people after the meeting, Jean McLean was heard to quip that she believed SOS on the night 'had as many converts as Graham'.[96]

***

In August 1968, several Sydney SOS women joined a Caravan Against Conscription which toured country NSW. It was organised under the auspices of the Abolish Conscription Campaign (ACC), a mixed group comprising representatives from a number of anti-war/conscription groups. In reality, it was SOS women who were largely responsible for its organisation. Sydney SOS committee member Ella Outhred was co-chair of the ACC and she was joined by SOS stalwarts Adele Pert, Noreen Hewett and Nora Mulheron, who brought along her young son Maurie. Conscientious objectors Rex Hewett and Alan Outhred also joined their mothers on the tour.[97]

The caravan was modelled on the 'freedom ride' of 1965 in which 29 students from Sydney University set out on a road trip through north-western New South Wales to raise awareness of Aboriginal rights. That trip, in turn, had been inspired by the 1961 Freedom Riders in the US.[98] The aim was to meet and discuss conscription and the Vietnam War with as many people in rural areas as possible. SOS women were particularly keen to spread their anti-conscription message to country areas, having been told by country members how difficult it was for draft resisters in those places. Before the group's departure, Ella Outhred stressed that activities would 'concentrate on exchange of opinions through friendly discussions rather than on protest demonstrations'.[99] Daytime street meetings and night meetings were planned and the aim was to make the caravan 'big enough to make an impact and representative enough to have an appeal to local communities'. To that end, ministers of religion were invited to speak, and performances by folk singers and other entertainers were planned. The 'headline act' was high-profile draft resister and journalist Simon

Townsend, who was honeymooning with his new bride Mary Jane. Maurie Mulheron recalled that posters were put up in towns in advance of the caravan's arrival. 'It was very theatrical, just the anticipation of it coming to town was like the circus coming'.[100]

In all, 34 people, and five or six vans, were involved in various stages of the tour which departed Sydney on 27 August 1968 visiting Goulburn, Wagga Wagga, Albury, Griffith, Forbes, Parkes, Orange and Bathurst before returning to Sydney on 7 September. Over the course of the trip, caravanners distributed thousands of leaflets, held 'talk-outs in the streets', screened the film *Inside North Vietnam* and held public meetings. There were some uncomfortable moments. In Wagga Wagga, the group was met by 'a group of bikies', Noreen Hewett recalled. 'The leader strode over, singled out Simon – to our apprehension – and shook his hand.' Later that night at a public meeting, the bikie leader and army men got into an argument. 'Insults were exchanged and a brawl looked like developing', Hewett said. 'Suddenly an onlooker shouted, "Sit down, Sergeant, and shut up". The belligerent soldiers left. The order was from an army captain with his own concerns about the war'.[101]

There were other attempts to disrupt the tour. 'Persons unknown' distributed bogus leaflets and urged the Returned and Services League (RSL) and army men to attend and disrupt events. This modus operandi was similar to tactics employed (and boasted about) by Australian Security Intelligence Organisation (ASIO) agents to disrupt a regional Queensland speaking tour by Brisbane peace activist Norma Chalmers a few years earlier.[102] In Wagga Wagga, members of the Caravan found one of the unauthorised leaflets discarded in a gutter. It claimed that the Caravan had been organised by the Communist Party of Australia (CPA) in conjunction with the 'peace front', the Association for International Co-operation and Disarmament (AICD).[103] By chance, a reporter from the local paper was with the Caravan group when the leaflet was found and a report appeared in that paper the next day under the heading 'A Bid to Sabotage Visit of Caravan', with a reply from a Caravan spokesperson.

Organisers also faced difficulty booking halls in Wagga. In the end a small anteroom was secured for a public discussion to which 'a small group of soldiers came to argue'. More bogus leaflets were distributed in Albury ahead of the Caravan's arrival with the local press warning that 'organised disturbances' could be expected.[104] During a Saturday morning 'talk-out' in Albury, the situation became heated when soldiers, both in uniform and civilian dress, surrounded the caravanners and peppered the discussions with hostile injections in what Ella Outhred later described as 'a concerted attack on anti-conscriptionists'.[105] Several caravanners were threatened with physical violence but, according to Outhred, 'the tempers of anti-conscriptionists remained unruffled' and eventually 'some, originally opposed, started to join in the debate on the side of the anti-conscriptionists'.[106] A public meeting held in the St Matthew's parish hall that night was well attended, despite the rival attraction of a Graham Kennedy show in the city. 'An air force bloke in uniform came up to Mum at the back of the hall with a $20 bill – which was a lot of money in those days – and donated it and said he would be deserting, getting out', Maurie Mulheron recalled. 'We never heard if he did.'[107]

Despite the disruptions and intimidation campaign, SOS leaders declared that the tour was 'highly successful', resulting in 'many excellent' articles in newspapers and on television and radio.[108] The public meetings also helped to stimulate discussion and raise awareness about the alternatives to conscription. The presence of SOS women alongside the draft resisters was important because it meant the group could not easily be dismissed as a bunch of student ratbags and gave the group multi-generational appeal as well as a sense of gravitas. SOS women also were heartened to hear that, as a result of the tour, women in Parkes were considering setting up their own group.

* * *

As the October 1969 federal election drew closer, there was renewed, if cautious, optimism among SOS groups, that the Gorton government could be defeated. There were promising signs. In August, US President Nixon had announced an immediate but gradual withdrawal of troops from Vietnam. While the Gorton government had shown no signs of following suit, Labor, under Gough Whitlam, was looking stronger and, if elected, had promised to withdraw Australian troops from Vietnam by the following June. The anti-war movement was reaching its peak, and moratorium committees were being formed throughout Australia, following the example of anti-war groups in the US. SOS was represented on all of these committees. Moreover, for the first time since the campaign began, a subtle change in public opinion had been identified. In August, a Morgan gallup poll found 55 per cent of those polled wanted Australian troops brought back. Only 40 per cent were in favour of continuing the war, while 5 per cent remained undecided.[109] All this gave SOS campaigners reason for hope.

SOS continued to work closely with other groups during this period. In July 1969, it was represented at a meeting at which the Committee in Defiance of the National Service Act was formed. This 'ad hoc' committee – comprising academics, resisters, politicians, clergymen, students and unionists – placed an advertisement in the *Australian* with

853 signatories from across Australia encouraging eligible young men to resist conscription. Other newspapers refused to run it. SOS women from around Australia were among the signatories, and some undertook to collect signatures.[110] The committee's actions were a deliberate breach of the federal *Crimes Act* and designed to force the government to take action against the signatories. The government, however, recognising a pre-election political gimmick, declined to prosecute the signatories. This led to one of the more bizarre actions of the era whereby committee members began to prosecute each other. The resulting chaos not only clogged up the courts system but made a public mockery of the government's conscription laws. Adele Pert and Ella Outhred were among those who were subsequently 'convicted' and fined for breaching the *Crimes Act*. In Wollongong, another signatory, Edna Gudgeon was also reported to be 'putting her house in order' in preparation for jail time. Her husband also signed the declaration. 'I don't know if you are even allowed to take clothes or even a toothbrush, but I guess I'll find out soon enough', she told a local reporter.[111] In the end, she never had to find out.

As the election drew closer, SOS groups redoubled their efforts. The Melbourne group announced it was seeking to raise $1000 'for an intensive campaign' for the repeal of the *National Service Act*. The committee also urged supporters to boycott goods advertised on radio stations that had made 'scurrilous attacks' on SOS and Jean McLean, personally.[112] Supporters were urged to 'work hard for any candidate who is against war and conscription' and to attend all court cases of conscientious objectors and draft resisters. Sydney SOS also appealed for funds, noting the cost of producing 50,000 copies of an election leaflet had largely drained the group's coffers.[113] Efforts were concentrated in swinging seats and where candidates were directly challenging government policy on Vietnam, including Wentworth, where non-complier Geoff Mullen was standing against the Minister for Labour and National Service.[114]

Again, the election result was disappointing, but it was not all gloom. The government was returned but had been 'badly mauled', losing 16 seats (15 of them Liberal) while its majority was reduced from 39 to just seven.[115] SOS took 'great heart' from the swing, immediately making plans for the future. Sydney's newsletter noted:

> Already there are signs of internal power and policy conflict in the ranks of our Government. It is showing weakness, while the peace and conscription movement shows consistency and strength.[116]

Melbourne's post-election newsletter claimed the fact that Labor had won 47 per cent of the total primary votes revealed a major shift in public opinion.

> NOW is our chance to drive home the attack on this hideously oppressive Act … lobbying will be increased and made more effective. Letters and demonstrations will have a more meaningful purpose. We must show our disgust with the crumbling government who, by virtue of its election by preferential votes, is the people's second choice.[117]

As Christmas approached, SOS members vowed to continue the fight into the new decade.

* * *

The 1960s were a period of development and consolidation for the SOS movement. By the end of the decade, it had evolved from a narrowly focused protest group to become an integral part of the broader anti-war movement, as demonstrated by its representation on a wide range of anti-war committees. There had been changes in leadership and fluctuations in membership along the way; Townsville SOS had all but folded, WA SOS had been absorbed into another anti-war group, and Brisbane's high-profile secretary Vilma Ward had 'retired', but the members of the new Wollongong SOS were reportedly showing plenty of 'vigour'. Tactics had also evolved. Civil disobedience was no longer off-limits and had proven to be an effective measure when used in well-controlled and peaceful circumstances. It had not been adopted uniformly by the SOS movement but embraced by different groups at various points of time as they responded to local circumstances and events. 'At first you did the right thing, you wrote letters to politicians and did it in the proper way, you wouldn't think about going out and putting up posters at night', Irene Miller recalled. 'You got more daring at doing things as time went on, things that you wouldn't have thought about doing at first ... we didn't necessarily want to get arrested but you didn't get taken much notice of otherwise.'[118] Joan Coxsedge believes SOS became more radical as its members accepted that the war in Vietnam could not be divorced from conscription.[119] Not everyone in SOS was happy with the new direction. Glen Tomasetti was one who expressed concern. 'I think she was a bit critical of our more radical actions, I don't think she was happy', Coxsedge reflected in 2014. 'There was this element that thought we should stay very polite and just march around the city square, but there were a few wild ones, and I'd have to say I was one of them.'[120]

But traditional methods of protest were not abandoned. As the decade drew to a close, vigils and letter-writing campaigns continued and delegations to Canberra were still being organised. Good manners and neat dress were also still important, but there was a new air of daring, as exhibited by the Melbourne Cup protest. According to

Melbourne committee member Chris Cathie, as the campaign progressed, women became more determined and prepared to do more. They 'lost faith in the parliamentary process, in democracy, in the idea that if you obeyed the laws and were good and rational ... that it would be listened to'.[121] Closer links with students and more militant members of the protest movement also influenced the women. 'It certainly started to become more militant and that was part and parcel of the pressures going on outside from other groups too', Coxsedge recalled. 'So people felt they had to take a more militant position.'[122] While SOS may not have received the same publicity as other protesters, its leaders in 1969 had no doubt that it had made a major contribution to the anti-conscription cause. As the Melbourne committee reminded its supporters shortly before the 1969 election – in underlined capital letters:

THE SAVE OUR SONS MOVEMENT HAS BEEN THE ONLY ORGANISATION THAT HAS CONSTANTLY CAMPAIGNED FOR THE REPEAL OF THE NATIONAL SERVICE ACT AND THE WITHDRAWAL OF AUSTRALIAN TROOPS FROM VIETNAM. The women of Save Our Sons have demonstrated, run meetings, run social functions, distributed leaflets, lobbied in Parliament, helped conscientious objectors, opposed American nuclear bases in Australia. WITHOUT US THERE WOULD NOT HAVE BEEN CONSISTENT AND SUSTAINED PROTEST.[123]

By the dawn of the 1970s, however, public opinion in favour of the war was still proving hard to shift. The moratorium movement was building but non-compliers and conscientious objectors were still being jailed, and the government had indicated that conscription could become a permanent part of Australian life.[124] Violent protests and support of the 'enemy' by 'ratbag' university students also had done little to engage the more conservative sections of the community.

Nevertheless, while the 1969 election may not have been the victory SOS had hoped for, as McLean later reflected: 'It was quite clear we had moved a hell of a long way on from '65'.[125] As Edna Gudgeon and the Wollongong 'chain gang' would underline the following year, however, there was still a long way to go.

Chapter 7

ON THE WORLD STAGE

> What we are doing here by way of protest
> is not enough ... we must do more in Australia
> to save our sons.
>
> *Jean McLean*[1]

Save Our Sons (SOS) groups maintained sporadic correspondence with peace organisations and other women's groups overseas from the beginning of their campaign. Some members already had links to these groups through the Union of Australian Women (UAW), the Women's International League for Peace and Freedom (WILPF) and other peace organisations. Other groups made contact after hearing of SOS's formation, and vice versa. In the late 1960s, there were opportunities to cement these links and make personal friendships when women represented SOS at international conferences. These experiences, shared with members and other groups on the women's return, boosted morale and the belief that SOS was part of a larger international women's coalition to end war and violence. It was through this process of internationalism that many SOS women came to see conscription as inextricably connected to the broader peace issues and the Vietnam War itself.

Two US women's peace groups that have been likened to the SOS are Another Mother for Peace (AMP) and Women Strike for Peace

(WSP). The SOS groups were in contact with both, and exchanged information, including newsletters and campaign literature. While there were strong similarities, not least the reliance on maternal rhetoric, there were also some striking differences, particularly in the women who joined the respective groups.

AMP was formed in 1967 by Barbara Avendon, a Hollywood television writer who later co-created the series *Cagney and Lacey*, after she invited 15 women to her home to discuss how they could influence public opinion about US military involvement in Vietnam. Like SOS, the group purported to represent middle-class housewives and mothers ('the nice lady next door'). But it also attracted strong celebrity support including actors Donna Reed, Debbie Reynolds, Joanne Woodward and Lauren Bacall, and former Miss America Bess Myerson, putting it in a different league to SOS, with access to powerful connections and, importantly, money.[2] Unlike SOS, the group also lobbied mainly on the sidelines, relying almost entirely on letter-writing campaigns, particularly targeting Mother's Day. One of its letter-writing campaigns was aimed at companies that profited from the war.[3] While it had a membership of more than 20,000 at its peak, Michelle Moravec argues it was largely ineffective and invisible, and that reliance on maternal rhetoric that emphasised women's position as mothers as 'gentle persuaders' and as 'ladylike protesters' was outdated and ineffective.[4] However, the group's material, much of it based on cards for Mother's Day, spread internationally, and was enthusiastically embraced by SOS in Australia. A yellow poster featuring a flower and the group's best known slogan 'War is not healthy for children and living things' was particularly popular. In 1969, AMP released its Pax Materna pledge, calling 'sisters in every land' to push for 'a permanent declaration of peace'.[5] It was translated into 17 languages and appeared on cards and posters that were also distributed by SOS.

Women Strike for Peace was created in November 1961 following a one-day national peace protest during which an estimated 50,000 women left their kitchens and their jobs to demand that President John Kennedy 'End the Arms Race – Not the Human Race'. Their campaign subsequently helped change the discourse of the Cold War and to bring about the ratification of a treaty that banned atmospheric nuclear testing. After 1963, the WSP changed its focus to the Vietnam War. The organisation was much larger than SOS and the majority of its members were college-educated women who had left the workforce after marriage and children. Like SOS, however, they employed maternal rhetoric to fight against the draft for Vietnam and to help organise and support resistance to it. According to Catharine R. Stimpson, WSP took on 'the supple role of the self-sacrificing, protective mother of young men'.[6] In this, they had much in common with SOS. WSP members formed links and friendships with Vietnamese women who were also fighting for peace, organising a number of joint initiatives. They also reached out to women's groups in other parts of the world, including SOS. The Sydney SOS women communicated with their WSP counterparts and included extracts from WSP newsletters in their own. SOS also had contacts with the Vietnam Women's Union, initially through the UAW, and exchanged letters and other written material.

SOS women had opportunities to meet like-minded women from other parts of the world face to face. In March 1968, Nora Mulheron represented SOS at an international conference in New Zealand concerning Vietnam, the Southeast Asia Treaty Organization (SEATO) and political stability in Asia. While strictly beyond SOS's statement of aims at the time, it was evidence of the movement's broadening agenda, and Mulheron's report on her return garnered much attention.[7] The following year, she travelled with Babs O'Sullivan to Helsinki to attend the World Congress of Women, where the pair met Madame Binh, one of the chief negotiators for North Vietnam in Paris.[8] The women paid for both trips themselves. In Finland, Mulheron addressed a session on anti-Vietnam and anti-conscription activities in Australia. She told SOS members on her return that many delegates, including those from the UK, had been 'shocked' to learn that conscripts were actually being required to fight in Vietnam.[9] While there, Mulheron was secretly presented with a film by the Vietnamese delegation to show audiences in Australia. It depicted a preschool teacher taking her class to an air raid shelter during a bombing raid. Fearful of it being confiscated upon her return to Australia, Nora hid it in her young son's suitcase which she correctly gambled would not be searched. 'Mum loved that film. She related to it on a number of levels and we showed that film all around the place', Maurie Mulheron recalled.[10]

In April that same year, Jean McLean travelled to France to represent SOS at the Paris Conference of Women to End War in Vietnam, a conference organised by WSP and co-sponsored by the Vietnam Women's Union. Australia was invited to send a number of delegates to the Paris conference and a fundraising committee was established to raise money for the airfares. SOS was represented on this committee, along with high-profile members of the arts community, including author Charmian Clift and folk singer Marian Henderson.[11] In the end, there was only enough money for one delegate and it was decided to send Jean McLean. SOS in Melbourne raised $1600 towards McLean's trip while Sydney SOS contributed $220. The decision was made to purchase an around-the-world fare, allowing McLean to visit peace groups in other regions, including the US. 'By doing this, Mrs McLean will make contacts with peace movements in all parts of the world', Melbourne's April newsletter enthused.[12]

The four-day conference was attended by women from North and South Vietnam, the United States, Australia, Canada, Great Britain, Japan, New Zealand and West Germany. WSP member Amy Swerdlow remembered it as 'an intense emotional, as well as political experience' for delegates as the Vietnamese women related graphic and 'agonising tales' of torture, repression and the bombing of civilians.[13] The conference concluded with a joint communiqué that demanded that the US government recognise the National Front for the Liberation of South Vietnam (NLF) in negotiations to end the war, and called on all women 'of different colours, religious and political backgrounds' throughout the world to join in a 'strong movement to support the Vietnamese children and children everywhere'. The SOS movement was one of a number of women's peace movements from nations involved in Vietnam who pledged to make 'every effort to help young people resisting military service'.[14]

McLean was deeply affected by the conference, which clarified her belief that more direct action was needed. In an interview with the *Australian* from London, she accused the Australian Government of being 'terrified' that the Paris peace talks between the US and North Vietnam might succeed because it was 'hell-bent' on keeping an Australian military presence in Asia.[15] Back home, she immediately embarked on a lecture tour of Sydney, Wollongong, Newcastle, Melbourne and Tasmania during which she relayed the Vietnamese women's stories of atrocities, attacked 'American imperialism', and courted controversy by stating her view that the young men who refused to be drafted were the 'true heroes'.[16]

In an ABC television interview in Hobart, McLean spoke of how impressed she had been by the North Vietnamese women she had met. She had returned, she said, believing 'it is very necessary for women to show their commitment and to speak as mothers' and that 'for too long women have left the politics to men'.

> They have a very, very important role to play in politics today and that their influence on both their children and menfolk could be very strong, if they are willing to use it. And Asian women, I believe, do much, much more so than in the Western world.[17]

On her way home from Paris, McLean also visited the United States as a guest of WSP where she was struck by the affluence of the group which included many wealthy women of high standing in the community. In New York, a suite at the Waldorf Astoria was reserved for the meeting, while in California she was flown by helicopter to Berkeley to give a speech at the University of California. 'They were women of means ... it was another world', McLean recalled.[18]

The trip seems to have been a turning point for SOS in Melbourne with McLean expressing frustration on her return about the lack of progress by the anti-conscription movement in Australia. At one well-attended SOS public meeting, she outlined some of the initiatives being undertaken by women elsewhere in the world. In Japan, she said, a million women could be called upon to demonstrate at any one time, while in America, organisations were teaching young men how to dodge the draft and paying for them to move to Canada, finding them employment there. 'What we are doing here by way of protest is not enough', she concluded. 'We must do more in Australia to save our sons.'[19] It was shortly after this trip that SOS became involved in the direct action campaign against By-law 418. A recruitment leaflet distributed by SOS in Melbourne around this time echoed McLean's call for a change of direction, declaring 'dissent alone has not been sufficient to defeat the forces of militarism'.[20]

But publicity surrounding the Paris visit paled by comparison to the controversy generated by McLean's next overseas trip to North Vietnam. An invitation to visit Hanoi had been extended in Paris by the Vietnam Women's Union. In July 1969, accompanied by UAW national president Freda Brown, McLean spent 10 days in and around Hanoi, touring hospitals and underground networks of shops and factories, and meeting leaders of the Provisional Revolutionary Government (PRG). The women were given 'a royal welcome' everywhere they went, with people on the streets clapping and waving. 'I felt like the Queen', McLean recalled later.[21] There was great interest in SOS, but McLean was surprised when her hosts updated her on an Australian demonstration held in her absence, evidence that the North Vietnamese were monitoring anti-war activity in Australia.

McLean returned home with her hand luggage bursting with souvenirs, including a pair of custom-made black Viet Cong 'pyjamas', a large NLF flag (a gift for student leader Harry van Moorst), a coolie hat, jewellery fashioned from downed American aircraft, and an anti-personnel bomb. A journalist who joined McLean on the last leg of her journey from Sydney to Melbourne announced 'Bombshell Jean is back', reporting, with some relief, that the souvenir bomb had been defused.[22] The trip received widespread media coverage, with McLean posing for photos in the hat, holding her pineapple bomb, and telling reporters that she had returned home 'with a much greater understanding of their determination to fight for reunification of their country'.[23]

In Melbourne, however, Commonwealth Police officers were waiting, keen to question McLean over her admission that she had presented the Viet Cong with $100 in medicines purchased in Australia. Under

Section 3 of the *Defence Forces Protection Act* of 1967, Australians were prohibited from sending or taking money or other financial assistance or goods to the North Vietnamese Government. If convicted, McLean faced a fine of up to $1000 or a year's jail. Aware of this, McLean had duly collected a 'receipt' from her North Vietnamese hosts, which clearly stated that her gift had included only medical supplies and 'that the money wasn't used for guns'.[24] In 1972, American film star Jane Fonda also made a controversial trip to Hanoi where she earned the moniker 'Hanoi Jane' and was accused of 'aiding and abetting the enemy'. Like McLean's trip, Fonda's was also organised through Madame Binh and the Vietnam delegation at the Paris peace talks. More than four decades later, Fonda was still receiving 'hate letters' from veterans.[25] McLean, who did not have Fonda's profile, was unrepentant, stressing she had no regrets and would do it all again. 'My reasons were not political', she told reporters in 1969. 'They were people, they were short of medical supplies – my motives were humanitarian.'[26]

In Australia, there was more interest than hostility. Few people at the time had had the opportunity to see firsthand the enemy's side of the war and McLean was once again in demand as a guest speaker in Melbourne and interstate. Among her insights about life in wartime North Vietnam were descriptions of how bomb craters were being used as fish farms. She also described a makeshift operating theatre in the jungle where 'a little nurse pedals like mad on a generator to keep the electric light going on the operating table'. Deeply impressed by the role of Vietnamese women in society, she stressed how, unlike women in Australia, they were not regarded as 'second-class citizens' but had 'attained complete equality, and at the same time have retained their femininity'. These observations were peppered with political insights about North Vietnamese attitudes to the Paris peace talks, the 'high morale' of the people, their determination never to give up their fight to rid their country of foreign invaders, and their belief that the Australians were 'just lackeys of the US'.[27] Her impression, she said, had been that 'they think Australia's policy is stupid rather than aggressive'.[28]

* * *

SOS was part of an international coalition of women working for peace and to end the Vietnam War. Their archives show they shared information while there were occasional opportunities to meet their international counterparts face to face. This exchange of information, particularly through WSP newsletters, helped to educate SOS women by providing access to information, research and political thought that was not available via the Australian media. The contact made SOS members feel part of something bigger and fed their conviction that they were on the side of right. It also helped to mould opinions on war and peace issues, expanding their original focus on conscription. As a result, SOS's attention increasingly turned to global issues rather than private family interests. But SOS's internationalism also provided further fuel for their opponents who accused them of being dupes of communism and, worse, gullible, uncritical mouthpieces of the enemy.

Chapter 8

'FAN MAIL'

> The frequent exhibitions your members put on
> in public is a disgrace to womanhood. Far better
> you stay home and look after your homes
> and make men of your sons …
>
> *A Proud Mother of a Proud and Loyal Son*[1]

Of the many letters of support Wollongong mother Helen Christofides received when her draft resister son Louis was in prison, the one she especially treasured came from a woman she had never met. 'This is from one mother to another, extending congratulations on having a fine son, who is prepared to sacrifice his freedom in the cause of peace', the note read.[2] But Christofides also had to withstand vitriol from those who viewed her son as a traitor and a coward. One anonymous ill-wisher sent her a white feather, the traditional symbol of cowardice, for 'your precious little Louie', suggesting 'a good swift kick in the balls and a belt under the left ear with the but [*sic*] of a military rifle … would do him the world of good'. The letter concluded with a sinister message for the Wollongong women who protested at Parliament House: 'What all you old trolls that chained yourselves to the rails need is a good boot in the smelly snatch'.[3]

These letters demonstrate the range of reactions that Save Our Sons (SOS) women encountered during their campaign against conscription.

While they drew strong support from trade unions, some church leaders, left-wing politicians, and the peace movement, they came under intense criticism from supporters of the war among their local communities, sometimes even within their own families. Surveillance by the Australian Security Intelligence Organisation (ASIO) and police was another unforeseen, and extremely stressful, cost of joining SOS. Criticism was particularly fierce in the early years when there was still strong support for Australia's involvement in Vietnam and the anti-conscription movement was struggling to find any momentum. 'War was popular then and most people were hostile to us', Sydney SOS's Noreen Hewett recalled.[4] While it was not unusual for anti-war protesters to attract hostility, there was a different – gendered – element to much of the criticism of SOS women that was frequently personal and vindictive, reflecting the broader changing time and roles of women in public life. Most members probably never knew the extent of the abuse. The Sydney women chose to preserve a sample of the worst in a file ironically labelled 'fan mail', which provides a glimpse of a malicious postal campaign that must have been truly frightening for those who received the letters. Yet there was never any mention of this in any other official document or correspondence. On the surface, SOS women adopted 'thick skins' and maintained a sense of humour, but this could not have been easy. In this chapter, letters, interviews, newspaper reports and official records highlight some of the typical reactions to the SOS movement and the impact these had on the women, both collectively and as individuals.

* * *

For SOS women the issue of conscription was not just political, it was deeply personal – and some paid a high price for their commitment. Like other anti-war and peace groups during this period, they were routinely accused on the streets of being unpatriotic, disloyal and communist sympathisers. But this criticism did not end when they turned in their sashes after each demonstration. It followed them into their communities and into their own homes, impacting on every aspect of their lives. It also affected those closest to them. While they did not dwell on this aspect of their activism in their newsletters, in private correspondence, interviews and memoirs, they recalled the hostility they encountered from neighbours, 'friends', work colleagues and even their own family members. Joan Coxsedge's neighbours in the middle-class Melbourne suburb of Balwyn, for example, used to cross the street to avoid her. 'I was living next door to Mr RSL, next door to him was Mr RSL, and opposite him was Mr RSL', she recalled. 'We just had to live with it, but it wasn't the easiest thing in the world living in a fairly conservative street.'[5] In Brisbane, a group of neighbours would shout out 'you commo so and so' whenever Gordon and Shirley Jamieson were within hearing distance. It made life very unpleasant, Gordon remembered. Years later, 'the ringleader' saw Gordon interviewed on television about his experiences as a Japanese prisoner of war and contacted the couple. 'She became Shirl's best friend', Gordon recalled. 'She would have remembered (the abuse) but I never discussed it with her.'[6]

Friendships were frequently strained or broken during this period. As a new arrival in Townsville, Margaret Reynolds became friendly with another young mother but was puzzled when, not long after SOS formed, the woman informed her they could no longer be friends because her priest had told her she should not associate with communists.⁷ Some of Dorothy Dalton's 'friends' did not speak to her until the war was over, others would inquire politely about her younger boy but never about her draft resister son. On one occasion, she sent a note of support to their local butcher's family whose son had resisted conscription and been subsequently jailed. The parents were not supportive of their son and the gesture was not appreciated. 'They didn't want to know me after that', she said.⁸

In Townsville, Esme Hardy encountered problems with her local priest who vehemently opposed communism and supported the Vietnam War. After the priest refused to support her son Tom's application for conscientious objection, the family became active in Pax Christi, the international Catholic Peace movement, which led to further tensions within their parish. Tom Hardy recalled the day his parents received an envelope that contained white powder and a note that read, 'Take this you Commie bastard'.⁹ He said his parents were 'quite disturbed by this sinister act', which he suspects came from one of their fellow parishioners. While the priest's pro-war stance did not affect Esme's faith, it did impact on her relationships with other church goers. One staunchly Catholic neighbour, a widow with 13 children, was particularly upset by the Hardys' stand against the Vietnam War. 'She did whatever the nuns told her to do and if the nuns told her that Henry and Esme Hardy were communists, she would believe it', Tom Hardy recalled. 'So, mum and dad had to have this discussion [with her] all the time. I think they had an effect on her. She was loyal to the last to her Catholic clergy but I know [mum and dad] rocked her thinking because they stood up for what they believed.'¹⁰ Despite her differences with the priest, Hardy said his mother always held on to her faith, insisting that her son apply for papal dispensation when he decided to marry a non-Catholic. He recalled: 'It meant a lot to Mum and Dad that I did the right thing as a Catholic. They would be the church's greatest critics … but they held on to those values, they were rock solid'.[11]

The younger children of SOS members frequently bore the brunt of opposition to their mothers' stand. At one parent–teacher night Irene Miller was 'taken aback' when a teacher suggested her son's lack of achievement in a particular subject might have been due the 'family atmosphere' and his mother's criminal record.[12] Coxsedge's daughter was given such a hard time by teachers over her mother's anti-war activities that she refused to return at the end of one term and had to be transferred to another school.[13] Esme Hardy's children were also targeted at their private Catholic school which her son sometimes found hard to bear. 'You wanted to be accepted by your peers', he recalled. '[But] we were always a subject of derision of most of our Tory friends.'[14] Joyce Golgerth's daughter Candy also experienced difficulties at school when her mother's activities became public. 'I was very conscious being at school that if I spoke too much about it then maybe I would be ostracised', she recalled. 'At the same time I felt very committed to what my mother was going through and I believed very strongly in what she believed in.'[15]

The women responded in their own, sometimes novel, ways. In Sydney, Nora Mulheron never missed an opportunity to raise conscription at school Parent & Citizens' meetings, which sometimes led to problems for her youngest son Maurie, who recalled one his teachers becoming 'very, very hostile'. On one occasion, a teacher tried to take his moratorium badge, sending him to the principal's office when he refused to hand it over. After being told to 'get out of my school before I smash your head against the wall', Maurie headed home and told the story to his shiftworker father who promptly drove him back to school. 'Mum then discovered that the guy who had sent me home was in charge of Inter-School Christian Fellowship', he recalled. 'So she got all these Christians Against War in Vietnam leaflets and for some time kept sending them to him on a regular basis anonymously.'[16]

While most of the high-profile SOS members had supportive families, some relatives and spouses were more circumspect. Joan Coxsedge said some women showed great bravery in becoming involved in the first place because most did not have independent means and, in some cases, their husbands were 'very hostile'.[17] Joyce Golgerth's husband never stopped her involvement but he made it known that he disapproved of some of the group's activities. Michael Golgerth recalled his father standing off to the side at SOS rallies with his arms folded, watching. 'I don't think he would have been able to stop her because she was quite strong-minded', daughter Sue Foster recalled. 'But I think there were certain things he didn't approve of. He probably thought this could bring some uncomfortable attention from some sorts of people and I don't think he liked the idea of that.'[18] One Victoria SOS woman described how her involvement in SOS caused friction at home. After her husband became 'quite icy', she no longer attended demonstrations, limiting herself to writing letters to politicians as 'my only protest'.[19] After the Vietnam War, she continued to write letters about other issues but never again took to the streets.

Some women were deeply concerned about the effect their involvement might have on their husbands' employment. Jean Bonner, in Bega, supported SOS financially but explained that personal circumstances prevented her from becoming an active member. 'My husband has quite recently been appointed as principal to the local high school', she wrote. 'At the moment he is treading very carefully 'til he gauges the local susceptibilities ... in the meantime I won't join any organisations of a controversial nature.'[20] In reply, Sydney's secretary Pat Ashcroft was sympathetic: 'We are much aware of the need to be circumspect – especially in such cases as yours. We too have to use discretion in some ways or find ourselves in the poor house.'[21]

In Wollongong, Edna and Mac Gudgeon's high-profile opposition to conscription made them unpopular with some segments of their local community. The Gudgeons received abusive letters and telephone calls from anonymous callers attacking them and their draft resister son. Mac senior, a World War II veteran, resigned from the Returned and Services League (RSL) after other members complained about his family's anti-war activities. On one occasion pro-war supporters even ordered a boycott of the family's pharmacy. In response, local unions instructed their members to purchase all their medicines from the Gudgeons. According to her son, while it was not easy, Edna refused to be intimidated. 'She just got stronger and stronger', he said.[22]

Others encountered hostility in the work place. As a trainee buyer at an upmarket Melbourne department store, one SOS woman was stunned by the response from the dining-room staff after she asked to address them about conscription. 'Some members were English and refused to serve me, branding me as a troublemaker with no idea of how important it was to have all young men do as was required by King and country', she recalled. 'Management was very good and tried to keep everyone happy; however, one day I was alone and one woman staffer spilt hot tea on me. I resigned at once.'[23] According to Corinne Kerby, her superiors made it clear they were not pleased by her public support of the anti-conscription movement. 'The ABC did not like it. I didn't say anything [on air] but I could have at any time and I was widely known and they were terribly uncomfortable about me', she said. 'I think they were very glad to see the end of me.'[24]

Kerby's mother was also horrified by her daughter's anti-conscription stance, afraid that she was following the same path as her unionist father, who lost his job with the tramways department after visiting Russia in the 1940s. 'She could see it all happening again', Kerby said. 'She wasn't nasty about it, but she was embarrassed and she was frightened.'[25] Other families became more supportive as time went by. Chris Cathie said her jailing with the Fairlea Five 'solidified' the support of her wider family. 'They thought [what we were doing] was slightly off but when that happened they more or less realised that it was what you had to do to get your message across and that you were entitled', she recalled. 'The main thing was that we weren't violent; we were non-violent, we weren't armed, [and] we weren't running around belting coppers or anything.'[26]

SOS women also had to contend with surveillance and police intimidation. Most undercover officers were well-known to the Melbourne and Sydney women. Indeed, Joan Coxsedge believed police made little effort to disguise themselves in order to intimidate those taking part in anti-war activities. 'They were very blatant, they'd sit at the back of meetings and take notes and photos', she recalled. 'Larkins of the Special Branch would come up and ask how your auntie and uncle were, what your kids were doing at school, to let you know he knew everything about you.' While such tactics did not concern Coxsedge 'one iota', she said others in the group were unsettled by them.[27] The Sydney women complained of similar treatment by the NSW Special Branch. After one demonstration, Pat Ashcroft reported that the officer-in-charge of the NSW Special Branch, Fred Longbottom, had spoken 'insultingly to one innocent woman' saying 'You think you are smart don't you? I've been watching you for years'.[28] Judging by the size of their individual ASIO files, in the case of some of the women this was almost certainly true.

The surveillance was conducted in every location where SOS was active. Some women chose to respond with humour. In WA, two plain-clothed officers, who spent hours sitting outside one SOS woman's home, were surprised when she appeared at the car window one afternoon offering them coffee and biscuits.[29] In Brisbane, Vilma Ward and a group of SOS women led 'two security boys' on a chase through the city streets. In a letter to Sydney SOS, Ward related how at one stage the women 'shot up a laneway and stood around the corner' so that 'the boys bumped straight into us'.[30] Not all surveillance could be laughed off. The activities of Nora Mulheron, also a member of the Communist Party of Australia (CPA), filled several volumes of ASIO files, and included mundane details of family events such as picnics in Centennial Park. The family adapted their lives to this surveillance. Believing their phone was tapped, for example, they had strict rules about what to say if one of the children answered when their parents were out. As a young boy, Maurie Mulheron found this very distressing. 'I used to hate to speak on the phone because I was always scared of what I could or couldn't say', he recalled. 'It took me years before I became comfortable answering the phone.'[31]

Joan Coxsedge was in an unusual situation because her brother was a policeman. This caused tensions within the family. 'He was not impressed at all and when I was marching he'd march alongside not saying a word to keep an eye on me so I didn't get into trouble', she recalled. 'But I had a different name so he'd always pretend to have nothing to do with us.'[32] Occasionally, police officers expressed sympathy for the women's cause. Chris Cathie recalled how 'appalled' a young policeman was when tasked with escorting the women to Fairlea prison. 'He was quite shocked, just walking down the stairs at the watch-house he said "this is wrong", or words to that effect, "this shouldn't happen"', she said. 'That was impressive.'[33]

Most of the written abuse SOS received was directed at the movement collectively, but secretary Adele Pert, whose name and address were listed on most of the Sydney group's literature, was often singled out for personal criticism. The irony of a purported 'commo' living in Anzac Avenue was frequently pointed out by outraged respondents who seemed to feel that such an iconic address should be reserved for only the most deserving of citizens. Most sinister, however, was a series of letters sent to Pert personally during the 1960s. These usually consisted of a one-line, frequently misspelt, handwritten note, accompanied by a photographic slide to illustrate the sender's often menacing message. One slide, for example, had a hole pushed through the image of a woman. The accompanying note read: 'Yet another old hag with a hole in the head'.[34] It must have been truly unnerving to receive these letters yet there is no mention of them in any minutes, newsletters or saved correspondence between SOS members. The only evidence that SOS women were concerned is a brief, undated, 'memo' in the SOS archives that suggests they may have complained to the postal authority. The note cryptically advises, 'if a prosecution was brought about it might do more harm than good to the movement'.[35] In 1970, Pert also noted in correspondence that a few leaflets had been returned with abusive remarks 'but the main objection seemed to be my address!'[36] SOS women appear to have countered such abuse in the best way possible, by ignoring the correspondence and keeping knowledge of its existence limited to as few as possible, thus avoiding creating any undue concern among the group's wider membership. It does, however, highlight the pressure some individual members were under, particularly Pert.

* * *

While SOS was routinely accused of having communist links and an unpatriotic agenda, there was another, gendered, dimension to much of the criticism directed at SOS that reflected broader societal unrest over what some viewed as a threat to the postwar ideal of the nuclear family. Although the numbers of women in paid work was increasing in the postwar years, they were still in a minority.[37] In most middle-class and some working-class families, it was still more common for women, if they were employed at all, to stop work after marriage or when they became pregnant. Popular women's magazines, such as the *Australian Women's Weekly*, idealised and promoted the idea of the middle-class housewife who devoted her waking hours to housework and childrearing.[38] Hence SOS women, in their middle-class uniforms, created a conflicting and unsettling image, standing out at a time when the public image of women was domestic, maternal and passive, rather than political and active. As women perceived to be acting outside their traditional domestic roles, they drew a strong current of disapproval that implied, both implicitly and explicitly, that they were 'bad mothers' and 'neglectful wives'. Irene Miller, who often took her youngest children to protests with her, was frequently singled out for such criticism. 'Many a time, men, mostly, would come up and say, "you should be home cooking your husband's dinner" and things like that', she recalled.[39] As Joyce Golgerth's daughter, Candy, explained, 'They were coming out of an era where women really didn't have a voice … they took a lot of battering from that and it was very hard.'[40]

Jean McLean, one of the younger members of SOS who later took part in the women's movement, explained that women in the 1960s were still mostly 'kept in their little suburban boxes, deprived of intellectual nourishment, in a world of wet nappies, pots and pans, and kids who needed constant attention'.[41] She had no doubt that some wanted to keep them there. In Townsville, Henry Reynolds' university colleagues expressed horror after learning via the local press that his wife Margaret had established a local branch of SOS. They were concerned that such an association would 'bring discredit to the university's good name'. To the couple's amusement, one even suggested that 'Reynolds should control his wife'. Margaret Reynolds later explained in her memoirs: 'This belief that men took responsibility for "managing" their wives was not uncommon in the 1960s and in the very macho environment of North Queensland it was assumed that Henry should have been able to prevent his wife from embarrassing him.'[42]

Some accused the women of taking their maternal roles too seriously; they were dismissed as selfish, over-protective mothers who mollycoddled their sons. In this vein, SOS was mocked by 'The Send Our Sons Committee, Sydney', which suggested the women had failed in their duty to bring up their sons as men. In a letter to a newspaper, the 'group' urged: 'If you do not wish your little darling to grow into a big darling, or if you are having difficulty distinguishing between your sons and daughters, join us in our crusade to Send Our Sons'.[43]

But it was not just men who accused SOS women of not acting like 'proper mothers'. Indeed, some of the most barbed criticism came from other women who also had sons of conscription age. While women's liberation did not really gain momentum until the SOS movement was winding down, there was still a sense of change in the air that not all women supported, something that is easy to forget when celebrating the advances of women during this period. Indeed, many women were very happy with the status quo and viewed motherhood in patriotic terms. In a typed response on one anti-conscription leaflet returned to the Sydney SOS group, for example, 'a proud mother of a proud and loyal son' demanded: 'What do you want your sons to be, weaklings, cowards?'

> Wake up to yourself and bring your Sons up to protect your daughters. The frequent exhibitions your members put on in public [are] a disgrace to womanhood. Far better you stay home and look after your homes and make men of your sons … Let us be thankful that there are 100 sensible women to every ratbag sending this out.[44]

Another mother of a teenage son suggested SOS women 'get into some housework and do some good for your family and those who are in need and keep your noses out of the Vietnam War'.[45] At national service intakes, SOS women also faced hostility from mothers, some of whom staged lavish champagne breakfasts with which to send off their sons. Many SOS women found criticism from other mothers particularly hard to reconcile. Dorothy Dalton, whose own son became a draft resister, recalled: 'The women, the mothers particularly, used to look at us as though we were the scum of the earth'. Dalton, for one, was not convinced by these shows of bravado. 'Well, I suppose if the boy was going in they had to bolster themselves up to try and put on the proud look.'[46]

At the heart of these gendered criticisms was a differing view on what constituted maternal duty. In the postwar period, the Menzies government had fostered the idea that this entailed women staying at home, bringing up children, supporting their husbands, and, by extension, keeping out of the public sphere.[47] Younger women who joined the anti-war protests and the women's movement rallied against this, at the same time dismissing the maternal rhetoric used by SOS and earlier women's peace groups as outdated and old-fashioned. SOS women were, in a sense, stuck in the middle of this changing world, pursuing a 'radical' agenda from a respectable platform. They did not set out deliberately to contest the status quo or to advocate radical feminism, rather they saw their actions as an extension of their maternal duty. Such thinking may have been viewed as 'old fashioned' in some quarters but, among SOS's target audience, it was particularly effective. SOS literature was designed to appeal to the sensibility traditionally ascribed to women, reinforcing the notion that 'good' mothers had a 'moral obligation' to make a stand against the government's policy. Moreover, a woman's innate understanding of others' suffering was portrayed as a strength that enabled women to be effective peacemakers in times of conflict. It was in this context that Nola Barber told the inaugural meeting of SOS in Melbourne that women had 'a moral obligation to stand together and fight conscription'.[48]

Unlike male protesters, SOS women also had to contend with criticism that they were overly sentimental and emotional. The gendered subtext here was that women were not capable of understanding rational arguments put forward in support of Vietnam and conscription. This was evident during the 1969 court appearance by Wollongong SOS members Edna Gudgeon and Flo Garber where the magistrate described them as 'excitable', concluding they had become 'so emotionally involved in the events on that day that they lost their control that they normally would have had'.[49] Likewise, when Elizabeth Jones in Sydney was charged with contempt of court for speaking up in support of her son, she was told that she was too emotionally involved.[50] Interestingly, female critics of SOS also targeted what they saw as an over indulgence in sentimentality. One woman wrote to Adele Pert, she said, in 'a vain attempt to place a rational fact somewhere in your head – quite obviously fogged in heavily with sentimentality, emotionalism and selfishness'.[51]

> Nothing on this earth would induce me to connect myself with a movement represented by the sloppy sickening tripe put forward in your leaflet. Do you really think the women of today are all sitting around weeping for a son, totally blind to the fact that quite possibly the main reason they have a son of age to be called up is that America stepped in and won the Second World War for us?[52]

As a woman already in the public domain, Councillor Nola Barber perhaps had an inkling of what was to come, cautioning at Melbourne's first SOS meeting that as women 'we should express our emotional nature with reason and intelligence'.[53] Nevertheless, SOS women found themselves frequently belittled on the basis of their perceived over sentimentality.

Gendered criticism was also evident in press reports. In 1966, Adele Pert complained to one supporter that much of the media coverage SOS had received to date had been 'misinformed'. 'We have variously been described as selfish or dominating mothers concerned only about our own sons ... as pacifists ... as unpatriotic ... as cranks', she said.[54] In 1968, Noreen Hewett sent an indignant letter to the manager of radio station 2UV after one of its presenters referred 'to women demonstrating only "wanting attention" that they had not had since the Yanks were here in the last war'. 'Our members are among thousands of women of unimpeachable character who demonstrate against the Vietnam War and conscription', she wrote.[55] SOS were also frequently ridiculed or caricaturised. As a result, they faced an additional hurdle in their campaign against conscription: a struggle to be taken seriously. In 1965, the *Sun* scoffed that 'people who see them are inclined to write them off as "a bunch of eccentrics"'.[56] In 1971, SOS women took umbrage at a cartoon appearing in the *Australian* about the latest road statistics that suggested troops in Vietnam were safer there than on

Australian roads. The cartoon included caricatures of SOS women as crones in hats and gloves holding a placard that read: 'Let them stay in Vietnam this Christmas'.[57] The SOS's president complained that the cartoon 'seems to question the worthiness of our policy'.[58]

* * *

While there are numerous examples of SOS women confronting male opponents who labelled them communists, SOS women rarely engaged their female critics, at least publicly. One high-profile female critic SOS did take on was Australia's most decorated World War II servicewoman Nancy Wake. The fearless French resistance fighter, who saved thousands of Allied lives by setting up escape routes and sabotaging German installations, was a national hero. She was also a member of the Liberal party.[59] In 1966, she was contesting the NSW seat of Kingsford Smith and campaigning in Albury where she was the guest speaker at a gathering of the local Liberal women's group. According to the local paper, Wake was 'very much against' SOS. 'She said that although most of the movement's members were quite sincere, they were becoming the tools of subversive groups, communists, who wanted Australia out of Vietnam'.[60] Sydney SOS was informed by its outraged supporters in Albury that Wake had made similar comments during an interview with the local radio station. In an angry letter to the Albury newspaper, Golgerth noted it was not the first 'attack' on SOS by Mrs Wake who she described as 'without a doubt the most ill-informed person as to the aims, objectives and constitution of the Save Our Sons movement'.

> It is highly likely that Mrs Wake, with an electioneering campaign imminent for the Kingsford Smith seat, believes that by

smearing an organisation such as Save Our Sons as unpatriotic, even subversive, she may steal a little added lustre for herself as the war heroine of World War II. For Mrs Wake's information, there are just as many women within Save Our Sons entitled to wear war medals as there are elsewhere.[61]

There is no evidence that Wake ever replied, though it is unlikely SOS women were sympathetic when she subsequently lost the election.

* * *

Fighting to save their sons was not a hobby for SOS women and, as this chapter has shown, their commitment often came at a personal cost. SOS women encountered hostility from neighbours, 'friends', work colleagues, other mothers and even their own family members. On top of this, they worried about the effect of their activism on their spouses' jobs, and on their children. Surveillance and intimidation only added to this pressure. To be sure, SOS women were not the only anti-war activists who experienced hostility during this period; however, there was a gendered dimension to much of the criticism aimed at them that reflected deeper fears about the changing social status of women. They were also easier targets for ridicule. Women coped with this in different ways, and some were more affected than others. Jean McLean, for example, was adamant that the support she received far outweighed any attacks. 'I have no regrets at all for that period of my life', she said. 'I feel that the friends I made then made up for any I might have lost, and the ones I lost weren't people I needed in my life anyway.'[62] SOS groups were close-knit units, and the women provided strong support for each other, but their greatest weapon proved to be their sense of purpose and deep-felt belief that what they were doing was 'the right thing'. Recalling the hostility her mother faced at this time, Joyce Golgerth's daughter said: 'It was disturbing for her but she was very focused in her belief and the fact that she felt that this was the right thing to be doing'.[63] Indeed the women's evident sincerity along with their respectable public image formed protective armour that even their most determined opponents found difficult to penetrate. Yet, as we will see, the impact of their activism did affect many long after their involvement in SOS ended.

Part 3

Keeping up Appearances, 1970s

Chapter 9

MORATORIUMS, CHAIN GANGS AND 'FALSIES'

> I will not sit idly by while young men are being gaoled because they refuse to kill ... I will defy the law as long as it conflicts with my conscience.
>
> *Flo Garber*[1]

The Wollongong women's 'chain gang protest' at Parliament House in June 1970 was evidence of just how far the movement – and its tactics – had changed and evolved since 1965. The 1970s heralded a new phase of direct action and civil disobedience during which Save Our Sons (SOS) women worked closely with other like-minded groups. They were involved with the moratorium movement in both leadership and 'backroom' positions; they actively incited youths to defy the *National Service Act*; and they assisted those who did by paying bails and fines, and helping to establish an 'underground' movement to hide and move them between a series of safe houses. Moreover, they became part of a vocal, radicalised mass movement – sometimes acting as a moderating force, at other times playing a lead role in directly challenging authorities.

Australia was also changing. The 1970s would witness an extraordinary era of social reform and the emergence of new social movements that would challenge fundamental ideas about postwar Australian society, including the role of women at work, home and in public life. Women's issues would be prominent in the 1972 election thanks in large part to the efforts of the newly formed Women's Electoral Lobby (WEL), which surveyed candidates on a range of issues of concern to women, including contraception, abortion, child care and equality.[2] Young women fed up with their treatment in mixed anti-war groups would also start linking their fight for equality to the political situation in Vietnam, marching under their own banners at demonstrations, while the Women's Abortion Action Campaign would stage noisy street marches and graphic demonstrations in what historian Marilyn Lake has described as a 'revolt against domesticity'.[3] For a movement with its roots firmly planted in the maternal peace rhetoric of the past, SOS did not fit easily into this narrative, then or since. But maternal imagery would still prove electorally potent during this period, especially when it came to leveraging the jailing of SOS women in 1971, now recognised as a pivotal moment in the anti-war movement.

While individual SOS women no doubt shared many or all of the concerns of WEL (and indeed some did later join the women's movement), collectively the movement, as it had done since its conception, stuck to its own race during this period, blinkered to all else but achieving its primary goal: the abolition of conscription. As such, SOS newsletters provide only glimpses of the parallel rise of second-wave feminism, and of other fights for lesbian and gay rights, Aboriginal land rights or environmental protections, which also emerged during this period. That is not altogether surprising; SOS was, after all, only active for a couple of years at the start of this tumultuous decade.

And they were busy years, as the next three chapters will show. They were also preoccupied with their own challenges. As the new decade dawned, behind the scenes, some SOS groups were battling for their own survival, under constant pressure to raise funds and to attract new members. Some would end up falling just short of the finishing line.

* * *

SOS began the new decade optimistically, dubbing 1970 the 'end the war year'. Sydney's first meeting was 'well-attended and enthusiastic', its leaders insisting there were many positive signs that victory was within reach.[4] The government's defence of conscription had changed, they argued. The public was no longer being 'battered by jingoistic statements' about the necessity of conscription for the nation's defence and even the party faithful were starting to openly question the policy.[5] At their annual convention, the Young Liberals, for example, had ignored a 'spirited defence' of conscription by Defence Minister Malcolm Fraser and voted instead for it to be 'rapidly' phased out.[6] The SOS women were also buoyed by plans for the upcoming moratorium that promised the widest participation in anti-war activities to date. But, as Melbourne's committee reminded supporters, the situation remained urgent: 'Remember when you feel weary of working for peace, that Australia is still involved to the hilt in killing Vietnamese people'.[7]

The SOS women continued to hold their usual vigils and to counsel young men, but most of their efforts during the first months of 1970 were devoted to the May moratorium. The idea for a nationwide action had first been mooted by the Victorian branch of the Committee for International Co-operation and Disarmament (CICD) at a national meeting held in Canberra in November 1969. It was attended by representatives from anti-war groups in NSW, Victoria, SA, NSW, Queensland and the ACT, who subsequently formed the Vietnam Moratorium Campaign (VMC).[8] Based on a similar movement in the United States, the VMC was a broad coalition of anti-war and anti-conscription groups, academics, trade unions, church groups and radical clergymen, and quickly established local committees in capital cities, suburbs and regional towns. Its aims were two-fold: the withdrawal of Australian troops from Vietnam and the repeal of the *National Service Act*. To these ends, VMC organised three moratoriums. The first, and largest, was held in May 1970, followed by two smaller actions in September 1970 and June 1971. SOS took part in all of them.

SOS was a sponsoring organisation of the VMC and its members were heavily involved in both leadership and back-room activities. A number of SOS women also became individual sponsors and joined local committees, helping to organise activities in their own suburbs and towns. In Melbourne, Jean McLean was elected joint deputy chair of the VMC committee under Jim Cairns. Joan Coxsedge, wearing 'two hats', represented both the Australian Labor Party (ALP) and SOS on the committee, with Jo Maclaine-Cross also serving on a sub-committee. Other Victoria SOS women, including Dorothy Dalton and Dorothy Gibson, were listed as contacts for the moratorium in their areas. In NSW, Ella Outhred represented SOS on the Sydney VMC secretariat while Edna Cullen chaired the Newcastle Moratorium Committee. Flo Garber and Edna Gudgeon were among several SOS women who joined Wollongong's committee.[9] Joan Davies and Marion Henderson were involved in the moratorium activities in Perth with several SOS members also providing 'loyal support' in Adelaide.[10]

The planned week-long program concluded on Mother's Day, making SOS's involvement particularly potent. Sydney SOS produced a special leaflet, titled 'Mothers in Mourning' using two black-and-white drawings donated by political cartoonist Bruce Petty that depicted an Australian mother and conscript son alongside a Vietnamese mother and child. The leaflet, which also included an anti-Vietnam poem, relied heavily on maternal rhetoric, and proved to be one of SOS's most popular.[11] In South Australia, Petty's illustrations were also used in a joint Women's International League for Peace and Freedom/SOS newspaper advertisement that urged women to take part in the moratorium.[12] The Victorian SOS women produced a special Mother's Day card that supporters were asked to sign and send to the prime minister and contributed to the printing and distribution of a million broadsheets explaining the background of the war.[13] Not everyone appreciated SOS's efforts. Some of the Sydney leaflets were returned bearing abusive messages, accusing the movement of spreading propaganda. 'I spent World War II in the RAAF to help keep this country safe for bitches like you', wrote one anonymous respondent. 'It was a mistake – we should have let the Japs loose at you and your kind.'[14]

While there was much enthusiasm for the moratorium, SOS women also hinted at the underlying tensions and 'difficulties' between the various representatives involved in the VMC. Sydney SOS's newsletter alluded to 'differences about dates and procedures' that had resulted in delays in finalising the program.[15] In private correspondence, SOS members in Sydney and Wollongong also expressed mutual frustration over the organisation of moratorium activities in their respective cities. 'This is off the record but it seems to me that the moratorium here is taking a long time to get off the ground', confided Sydney's secretary Adele Pert. 'But I hope it picks up. It is very necessary to make it a success.'[16] In Adelaide, there were concerns expressed about the 'worrying' language of some of the student members.[17] There was also frustration in Melbourne. Joan Coxsedge later described the Victorian committee as 'a motley crew of warring factions', made up of 'a wide range of ages and opinions from "old left" working-class communists to "new left" university types, including a swathe of religiosos, and everything in between'.[18] At meetings, some student members 'spoke frequently and strongly', arguing that the major objective of the moratorium should be the smashing of US imperialism.[19] In stark contrast to the well-organised SOS meetings, VMC gatherings would go on 'for hours and hours while people would argue over one word for a slogan'. Coxsedge recalled: 'It would drive you demented … to get agreement was pretty amazing'.[20]

Veteran peace campaigner and SOS foundation member Dorothy Gibson was instrumental in the formation of a local VMC committee in her suburb where she observed with concern the clashes between the 'old' campaigners and the younger members.[21] While relatively small, the Oakleigh Moratorium Committee included a number of 'active young people' with 'ultra-left views' who had clear differences on what the aims of the peace movement should be and on the tactics it should employ. Some of them believed that Jim Cairns, the CICD, and the Communist party were 'holding the movement back', while old time peace campaigners, like Dorothy and her husband Ralph, were concerned that the radical youth wanted to turn the anti-war movement into a revolutionary party that 'ran counter to all our ideas'. While diplomatic, Gibson made it clear she would not be silenced. 'We have much to learn from the youth', she advised at the time. 'But that does not mean that we trail behind … First, listen and understand what they are driving at. Support what's good. Challenge and discuss what's not.'[22]

Organisers had more to worry about than internal politics. In the lead-up to the May moratorium, public officials ran a fear campaign, warning it would result in 'blood in the streets'.[23] Some of these fears were real, especially after the violent events in the US on 4 May where the National Guard opened fire on an anti-Vietnam protest at Kent State University killing four students and wounding several others. Others were concocted, designed to discredit organisers and discourage 'ordinary' Australians from taking part. The prime minister, John Gorton, and the Victorian premier, Sir Henry Bolte, both 'fiercely attacked' the moratorium with Gorton accusing Jim Cairns of inciting anarchy and of forming 'an alliance with the Communist Party'.[24] However, it was Minister for Labour and National Service Billy Snedden's description of organisers as 'political bikies pack-raping democracy' that SOS women found particularly offensive.[25] In response, one Victorian SOS woman booked an appointment with her hairdresser for the morning of the march and 'wore my new patent shoes which wore a blister on my left heel as big as a ten cent piece'. She recalled: 'It seemed important to look like an ordinary middle-class housewife demonstrating agreement with the long-hairs, hippies, yippies, students and whatever else the Liberals choose to call those who do not agree with them'.[26] If the nation was in the midst of a 'revolt against domesticity', clearly this proud housewife was unaware of it. Irene Miller, who usually protested alongside her children, decided to leave her youngest at home 'because of the talk of violence'.[27] Some intimidation was more direct. The evening before the moratorium, Jean McLean was visited at her home by three plain-clothed policemen who asked her to call off the 'irresponsible' moratorium. She told them it was impossible, reiterating that organisers did not want violence. 'How do you call off something you've spent five months organising?' she asked.[28]

On the morning of the march, McLean recalled that organisers were 'pretty anxious', unsure how many people would actually heed the call to 'occupy the streets'.[29] They were euphoric when an estimated 200,000 people turned out nationwide, including an estimated 100,000 in Melbourne, twice the number predicted by Cairns. 'We felt terribly excited and very pleased and vindicated', McLean said. 'It was an incredible feeling because we believed that what we were doing was right.'[30] She said many police officers were 'very sympathetic and friendly' during the march. 'Some had moratorium badges under their lapels which they flashed furtively, with a smile.'[31] The only exception was Adelaide where a Radical Alliance demonstration associated with the moratorium was 'attacked' by a group of soldiers on leave from Woodside Barracks. Five soldiers were arrested. The local VMC committee believed the attack was premeditated.[32] Nevertheless, the SOS committee in Adelaide reported that the moratorium had, overall, gone 'extremely well', attracting a lot of new interest.[33] For Sydney SOS women, the highlight was a 20,000-strong rally outside the town hall where their vice president Alma Scaysbrook, mother of five boys, delivered 'a magnificent speech' on 'the evil force' of conscription and the immorality of Australia's involvement in Vietnam.[34] Scaysbrook's passionate entreaty reportedly 'made every member present very proud'.[35]

While the marches and rallies in the capital cities were the most high-profile events, there were moratorium activities throughout the week, including folk concerts, theatre productions, church services and smaller rallies in suburban and regional areas. The day after the occupation of Melbourne's streets, the *Age* reported 'the moratorium came to the housewives' with demonstrators, including SOS, covering every main shopping centre in the metropolitan area.[36] In Newcastle,

SOS women handed out pamphlets to church-goers attending Mother's Day services.[37] While the moratorium did not succeed in achieving its aims, its size and the diversity was immensely gratifying for the SOS movement. Sydney SOS leaders declared it 'an overwhelming success', arguing 'every Australian in some way was made to think'.[38] Scaysbrook saw it as 'evidence that the nation's conscience [was] at least stirring'.[39]

SOS was just one organisation involved in the moratorium, but members believed their role was significant, even if their contributions were not always recognised, even by other members of the VMC. 'It has taken several years to build up the present strong opposition to conscription … but as one of the first groups formed for this purpose, SOS can take a fair share of the credit for the change in attitudes of a large number of Australians', Adele Pert told Sydney's annual general meeting the following month.[40] Joan Coxsedge said representation on the Victorian committee, including McLean's election as Cairns' deputy, was certainly 'recognition that we did play a very important role, without a doubt', not just in backroom positions but in leadership roles.[41] Cairns' biographer Paul Ormonde supported this view, arguing that 'contrary to popular opinion, Cairns played little part in getting the numbers into the streets'. Cairns may have had the chairmanship 'thrust' upon him, but Ormonde argued that 'the main drive' came from his three deputies – McLean, along with Sam Goldbloom and John Lloyd, both from CICD.[42] Asked in 1998 what his particular contribution to the moratorium had been, Cairns himself observed: 'I often wonder if it was anything at all. You see even in the end, in that part, I was not an organiser. I have never been an organiser. I have never organised more than one person in all my life. I have been a writer and a talker. That is all'.[43] McLean frequently had to step in for Cairns and speak on his behalf at events. 'People would ask Jim Cairns to speak at a meeting but he always promised everybody and then of course he couldn't go so I'd get a phone call, "Jean, could you go?"' she recalled. 'They'd all be there to hear Jim and I'd go out and say, "Terribly sorry, I have just had a call from Dr Cairns ..." That happened quite a bit, it was a bit nerve-wracking.' However, McLean said some of the male members of the VMC were reluctant to share the limelight. 'Sam Goldbloom, for instance, bless his heart, he sort of expected you to do all the work and then he was leading the march, he'd push you out of the way, he was going to be in the front ... it did get a bit better but at the first moratorium he refused to even allow me in the front row.'[44] Some of the female students later complained about male student leaders in the anti-war movement expecting them to be the 'shitworkers', doing the admin work and making the tea.[45] However, McLean said she had been too busy to dwell on what was a fairly normal state of affairs in those days. 'I didn't spend a lot of time feeling we were being ignored or we did all the work and nobody cared', she said. 'I suppose I just thought, "That is typical of those bastards".'[46]

* * *

In the immediate aftermath of the first moratorium, Jim Cairns warned protestors against future acts of 'non-compliance and obstruction', such as 'sitting in' government offices, filling in false national service registration cards or blocking traffic, arguing such tactics were unlikely to change the government's mind but very likely to turn people 'against us'.[47] His message did not get through to Wollongong SOS president, Flo Garber, who, just weeks after the first moratorium, led the so-called 'chain gang protest' in Canberra. 'I will not sit idly by while young men are being gaoled because they refuse to kill', she declared. 'I advocate and practice non-violent civil disobedience as a method of causing people to know the perils to which this world is exposed.'[48]

The trigger for the Canberra protest was the arrest in early June of local draft resister Louis Christofides for failure to pay fines of $102 imposed for offences against the *National Services Act*. According to the Australian Security Intelligence Organisation (ASIO), members of the Wollongong SOS and the South Coast Citizens Against Conscription (SCCAC) subsequently called a meeting in the boardroom of the trade union centre to discuss what action to take. It was here that Garber first mooted an SOS 'sit-in' in Canberra, telling the meeting 'she would have to be removed forcibly as she would not be moving otherwise'. A SOS 'sit-in' at the local Commonwealth offices followed by a demonstration outside was also proposed for the week before the Canberra trip. According to ASIO's source, it was decided that if the Commonwealth buildings were closed, then the demonstrators would lie down across the exits to prevent the staff from leaving at closing time and so that the Commonwealth police would have to remove them.[49] Despite being forewarned, ASIO apparently did nothing to prevent the Canberra demonstration going ahead. Stan Woodbury, secretary of the Combined Waterfront Group of Unions, later told a local newspaper that he was one of three men who drove the 12 women from Wollongong for the carefully planned protest.[50] To ensure maximum publicity, the group went via the local Australian Broadcasting Corporation (ABC) offices, tipping off journalists about its intentions.

Victoria's SOS committee also ignored Cairns' directive and continued to engage in acts of civil disobedience. In July 1970, seven SOS mothers were arrested after a sit-in at the offices of the Department of Labour and National Service. Hosting 'fill in a falsie' parties were also popular during this period. The idea was to obtain and fill out as many national service registration forms as possible using false names in order to 'gum up the system'. 'We used to go along to post offices and take great supplies of registration papers', Dorothy Dalton said. 'A group of people would then get together, have a few drinks and fill them in. Clifton Pugh's wombat's marble was once pulled out of the barrel, people's cats were called up, and a few Liberal politicians.'[51] The SOS women made no secret of what they were doing, advertising the campaign in its newsletter and distributing detailed instructions on how to fill out forms in order to escape detection. In May 1970, Melbourne's newsletter urged supporters to help make this 'the largest registration on record … think of your friends and register them too'.[52] The women even invited the media to cover their 'law-breaking'. At one 'party' at McLean's home, two television news crews filmed as partygoers sat around filling out forms.[53] A polite return letter to Irene Miller from the Department of Labour and National Service showed how time consuming such tactics could be for officials. Addressed to Mr Miller, it drew attention to several incomplete questions on the original form, and included a new form with a reply paid envelope 'for your convenience'.[54] While it is impossible to know how effective the campaign was in slowing the wheels of bureaucracy, the SOS committee claimed that in one registration period in Victoria alone, 9500 'falsies' had been submitted. As a result, the Department was forced 'to spend a considerable amount of time and money trying to ferret out all the old age pensioners, dogs, cats and assorted menagerie from their intended victims'.[55] On another occasion, the Victorian SOS committee urged mothers to protest by not filling out the Census form, an offence that carried a $20 fine.[56] It is not known how many, if any, heeded the call.

Moratoriums, Chain Gangs and 'Falsies'

SOS newsletters generally became more militant in tone after the May moratorium, making some of the movement's more conservative members uneasy. In June 1970, Victoria SOS's newsletter welcomed the formation of the Draft Resisters Movement observing that 'the true heroes of this war are the young men who are determined not to become part of the killing machine that produces My Lai situations'.[57] The same edition focused on atrocities allegedly committed in Vietnam by US and Australian soldiers and declared that SOS's duty now was 'to make the public realise that Vietnam is one big "My Lai" and we are party to every slit gut and rape that the US perpetuates'.[58] One supporter took issue with such vivid imagery, wondering if a man might have written it ('it couldn't ever have been written by a woman could it?') and suggested the author should meet his readers, 'then he may discover how repugnant his words are'.[59] Joan Coxsedge suspects she was probably the author. 'It sounds a bit like me doesn't it?' she said in a 2014 interview. 'You did upset the niceties ... there was that element, "keep yourself nice, Mrs Bouquet".'[60]

Sydney SOS's newsletters also became more strident, with articles mirroring the imperialistic language of the student protest movement in stark contrast to the 'gentler' language of earlier editions. In September 1970, the newsletter drew readers' attention to a recent manslaughter case where a 23-year-old soldier had been found guilty of strangling a 30-year-old mother with his bare hands. The presiding judge had noted that the method of killing was one which the soldier had been 'encouraged to learn' in the course of his military training. For SOS, this was an example of 'the brutalising effect of military training' that underlined the need to 'further strengthen our efforts to oppose this apparently people-hating government responsible for such a course of human demoralisation'.[61]

In September 1970, the second moratorium was held. Smaller than the May event, it was marred by violence in Sydney and Adelaide. The largest rally in Melbourne, which attracted about 70,000 people, was mostly peaceful despite the arrest of four people. In Sydney, however, 200 people were arrested after clashes with police, while in Adelaide, Premier Don Dunstan ordered a Royal Commission to seek the cause of violence that resulted in 130 arrests.[62] The SA SOS group gave 'loyal support' to the moratorium with one of its members Sadie Pritchard providing a statement to the Royal Commission in support of those arrested. 'The SOS, in general, has remained actively involved with the VMC and is proud of the fact that in doing so it is supporting the vanguard of the peace movement and supporting young people who are directly affected by conscription and the war in Vietnam', Adelaide's secretary Audrey Potticary reported.[63]

Members of Sydney SOS, who were eyewitnesses to the violence in that city, were outraged by police tactics, declaring Australia had moved 'a step closer to becoming a police state'.[64] Sydney's October newsletter recognised that 'the confidence in our beliefs is being severely tested' but warned 'we must stand for our beliefs or yield to pressure and become servants of a despotic state'.[65] When the Returned and Services League (RSL) subsequently demanded that the government organise a pro-Vietnam march in response to the moratoriums and 'stamp out subversive literature', SOS publicly accused the veterans' group of being 'tyrannical' and 'intolerant'.[66] Some long-time SOS supporters, however, were dismayed by tactics adopted by protesters with whom SOS was now working closely. Lilli Heyde, of Double Bay, wrote that she had been 'to every demonstration I can remember' but was 'angry and disappointed' by the organisation of the moratorium. Specifically, she believed organisers had played into the government's hands by their 'childish' refusal to follow the route proscribed by the police. 'A bit more pragmatism would have frustrated (Premier) Askin's obvious intention – which everybody now so cleverly spells out – that he did NOT want a peaceful demonstration', she wrote.[67] She was also furious that flags supporting the Viet Cong had been carried. 'If we call it a peace march, we cannot allow flags saying "Victory to the NLF"', she wrote. 'Do we want more people on our side? Then we must be seen to be peaceful ... we may scream police brutality; no one will believe us ... we put ourselves legalistically in the wrong and have harmed our cause, I believe.'[68] It is not known how SOS leaders responded or how common Heyde's concerns were among supporters.

* * *

Despite the excitement over the moratoriums, 1970 ended in frustration. The war was not over and there were new signs that the government was cracking down not just on draft resisters but on those who incited them to disobey the *National Service Act*.[69] There were also internal pressures with leaders in Sydney, Adelaide and Newcastle lamenting the lack of 'active' members while struggling to raise funds. At Sydney's first meeting in 1971, there was the disappointing confirmation that the Newcastle group had folded. While Melbourne was never short of active members, its committee was constantly looking for new ways to raise funds to pay the soaring costs of fines, bails and legal fees. In March, the federal government announced a further withdrawal of Australian troops from Vietnam, but SOS took no comfort from this, pointing out that 6000 soldiers were still there, and that conscription was continuing.

Chapter 10

THE FAIRLEA FIVE AND THE 'UNDERGROUND'

> The organisation of the underground wouldn't have worked without a group like Save Our Sons ...
>
> Sue McCulloch, Draft Resisters' Union[1]

The following year, 1971, would prove to be a pivotal year for the anti-war movement – and Save Our Sons (SOS). The Victorian women vowed to 'unite behind the courageous young men' who were refusing to be conscripted. 'We cannot continue to lamely "Oppose Conscription"', the February newsletter warned. 'The time has come for a more positive, more militant line'.[2] In February, SOS women joined the Draft Resisters' Union (DRU) at the Melbourne GPO where, in blatant violation of the *Crimes Act*, they encouraged young men not to register. The following month, ten SOS women dressed in death masks and black robes stuck posters that read 'Get out of Laos, get out of Cambodia' on the windows of the US Consulate, the American Australian Club and the Pan Am building. They then entered the bar of the Southern Cross Hotel and handed out leaflets to visitors questioning the role of the US oil interests. When asked to leave, they picketed outside. However, response to the demonstration was disappointing. According to Irene Miller most passers-by just ignored the group.[3]

In April, SOS was back in the national headlines when the 'astonishing' news broke that five Melbourne mothers had been jailed for 14 days. The women – Jean McLean, Joan Coxsedge, Irene Miller, Chris Cathie and Jo Maclaine-Cross – had been arrested and charged with wilful trespass in February, following a 'sit-in' in the lift lobby outside the 10th floor office of the Department of Labour and National Service in Flinders Street. It was the second time the women had staged a sit-in on the premises. The first time, they had escaped penalty on 'a technicality' after their solicitor successfully argued that the person who had ordered them to leave had not had the proper authority. A subsequent amendment to the Victorian *Summary Offences Act* ensured the women would not escape punishment twice. At the second 'sit-in', the women directly approached young men arriving to lodge their registration forms, urging them 'to think again'. Despite their arrests, the women reported back that it had been 'an extremely valuable exercise'.

> None of the young men wanted to go to Vietnam, nor did they support the war but they just did not know what action to take. When the alternatives were explained to them, they were anxious to take a Conscientious Objectors stand ... we were arrested because we were being so effective.[4]

Joan Coxsedge said that after 'getting off' the first time, the women expected nothing more than a fine when they faced court again.[5] The magistrate, however, had other ideas, sentencing them to 14 days in the Fairlea women's prison. McLean remembered that 'as the last words of the sentence were uttered, the magistrate fled from the court as though he wore running shoes'.[6] Angry supporters of the women shouted insults in his wake.[7] Chris Cathie said the sentence caught all of them unawares. 'We were all going away for Easter to have a rest from the damn campaign', she recalled.[8] Hasty arrangements had to be made for cars to be collected, husbands to be informed and children cared for while the women were 'away'. Coxsedge remembers worrying that her husband would not be able to find where she had hidden the children's Easter eggs.[9] Shocked as they were, the women were savvy enough to understand that the sentence was 'a show of strength by the Government and that our answer could only be to accept our sentences and not to appeal'.[10]

The women's case was the last to be heard on the Thursday before Easter, deliberately timed, they believed, to minimise publicity given there would be no newspapers printed on Good Friday. But a lone Australian Broadcasting Corporation (ABC) radio court reporter ensured the case became the top news story for that evening's bulletin. One of Irene Miller's sons, Bill, then 16, was on his way with friends to a weekend sailing regatta when he heard the news on the car radio. 'It was a shock that (the court) had gone over the top … it was just trespass and not too many people are jailed for that', he recalled.[11] As a teenager, however, he was not overly worried about his mother; there were even some advantages. 'I remember telling my friend's older brothers, "You'd better give me a beer because my mother's in prison"', he said.

Others were shocked and outraged. Many supporters who heard the news on Thursday night cancelled their holidays and returned to Melbourne to take part in demonstrations outside the prison. A press release distributed on Good Friday noted it was 'rather ironic that on the day when the Christian World still mourns the crucifixion of a "man of peace" these women should be spending their first day behind jail for "wilful trespass" in the cause of peace'.[12] On Easter Saturday, 350 people carrying banners held a protest rally outside the prison gates where Australian Labor Party (ALP) and union officials lined up to express their horror that 'respectable married women' had been jailed for taking part in a peaceful demonstration.[13] Jim Cairns told demonstrators it was the first time that trespass had been made a criminal offence and further proof that the civil rights of Australians were being steadily eroded.[14] On Easter Sunday, almost 500 people attended a joint church service outside the prison presided over by clergy from Catholic, Anglican and Methodist churches.[15] After the service, protesters marched to the City Square to begin a vigil that continued until the women were released. Industrial action brought Melbourne's waterfront to a virtual standstill and copy-cat protests were held at the national service offices when they reopened after the Easter break.[16]

Protests were not limited to Melbourne. SOS groups in Wollongong, Adelaide and Sydney protested to Victorian and federal politicians and sent telegrams of support to the 'Fairlea Five'. On Easter Monday, SOS members demonstrated at the Adelaide Railway Station.[17] The following Thursday, Sydney members protested outside the state office buildings and distributed leaflets 'informing citizens of Sydney about repressive measures increasingly being forced upon the individual'.[18] At its conclusion, five members delivered a letter to the Premier, Robert Askin, stating 'our opposition to the ever mounting erosion of civil liberties'.[19]

The women's jailing rapidly turned into a public relations disaster for both the Victorian and federal governments. The media, delighted to have a story over the normally quiet Easter period, initially emphasised the fact that the women were all members of the ALP. Later reports downplayed this angle, highlighting instead that the women had 25 children between them who would be without their mothers at Easter. Maternal rhetoric may have been viewed as outdated in other quarters, but stories on motherhood apparently still sold papers. Daily reports portrayed the women as a group of sincere, ordinary mothers jailed for expressing their concerns about conscription.[20] Photographs tugged at the nation's collective heartstrings, showing the women's young children protesting outside of the jail, dwarfed by placards that read 'Our Mother Is A Political Prisoner'.[21] Other articles focused, to Bill Miller's annoyance, on how husbands and children were surviving on the domestic front while the women were away.[22] 'Though the papers made out it was "shock, horror, who was going to cook dinner?" the fact was my father always did breakfast and stuff and we all had our chores to do … so it wasn't quite like it was portrayed', he said.[23] The coverage also had a political edge. An editorial in the *Australian* accused the government of overreacting to threats of 'law and order'. 'These women are non-violent political activists. They are not criminals', it stated. 'Their offences have earned them a much too severe penalty. The public counter-reaction to the government's draconian attempts to impose law and order is creating wider disruption.'[24]

The women, themselves, had little knowledge of what was occurring outside the prison. Housed together in a dormitory of 19 beds, they were allotted daily jobs and not allowed to read newspapers or anything with 'political content'. Telegrams and letters were also withheld until their release although Irene Miller's husband managed to smuggle in some newspaper articles by sticking them inside the pages of old magazines.[25] On Easter Sunday, demonstrators organised high-powered amplifiers so that the women inside could hear the speeches. Instead, the women were awoken at 6am by the prison loudspeaker system blasting music. Chris Cathie said the aim had not only been to prevent the women hearing supporters outside but also to turn the other prisoners against them. Instead, she said, 'den mother' Jo Maclaine-Cross, who had experienced similar shows of authority during World War II, explained to the other prisoners that it was a ploy to upset them. It also gave the women an opportunity to talk about their aims. According to Cathie, everyone would probably have slept through the demonstration otherwise.[26]

The women were released on 18 April, three days early for 'good behaviour', describing their experience in prison as 'hell'.[27] Indeed in subsequent interviews, it became clear that the Bolte government had unwittingly given SOS another cause, as the women sought to draw attention to appalling conditions inside Fairlea.[28] To this end, they met with the Minister for Social Welfare, Ian Smith, presenting him with a list of suggestions to improve conditions at the prison. Smith, at the time, was looking for a new deputy governor for Fairlea and sarcastically suggested the women take the job, stating 'it would be a good thing for them to do something constructive instead of sitting around offices wasting people's time'.[29] Coxsedge promptly applied for the position but Smith, not surprisingly, later reneged on his offer.[30]

The following month, SOS members were heartened by a poll showing only 37 per cent of Australians now supported the war and that 48 per cent wanted the war stopped and troops withdrawn.[31] Coxsedge believed the jailing of the Fairlea Five was a catalyst in galvanising public opinion, 'Public opinion was changing but that was icing on the cake', she said.[32] Jim Cairns also endorsed this view, describing the jailing as a turning point in the fight for public opinion.[33] It also boosted SOS's profile, positively reinforcing its image as a body of concerned mothers in contrast to the more radical elements of the anti-war movement. Moreover, it strengthened the relationship between SOS and other protest groups. 'On reflection that decision to stay in Fairlea and the continuous protest and vigil which hailed our incarceration brought a new militancy to the anti-conscription campaign', Jean McLean said in 1973. 'It strengthened our bond with resisters, jailed or threatened with jail.'[34] It also reinforced the rights of citizens to protest against government policy. The day after the women's release, Jim Cairns and his wife staged a protest in the same location but were not arrested.[35] During the next registration period, another anti-conscription group was even permitted to set up a table in the foyer of the national service department building to counsel young men. SOS women were among those who volunteered to take part. There were no arrests.

The Melbourne women were not the only SOS members jailed that year. In March, Wollongong's Flo Garber was arrested under the NSW *Summary Offences Act* while speaking against conscription outside Sydney's Phillip St Court. In July, after refusing to pay the $5 fine, Garber was arrested at her home and taken to Silverwater women's prison where she spent a night before being released the next day. She instructed her husband that under no circumstances was he to pay the fine. 'The non-compliers are going to gaol and I will go too', she told him.[36] Supporters held a late-night vigil outside the Wollongong office of the Department of Labour and National Service in protest and several Sydney SOS members were among those waiting outside the jail when Garber was released, congratulating her on 'her brave stand' and 'courageous spirit'.[37] The local paper reported the jailing would not stop Mrs Garber demonstrating against the war in the future. 'It's a matter of conscience', she said.[38] Unlike the Fairlea Five, however, Garber's jailing was mostly ignored by other state and national news outlets.[39]

* * *

The Fairlea Five and the 'Underground'

One of SOS's least publicised – but arguably one of its most significant contributions to the anti-war/anti-conscription movement – was its role in the formation and operation of an organised safe house network that became known as 'the underground'. Operating from late 1969 to December 1972, it involved SOS supporters, and others, helping to hide and move draft resisters between a series of 'safe houses' that stretched from Adelaide to Queensland. A few young men were even sent by boat to Tasmania and New Zealand. While it was the draft resisters themselves who attracted the media attention, it was the women working tirelessly behind the scenes that kept the operation going. According to Sue McCulloch, a university student and treasurer of the Draft Resisters' Union (DRU), SOS's organisation of the underground was vital. 'They organised all of that underground stuff', she said. 'Really, the organisation of the underground wouldn't have worked without a group like Save Our Sons because it wasn't just [financial] support it was actual organisation ... doing it cleverly so that one lot of people didn't know what the other lot was doing and things like that. There wasn't one person, I don't think, who knew everything.'[40]

In October 1970, the DRU's newspaper *Resist* announced that an underground had been established with support from SOS, the VMC and Catholic groups.[41] That same month, SOS women were signatories to a statement that pledged to provide 'sanctuary in the form of shelter, work and sustenance to all young men who courageously defy the *National Service Act*'.[42] According to McLean, the SOS committee had first devised a plan to conceal resisters in 1969 with a fund established specifically for this purpose to cover bail monies and other expenses. This claim is supported by a September 1969 security intercept in which McLean was recorded telling Tony Dalton that she had a lot of 'important contacts' who were willing to 'look after' draft resisters.[43]

The following year, the Australian Security Intelligence Organisation (ASIO) also reported that an ABC technician who had contacted McLean for 'advice on how to evade National Service' had been told 'that if things should get "too hot" she could arrange for him to stay clandestinely' at her sister's home.[44] In October 1969, news also broke of 'Wollongong's organised underground', which was blamed for hiding two army deserters.[45] The Gudgeons, who later supplied Jean McLean with wigs for Victorian draft resisters, were rumoured to be involved. The underground was remarkably successful. 'We had a rule that we didn't lose anyone when we agreed to find somewhere for them to stay', McLean said.[46]

Initially, however, there was little need for an underground with the government appearing reluctant to jail resisters and risk making martyrs of them. According to McLean, this meant that many men who refused call-up notices went for years without being summonsed. However, from mid-1971 the government began acting 'more vigorously' and the underground movement gathered pace. Resisters then faced a choice: to go to jail or go underground. McLean recalled there were different attitudes among resisters and others about 'the morality and the political effectiveness of the two paths of resistance'.[47] Both meant 'a gap' in a man's life. 'Each decision was a personal one, usually reached after much discussion amongst resisters and their supporters', McLean said. 'Often these discussions were deeply moving. On one occasion the choice was debated between the resister, his family, a priest, myself, and other activists. The resister finally chose the underground against family wishes.'[48]

In 1969, this choice was put to Brian Ross, a young farmer from East Gippsland. In a letter to McLean, he gave his reasons for not taking the underground option:

> I can see the value of your suggestions ... although in one way, I feel that I should accept your very good offer, I find it more consistent with what I have done in the past to go to court in Orbost ... it will show that it is not just radical students in the cities that think this way but people from other environments as well ... so this is what I intend doing. I am certainly not sure that I am doing the best thing and if I change my mind by the 29th I will let you know.[49]

Ross did not change his mind and was sentenced to two years' jail under the Commonwealth *Crimes Act*. He was released 11 months later after public pressure prompted a Supreme Court inquiry into his case that found that he was indeed a conscientious objector.[50] SOS groups campaigned strongly for his release, holding various events and producing a pamphlet that asked 'Why is Brian Ross in Jail?' McLean also wrote an article for a Melbourne newspaper after visiting Ross in prison, describing his daily routine and noting with concern his declining health.[51]

Another draft resister, Bob Scates, did take the underground option. In March 1972, he was arrested at his workplace and subsequently bailed. Victorian State Opposition Leader and lawyer Clyde Holding offered to defend Scates along with other draft resisters in a bid to seek an adjournment of the case until after the federal election. Scates later said he had been persuaded to take part in the test case until he met with members of SOS and the VMC and was convinced this course of action would be 'a mistake'.[52] He initially stayed with McLean's family but had to be moved on quickly because he insisted on going out in a car that was well-recognised.

Most of those who offered safe houses were known to the SOS leaders. One of McLean's neighbours approached her on the beach and gave her a key to his house. The draft resister housed there would walk down two doors to have dinner with McLean's family. Others were sent to factories in Eden on the NSW south coast or whisked by boats to other locations interstate. Plans to send draft resisters further afield were thwarted because it turned out to be too difficult to secure false passports. According to McLean, shelter was provided by people who 'for one reason or another' did not want to make their opposition to the war public. 'They were either university academics or business people working for large firms or multinationals who felt that it could jeopardise their jobs if they came out publicly', she said. 'But they supported us privately and they'd give us money, buy raffle tickets, or whatever and were also willing to host people for a limited amount of time.'[53] Despite her high profile, Joan Coxsedge also hosted about half a dozen young men at different times.[54] According to McLean there was 'a particularly good Victoria–NSW coastal underground'. In November 1971, the *Age* reported that 'a highly organised underground' was protecting six draft resisters, three in Melbourne, two in NSW and one in Adelaide.[55] Sometimes there were unforeseen consequences. McLean said one student, who was sent to Eden on the NSW coast where he worked under an assumed name on scallop boats, never returned to city life. 'He decided that was a much better lifestyle than architecture and stayed there after it was all over.'[56]

The young men were moved between houses every two to three weeks so as not to inconvenience the hosts or rouse the suspicions of neighbours. Sometimes they had to be moved more frequently. 'I had a few instances of being telephoned at one or two o'clock in the morning by young men saying, "there are people hanging around outside, I'm getting nervous, come and get me"', she recalled. 'So I used to do some funny drives, leaving my two small children home while I went and moved them. Of course, I had a husband looking after them.'[57]

But those being hidden did not always make it easy. After he lost his camera, one draft resister in hiding rang the police to report it stolen. Upon realising his mistake, he alerted McLean and was swiftly moved to another location. On another occasion, McLean was asked to move a draft resister's car which had been parked in a street for too long and risked being identified. 'My task was to drive up to park my car and then move the car belonging to him ... which I did', she recalled. 'Then the phone call came, "why haven't you picked up the car?" Turned out I had taken the wrong car. So, I then had to take the first one back but when I went back there was no parking spot, so I had to drive around and wait before putting it back in the original space.'[58]

The draft resisters did not just 'hide', they led police on highly publicised 'cat and mouse' chases, appearing in the media and at anti-war events, then 'escaping' before police arrived. 'We would have people on the run and popping up from time to time to keep the pressure on police', recalled draft resister Tony Dalton, whose mother, Dorothy, was a SOS member. 'In this way, we discredited the Act and all its penalties.'[59] The Victoria SOS women choreographed many of these activities, including taking reporters covered in blankets in the back seat of cars to meet draft resisters at safe houses. Sometimes the men were dressed in women's clothes and wigs to disguise their appearance. Discretion was stressed. Sydney SOS leaders issued a 'special warning' to members and friends to be 'on their guard if asked, particularly on the telephone, about the movements and addresses of conscientious objectors, non-compliers, etc.' as 'a subterfuge' had recently been employed by authorities to gain information on some non-compliers.[60]

However, many within the anti-war movement believed police were never serious in their efforts to find the young men. After declaring himself a draft resister, law student Mac Gudgeon, for example, spent six months in Sydney then started travelling around the country working quite openly on the wharves in Melbourne, Adelaide, and Port Kembla. He was never arrested, despite being sentenced to two months' jail in his absence.[61] While former Commonwealth policeman Peter O'Brien later confirmed that McLean and Coxsedge's homes and vehicles were under surveillance during this period, he stressed that catching draft resisters was just one small part of the force's duties.[62] McLean, however, believed police were simply outmanoeuvred. 'We had mobilised such a wide cross section of people spread over sprawling suburbia that their task was almost a hopeless one', she said.[63] Ceci Cairns argued that even if it were true that Commonwealth police did not try very hard to track down the men, it did not diminish what the women had done. 'We weren't actually saving boys from the hands of the police. That wasn't what we were doing. It was a political exercise to raise publicity for a cause and it was a highly sophisticated exercise.'[64] It was also expensive. As more bails were forfeited, fundraising became more urgent. In May 1972, Jean McLean and 'Friends of the Underground' organised a fundraising dinner after draft resisters Bob Scates and Bob Bissett forfeited $400 bail and $400 security each. 'There's more to come if the Draft Resistance movement is to survive', a flyer for the dinner warned. 'We must have money – money for bail, money for legal expenses and money to keep these young men alive and out of prison.'[65]

Ahead of the third moratorium in June 1971, the Victorian SOS launched a 'Hunt the Michael' campaign, a reference to draft resister Michael Hamel-Green who had recently joined the underground. Hamel-Green planned to make an appearance at the moratorium where he would defy the police to arrest him. Melbourne's newsletter informed its supporters that the moratorium organisers and SOS had 'agreed to give Michael and other resisters maximum support – including preventing any arrests'.[66] In the end, the moratorium was somewhat overshadowed by world events, including the deaths in space of three Russian Cosmonauts, and the controversial tour of the South African Rugby Union team, which attracted violent protests everywhere it was scheduled to play.[67] Marches in Melbourne, Sydney, Perth, Hobart and Adelaide attracted smaller crowds but were mostly peaceful except in Adelaide where there were 'wild scenes' that resulted in the arrest of 38 people. Violence also 'erupted briefly' in Brisbane where protesters tried to seize a 'Red Rats' placard from a 'uniformed Nazi'. In Melbourne, 20,000 marched to Parliament House where they were addressed by renowned American paediatrician and anti-war campaigner Dr Benjamin Spock and four 'underground' draft resisters. An 'orderly crowd' of 10,000 was reported in Sydney while, in Perth, newly elected Labor Premier John Tonkin led a march of about 5000.[68]

* * *

Yet despite all the activity, at the end of 1971 SOS women felt no closer to achieving their goals. They were not even cheered by the announcement in August that Australia, following the US lead, would bring most of its troops home by Christmas, and reduce conscription to 18 months. On the contrary, Sydney SOS leaders warned this was 'a deception ... of the worst order'. 'Many people are of the opinion that now, with the withdrawal of our troops from Vietnam and the reduction in the period of military training, that all is now well again', its newsletter stated. 'This, however, is purely a political manoeuvre to lull the apathetic into a false sense of security'.[69] The SOS women firmly believed that as long as conscription continued, it was highly probable that young men would be sent to other conflicts. Their fears were further heightened when the Minister for Labour and National Service, Phillip Lynch, argued that conscription was still 'essential in the national interest', filling 'a significant role in the provision of manpower for the armed forces of this country'.[70] Clearly, the fight was not yet over.

Chapter 11

THE FINAL PUSH

HOW MUCH LONGER
NEED WE PROTEST?

Sydney SOS[1]

At the beginning of 1972, there was still no end to conscription in sight and almost seven years of continuous protest activity, combined with two disappointing election results, were taking its toll on some Save Our Sons (SOS) groups. Members no long naïvely clung to the hope that education alone could change the wider public's view of conscription and the war. SOS Sydney noted after the withdrawal of Australian troops from Vietnam, 'the feeling of the public against conscription lost its urgency'.[2] Some of SOS's own supporters felt the same way, with renewed debate in Sydney and Adelaide over whether the time had come for SOS to roll up its banners or find a new direction. In Sydney, it was suggested the group change its name, but this was unanimously rejected in favour of refocusing on 'how can we stir the apathetic masses?'[3] However, the group did widen its agenda, lending its support to action for other causes, including women's liberation and Aboriginal land rights.

Sydney SOS was also facing financial pressures. It reduced its monthly newsletter to six publications a year and raised subscription fees, but this was countered by declining membership. In June, frustration boiled over in an editorial that demanded, in capital letters for emphasis, 'HOW MUCH LONGER NEED WE PROTEST?' It noted that SOS had held vigils at each of the four annual intakes for the past seven years. 'We have distributed thousands of leaflets and our placards have been seen by thousands more people. Could the next intake … be the last? We sincerely hope so.'[4] In Melbourne, there were similar appeals to the membership to 'keep the faith' amid warnings that sons, however young now, might one day be conscripted.[5] But attempts to keep the South Australian group going faltered. In June, its committee advised Sydney SOS that it had been put in 'caretaker mode'.[6] Another discussion about Sydney's future was also held at this time. It was decided to continue to be as active as possible for the rest of the year and to reconsider the matter after the election.[7] Wollongong, with its smaller membership base, likely had similar issues but by 1972 it was working in close association with South Coast Citizens Against Conscription (SCCAC). By contrast, the Victorian SOS committee remained steadfast, though the pressure to raise money continued.

These ongoing frustrations formed the backdrop to SOS's last full year of activity but there were also reasons to be optimistic. The focus was now on the December election with hopes high that Labor could finally win government under Gough Whitlam. There was pressure from Labor leaders, however, to play down anti-war protests, amid fears they could be a distraction for electors.[8] As before, SOS leaders refused to comply, confident that conscription would be the major issue of the election.[9] SOS women subsequently took part in a national anti-conscription campaign of 'public incitement' held in July. As part of this, Sydney SOS members helped distribute thousands of 'Don't Register' leaflets, in defiance of the *Crimes Act* but were disappointed when authorities took no action against them. Alma Scaysbrook and

Adele Pert noted it was the same leaflet handed out at a rally a week earlier when 13 men were arrested. 'We committed the same offence. All those at the rally did – thousands committed the same offence, yet only a few have been prosecuted', they said.[10]

In Melbourne, the SOS women were kept busy helping draft resisters evade police, but they were unable to keep one of their own from being jailed again. At 2pm on 18 October, Jean McLean was arrested at her home for refusing to pay fines imposed for handing out 'Don't Register' leaflets.[11] There was some disagreement on the committee about whether this was a useful tactic. Joan Coxsedge said she personally thought that McLean should have paid the fine.[12] This time, the sentence came as no surprise. Dorothy Dalton recalled that McLean invited a group of SOS women around to her home for a 'farewell lunch'. 'We had champagne, we had a lovely time and, at the arranged time, the police came for Jean … and we all stood up and waved her off', she said.[13] Later that night in Canberra, three Australian Labor Party (ALP) Senators spoke in defence of McLean's actions, calling on the Attorney-General to show leniency to a 'young mother of two' and 'woman of great principle'. ALP Senator Cyril Primmer stated that in his opinion 'there is no law under which it is justifiable to gaol a person of the moral character and fibre of Mrs McLean'.[14]

> Mrs McLean has been one of the few people responsible for drawing to the attention of the Australian people the horrors and futility of the Vietnam War. Quite frankly I believe that her action and similar action by other people has caused the Government to reconsider its Vietnam commitment and, consequently, possibly has saved at least 500 young Australian lives in that conflict.[15]

But the Attorney-General, Senator Ivor Greenwood, showed no sympathy, dismissing McLean as 'an acknowledged, prominent member of this notorious Victorian Labor Party' who had 'gone out of her way to defy the law'. Her decision to go to jail rather than pay the fine, he said, amounted to nothing more than 'a cheap political trick'.[16]

Ahead of the 1972 election, Sydney SOS decided once again to target swinging seats and urged supporters to 'vote and work for parties who are opposed to conscription', though it again stopped short of endorsing the ALP. While hopes were high of a change in government, previous disappointments meant nothing was taken for granted. 'Until the results of the election are known, we must obviously advise them to act on the assumption that the government will be returned to power', leaders warned.[17] The last draft intake before the election was held on 27 September. Despite the short notice, Sydney's newsletter reported 'our faithful members were at the gates shortly after 7.30 am, distributing leaflets to conscripts, their friends and families but also to people passing by'.[18] While the women did not know it at the time, this would be the last intake of conscripts during the Vietnam War.

The Victorian SOS again publicly supported the ALP. They were also closely involved in the unusual campaign of draft resister Barry Johnston, who was the endorsed Labor candidate for the federal seat of Hotham held by the Minister for Customs, Don Chipp. In February 1972, Johnston joined the underground after a warrant was issued for his arrest. The 22-year-old primary school teacher had already spent one week in Pentridge prison for failing to register and another for refusing to attend an army medical registration. He now faced an 18-month sentence for refusing to obey his call-up notice.[19] SOS women were among 30 supporters who attended court on the day he failed to appear. Led by McLean, the women waited until his name was called, then stood and began reading aloud from a typewritten statement. The magistrate ordered them all from the court and McLean was arrested. She was held in custody for two hours but was released after apologising to the court.[20]

Johnston conducted his campaign from the underground where Jean McLean took overall responsibility for his safekeeping. Though she is absent from media reports, according to McLean, she served, for all intents and purposes, as Johnston's 'right hand' during the campaign. When Johnston's election campaign was officially launched at the Moorabbin Town Hall in July 1971, 600 people, including five Commonwealth policemen, listened to a tape-recorded speech in which the candidate accused police of bungling his arrest and intimidating his family.[21] 'We would have an empty chair on the platform whenever he was supposed to appear because he couldn't', McLean recalled. 'I went in place of him to speak when he was asked to speak, and I would take letters from him and I'd read it to them. I'd say that he couldn't come because he was in the underground. I moved him around and did quite a bit to keep his campaign going.'[22] On one occasion, Johnston appeared on the Australian Broadcasting Corporation's (ABC) current affairs program *This Day Tonight* after 'someone' rang the studio and told them to send a crew to a Melbourne street corner. The crew were apparently then picked up in a car and taken to Johnston, but not before 'being driven around the city for some time'.[23] During the 10 months he was on the run, Johnston stayed in about 30 houses, sleeping during the day because police raids were usually conducted in the early hours of the morning. 'You never knew when the knock on the door would come', he said later.[24]

Whitlam was initially unhappy about Johnston's candidature, publicly complaining that it was a distraction from any serious discussion about conscription.[25] According to McLean, both Whitlam and Bob

Hawke came to her and 'demanded I get [Johnston] to resign … because we'd lose the election'. McLean fervently believed Johnston could win his seat and told the men they were 'wrong'. She said Whitlam also demanded that McLean cease making conscription an issue ahead of the election. 'Gough said, "Don't mention conscription any more", he said. "Wait until after we have won and we will fix it all up". I got an awful lot of that', she said.[26] Not to be intimidated, SOS continued to loudly, and rigorously, oppose conscription and to assist draft resisters. 'To those who suggest that it could hurt the ALP's chance of election, we would like to point out that the protest movement has enhanced the ALP prestige, it is ALP policy to oppose the war and end conscription', declared Melbourne's last newsletter before the election. 'We believe it is our duty and moral obligation to continue the struggle unabated.'[27]

In the end, Johnston ran a close second to Chipp, polling 21,796 votes to Chipp's 25,242.[28] McLean, who threw a huge party at her home on election night, said at one point during the evening it even looked like he might win. On the 30th anniversary of Whitlam's election in 2002, Johnston spoke to the *Age* about his experiences as a draft resister. On election day, he estimated there had been about 20 activists underground and six in prison, all of whom were released within a few days of the election. That night he went openly to McLean's party where he was the guest of honour, receiving cheers from the crowd of nearly 200 and fielding questions at an impromptu press conference.[29] 'We (draft evaders) were the first to benefit from the Whitlam government because on the night of the election the people who had gone underground came out', he said.[30] McLean's party has become part of Australian political legend, attended by a veritable 'who's who' of left-wing identities. When Whitlam died in October

2014, playwright David Williamson, who attended the party with his wife Kristin, recalled the excitement. 'When Billy McMahon conceded defeat at 11 o'clock, a roar of elation went up from the guests that wasn't equalled until Collingwood broke its premiership drought in 1990', he wrote.[31] Bob Scates, who spent election night in Pentridge, said visitors the next day regaled those inside with stories from the party.[32] 'It was an unbelievable feeling on that night, we were ecstatic', McLean later recalled.[33]

It is not known how Sydney SOS members spent election night but at their next meeting on 16 December, they indulged in a 'short celebration' where a toast was proposed 'to peace' and the end of conscription. 'It is with great joy and relief that we of the Save Our Sons movement received the results of the federal election', reported president Alma Scaysbrook. 'It has taken almost eight years of very hard work by this small band of dedicated women to help change public opinion.'[34] The women rejoiced that the new prime minster had acted quickly to honour his election promise to withdraw prosecutions under the *National Service Act*, release jailed draft resisters, and end the nation's commitment to Vietnam, but were concerned that conscription had not been officially abolished. Ella Outhred dampened the party mood by cautioning that Labor might not repeal national service as it could be deemed useful in an emergency: 'As long as this Act remains, any future government would do exactly the same as the Menzies government did in 1965', she said.[35]

Whitlam did not renege, taking immediate action to terminate conscription. It was officially abolished in June 1973 with the passing of the *National Service Termination Bill*.[36] After much debate, Sydney women voted that SOS should go into 'indefinite recess' in April 1973.[37] It is not known when the Wollongong group folded but, according to Melbourne's last newsletter, by August 1973 Victoria SOS was the only group remaining. It forged on for another four months to witness the official demise of the *National Service Act*, after which members also came to the conclusion that 'as an anti-conscription organisation our job is finished'.[38]

Chapter 12

ROLLING UP THE BANNERS

> At demonstrations the SOS women gave things a sense of gravity and solidity ... You always felt that their presence was a validation that you were on the side of decency.
>
> *Mac Gudgeon, draft resister*[1]

In the aftermath of the 1972 election, Sydney Save Our Sons' (SOS) last president Alma Scaysbrook reflected on the group's 'eight years of very hard work'. While there was satisfaction that conscription was set to be abolished, this was tempered by how long the campaign had taken, resulting in the unnecessary and 'reckless waste of Australian lives' and 'the terrible suffering of the Vietnamese'.[2] Nevertheless, Scaysbrook looked back with pride on the conduct of the 'close-knit group' of SOS women who, she said, had displayed 'integrity and faithfulness' in all their endeavours. 'It has been a wonderful enriching experience to have belonged to SOS', Scaysbrook concluded. 'We have all done our very best with dedication and zeal.'[3]

Five decades after the SOS founders first issued their 'distress call', the 'dedication and zeal' of those who answered it still stands out. Indeed, it is palpable in the array of correspondence, pamphlets, newsletters and oral testimonies gathered for this book. SOS supporters were among the first to protest publicly at a time when the vast majority of Australians supported their government's stand on national service and the Vietnam War – and they were among the last to roll up their banners and put away their placards, long after the moratorium crowds had returned home. During this time, supporters endured abuse, intimidation and, sometimes, personal hardship but they never deviated from their original aim – to end the conscription of young Australian men. 'I feel that the integrity and faithfulness of our close-knit group could serve as an inspiration to others', wrote Scaysbrook.[4]

But despite its schedule of constant, almost daily, activities over an eight year period, assessing the effectiveness – and legacy – of SOS's campaign is difficult. While conscription was eventually abolished and Australian troops were withdrawn from Vietnam, the degree of influence exercised by the anti-war movement over political and public attitudes is still contested today. Opinion polls from the period show the majority of Australians continued to be hostile towards the anti-war movement – even after the hugely popular moratorium campaigns of the 1970s.[5] Moreover, some, like Peter Edwards, continue to argue that while the anti-war movement 'claimed Australia's withdrawal as a victory for their cause ... their claims were exaggerated'.[6] While Prime Minister McMahon was 'obviously sensitive' to the unpopularity of the war by 1971–72, according to Edwards, Australia's eventual exit from Vietnam was in response to changes in the policy of the United States, not to domestic dissent.[7] Hence, it is difficult to draw any conclusion that SOS – as 'one small chip' in the mosaic of the anti-war movement – had a significant degree of direct influence on the federal government's policy on conscription.

There are other ways of assessing the effectiveness of SOS, although some of these are also difficult to quantify. It is impossible to say, for example, exactly how many potential conscripts may have been directly 'saved' by the actions of SOS, either through its counselling services, pamphlets, or other assistance that its members rendered conscientious objectors or draft resisters.[8] However, there is anecdotal evidence that suggests that some young men who had contact with SOS members did subsequently decide not to register for national service or to opt instead to lodge a conscientious objection. As well as witnessing these 'changes of heart' firsthand, SOS women interpreted a later crackdown on their activities as proof that their methods were having an effect. Some draft resisters and conscientious objectors, like Mac Gudgeon, Bill White and Louis Christofides, have also expressed their appreciation for SOS's assistance. Gudgeon had no doubt that an early encounter with women in Sydney influenced his political thinking:

> I was in the centre of Sydney on day leave from boarding school and I came across a couple of middle-aged women with anti-conscription placards. One thing led to another and I got into a debate with them. I was a 'know nothing' who thought we were doing the right thing in Vietnam. The debate ended when one of the women said, 'If you are so keen on the war, why don't you have the courage of your convictions and enlist?' She slapped a pamphlet in my hand and I remember heading back to Parramatta to school on the train and reading it and thinking there's another side to this debate. That was the beginning of my journey from supporter to resister.[9]

Jean McLean believes 'very strongly' that there would not have been anywhere near as many conscientious objectors and draft resisters if SOS had not existed to provide financial and legal support.[10] Unfortunately, records do not exist to enable this to be quantified in any meaningful way. McLean also argues that Victoria SOS never 'lost' any of the young men it assisted.[11] They may have been jailed for offences relating to their refusal to obey the *National Service Act*, but they were not forced to fight in Vietnam. Again, this is difficult to verify without a complete list of those who sought assistance from SOS. However, newspaper reports of the more high-profile cases do tend to support McLean's claim.

Among some SOS women there was a strong suspicion that their activism may have contributed to their own sons avoiding national service but there is no archival evidence for this. This suspicion, however, did not hurt recruitment. Noting her own son had received an indefinite deferment, Sydney secretary Pat Ashcroft confided in an interstate colleague: 'We are not saying this too loudly, but it seems this is happening to sons of most SOS mothers'.[12] A number of sons of SOS women interviewed for this thesis also expressed suspicions that their mother's activism may have played a role in their success in gaining deferrals, or avoiding active service. 'I always wondered if Mum's background helped me not go to Vietnam', said Ken Jack, an engineer who, after having his initial deferment cancelled at short notice, spent his time in the army at a base in Townsville where his mother was active with the local SOS.[13] While SOS records show that several sons of high-profile members, including the sons of Joyce Golgerth, Ella Outhred, Pat Ashcroft and Nora Mulheron, did receive deferrals or fail army medicals, it is difficult to know whether this was part of a larger pattern or just coincidence. Sons of other SOS supporters certainly were conscripted, and served in Vietnam. These young men came from a variety of backgrounds and it did not appear to make a scrap of difference how rich, poor, influential or, indeed, how active in antiwar protests their parents were. Australian Security

Intelligence Organisation (ASIO) files examined for this thesis also make no mention of any 'scheme' to reject the sons of known activists, although common sense suggests such 'troublemakers' might not have made the most ideal candidates for military service.

Despite these difficulties in quantifying effect, it is clear that SOS played a significant role in the anti-conscription debate during the Vietnam era. There can be no doubt, for example, that SOS women did provide valuable practical and moral assistance to many young men who opposed national service. Some of this was in the form of financial assistance for bails and legal fees. They provided counselling services and basic information about the rights of would-be conscripts, including their right to lodge a conscientious objection. They also produced literature and held demonstrations in support of individual conscientious objectors and resisters, drawing public attention to their cases. Other support included housing and moving draft resisters between 'safe houses' along the east coast of Australia. In Victoria alone, Jean McLean estimates dozens of young men were assisted in this way.[14]

The importance of moral support provided by SOS also should not be overlooked. SOS women spent many hours inside and outside courtrooms supporting young men in their legal battles. SOS counsellors, in conjunction with other groups, also helped prepare these men for their court appearances, organised legal representation and made sure that they and their families fully understood their legal options. SOS women everywhere made a point of attending every court case they could, supporting young men from the public gallery, many of whom did not have the support of their families. 'We of the SOS felt that our presence and support helped these young men to feel less lonely', Scaysbrook said.[15] Moral support also extended to checking up on the mental health of mothers distraught at the call-up of their children, and mediating between young objectors and their families. In this respect, SOS women acted not only as morale boosting cheerleaders but as family counsellors and, sometimes, substitute parents.

Politically, SOS also can be seen to have had an effect. The jailing of five suburban 'mums' in Fairlea women's prison became a potent symbol of middle-class dissent ahead of the 1972 election. While this event may have occurred at a time when public opinion on the war and conscription was already starting to change, it was, as Joan Coxsedge describes, 'the icing on the cake' that focused national media attention on these issues. 'That was very, very important because it was five women with lots of kids prepared to go to jail for only telling young men their rights so that upset a lot of people', she said.[16] Jim Cairns concurred, describing the event as a significant turning point in the campaign for public opinion.[17] The effect of their jailing did not end when the women were released from prison. According to Jean McLean, former Prime Minister Billy McMahon later told her that when he saw the Fairlea Five women sitting in the front row of a public rally with black veils on their heads he knew the government would lose the election.[18] She said McMahon also told her that he had wanted to abolish conscription ahead of the 1972 election, believing the government would lose otherwise, but that the leader of the National Party had threatened to break the Coalition if he did.[19] SOS's effect might not have been discernible in opinion polls at the time but if the above story is true, it seems that at least some of the nation's elected officials regarded it as a barometer of the electoral climate.

SOS was important in other ways. Highly visible at protests, SOS supporters stood out at a time when 'respectable' women were only just starting to break free of the domestic sphere. While their maternal rhetoric may have been regarded as past its use-by date by more radical elements of the emerging feminist movement, motherhood was still a powerful image that resonated with a large section of Australian society during this period. The very presence of these women at demonstrations served to broaden the appeal of the anti-war movement and reach segments of society that the peace movement had previously been unable to penetrate. 'They tried to denigrate us and in the end they couldn't so then they said we were just naïve women. But people started to listen', Jean McLean recalled. 'And they thought, "Gosh, if they are willing to do it, so are we", and as more and more sons got conscripted they started to think about the issues.'[20] According to Jim Cairns, SOS was particularly 'significant' in bringing the middle class into the broader anti-war movement. 'I don't say that middle-class people didn't feel for peace but they had their own way of giving expression to those feelings and it didn't involve getting out on to the streets and fronting a peace walk', he said. '[But] they could see that women were there and that in a way it was safe for women to be there and therefore more women came.'[21] SOS also had some unlikely converts. Former Commonwealth policeman Peter O'Brien, whose tasks during the Vietnam War included 'spying' on and arresting SOS members, later claimed that the presence of so many respectable and sincere middle-class women at demonstrations had a huge influence on his own views about the validity of the war and conscription. 'That is what impacted on me', he said. 'Suddenly I started to realise that it wasn't as straightforward as what it seemed.'[22]

SOS played an important part in the fight for civil liberties too. In Melbourne, SOS's contribution to the By-law 418 campaign helped in securing the basic right of citizens to demonstrate on the streets. The women repeatedly broke the law and were arrested, helping to raise public attention about the issue. The fact that their 'crimes' were frequently ignored, even though they were committed alongside students who were subsequently arrested, also drew attention to the inequity in the enforcement of this law. The eventual backdown by the Melbourne City Council was publicly attributed in part to the actions of the SOS women.[23] Jean McLean argued that SOS's initial refusal to abide by the rules was an important factor in creating a 'public political debate' that eventually led to change in the law. 'People suddenly realised that Anzac Day marches and stopping all the traffic for military parades, which was always accepted, was also our right and I think that the message that got through has never changed since then', she said. 'I think it was a very, very healthy political change that came out of the anti-conscription movement which I believe started with Save Our Sons. Well, I know it did because I was there.'[24]

SOS was also recognised as being an important part of a much wider international movement that emerged in the 1960s and 1970s in opposition to the war in Vietnam. The fires of this international pressure were deliberately and systematically fanned by the NLF/PRG (the Vietnamese National Liberation Front which later formed the Provisional Revolutionary Government).[25] In her 2013 autobiography, Nguyen Thi Binh (also known as Madame Binh), who headed the PRG's delegation at the Paris peace talks, described how this strategy of 'people diplomacy' was used to harness international public opinion against the war, increasing pressure on the US government to change its policy. 'We took advantage of worldwide sympathy and the call for justice', she wrote. 'Using this approach we elicited sympathy and won over people with differing points of views, thereby creating a strong, widespread, international movement of support.'[26] Women's groups worldwide, including SOS, played a strong role in creating this support network. In her autobiography, Madame Binh expressed gratitude to women throughout the world who supported 'Vietnam's struggle'.[27] While she did not single out the SOS women in her memoirs, in 2001 the Fairlea Five women were invited to Hanoi where Madame Binh (by then Vietnam's vice-president) presented them with medals of peace and friendship.[28] The women spent a week in Hanoi during which they met children with severe deformities, a legacy of the herbicide Agent Orange that had been sprayed on the countryside.[29] For some of their critics this trip no doubt reinforced their belief that SOS women had been communist supporters. For the women, seeing the young victims underlined the importance of the stand they had taken in opposing conscription and Australia's involvement in the Vietnam War. 'It was very moving', Coxsedge recalled in 2014. 'I had never seen children so badly malformed ... to me that was a war crime [and] the thing that really justified what we had been fighting for.'[30]

While a foreign government may have recognised SOS's contribution, it was not always recognised, or appreciated, among other members of the protest movement. Sue McCulloch, a younger woman involved with the student movement in Melbourne, recalled that some of the male 'gungho radicals' regarded them 'in a very patronising way as the "silly old dears"'.[31] But she said with hindsight it was clear that SOS had 'enormous significance'. As well as providing practical support to the moratorium movement, organising demonstrations, protecting and moving draft resisters around the underground, and raising much-needed funds, SOS's high public profile also helped to further debate and broaden the appeal of the anti-war movement. 'In the media's and public's eyes, I think they were enormously important because it [showed it] wasn't just students who were involved', she said. 'It broadened the whole aspect because it was just ordinary people and women and mothers who were concerned about the fate of their children.'³² Hugh Outhred, son of SOS member Ella Outhred and a student protester in Sydney, said SOS had provided 'a great counterfoil to the younger wilder type of stuff'. '[Student activism] was the 1960s version of Schoolies ... it was fun but was it politically productive? That is the big question in my mind', he said. 'In a political sense ... seeing that more mature group out there – determined, coherent and articulate – was probably a greater threat than the young people running around doing their thing.'³³

However, other former anti-war protesters stressed that SOS was just one of a number of groups involved in the anti-conscription campaign. In a 1991 letter to Pauline Armstrong, former draft resister Barry York disagreed that SOS had been 'overlooked and ignored' in research on the anti-war movement. 'My view, in hindsight, is that SOS was an important part of the anti-war and anti-conscription movement because it brought together women as a separate entity and also because it appealed to the sense of motherhood which was strong in the society at large', he said. 'In rating it as an important organisation, however, I would attempt to be balanced about it. There were more important male-dominated, anti-war organisations and SOS was only one part of a very diverse movement.'³⁴ York said he also could not recall SOS being part of the By-law 418 campaign, despite being actively involved in it himself. 'Perhaps that indicates a "blind spot" on my part or perhaps it indicates that SOS was standing at a different end of the City Square!' he said.³⁵

Sam Goldbloom, who headed the Campaign for International Co-operation and Disarmament during the Vietnam era and worked closely with Jean McLean when both were deputy chairs of the moratorium campaign, was also circumspect, remembering the SOS women as being 'to a very considerable degree ... middle class, nice, blue-tinted hair, very polite ladies'.[36] While stressing he did not wish to elevate their contribution above other groups, he did allow that SOS's high public profile had 'made an inordinately large contribution to the raising of the issue … and helping to inform public opinion'.[37] However, Wollongong draft resisters Lou Christofides and Mac Gudgeon argued the women's involvement was extremely valuable. 'In many cases, the women displayed more guts than men', Christofides recalled.[38] Gudgeon said that the presence of SOS women at demonstrations gave them 'a sense of gravity and solidity':

> The rest of us could be dismissed by our foes as "young, idealistic and naïve"; they couldn't dismiss those women so easily because they were mature and had a lot at stake – their sons' lives and futures. You always felt that their presence was a validation that you were on the side of decency.[39]

As an observer on the other side of the conscription debate, former Commonwealth policeman Peter O'Brien said he believed SOS's contribution had been vastly underestimated and that the women had 'a more profound effect on the society at that time' than students or the trade union movement, and could be compared to the women who campaigned against conscription during World War I. 'I would be prepared to say that without the contribution of the women, there would have been no moratoriums', he said. 'The women's contribution was vital because my observations were that they dragged the male population into an act of conscience … they stirred the conscience of the nation as [women] did in 1917 and 1916.'[40]

Yet SOS's role in the anti-conscription debate still stirs controversy. Retired army officer Kevin Gillett has never deviated from his belief that SOS was a communist front. In a 2014 post on his blog commenting on the legacy of Gough Whitlam, he wrote: 'The women who marched behind these women were looking to save their sons. The women at the front were looking to help the communists win the war and this was a good way to do it'.[41] Another ex-serviceman, who served in the regular troops in Vietnam, recalled one conscript in his unit having to 'sneak past' his mother after recognising her among a group of SOS protesters in Brisbane. He said the four conscripts under his command all 'agreed that the service experience helped them to become more self-reliant' and that SOS 'was just a case of ill-informed mothers being overly protective'.[42] These differing recollections underline the fact that collective memory for this period is still in the process of being formed. Given this, it can be expected that the contribution and legacy of the SOS movement will continue to be contested for some time to come.

One point that is not contested is that the SOS movement provided a segment of women who were new to activism with a safe, non-political vehicle and a supportive collegiate environment through which they could register their dissent. According to Noreen Hewett, most Sydney members were politically inexperienced. 'To me the SOS women showed how even apolitical women, initially dedicated to a single issue – conscription – through action and debate, came to understand the unjust nature of the Vietnam War itself and were confident in articulating the broader issues', she said.[43] SOS leaders never pushed their members to be involved any further than they felt comfortable; the wishes of those who did not want to be involved in civil disobedience campaigns were always respected. The experiences of SOS women during this period were subsequently more positive overall than of those reported by younger women involved in male-dominated anti-war groups who often complained of being relegated to auxiliary roles, often menial ones, while the men took the leading roles. As a study by Ann Curthoys has noted, the effect of feeling marginalised led many of these women to value collective female action, going on to build a new movement for the liberation of women during the 1970s.[44] But this was not the experience of those who joined SOS groups. Women in SOS, for example, 'did not have to fight for a hearing ... as they so often did in the student and youth organisations'.[45] 'SOS was important because it provided a place for women to take part in stuff at their own level that they felt comfortable with', Joan Coxsedge recalled.[46] But SOS also played a role in challenging expected gender roles of the day. Reflecting on her experience in SOS, Corinne Kerby argued that it should never be underestimated how much SOS had accomplished by 'breaking free' of the expected codes of behaviour of the day. 'Women weren't taken any notice of at all', she said. 'They were just decorative things in the background. [SOS women] made themselves known, and their opinions known.'[47]

Several SOS women, including Scaysbrook, noted the camaraderie among the women and the fact that unlike other protest groups they never had to deal with 'a power struggle within our ranks'.[48] However, there was not always harmony. In the early years, after a disagreement with Pat Ashcroft over the direction of the group, Joyce Golgerth resigned.[49] A delegation of SOS committee members was duly dispatched and succeeded in changing her mind. Internal 'politics' were also partly blamed for the eventual demise of the Newcastle group. Nonetheless, SOS was notably free of the sometimes bitter power struggles and disagreements over politics that beset some of the male-dominated anti-war groups.[50] Given the length of time SOS existed, this in itself was no small feat.

* * *

The effect on the women themselves is more tangible. As previously discussed, many faced hostility in their communities, workplace and even within their own families. But while SOS may have folded in 1973, the effect on those involved did not end there. Indeed for many women 'draft counselling, hiding draft resisters, fighting court cases, and marching in street demonstrations had become a way of life'.[51] Once it was over some immediately adopted another cause, formed new groups or continued in the peace movement. A few – Joan Coxsedge, Jean McLean and Margaret Reynolds – went on to hold public office. Others, like Edna Gudgeon, were happy to return to their domestic sphere and pick up the threads of their disrupted lives. 'After it was all over [my parents] had had enough', Mac Gudgeon said. 'They were still strong Labor supporters but they sort of stepped back a bit. I think it had been a bit traumatic for them, much more traumatic than for me actually because I was elsewhere most of the time and they had to face quite a bit of resentment.'[52]

Founder Joyce Golgerth also 'retired' from activism. 'She was there to the end … but that was it', son Michael recalled. 'She was quite set in what she believed in and what she had to do to make it come about and that is exactly what she did and then stopped.'[53] But daughter Candy Cole said her mother's stand had affected her children in a positive way. 'It certainly made you question a lot in life', she said. 'The one thing my mother told me was never to accept it like it is but to have a brain and have a thought of your own.'[54] Nora Mulheron's son Maurie, who went on to head the New South Wales Teachers Federation, also credits his mother's activism for having had a huge effect on his own outlook and career choices. 'The Vietnam protests informed what I am today because from nine or ten until I went to uni, it dominated our whole existence', he said.[55]

Some SOS women saw the anti-conscription campaign as an extension of their work within the peace movement and when the movement folded many continued their work in other groups. In their last letter to SOS members, Sydney committee members Alma Scaysbrook and Nora Mulheron took it for granted that there would be a 'continuing association' with their former colleagues through the wider peace movement.[56] This was not an unreasonable assumption. Many Sydney members were already members of the Association for International Co-operation and Disarmament and continued to work together on other peace issues. The remaining Sydney SOS funds were also transferred to this group. Women who were not already members were encouraged to join this or other groups, including the Women's International League for Peace and Freedom, the Federal Pacifist Council, Christian Women Concerned, and Another Woman for Peace.[57]

Vietnam was not forgotten. Sydney women were encouraged to campaign for the freedom of political prisoners in South Vietnam while Melbourne's committee, including Coxsedge, McLean, Irene Miller and Chris Cathie, immediately formed a new group to push for recognition of the Provisional Revolutionary Government.[58] The South Australian SOS group donated its remaining funds to assist Vietnamese women.[59] After the Vietnam War officially ended in 1975, Jean McLean also convened the Australia–Vietnam Association, a 'friendship group' that promoted visits and links between government and business leaders of both countries.[60] These visits were not popular among South Vietnamese now resident in Australia.[61]

For those who opted to join other groups, there was no shortage of 'causes' to choose from; Indigenous issues, multiculturalism, women's rights and environmentalism all gained prominence during the 1970s and 1980s. Former SOS women Dorothy Dalton, Flo Garber, Chris Cathie and Irene Miller were subsequently to be found campaigning against uranium mining in Kakadu, for better health services for Aboriginal Australians, and improved working conditions for women. Many of the women later spoke about the confidence they had gained through their involvement with SOS. 'I don't think SOS changed me', Miller reflected. 'It just made me realise that I could do stupid things like stand in streets and hold placards or chalk up messages in the streets.'[62] Ceci Cairns, on the other hand, said SOS 'totally altered my whole life'. She credited the movement for instilling her with the confidence and skills to become involved in other political campaigns. 'It taught me how to run a campaign, all those nitty-gritty things about grass roots' work … it was a wonderful learning experience', she said.[63]

Brisbane's energetic SOS leader Vilma Ward did not fade away either, continuing to campaign for causes close to her heart for the rest of her life. In the 1970s and 1980s, she was involved with CARP (Consumers Against Rising Prices), leading a 'consumer war against rising prices for basic products such as bread and milk'. This led to a five-year job as a consumer reporter for Channel 9's *Brisbane Extra*, where she became known as 'a champion of "the battler"'.[64] She also founded the Queensland Branch of the Sudden Infant Death Syndrome Foundation in 1978, and was an active president of her local senior citizens and community centre in Brisbane. In 2014, she grabbed national headlines again as the 'cranky granny who grilled PM Tony Abbott' on live national TV about changes in his unpopular Budget that she said would penalise 3.7 million pensioners. (The Liberal party hit back, accusing the then 85-year-old great-grandmother of being a Labor party "stooge", releasing photos of her campaigning with her local member Kevin Rudd).[65]

Noreen Hewett never ran for public office, but she became a noted advocate for the rights of older women and was still attending demonstrations on a range of issues in her late seventies. Given she had been a 'spirited activist' long before she helped found SOS, it is unlikely that her involvement in this one group altered her outlook.[66] Similarly it is difficult to know whether the lives of the women who entered politics would have still followed the same trajectory had they not been involved in SOS. Jean McLean, who was elected as an Australian Labor Party (ALP) member of the Victorian Legislative Council in 1985, said everybody who crossed the line between staying home and marching on the streets could probably identify some 'trigger' that personally affected them 'either morally, physically or financially'.[67] For McLean it was conscription and the Vietnam War, although she stressed that her interest in foreign affairs extended back to childhood. However, her involvement in SOS most certainly helped to boost her public profile, expand her network of contacts, and hone her political skills, assisting in her eventual transition to elected office.

Margaret Reynolds, on the other hand, claimed SOS was 'a significant contributing factor' in her 'coming of age as a community activist'.[68] In her autobiography she noted 'this small initiative was to set the future of my political career and my commitment to the peace movement'.[69] After SOS, she helped set up the Headstart Kindergarten program for Indigenous children in Townsville with fellow SOS members and 'mentors' Loma Thompson and Esme Hardy. She then served on the Townsville City Council before being elected to the Australian Senate in 1983, where she became a minister in the Hawke government. While the short-lived Townsville SOS group may not have had a great effect at the time, Reynolds said it had a great impact on her personally, heightening her political awareness and giving her insights into the political process. At the same time it also influenced the development of her own identity 'in a community that defined a woman by her husband's career' and showed her it was possible to combine her roles 'as wife and mother while being involved in the community'.[70] 'Conscription was really one of the first political issues I felt strongly about', she said in 2012. 'Looking back, it was a very tentative beginning of my activism. If I had to name some of my major successes, I wouldn't name Save Our Sons although just to have it operating in *the* military town was quite an achievement, I can see that now.'[71]

Joan Coxsedge also believes her anti-Vietnam activities accelerated her 'politicisation'. As a protester, she learned 'how to suss out the facts, marshal them in a coherent way and persuasively argue a case'. It was also an 'excellent way' to improve writing and public speaking skills. 'I was always nervous talking at large public meetings and rallies, but when you talk about things that really matter, you usually manage to put butterflies to flight', she said.[72] When SOS folded, Coxsedge did not pause. 'Fed up to the back teeth' by the secret surveillance of anti-war protesters, she and a 'few hardies' formed CAPP – the Committee for the Abolition of Political Police. The group set about reversing roles with 'the snoopers', photographing ASIO officers entering and leaving their Melbourne headquarters and publicising their names and addresses on posters and leaflets.[73] One of its more 'outrageous' stunts was the mock auction of the home of former ASIO Director-General, Peter Barbour; it proved so disruptive that the actual auction had to be abandoned.[74]

As a member of the Socialist Left of the ALP, Coxsedge also campaigned against uranium mining and, in 1974, became the first president of the Status of Women Committee which lobbied for, among other things, the decriminalisation of prostitution and the fundamental right of women to contraception and abortion (a 'hot potato back then').[75] In 1979, she was elected to the Victorian Legislative Council, one of the first two women to enter the state's Upper House where facilities did not yet include 'a female loo'.[76] While a parliamentary profile listed her occupation as 'artist', it had been a long time since she had painted full-time. 'I packed away my oil paints and brushes to become a protester', she later recalled of her time with SOS. 'When the soldiers came home, I kept going.'[77] While not all 'kept going', the lives of SOS women were certainly disrupted and changed during their involvement with the movement, and some were changed for good. If there were any regrets, it was the time spent away from their own families. Volunteering with SOS 'became a full-time job', according to Joan Coxsedge, who had a young family during this period. 'We spent such a lot of time at meetings and because we were telling young men not to register, we felt an obligation to roll-up at the magistrates' court and so on to give them support', she said. 'I really felt I would have liked to have spent more time with the children. That was something I do regret. I think a lot of activists do actually.'[78]

* * *

The Save Our Sons movement was a product of its time. The issue of conscription made the political personal for hundreds of women and motivated them to take a public stand against a government that had enjoyed long-term support. In 1965, their stand was considered brave, noteworthy and slightly puzzling to those who encountered them. As the Vietnam War continued, they became an important part of the larger moratorium movement. However, while its supporters worked closely with other groups, SOS always maintained its own identity.

Jean McLean believes it would be unlikely that a movement like SOS could be replicated in today's world where maternal rhetoric has come to be regarded as outmoded and where social media has replaced 'old fashioned' face-to-face campaigning and public meetings. 'I think it was a very important movement and an important forerunner for people to organise for particular issues until it was buggered up by computers', she said.[79] In any case, she is hopeful that a movement like SOS will never be needed again, pointing out that no government since Gough Whitlam's election has 'dared' reintroduce conscription in any form.[80] This does not mean one could not. Under the Keating Labor government's *Defence Legislation Amendment Act* of 1992, the government still has the power to introduce conscription in time of war, though only with the approval of both Houses of Parliament.[81] Introducing the legislation, which also included changes that would make it easier to claim conscientious objection, then Attorney-General, Peter Duncan, said it was the government's aim 'to preserve the capacity to introduce conscription for the protection of Australia, but to ensure that those claiming exemption would receive a rapid and fair hearing'.[82] The spectre of national service was briefly raised when the Howard government was preparing to send peacekeeping troops to East Timor in the late 1990s but was deemed unnecessary.[83] So, while there are greater safeguards in place than existed before the Vietnam War, it is conceivable that young Australians might one day be told to register for national service again.

Even in post-election euphoria of 1973, some members of the Sydney SOS committee remained uneasy; they were not convinced that the threat of conscription was over forever. 'The waters may appear calm but it is the damnable undercurrents that can lead to turbulence', warned one member.[84] It was for this reason that the committee decided not to officially disband SOS but to place it 'into indefinite recess'. In theory at least, 'should the need arise', the Save Our Sons movement could be reconvened to 'go into action' once more.

NOTES

Prologue

1. 'Women for Peace: why we chained ourselves' [Pamphlet], 1970. *Garber Collection*. Wollongong City Library (WCL) DMSS 225/1.
2. Commonwealth, *Parliamentary Debates* [CPD], House of Representatives, no.24, 11 June 1970, 3361.
3. 'Women in Chains Protest', *Canberra Times*, 12 June 1970.
4. 'Women for Peace' Pamphlet.
5. CPD, House of Representatives, no.24, 11 June 1970, 3352-3353.
6. Australian War Memorial, http://www.awm.gov.au/encyclopedia/vietnam/statistics, accessed 5 November 2013.
7. 'Women for Peace' Pamphlet.

Introduction

1. 'Those Women with Banners', *Sun*, 14 December 1965.
2. 'Mothers Oppose Call-Up', *Australian*, 19 May 1965.
3. Under the National Service Scheme, all 20-year-olds were required to register for national service and then went into a 'birthday ballot'. Every six months, marbles marked with a date were drawn out of a Tattersalls' lottery barrel, dubbed by the Leader of the Opposition, Arthur Calwell, as 'the lottery of death'. There was about one in 12 chance of being conscripted. See: Paul Ham, *Vietnam: The Australian War* (Sydney: Harper Collins, 2008), 169.
4. Letter from P. Ashcroft to R. Collie, 13 April 1966. NLA: MS 3821-2.
5. Sydney SOS, Statement of Aims, 1965. NLA: MS 3821-25.
6. 'Those Women with Banners', *Sun*, 14 December 1965.
7. See, for example: Barry York, *Student Revolt! La Trobe University 1967–73* (Campbell, ACT: Nicholas Press, 1989); Michael Hyde, ed., *It is Right to Rebel* (Canberra: The Diplomat, 1972); Michael Hamel-Green, 'The Resisters: a history of the anti-conscription movement 1964–1972', in *Australia's Vietnam*, ed. Peter King (Sydney: Allen & Unwin, 1983), 100-128.
8. See for example, Ann Curthoys, '"Shut Up, You Bourgeois Bitch": sexual identity and political action in the anti-Vietnam movement', in *Gender and War: Australians at War in the Twentieth Century*, ed. Joy Damousi and Marilyn Lake (Cambridge: Cambridge University Press, 1995); and the first edition of Siobhan McHugh's book, *Minefields and Miniskirts: Australian Women and the Vietnam War* (Sydney: Doubleday, 1993). Ann-Mari Jordens, 'Conscription and Dissent: the genesis of anti-war protest', in *Vietnam Remembered*, ed. Gregory Pemberton (Sydney: New Holland Publishers, 2009), 60-81; Pauline Armstrong, 'A History of the Save Our Sons Movement of Victoria: 1965–1973', (MA thesis, Monash University, 1991).

9   Rebecca McLean, S.O.S [Documentary], (Canberra: Ronin Films, 1997).
10 Maurie Mulheron, interviewed by author, 20 October 2012. [All interviews unless otherwise denoted are by the author].
11 'The Rude Awakening of Vilma', *Sunday Truth*, 15 October 1967.
12 Peter O'Brien interviewed by P. Armstrong, 16 June 1991. NLA: MS 9878-3-3.
13 Jean McLean interview, 2 October 2014.
14 Jim Cairns, *Silence Kills: Events Leading Up to the Vietnam Moratorium on 8 May* (Melbourne: Vietnam Moratorium Committee, 1970).
15 Jim Cairns interviewed by P. Armstrong, 5 August 1990. NLA: MS 9878-3-2.
16 Amy Swerdlow, *Women Strike For Peace: Traditional Motherhood and Radical Politics in the 1960s* (Chicago: The University of Chicago Press, 1993), 1.
17 Curthoys, '"Shut Up, You Bourgeois Bitch"', 322, 338, 335.
18 Michael Caulfield, *The Vietnam Years: From the Jungle to the Australian Suburbs* (Sydney: Hatchette Australia, 2007), 116.
19 Note from 'A Proud Mother of a Proud and Loyal Son' to A. Pert, n.d. NLA: MS 3821-10.
20 Maurie Mulheron interview, 20 October 2012.
21 For an understanding of how ASIO operated see: David Horner, *The Spy Catchers. Volume I: The Official History of ASIO 1949–1963* (Crows Nest, NSW: Allen & Unwin, 2014); Frank Cain, *ASIO: An Unofficial History* (Richmond, Victoria: Spectrum Publications, 1994); Michael Tubbs, *ASIO: The Enemy Within* (Croydon Park, NSW: Michael Tubbs, 2008); David McKnight, *Australia's Spies and Their Secrets* (St Leonards, NSW: Allen & Unwin, 1994); John Blaxland, *The Protest Years. Volume II: The Official History of ASIO 1963–1975* (Crows Nest, NSW: Allen &Unwin, 2015).
22 Margaret Reynolds interview, 2 November 2012.
23 Rick Feneley, 'ASIO Files: that looks suspicious doesn't it?' *Sydney Morning Herald*, 4 January 2014.
24 Vince Prasser interview, 4 March 2013; 'SOS Townsville Member', 23 December 1966. NAA: A6122, 1680/21.
25 Jean McLean, 'My Life in a Distorting Mirror', in *Dirty Secrets: Our ASIO Files*, ed. Meredith Burgmann (Sydney: NewSouth Publishing, 2014), 184.
26 'Those Women with Banners', *Sun*, 14 December 1965.
27 Dorothy Cora, *Noreen Hewett: Portrait of a Grassroots Activist* (Sydney: Older Women's Network of NSW, 2010), 24.
28 Louis Christofides quoted in Greg Langley, *A Decade of Dissent: Vietnam and Conflict on the Australian Homefront* (Sydney: Allen & Unwin, 1992), 223.

Chapter 1: Dress Rehearsal

1   'I Didn't Raise My Boy to Be a Soldier', lyrics by Alfred Bryan and composed by Al Piantodosi (1915), was an American protest song, popular among those who opposed the United States joining World War I. It was outlawed in Australia under the *War Precautions Act* of 1915 but this did not stop strident anti-conscriptionists Adela Pankhurst and Cecilia John from singing it at public meetings. See: Carmel Shute, 'Heroines and Heroes: sexual mythology

in Australia 1914–18', in *Gender and War*, ed. Joy Damousi and Marilyn Lake (Cambridge: Cambridge University Press, 1995), 29.

2   On 10 November 1964, Prime Minister Robert Menzies made a statement on defence to the House of Representatives in which he announced the introduction of a compulsory selective National Service Scheme, in light of recent 'aggressive Communism' developments in Asia. (See: *CPD*, House of Representatives, vol.46, 10 November 1964, 2715-2724.) The *National Services Act 1964*, passed on 24 November, required selected 20-year-old males to serve for two years full-time in the regular army followed by three years part-time in the reserves. There was no mention at this time of conscripts serving overseas.

3   'Women in Black Hoods Fail to Shake Menzies at Poll Rally', *Sydney Morning Herald*, 24 November 1964.

4   Michelle Cavanagh, *Margaret Holmes: The Life and Times of an Australian Peace Campaigner* (Sydney: New Holland, 2006), 214.

5   Bertha Walker, *How to Defeat Conscription: A Story of the 1916 and 1917 Campaigns in Victoria* (Northcote, Victoria: Anti-Conscription Jubilee Committee, 1968), 4.

6   John Barrett, *Falling In: Australians and 'Boy Conscription' 1911–1915* (Sydney: Hale & Iremonger, 1979), 102.

7   K. S Inglis, 'Conscription in Peace and War, 1911–1945', in *Conscription in Australia*, ed. Roy Forward and Bob Reece (St Lucia, Queensland: University of Queensland Press, 1968), 29.

8   Ann-Mari Jordens, 'Conscription and Dissent: the genesis of anti-war protest', in *Vietnam Remembered*, ed. Gregory Pemberton (Sydney: New Holland Publishers, 2009), 64.

9   Walker, *How to Defeat Conscription*, 18–20.

10 Jordens, 'Conscription and Dissent', 63–64.

11 Joy Damousi, *Women Come Rally: Socialism, Communism and Gender in Australia 1890–1955* (Melbourne: Oxford University Press, 1994), 14; Malcolm Saunders and Ralph Summy, *The Australian Peace Movement: A Short History* (Canberra: Peace Research Centre, Australian National University, 1986), 19.

12 Shute, 'Heroines and Heroes', 28.

13 Sir William Irvine, Address to the Millions Club in Sydney, 8 November 1917, cited in Leslie C. Jauncey, *The Story of Conscription in Australia* (South Melbourne: Macmillan, 1968), 275.

14 Eleanor Moore, *The Quest for Peace as I Have Known it in Australia* (Melbourne: Wilke & Co., 1949), 22.

15 Moore, *Quest for Peace*, 39.

16 Moore, *Quest for Peace*, 27.

17 Moore, *Quest for Peace*, 27.

18 Moore, *Quest for Peace*, 27.

19 Mimi Colligan and Malcolm Saunders, 'Moore, Eleanor May (1875–1949)', *Australian Dictionary of Biography*, http://adb.anu.edu.au/biography/moore-eleanor-may-7635/text13349, accessed 15 June 2015.

20 Moore, *Quest for Peace*, 28.

21 Janice N. Brownfoot, 'Goldstein, Vida Jane (1869–1949)', *Australian Dictionary of Biography*, http://adb.anu.edu.au/biography/goldstein-vida-jane-6418/text10975, accessed 15 June 2015.
22 Jauncey, *Story of Conscription*, 106.
23 Jauncey, *Story of Conscription*, 106.
24 Moore, *Quest for Peace*, 36.
25 Shute, 'Heroines and Heroes', 28.
26 Shute, 'Heroines and Heroes', 29.
27 Raymond Evans, 'Conscription Riot', in *Radical Brisbane: An Unruly History*, ed. Raymond Evans and Carole Ferrier (Carlton North, Victoria: The Vulgar Press, 2004), 156.
28 Evans, 'Conscription Riot', 158.
29 Walker, *How to Defeat Conscription*, 7–8.
30 Vida Goldstein, 'Manifesto Australia's Women's Peace Army', *The Woman Voter*, 5 October 1916. *Reason in Revolt: Source Documents of Australian Radicalism*, http://www.reasoninrevolt.net.au/bib/PR0000330.htm, accessed 28 February 2013.
31 Shute, 'Heroines and Heroes', 24.
32 Shute, 'Heroines and Heroes', 26.
33 Shute, 'Heroines and Heroes', 26.
34 'Sister of Soldiers' [Letter to the Editor], *Brisbane Courier*, 12 July 1916.
35 'Australian Nationalists. Vote Yes' [Leaflet], Melbourne, 1916. Australian War Memorial (henceforth AWM) Leaflet Collection: 2/1/1 RC00305.
36 J. M. Main, ed., *Conscription: The Australian Debate, 1901–1970* (Melbourne: Cassell, 1970), 89.
37 'The Mothers' [Leaflet], 1914–1918, AWM Leaflet Collection: 2/1/1 RC00335.
38 'The Blood Vote' [Leaflet], c. 1916, AWM Leaflet Collection: 2/1/1 RC0037.
39 E. J. Holloway, 'The Australian Victory Over Conscription in 1916–17', cited in Walker, *How to Defeat Conscription*, 12.
40 Women's International League for Peace and Freedom (WILPF). http://wilpf.org/US_WILPF, accessed 28 February 2013.
41 Colligan and Saunders, 'Moore, Eleanor May (1875–1949)', *Australian Dictionary of Biography*, http://adb.anu.edu.au/biography/moore-eleanor-may-7635/text13349, accessed 28 February 2013.
42 Eleanor Moore, 'Conscription and Women's Loyalty' [Leaflet], 1916, reproduced in Leslie. C. Jauncey, *Story of Conscription*, 201.
43 Prime Minister Robert Menzies, Statement to Parliament, *CPD*, House of Representatives, no.46, 15 November 1939, 1133.
44 Inglis, 'Conscription in Peace and War', 51.
45 Inglis, 'Conscription in Peace and War', 56.
46 Malcolm Saunders and Ralph Summy, 'Odd Ones Out: the Australian section of the Women's International League for Peace and Freedom, 1919–41', *Australian Journal of Politics and History* 40, no.1 (1994): 83.
47 'National Service, 1951–59 [Fact Sheet 163]', National Archives of Australia [NAA] http://www.naa.gov.au/collection/fact-sheets/fs163.aspx.
48 Ann-Mari Jordens notes that 'In 1950, 87 per cent of those polled approved of

the reintroduction of compulsory military training'. Jordens, 'Conscription and Dissent', 65.
49 Peter Edwards, *A Nation at War: Australian Politics, Society and Diplomacy During the Vietnam War 1965–1975*. (Sydney: Allen & Unwin, 1997), 21.
50 Les Dalton, 'Politics of the Australian Peace Movement: 1930s to 1960s', *Centre for Dialogue Working Paper Series, No. 2011/1* (Melbourne: LaTrobe University, 2011), 7. Available from http://www.latrobe.edu.au/dialogueOLD/publications/working-paper-series/past-issues, accessed 5 March 2013.
51 Dalton, 'Politics of the Australian Peace Movement', 25.
52 Cavanagh, *Margaret Holmes*, 182.
53 Cavanagh, *Margaret Holmes*, 183.
54 McHugh, *Minefields and Miniskirts*, 203.
55 Barbara Curthoys and Audrey McDonald, *More than a Hat and Glove Brigade: The Story of the Union of Australian Women* (Sydney: Bookpress, 1996), 1; Zora Simic, 'Butter Not Bombs: A short history of the Union of Australian Women', *History Australia* 4, no.1 (2007), 71.
56 Simic, 'Butter Not Bombs', 71.
57 'Minister Sends Back Peace Notes', *Sydney Morning Herald*, 11 May 1954; 'Union of Australian Women is "Red-Controlled"', *Advertiser*, 11 May 1954.
58 Suzane Fabian and Morag Loh, *Left-Wing Ladies: The Union of Australian Women in Victoria, 1950–1998* (Flemington, Victoria: Hyland House Publishing, 2000), 34.
59 Curthoys and McDonald, *More than a Hat and Glove Brigade*, 73.
60 Margaret Frazer quoted in Greg Langley, *A Decade of Dissent: Vietnam and Conflict on the Australian Homefront* (Sydney: Allen & Unwin, 1992), 4.
61 Curthoys and McDonald, *More than a Hat and Glove Brigade*, 76.
62 Curthoys and McDonald, *More than a Hat and Glove Brigade*, 76.
63 Frazer quoted in Langley, *Decade of Dissent*, 4.
64 Cavanagh, *Margaret Holmes*, 213.
65 Margaret Holmes, 'Supplement to Peace and Freedom', 30 October 1964. NAA: A6119, 3363/2.
66 Edwards, *Nation at War*, 25.
67 Edwards, *Nation at War*, 21.
68 Australian Gallup Polls, No. 1789–1803, October–November 1964, 2.
69 Margaret Holmes, 'Letter to Federal MPs', in Cavanagh, *Margaret Holmes*, 215.
70 'Women for Peace: why we chained ourselves', 1970 [Pamphlet]. *Garber Collection*. Wollongong City Library (WCL) DMSS 225/1.
71 Edwards, *Nation at War*, 369.
72 Amy Swerdlow, *Women Strike For Peace: Traditional Motherhood and Radical Politics in the 1960s* (Chicago: The University of Chicago Press, 1993), 28.

Chapter 2: Rebels with a Cause

1 J. Harrison, 'Letter to the Editor', *Australian*, n.d. NLA: MS 3821-3.
2 E. Ebere, 'Letter to the Editor', *Armidale Express*, 12 July 1965.
3 E. Deakin, 'Letter to the Editor', *Sydney Morning Herald*, 26 August 1969.

4   'Don't Send Compulsory Trainees to Vietnam', *Gallup Poll*, 10 January 1966. National Library of Australia (henceforth NLA): MS 9152-3.
5   See Peter Edwards, *A Nation at War: Australian Politics, Society and Diplomacy During the Vietnam War 1965–1975*. (Sydney: Allen & Unwin, 1997), 369.
6   E. Cullen, 'Conscripts' [Letter to Editor], *Newcastle Morning Herald*, c. August 1966. NLA: MS 3821-1.
7   Letter from J. Bonner to P. Ashcroft, 16 August 1965. NLA: MS 3821-3.
8   In 1971, this was reduced to 18 months.
9   Letter from C. Gray to Menzies, 14 November 1964. NAA: A463, 1962/3685 Part I.
10 P. Rose, 'Letter to the Editor', *Sydney Morning Herald*, 24 July 1969.
11 Letter from Mrs Johnston to Menzies, 9 November 1964. NAA: A463, 1962/3685. Part I.
12 E. Deacon, 'Letter to the Editor', *Sydney Morning Herald*, 26 August 1969.
13 Letter from I. McArthur to J. Golgerth, 26 June 1965. NLA: MS 3821-1.
14 'Mother's Defiance', *Sunday Truth*, 17 October 1965.
15 'Mother's Defiance', *Sunday Truth*, 17 October 1965.
16 E. Ebere, 'Letter to the Editor', *Armidale Express*, 12 July 1965.
17 E. Ebere, 'Letter to the Editor', *Armidale Express*, 12 July 1965.
18 J. Harrison, 'Letter to the Editor', *Australian*, n.d. NLA: MS 3821-3.
19 C. Atkins, 'Letter to Editor', *Australian*, n.d. NLA: MS 9152-2.
20 Letter from G. Walter to P. Armstrong, 7 December 1990. NLA: MS 9878-2.
21 Letter from I. Miller to I. Dunn, 29 May 1984. NLA: MS 9878-4.
22 'Draft Resisters', *ABC Online*. http://www.abc.net.au/gnt/history/Transcripts/s1162103.html, accessed 25 April 2012.
23 'German-Born Couple Won't Be Silent', *Illawarra Mercury*, 6 May 1970.
24 Ralph Gibson, *One Woman's Life: A Memoir of Dorothy Gibson* (Sydney: Hale and Iremonger, 1980), 9.
25 Nita Murray-Smith, 'Gibson, Dorothy (1899–1978)', *Australian Dictionary of Biography*, http://adb.anu.edu.au/biography/gibson-dorothy-10297/text18219, accessed 8 August 2012.
26 Gibson, *One Woman's Life*, 91–92.
27 Gibson, *One Woman's Life*, 93.
28 'A Counsellor for Prisoners of Conscience', *Canberra Times*, 4 March 1969.
29 'A Counsellor for Prisoners of Conscience', *Canberra Times*, 4 March 1969.
30 Clare Land, 'Abraham, Vivienne', *The Australian Women's Register*, http://www.womenaustralia.info/biogs/AWE0183b.htm, accessed 26 April 2012.
31 Bobbie Oliver, 'Exploring the Vivienne Abraham Collection: resources, issues, responsibilities', in *Perth Congress 2000: Let Records Speak* (27 September – 1 October 2000): 119–120.
32 'A Counsellor for Prisoners of Conscience', *Canberra Times*, 4 March 1969.
33 Mac Gudgeon interview, 17 November 2012.
34 E. Jones, 'Letter to the Editor', *Australian*, 19 March 1969.
35 Dorothy Dalton interviewed by P. Armstrong, 23 August 1990. NLA: MS 9878-3-2.

36   Dorothy Dalton and Les Dalton, 'Anti-Uranium Activists', 99–102.
37   Louis Christofides interview, 22 November 2012.
38   'Women for Peace: why we chained ourselves', 1970 [Pamphlet]. *Garber Collection*. Wollongong City Library (WCL) DMSS 225/1.
39   Christofides interview.
40   Gudgeon interview.
41   Gudgeon interview.
42   'A Mother Weeps for Son in Gaol', *Illawarra Mercury*, 10 June 1970.
43   Suzane Fabian and Morag Loh, *Left-Wing Ladies: The Union of Australian Women in Victoria, 1950–1998* (Flemington, Victoria: Hyland House Publishing, 2000), 27.
44   Neal Sellars, *Fred Thompson, Communist, Union Organiser, Humanist: A Biography* (Townsville: Neal Sellars, 2012), 137–148.
45   Loma Thompson interview, 7 December 2012.
46   Val Reid, 'How to Vote Card', n.d. NLA: MS 3821-6.
47   Letter from Mrs D. J. Simes to H. Holt, 26 October 1966. NAA: A463 1966/1952.
48   Letter from Mrs D. J. Simes to H. Holt, 26 October 1966.
49   Letter from M. Boddy to H. Holt, 14 November 1966. NAA: A463 1966/1957.
50   Letter from M. Cornell to Mr and Mrs O'Neil, n.d. NLA: MS 3821-2.
51   Letter from M. Cornell to Mr and Mrs O'Neil.
52   E. Ebere, 'Letter to the Editor', *Armidale Express*, 12 July 1965.
53   'Australia On the Road to War, Says Churchman', *Canberra Times*, 23 November 1964.
54   Michelle Cavanagh, *Margaret Holmes: The Life and Times of an Australian Peace Campaigner* (Sydney: New Holland, 2006), 227.
55   Margaret Holmes, 'Letter for Primate', *Anglican*, 18 November 1965.
56   Dorothy Cora, *Noreen Hewett: Portrait of a Grassroots Activist* (Sydney: Older Women's Network of NSW, 2010), 25.
57   Letter from V. Reid to A. Pert, 22 May 1967. NLA: MS 3821-3.
58   V. Reid, 'Open Letter to a Neighbour', 28 October 1966. NLA: MS 3821-3.
59   Reid, 'Open Letter to a Neighbour'.
60   Reid, 'Open Letter to a Neighbour'.
61   Thomas Hardy interview, 22 November 2012.
62   Alma Scaysbrook, 'A Mother Speaks' [Pamphlet]. NLA: MS 3821-16.
63   'Eulogy for Ella Outhred', Private papers of Alan Outhred.
64   Hugh Outhred interview, 28 November 2013.
65   'TV's Clever Career Mother', *Australian Women's Weekly*, 10 January 1962, 18.
66   Corinne Kerby interviewed by P. Armstrong, 30 September 1990. NLA: MS 9878-3-3.
67   Philip Jones, 'TV Star's Gift for Words that Moved on to Poetry', *Age*, 2 September 2003.
68   Jones, 'TV Star's Gift for Words'.
69   Jones, 'TV Star's Gift for Words'.
70   Corinne Kerby, *Mainly Affirmative* (Melbourne: Georgian House, 1968), 28–31.
71   Jones, 'TV Star's Gift for Words'.

72 'Women Say a Word on War', *Tribune*, 29 November 1967.
73 Jones, 'TV Star's Gift for Words'.
74 Jones, 'Brains, Beauty and Heart', *Australian*, 24 July 2003.
75 'Singer Holds Back Tax in Protest Over War', *Australian*, 18 November 1967.
76 Claire Wright, 'A Life's Song for the Heart and Soul of Australia', *Age*, 1 August 2003.
77 Wright, 'A Life's Song'.
78 Cora, *Noreen Hewett*, 24.
79 'Women for Peace' Pamphlet.

Chapter 3: The 'Founding Mothers'

1 'SOS First Press Release', May 1965, NAA: A6126, 1338/45.
2 Candy Cole interview, 11 November 2013.
3 'Mothers Oppose Call-Up', *Australian*, 19 May 1965.
4 'Silent 300 in Protest on Vietnam', *Sydney Morning Herald*, 21 May 1965; Dorothy Cora, *Noreen Hewett: Portrait of a Grassroots Activist* (Sydney: Older Women's Network of NSW, 2010), 24.
5 'Night in Canberra', *UAW Newsletter*, May 1965. NAA: A6126 1338/47.
6 'Vietnam Act by Australia Lacks Respect', *Sydney Morning Herald*, 31 May 1965.
7 'SOS Stand on Draft', *Australian*, 24 June 1965.
8 Sydney SOS Newsletter, September 1965.
9 Sydney SOS Newsletter, September 1965.
10 Sydney SOS, First Annual Report, 5 June 1966. NLA: MS 3821-23.
11 Sydney SOS Newsletter May 1966. NLA: MS 3821-20.
12 'Joyce Mary Golgerth', 15 October 1965. NAA: A6126, 1338/32.
13 'SOS First Press Release', May 1965. NAA: A6126, 1338/45; Michael Golgerth interview, 21 October 2013.
14 'Joyce Mary Golgerth', 15 October 1965. NAA: A6126, 1338/32.
15 See, for example: Ann-Mari Jordens, 'Conscription and Dissent: the genesis of anti-war protest', in *Vietnam Remembered*, ed. Gregory Pemberton (Sydney: New Holland Publishers, 2009), 79.
16 Sue Foster interview, 29 October 2013.
17 Foster interview.
18 Foster interview.
19 'SOS First Press Release', May 1965, NAA: A6126, 1338/45.
20 'Those Women with Banners', *Sun*, 14 December 1965.
21 J. Golgerth, 'Letter to the Editor', *Bulletin*, 9 April 1966.
22 Bob Gould, 'Recollections of the Struggle Against the Vietnam War', *Green Left Weekly*, 10 May 1995. www.greenleft.org.au.node9309, accessed 19 September 2014.
23 Cora, *Noreen Hewett*, 3–10.
24 'Spirited Activist Never Gave Up Fight', *Sydney Morning Herald*, 24 April 2012.
25 Cora, *Noreen Hewett*, 11.
26 'Spirited Activist Never Gave Up Fight', *Sydney Morning Herald*, 24 April 2012.
27 Cora, *Noreen Hewett*, 20.
28 Cora, *Noreen Hewett*, 15.

29   Cora, *Noreen Hewett*, 19–20.
30   Noreen Hewett, 'The Anti-Vietnam War and Anti-Conscription Movements', in *A Turbulent Decade: Social Protest Movements and the Labour Movement, 1965–1975*, ed. Beverley Symons and Rowan Cahill (Newtown, NSW: Australian Society for the Study of Labour History (Sydney branch), 2005), 11.
31   'Save Our Sons Meeting', 2 September 1965. NAA: A6119, 4102/51.
32   'Spirited Activist Never Gave Up Fight', *Sydney Morning Herald*, 24 April 2012.
33   Golgerth interview; Cole interview; Foster interview.
34   'Government Challenged on Call-Up', *Canberra Times*, 17 November 1964; Noreen Hewett, 'The Anti-Vietnam War and Anti-Conscription Movements', 11.
35   Cora, *Noreen Hewett*, 23.
36   Noreen Hewett, 'The Anti-Vietnam War and Anti-Conscription Movements', 11.
37   Siobhan McHugh, *Minefields and Miniskirts: Australian Women and the Vietnam War* (Sydney: Doubleday, 1993), 206.
38   Cora, *Noreen Hewett*, 23. [Emphasis is the author's.]
39   Cora, *Noreen Hewett*, 23.
40   'SOS Meeting', 2 September 1965. NAA: A6119, 4102/51.
41   'SOS Meeting', 2 September 1965. NAA: A6119, 4102/51.
42   'SOS Meeting', 16 September 1965. NAA: A6119, 1338/36.
43   'SOS First Annual Meeting', 5 June 1966. NAA: A6126, 1338/17.
44   'Union of Australian Women NSW Branch's Management Committee Meeting', 7 May 1966. NAA: A6122, 1853/123.
45   Sydney SOS, First Annual Report, 5 June 1966. NLA: MS 3821-23.
46   'John (William John) Ashcroft', 12 November 1964. NAA: A6119, 5787/41.
47   'Australian Congress for International Co-Operation and Disarmament', 15 October 1964. NAA: A6119, 5787/27/40.
48   'Background Check On William John Ashcroft and Patricia Ashcroft', 19 October 1962. NAA: A6119, 5787/10.
49   'UAW NSW Annual Meeting', 21 December 1964. NAA: A6119, 5787/45.
50   'Report on AICD Peace Delegation to Canberra', 23 April 1965. NAA: A6119, 5787/49.
51   'SOS', *Our Women*, April–June 1966.
52   'Dorothy Bendick', 1982. NAA: D4881; Barbara Curthoys and Audrey McDonald, *More than a Hat and Glove Brigade: The Story of the Union of Australian Women* (Sydney: Bookpress, 1996), 82.
53   'Basic Particulars', 19 November 1982. NAA: A6119, 6238/83.
54   'UAW Meeting', 20 November 1965. NAA: A6119, 4923/77.
55   'A Cry for the Children from an American-Australian Mother', *Tribune*, 7 April 1965.
56   'Helen Palmer', 27 April 1965. NAA: A6119, 6238/13; 'An American View', *Peacemaker*, May 1965.
57   'Dorothy Bendick', 15 June 1965. NAA: A6119, 6238/22.
58   Curthoys and McDonald, *More than a Hat and Glove Brigade*, 82.
59   Curthoys and McDonald, *More than a Hat and Glove Brigade*, 83.
60   'UAW Meeting', 20 November 1965. NAA: A6119, 4923/76.

61 'Dorothy Bendick', 5 August 1965. NAA: A6119, 6238/24.
62 'Kuring-gai Branch CPA', n.d. c. 1965. NAA: A6119, 6238/23.
63 The UAW's newsletter in July 1966 mentioned that Bendick had been forced to return 'unexpectedly' to the USA. NAA: A6119, 6238/76.
64 Philip Decker interview, 2 December 2013.
65 'Councillors of Sutherland Shire 1906 and Onwards', *Sutherland Shire Council*, https://www.sutherlandshire.nsw.gov.au/files/sharedassets/website/document-library/information-management/council-online/history-of-councillors-web-version.pdf, accessed 22 September 2014.
66 'Shorthand Record of Chou En-lai Interview', *St George and Sutherland Shire Leader*, 2 June 1971.
67 'China Trip', *St George and Sutherland Shire Leader*, 14 April 1971.
68 'Shorthand Record of Chou En-lai Interview', *St George and Sutherland Shire Leader*, 2 June 1971.
69 Decker interview.
70 Decker interview.
71 SOS, 'Press Release: Canberra delegation', 21 May 1965. NLA: MS 3821-25.
72 Hon J. W. Shaw, 'Death of the Honourable John Davis Garland', *NSW Legislative Council Hansard*, 7 September 1993. www.parliament.nsw.gov.au/prod/parlment/hansart.nsf/V3Key/LC19930907035, accessed 26 September 2013.
73 Barbara Curthoys, 'The Union of Australian Women: a celebration', *The Hummer* 2, 7 (Summer 1996/97). *Australian Society for the Study of Labour History*, https://asslh.org.au/hummer/vol-2-no%20-7/australian-women/, accessed 7 September 2014.
74 'Memo from Australia House', 20 July 1960. NAA: A6119, 4102/2.
75 Mark Gregory Interview, 6 November 2013.
76 'Elizabeth Ann Gregory', 20 July 1960. NAA: A6119, 4102/2.
77 'Elizabeth Ann Gregory', 20 July 1960. NAA: A6119, 4102/2.
78 'Ann Gregory', 16 February 1965. NAA: A6119, 4102/12.
79 Gregory interview.
80 'Balmain Branch CPA Meeting', 11 March 1965. NAA: A6119, 4102/21.
81 Gregory interview.
82 Gregory interview.
83 SOS, 'Press Release: Canberra delegation', 21 May 1965. NLA: MS 3821-25.
84 'Elizabeth Ann Gregory', 21 June 1967. NAA: A6126, 1338/3.
85 'Elizabeth Ann Gregory', 21 June 1967. NAA: A6126, 1338/3.
86 'Margaret Rae Lee', 27 April 1966. NAA: A6119, 6149/26.
87 'SOS Meeting', 17 June 1965. NAA: A6119, 4102/31; Cole interview.
88 'Ruby O'Sullivan', 4 November 1970. NAA: A6119, 6283/169.
89 'John Patrick O'Sullivan / Ruby O'Sullivan', 28 August 1959. NAA: A6119, 6283/31.
90 Foster interview.
91 'SOS Meeting', 16 September 1965. NAA: A6119, 4102/62.
92 'A Life Devoted to the Rights of Others', *Sydney Morning Herald*, 23 January 2013.
93 'A Life Devoted to the Rights of Others', *Sydney Morning Herald*, 23 January 2013.

94 'ASIO Report on Save Our Sons', 1 June 1965. NAA: A6119, 4102/29.
95 'ASIO Report on Save Our Sons', 1 June 1965.
96 'Letter from ASIO to the Prime Minister', 20 September 1965. NAA: A6122, 1665/147.
97 'ASIO Reply to Ministerial Enquiry', 28 August 1968. NAA: A6119, 1758/145.
98 'Meeting of Communist Party of Australia Faction in Union of Australian Women', 6 October 1965. NAA: A6119, 4923/39.
99 'Letter to Editor from G. H Yates', *Sydney Morning Herald*, 1 October 1965.
100 Cora, *Noreen Hewett*, 25.
101 Cole interview.
102 Cora, *Noreen Hewett*, 25.
103 'Save Our Sons Meeting', 1 July 1965, NAA: A6126, 1338/49.
104 'Save Our Sons Meeting', 1 July 1965.
105 'Save Our Sons Membership List'. NAA: A6122, 1668/33-39.
106 'Memo Re: Save Our Sons Membership List'. NAA: A6119, 5787/89.
107 Sydney SOS, First Annual Report, 5 June 1966. NLA: MS 3821-23.
108 'SOS First Press Release', May 1965. NAA: A6126, 1338/45.
109 Maurie Mulheron interview, 20 October 2012.
110 I. Hogbin, 'Handwritten Note, Including Underlining, On Form for SOS National Petition to Prime Minister Against Conscription for Overseas Service', 9 March 1966. NLA: MS 9878-7.
111 Cora, *Noreen Hewett*, 23–24.
112 'SOS Statement of Aims'. NAA: A6122, 1665/54.
113 Letter from P. Ashcroft to J. Ralfs, 6 October 1965. NLA: MS 3821-3.
114 Sydney SOS Newsletter, September 1965.
115 'SOS First Press Release', May 1965. NAA: A6126, 1338/45.
116 'SOS First Press Release', May 1965.
117 'SOS First Press Release', May 1965.
118 Cole interview.
119 Letter from P. Ashcroft to R. Fitzgerald, 7 October 1965. NLA: MS 3821-20.
120 Cole interview.
121 Letter from P. Ashcroft to J. Ralfs, 6 October 1965. NLA: MS 3821-3.

Chapter 4: 'Mothers Are on the March'

1 'Quote by Juan Regano from SOS Recruitment Leaflet', 1965, NAA: A6122, 1665/109.
2 Anna Vroland, *Calling All Women* [Newsletter]. NLA: MS 9878-2.
3 Vroland, *Calling All Women*.
4 Letter from J. McLean to P. Ashcroft, 5 July 1965. NLA: MS 3821-4.
5 Letter from V. Ward to P. Ashcroft, 15 June 1965. NLA: MS 3821-5.
6 Letter from I. McArthur to J. Golgerth and Ashcroft, 26 June 1965. NLA: MS 3821-1.
7 Letter from R. Fitzgerald to P. Ashcroft, 9 July 1965. NLA: MS 3821-3.
8 'Union of Australian Women Statement on Airport Protest', 8 July 1965. NLA: MS 3821-2.

9   'Sydney SOS Anti-Conscription Leaflet', 29 July 1965. NAA: A6122, 1665/82.
10 Sydney SOS Newsletter, September 1965.
11 Sydney SOS, First Annual Report, 5 June 1966. NLA: MS 3821-23.
12 'SOS First Press Statement', May 1965. NAA: A6126, 1338/45.
13 John Murphy, *Harvest of Fear: A History of Australia's Vietnam War*. (Sydney: Allen & Unwin, 1993), 141.
14 Letter from V. Ward to P. Ashcroft, 15 June 1965. NLA: MS 3821-5.
15 Letter from V. Ward to P. Ashcroft, 9 July 1965. NLA: MS 3821-5.
16 Letter from V. Ward to P. Ashcroft, 23 July 1965. NLA: MS 3821-5.
17 Open letter from Brisbane SOS, n.d. c. July 1965. NAA: A6122, 2010/81.
18 Letter from V. Ward to P. Ashcroft, 16 July 1965. NLA: MS 3821-5.
19 'SOS Qld', 1 June 1966. NAA: A6122, 2010/125; 'SOS Movement Offers FREE Legal Aid' [Advertisement], *Truth*, 20 March 1966.
20 Letter from V. Ward to P. Ashcroft, 19 November 1965. NLA: MS 3821-5.
21 Pam Young, *Daring to Take a Stand: The Story of the Union of Australian Women in Queensland* (Wavell Heights, Queensland: Pam Young, 1998), 93.
22 'Visit to Australia of Prime Minister Ky', 18 January 1967. NAA: A6119, 2659/104.
23 Letter from V. Ward to P. Ashcroft, 9 July 1965. NLA: MS 3821-5.
24 Letter from V. Ward to P. Ashcroft, 9 July 1965.
25 'CPA Interest in Vietnam Save Our Sons Movement', 13 July 1965. NAA: A6122, 2010/1.
26 'Grievance Meeting – For Women Only', *Australian Women's Weekly*, 3 May 1967.
27 Letter from V. Ward to P. Ashcroft, 5 July 1965. NLA: MS 3821-5.
28 'Vale Margaret Baxendell', *Newsletter of Women's International League of Peace and Freedom (QLD)*, April 2012.
29 'Social Experiment in Tiny Quaker Settlement', *Telegraph*, 27 November 1943.
30 'Shirley Jamieson – Ace Chicken Sexer', n.d., publication unknown, in Private Collection of Gordon Jamieson.
31 Gordon Jamieson interview, 10 August 2013.
32 Jamieson interview.
33 'Interstate Movement of Persons of Security Interest', 21 September 1965. NAA: A6119, 2010/23.
34 'Conscripts' [Letter to the Editor], publication unknown, c. June 1966, in Private Collection of Gordon Jamieson.
35 'Visit to Australia of Prime Minister Ky', 18 January 1967. NAA: A6119, 2659/104.
36 Sydney SOS Newsletter, September 1965.
37 Joan Ross interview, 27 November 2013.
38 'Visit to Australia of US President', 19 October 1966. NAA: A6122, 2010/198.
39 Letter from P. Ashcroft to V. Ward, n.d. c. 1966. NLA: MS 3821-5.
40 Letter from V. Ward to P. Ashcroft, n.d. c. January 1966. NLA: MS 3821-5.
41 Letter from V. Ward to A. Pert, 7 July 1966. NLA: MS 3821-5.
42 Letter from A. Pert to V. Ward, 19 July 1966. NLA: MS 3821-5.

43 Letter from V. Ward to A. Pert, n.d. c. 1967. NLA: MS 3821-5.
44 'The Rude Awakening of Vilma', *Sunday Truth*, 15 October 1967.
45 'The Rude Awakening of Vilma', *Sunday Truth*, 15 October 1967.
46 Letter from V. Ward to Sydney SOS, 17 April 1967. NLA: MS: 3821-5.
47 Letter from V. Ward to Sydney SOS, 17 April 1967. NLA: MS: 3821-5.
48 Letter from A. Pert to V. Ward, 26 June 1967. NLA: MS 3821-5.
49 'Queensland Peace Committee liaison committee meeting', 30 November 1967. NAA: A6122, 2010/74.
50 Jamieson interview.
51 Margaret Reynolds interview, 2 November 2012.
52 Letter from M. Reynolds to Sydney SOS, n.d. 1966. NLA: MS 3821-7.
53 Reynolds interview.
54 Reynolds interview.
55 Reynolds interview.
56 Margaret Reynolds, *Living Politics* (St Lucia, Queensland: University of Queensland Press, 2007), 53.
57 Reynolds interview.
58 Thomas Hardy interview, 22 November 2012.
59 Jim McIlroy, *The Red North: Queensland's History of Struggle* (Chippendale, NSW: Resistance Books, 2001), 4.
60 McIlroy, *The Red North*, 3.
61 Diane Menghetti, *The Red North: The Popular Front in North Queensland* (Townsville: James Cook University, 1981), 95.
62 Email from E. Hannay to the author, 1 June 2013.
63 Reynolds interview.
64 Reynolds, *Living Politics*, 47.
65 Letter from M. Reynolds to P. Ashcroft, n.d. (early 1966). NLA: MS 3821-7.
66 'Wants to Form Branch of SOS', *Townsville Daily Bulletin*, c. 1966, cited in Reynolds, *Living Politics*, 54.
67 Reynolds interview.
68 Reynolds interview.
69 Letter from M. Reynolds to P. Ashcroft, 23 May 1966. NLA: MS 3821-7.
70 Reynolds interview.
71 Neal Sellars, *Fred Thompson, Communist, Union Organiser, Humanist: A Biography* (Townsville: Neal Sellars, 2012), 137-141.
72 Loma Thompson interview, 7 December 2012.
73 Thompson interview.
74 Hardy interview.
75 Reynolds, *Living Politics*, 54.
76 Reynolds interview.
77 Reynolds, *Living Politics*, 56; Letter from M. Reynolds to A. Pert, 29 October 1966. NLA: MS 3821-7.
78 Vince Prasser interview, 4 March 2013.
79 'Ethnee Joyce Brunker'. NAA: A6122, 1680/21.
80 'Ethnee Joyce Brunker'. NAA: A6122, 1680/21.

81 Prasser interview.
82 'Prasser interview.
83 Paul D. Williams, 'Keeffe, James Bernard (1919–1988)', *Australian Dictionary of Biography*, National Centre of Biography, Australian National University, http://adb.anu.edu.au/biography/keeffe-james-bernard-jim-12718/text22933, accessed 4 November 2012.
84 Letter from M. Reynolds to P. Ashcroft, 28 May 1966. NLA: MS 3821-7.
85 Letter from M. Reynolds to P. Ashcroft, 23 May 1966. NLA: MS 3821-7.
86 Letter from M. Reynolds to A. Pert, 29 October 1966. NLA: MS 3821-7.
87 Letter from M. Reynolds to A. Pert, 29 October 1966.
88 Letter from M. Reynolds to A. Pert, 29 October 1966.
89 Letter from P. Ashcroft to M. Reynolds, 28 March 1966. NLA: MS 3821-7.
90 Letter from M. Reynolds to A. Pert, 29 October 1966.
91 Reynolds interview.
92 Letter from A. Pert to M. Reynolds, 4 November 1966. NLA: MS 3821-7.
93 'Save Our Sons Movement, Townsville Branch'. NAA: A6122, 1680, 37.
94 Reynolds interview.
95 Letter from I. McArthur to J. Golgerth, 26 June 1965. NLA: MS 3821-1.
96 Letter from I. McArthur to J. Golgerth, 26 June 1965.
97 Letter from I. McArthur to P. Ashcroft, 5 August 1965. NLA: MS 3821-1.
98 Letter from I. McArthur to P. Ashcroft, 5 August 1965.
99 Edna Cullen, 'Conscripts' [Letter to Editor], *Newcastle Morning Herald*, c. August 1966. NLA: MS 3821-1.
100 SOS Newcastle, 'Mothers' [Leaflet], c. June 1966. NAA: A6122, 1668/71.
101 'Doyen of Urban Committees', *Newcastle Morning Herald*, 17 March 1966.
102 Letter from R. Hobson to P. Ashcroft, 27 August 1965. NLA: MS 3821-1.
103 Letter from E. Warburton to SOS, n.d. c. 1966. NLA: MS 3821-2.
104 'SOS', 5 August 1970. NAA: A6122, 2649/2.
105 'SOS Meeting', 13 February 1971. NAA: A6119/1813/138.
106 'Complaint by RSL', *Illawarra Mercury*, 26 June 1965.
107 'Letters to Wollongong', 15 March 1966. NLA: MS 3821-3.
108 'Women Against Conscription', *Illawarra Mercury*, 31 March 1966.
109 'Communist Party of Australia Interest in the Wollongong Branch, Save Our Sons', 12 April 1966. NAA: A6122, 1853/82.
110 'Communist Party of Australia Interest in the Wollongong Branch, Save Our Sons', 12 April 1966.
111 'The Vietnam Protest and Anti-Conscription Movements in Australia, Save Our Sons', 10 May 1966. NAA: A6122, 1853/118.
112 Letter from N. Davenport to N. Hewett, 1 April 1966. NLA: MS 3821-3.
113 Letter from N. Thomas to N. Hewett, 11 April 1966; 'Vietnam: War of Useless Sacrifice Signed by Citizens of Greater Wollongong' [Advertisement], *South Coast Times*, 10 August 1967.
114 'Youths Leave for Training', *South Coast Times*, 21 April 1966.
115 'Save Our Sons Report on Canberra Deputation', 27 April 1966. NAA: A6122, 1853/102.

116 South Coast Waterside Workers' Women's Committee, *Roundabout* [Newsletter], October 1967. *Garber Collection*. Wollongong City Library (henceforth WCL): DMSS 225/1.
117 Letter from F. Garber to A. Pert, 11 March 1969. NLA: MS 3821-3.
118 'Vietnam: War of Useless Sacrifice' [Advertisement], *South Coast Times*, 10 August 1967.
119 South Coast Waterside Workers' Women's Committee, *Roundabout* [Newsletter], October 1967. WCL: DMSS 225/1.
120 South Coast Waterside Workers' Women's Committee, *Roundabout* [Newsletter], May 1967. WCL: DMSS 225/1.
121 'South Coast Citizens Against Conscription', c. 1969, publication unknown. WCL: DMSS 225/2.
122 Mac Gudgeon interview, 17 November 2012.
123 'Bowen, Sally (1918–1999)', *Australian Women's Register*. http://nla.gov.au/nla.party-741073, accessed 10 February 2012.
124 Frances Laneyrie, 'Between Class and Gender: female activists in the Illawarra 1975–1980', (PhD thesis, Auckland University of Technology, 2010), 131.
125 'Women for Peace: why we chained ourselves', 1970 [Pamphlet]. *Garber Collection*. Wollongong City Library (WCL) DMSS 225/1.
126 'Letter to the Editor', n.d., publication unknown. *Garber Collection*. WCL: DMSS 225/2.
127 Letter from F. Garber to A. Pert, 27 August 1969. NLA: MS 3821-3.
128 Letter from F. Garber to A. Pert, 9 September 1969. NLA: MS 3821-3.
129 Jean McLean interview, 2 October 2014.
130 Gudgeon interview.
131 'SOS SA recruitment letter', 29 June 1965. NAA: A6122, 1813/1.
132 'SOS', 2 July 1965. NAA: A6122, 1813/2.
133 'Women Demonstrate: silent airport vigil', *News*, 1 July 1965.
134 Audrey Potticary, 'Save Our Sons Remembered' in *Years of Struggle: Reminiscences of the Union of Australian Women in South Australia, 1950–2005*, Beryl Miller and ed. Susan Marsden (Adelaide: Union of Australian Women (SA), 2005), 46.
135 'Women Demonstrate: silent airport vigil', *News*, 1 July 1965.
136 'Women Demonstrate: silent airport vigil', *News*, 1 July 1965.
137 'CPA Interest in Vietnam', 1 July 1965. NAA: A6122, 1813/5.
138 Miller and Marsden, *Years of Struggle*, 19.
139 Beryl Miller interview, 8 April 2014.
140 Valerie Howe, 'Early Days in the UAW', in *Years of Struggle*, 45.
141 'Report from South Australian Branch of UAW', 8 July 1965. NLA: MS 3821-2.
142 'Report from South Australian Branch of UAW', 8 July 1965.
143 Letter from P. Ashcroft to H. Hoare, 31 September 1965. NLA: MS 3821-2.
144 Potticary, 'Save Our Sons Remembered', in *Years of Struggle*, 46.
145 Potticary, 'Save Our Sons Remembered', in *Years of Struggle*, 46.
146 'Viet. Key to Vote', *News*, 22 November 1966.
147 SA SOS Minutes, 3 May 1971. State Library of South Australia (henceforth SLSA): SRG 555.

148 Eulalie Tapp, 'SOS South Australia'. NLA: MS 9878-2.
149 'Viet. Key to Vote', *News*, 22 November 1966.
150 'Viet. Key to Vote', *News*, 22 November 1966.
151 Letter from M. Wharton to A. Pert, 22 May 1967. NLA: MS 3821-2; Eulalie Tapp, 'SOS South Australia'. NLA: MS 9878-2.
152 Letter from H. Hoare to J. Golgerth, 15 September 1965. NLA: MS 3821-2.
153 Letter from P. Ashcroft to H. Hoare, 31 September 1965. NLA: MS 3821-2.
154 Letter from M. Wharton to A. Pert, 22 September 1967. NLA: MS 3821-2.
155 Tapp, 'SOS South Australia'. NLA: MS 9878-2.
156 SA SOS minutes, 26 September 1966. SLSA: SRG 555.
157 Letter from M. Wharton to A. Pert, 3 May 1967. NLA: MS 3821-2.
158 Tapp, 'SOS South Australia', NLA: MS 9878-2.
159 Tapp, 'SOS South Australia', NLA: MS 9878-2.
160 SOS SA Minutes, 27 May 1968. SLSA: SRG 555.
161 Letter from A. Potticary to A. Pert, 11 July 1968. NLA: MS 3821-2.
162 Letter from A. Potticary to A. Pert, 12 June 1969. NLA: MS 3821-2.
163 A. Potticary, 'Memo to Members', n.d. c. 1968. SLSA: SRG 555.
164 Campaign for Peace in Vietnam Newsletter, 6 July 1968. SLSA: SRG 781/26/3.
165 A. Potticary, 'Secretary's Report', 28 July 1969. SLSA: SRG 555.
166 J. L. Darling, 'Notes on SOS Leaflet Distributed to Members', July 1970. SLSA: SRG 555.
167 A. Potticary, 'Secretary's Annual Report 1970–71', June 1971. SLSA: SRG 555.
168 SOS SA Minutes, 27 March 1972. SLSA: SRG 555.
169 Letter from R. Gilchrist to P. Ashcroft, 2 February 1966. NLA: MS 3821-2.
170 'UAW Management Meeting', 8 June 1965. NAA: A6119, 5671/27.
171 'UAW Management Meeting', 8 June 1965.
172 Letter from M. Henderson to Sydney SOS, c. 1966. NLA: MS 3821-2.
173 'Report of Union of Australian Women Meeting', n.d. NAA: A6119, 5671/45.
174 'Minutes of Citizens' Meeting Held at the Railway Institute', 29 March 1966. NAA: A6119, 5703/35.
175 'Minutes of Citizens' Meeting Held at the Railway Institute', 29 March 1966.
176 'Report on Combined Meeting of Belmont/Midland Junction Branches of CPA', 29 March 1966. NAA: A6119, 5671/51.
177 Ray Collie interviewed by Stuart Reid, 1988, State Library of Western Australia: OH 2057.
178 Letter from M. Henderson to Sydney SOS, c. 1966. NLA: MS 3821-2.
179 Letter from P. Ashcroft to R. Collie, 13 April 1966. NLA: MS 3821-2.
180 Letter from P. Ashcroft to R. Collie, 13 April 1966.
181 Letter from M. Henderson to Sydney SOS, c. 1966.
182 'WA Special Branch Report on SOS Protest', 2 April 1966. NAA: A6119, 5671/58.
183 'Marchers Protest', *Weekend News*, 2 April 1966.
184 'Anti-Vietnam Marchers', *Sunday Times*, 3 April 1966.
185 'ASIO Report re: SOS March', 2 April 1966. NAA: A6119, 5671/55.
186 'SOS Meeting', 4 April 1966. NAA: A6119, 5671/49.

187 Letter from M. Henderson to Sydney SOS, c. 1966. NLA: MS 3821-2.
188 'WA Special Branch Report on SOS Protest', 2 April 1966. NAA: A6119, 5671/58.
189 'Sapper McIlroy Off to Vietnam', *Daily News*, 4 April 1966.
190 'ASIO Report on SOS Public Meeting', 4 April 1966. NAA: A6119, 5671.
191 'WA SOS', 15 December 1966. NAA: A6122, 1682/189.
192 'Report on Proposed Constitution of WA SOS', 1 May 1966. NAA: A6122, 1682/69.
193 J. Kane, 'Letter to Editor', *West Australian*, 28 April 1966.
194 'UAW National Conference', 27–31 May 1967. NAA: A6119, 5671/81.
195 'SOS WA Minutes', 5 May 1966. NAA: A6122, 5703/3.
196 'WA SOS', 15 December 1966. NAA: A6122, 1682/189.
197 'Report on SOS WA', 4 April 1966. NAA: A6122, 1682/45.
198 'WA SOS', 15 December 1966.
199 Stuart Wearne interview, 14 May 2013.
200 'WA SOS', 15 December 1966. NAA: A6122, 1682/189.
201 'SOS Demonstration', 21 May 1966. NAA: A6119, 5671/61.
202 'Security Check', 11 May 1967. NAA: A6122, 2008/20, 36.
203 'WA SOS', 15 December 1966.
204 'UAW Executive Management Meeting', 9 May 1966. NAA: A6119, 5671/68.
205 'UAW Executive Management Meeting', 19 May 1966. NAA: A6119, 5671/69.
206 'SOS WA Minutes', 9 March 1967. NAA: A6119, 5703/48.
207 J. Keady, D. Whyte and B. Ewing, 'Save Our Sons Policy' [Letter to the Editor], *Daily News*, 1 August 1966.
208 'SOS Meeting', 9 February 1967. NAA: A6119, 5671/121.
209 'UAW Meeting', March 1967. NAA: A6119, 5702/6.
210 'SOS Special Meeting', 6 June 1967. NAA: A6119, 5702/18.
211 'SOS Special Meeting', 6 June 1967.
212 'SOS General Meeting', 13 June 1967. NAA: A6119, 5702/20.
213 'Combined Meeting of SOS and VAC', 27 June 1967. NAA: A6119, 5702/21-22.
214 'Combined Meeting of SOS and VAC', 27 June 1967.
215 'Combined Meeting of SOS and VAC', 27 June 1967.
216 'Combined Meeting of SOS and VAC', 11 July 1967. NAA: A6119, 5702/23.
217 'Minutes of SOS WA Meetings', March 1966 – July 1967. NAA: A6119, 5703.
218 Wearne interview.
219 'UAW lunch', 29 February 1972. NAA: A6119, 5704/8.
220 Letter from M. Henderson to A. Pert, n.d. c. November 1967). NLA: MS 3821-2.
221 'VOC General Meeting', 23 April 1968. NAA: A6119, 5702/67.
222 Letters from Victorian women to SOS Sydney. NLA: MS 3821-4.
223 Letter from N. Walsh to A. Gregory, 2 June 1965. NLA: MS 3821-4.
224 Vroland, *Calling All Women*.
225 Letter from D. Gibson to Ailsa, 17 June 1965. NLA: MS 9878-4.
226 Letter from D. Gibson to Ailsa, 17 June 1965.
227 Jean McLean, 'Anti-Vietnam War Activist', in *Protesters*, ed. Gloria Frydman (Blackburn, Victoria: Collins Dove, 1987), 16.
228 Jean McLean interview, 2 October 2014.

229 Pauline Armstrong, 'A History of the Save Our Sons Movement of Victoria: 1965–1973', (MA thesis, Monash University, 1991), 26.
230 Vroland, *Calling All Women*.
231 Letter from J. McLean to P. Ashcroft, 5 July 1965. NLA: MS 3821-4.
232 Vroland, *Calling All Women*.
233 Women of the Australian Labor Party, 'Who's Afraid of Total War?' [Leaflet], n.d. c. July 1965. NLA: MS 3821-4.
234 Letter from J. McLean to P. Ashcroft, 3 August 1965. NLA: MS 3821-4.
235 Letter from M. Mason to J. Golgerth, 3 August 1965. NLA: MS 3821-4.
236 Letter from M. Mason to J. Golgerth, 3 August 1965. Bob Santamaria was an Australian Roman Catholic anti-Communist political activist and journalist who supported the Vietnam War.
237 Letter from J. McLean to P. Ashcroft, 3 August 1965. NLA: MS 3821-4.
238 Letter from J. McLean to P. Ashcroft, 19 August 1965. NLA: MS 3821-4.
239 Dorothy Foster, 'Looking at Kitchens: Monastic and magnificent', Unidentified newspaper clipping, 29 May 1968, NAA A6119, 1758/101.
240 McLean, 'Anti-Vietnam War Activist', in *Protesters*, 16.
241 McLean, 'Anti-Vietnam War Activist', in *Protesters*, 16.
242 'Jean McLean – My Life in Photos', *Dimensions in Time*, 19 February 2002, Australian Broadcasting Corporation (ABC), formerly available from http://www.abc.net.au/dimensions_in_time/transcripts/s485125.htm, accessed 25 April 2012.
243 'Jean McLean – My Life in Photos'.
244 McLean, 'Anti-Vietnam War Activist', in *Protesters*, 6.
245 Victoria SOS Newsletter, 18 August 1965.
246 Victoria SOS Newsletter, 18 August 1965.
247 Victoria SOS Newsletter, 18 August 1965.
248 McLean interviewed by P. Armstrong, 26 June 1990. NLA: MS 9878-3-2.
249 Victoria SOS Newsletter, 18 August 1965.
250 Victoria SOS Newsletter, 18 August 1965.
251 Armstrong, 'A History of the Save Our Sons Movement of Victoria', 36.
252 Joan Coxsedge interview, 3 April 2014.
253 McLean interviewed by Armstrong.
254 McLean interview by author.
255 Coxsedge interview.
256 Coxsedge interview.
257 McLean interview.
258 McLean interview.
259 Coxsedge interview.
260 Coxsedge interview.
261 McLean interviewed by Armstrong.
262 Coxsedge interview.
263 Jean McLean, 'Notes', 1973. NLA: MS 9878-4.
264 McLean interview.
265 Letter from A. Pert to M. Reynolds, 4 August 1966. NLA: MS 3821-7.

Chapter 5: 'Heads Bowed, Hands Clasped', 1965–66

1. Irene Miller interview, 31 July 2014.
2. Letter from V. Ward to P. Ashcroft, 12 July 1965. NLA: MS 3821-5.
3. Jean McLean interview, 2 October 2014.
4. Jean McLean, 'Notes', 1973. NLA: MS 9878-4.
5. Jean McLean interviewed by P. Armstrong, 26 June 1990. NLA: MS 9878-3-2.
6. McLean interviewed by Armstrong.
7. McLean interviewed by Armstrong.
8. SOS, the WILPF and the UAW all held vigils during the Vietnam War. Women from these groups supported each other's events. Media coverage of these events frequently confused these groups.
9. Victoria SOS Newsletter, November 1965.
10. 'Wild Farewell for Servicemen', *Daily Telegraph*, 1 July 1965; 'Protest on Conscription', *Sydney Morning Herald*, 1 July 1965.
11. 'Protests as Call-Up Youths Leave', *Age*, 1 July 1965.
12. Sydney SOS Minutes, 1 July 1965. NLA: MS 3821.
13. Commissioner of Police, 'SOS Rally Perth', 16 April 1966. NAA: A6119, 4570/27.
14. Letter from V. Ward to P. Ashcroft, 12 July 1965. NLA: MS 3821-5.
15. Victoria SOS Newsletter, November 1965.
16. Miller interview.
17. Letter from P. Ashcroft to V. Ward, 22 August 1965. NLA: MS 3821-5.
18. McLean interview.
19. Letter from V. Ward to P. Ashcroft, 21 August 1965. NLA: MS 3821-5.
20. Dorothy Dalton interviewed by P. Armstrong, 23 August 1990. NLA: MS 9878-3-2.
21. Irene Miller interviewed by P. Armstrong, August 1990. NLA: MS 9878-3-2.
22. Joan Coxsedge interview, 3 April 2014.
23. 'May Day Celebrations', 9 May 1966. NAA: A6122, 1680/135.
24. 'Save Our Sons', *Herald*, 11 November 1965.
25. Sydney SOS Newsletter, June 1966.
26. Sydney SOS Minutes, June 1966. NLA: MS 3821.
27. 'Save Our Sons', 27 May 1966. NAA: A6122, 1680/120-123.
28. SA SOS Minutes, 31 October 1966. SLSA: SRG 555.
29. Sydney SOS Minutes, 27 October 1966. NLA: MS 3821.
30. Sydney SOS Newsletter, July 1966.
31. Noreen Hewett, 'The Anti-Vietnam War and Anti-Conscription Movements', in *A Turbulent Decade: Social Protest Movements and the Labour Movement, 1965–1975*, ed. Beverley Symons and Rowan Cahill (Newtown, NSW: Australian Society for the Study of Labour History (Sydney branch), 2005), 12–13.
32. Pam Young, *Daring to Take a Stand: The Story of the Union of Australian Women in Queensland* (Wavell Heights, Queensland: Pam Young, 1998), 69.
33. Brisbane SOS, 'Petition Against War Toys'. NLA: MS 3821-5.
34. Letter from V. Ward to P. Ashcroft, n.d. c. 1966. NLA: MS 3821-5.
35. 'War Toys Losing the Sales Battle', *Sun News-Pictorial*, 12 March 1968.

36   Letter from A. Pert to the Council of Civil Liberties, 20 July 1966. NLA: MS 3821-7.
37   Sydney SOS Minutes, 10 February 1966. NLA: MS 3821.
38   Sydney SOS Minutes, 23 June 1966. NLA: MS 3821.
39   Sydney SOS Newsletter, May 1966.
40   Sydney SOS Newsletter, May 1966.
41   Letter from A. Pert to N. Jensen, 16 June 1966. NLA: MS 3821-8.
42   Letter from N. Jensen to A. Pert, 28 June 1966. NLA: MS 3821-8.
43   Marion Henderson, 'History of SOS Perth', n.d. NLA: MS 3821-2.
44   Shelley Davies interview, 25 July 2013.
45   Davies interview.
46   Davies interview.
47   Email from Wendy Kendrick to author, 7 August 2013.
48   Henderson, 'History of SOS Perth'.
49   ASIO, 'SOS Demonstration', 21 April 1966. NAA: A6119, 5671/61; 'Varied Peace Reactions', *Tribune*, 27 April 1966.
50   'A Mother Says … I Want to Keep My Son Pale and Sickly', *Herald*, 22 August 1967.
51   Sydney SOS Newsletter, September 1965.
52   'You Didn't Fight, So Why Our Sons?' *Australian*, 2 June 1966.
53   Victoria SOS Newsletter, November 1965.
54   Sydney SOS, 'SOS Canberra Lobbying Mission Report', October 1965. NLA: MS 3821-12.
55   'Obstacles to Protest', *Canberra Times*, 22 September 1965.
56   Sydney SOS, 'SOS Canberra Lobbying Mission Report', October 1965. NLA: MS 3821-12.
57   Sydney SOS, 'SOS Canberra Lobbying Mission Report'.
58   Sydney SOS, 'SOS Canberra Lobbying Mission Report'.
59   Pat Ashcroft, 'SOS at Canberra', October 1965. NLA: MS 3821-12.
60   Ashcroft, 'SOS at Canberra'.
61   Sydney SOS, 'SOS Canberra Lobbying Mission Report'.
62   Letter from R. Fitzgerald to P. Ashcroft, 27 September 1965. NLA: MS 3821-3.
63   Letter from P. Ashcroft to R. Fitzgerald, 7 October 1965. NLA: MS 3821-3.
64   Letter from P. Ashcroft to Mrs Wallace, 7 October 1965. NLA: MS 3821-3.
65   Letter from J. Maclaine-Cross to P. Armstrong, 31 August 1990. NLA: MS 9878-2.
66   Sydney SOS, 'Report on Canberra Deputation'.
67   Sydney SOS, Second Annual Report, June 1967. NLA: MS 3821-23.
68   Reynolds interview.
69   Letter from P. Ashcroft to Adelaide SOS, 5 March 1966. NLA: MS 3821-2.
70   'Test for Call-Up Policy', *Daily Mirror*, 15 March 1966.
71   'Court Test of Call-Up', *Australian*, 15 March 1966.
72   Letter from P. Ashcroft to Newcastle, Brisbane, Victoria SOS groups, 5 March 1966. NLA: MS 3821-19.
73   Telegram from V. Ward to Sydney SOS, 7 March 1966. NLA: MS 3821-19.

74　Letter from V. Ward to Sydney SOS, 7 March 1966.
75　Letter from P. Ashcroft to Newcastle SOS, 11 March 1966.
76　Letter from Sydney SOS to other SOS groups, n.d. (1966). NLA: MS 3821-19.
77　Letter from E. Outhred to Adelaide SOS, 25 April 1966. NLA: MS 3821-19.
78　Letter from E. Outhred to Adelaide SOS, 25 April 1966.
79　Ella Outhred, Legal Aid Report, 14 June 1967. NLA: MS 3821-16.
80　Letter from E. Outhred to A. Potticary, n.d. NLA: MS 3821-16.
81　'SOS Secretary Says', *Queensland Guardian*, 8 December 1965.
82　Letter from E. Outhred to A. Potticary, n.d. NLA: MS 3821-16.
83　Joan Ross interview, 27 November 2013.
84　Victoria SOS Newsletter, September 1966.
85　Jean McLean quoted in Greg Langley, *A Decade of Dissent: Vietnam and Conflict on the Australian Homefront* (Sydney: Allen & Unwin, 1992), 32.
86　Maurie Mulheron interview, 20 October 2012.
87　Sydney SOS Newsletter, September 1965.
88　Sydney SOS, Second Annual Report, June 1967. NLA: MS 3821-23.
89　Victoria SOS, 'Christmas' [Leaflet], December 1965. NLA: MS 9878-5.
90　'Emigrate to Vietnam' [Letter to the Editor], *Freedom Anarchist Weekly*, 16 July 1966.
91　Newcastle SOS, 'Save Our Sons in the Name of Humanity' [Advertisement], *Newcastle Daily Herald*, n.d. c. 1966. NLA: MS 3821-1.
92　'Opinions on Conscription', *Townsville Daily Bulletin*, 1 August 1966.
93　'SOS Townsville', 30 July 1966. NAA: A6122, 1680/168.
94　Letter from V. Reid to J. Clark, 29 September 1966. NLA: MS 3821-3.
95　Val and Clive Reid, 'In Sympathy' [advertisement], *Border Morning Mail*, 17 November 1966. NLA: MS 3821-3.
96　Newcastle SOS, 'We Nurtured Him Through Childhood' [Leaflet], c. 1966. NLA: MS 3821-1.
97　Wollongong SOS, 'Mother's Day' [Leaflet], May 1970. NLA: MS 3821-3.
98　Corinne Kerby interviewed by P. Armstrong, 30 September 1990. NLA: MS 9878-3-3.
99　Corinne Kerby, 'Lines Written on the Picture of a Vietnamese Child Burned by Napalm', *Mainly Affirmative* (Melbourne: Georgian House, 1968), 28.
100　Letter from V. Reid to A. Pert, 12 June 1967. NLA: MS 3821-6.
101　Letter from L. Fisher to P. Ashcroft, n.d. 1965. NLA: MS 3821-6.
102　Glen Tomasetti, 'No!', *Broadside*, 92 (June 1968). https://singout.org/downloads/broadside/b092.pdf, accessed 6 April 2015; Victoria SOS Newsletter, 18 August 1965.
103　Glen Tomasetti, 'The Army's Appeal to Mothers 1968', in *The Vietnam Song Book*, ed. Barbara Dane and Irwin Silber (New York: The Guardian, 1969), 148–149.
104　Phyl Lobl, 'Tribute to a Rebel Girl', *Australian Folk Songs*, http://folkstream.com/reviews/glen/, accessed 2 April 2015.
105　Victoria SOS Newsletter, November 1965, December 1966.
106　Morgan Gallup Poll: APOP Subscribers' reports [table], cited in Murray Goot and Rodney Tiffen, 'Public Opinion and the Politics of the Polls', in *Australia's Vietnam*, ed. Peter King (Sydney: Allen & Unwin, 1983), 135.

107 Victoria SOS, 'Federal Election' [Leaflet], October 1966. NLA: MS 9878-4.
108 Letter from A. Pert to supporters, 13 October 1966. NLA: MS 3821-6.
109 Sydney SOS Newsletter, October 1966.
110 Mulheron interview.
111 Letter from D. Giles to A. Pert, 8 June 1966. NLA: MS 3821-9.
112 Victoria SOS Newsletter, October 1966.
113 Victoria SOS Newsletter, November 1966.
114 Sydney SOS Newsletter, July 1966.
115 Leonard Radic, 'An Evening of Dissent', *Age*, 14 November 1966.
116 Ann-Mari Jordens, 'Conscription and Dissent: the genesis of anti-war protest', in *Vietnam Remembered*, ed. Gregory Pemberton (Sydney: New Holland Publishers, 2009), 71.
117 'Police Carry White into the Army', *Australian*, 23 November 1966.
118 'Protest on White', *Sun News-Pictorial*, 22 November 1966; Ceci Cairns quoted in Langley, *Decade of Dissent*, 36.
119 Sydney SOS Newsletter, August 1966.
120 Bill White quoted in Langley, *Decade of Dissent*, 61.
121 McLean interview.
122 Bob Scates, *'Draftmen Go Free': A History of the Anti-Conscription Movement in Australia* (Richmond, Victoria: R. Scates, 1988), 23.
123 Scates, *Draftmen Go Free*, 29.
124 Miller interviewed by Armstrong.
125 Mulheron interview.
126 McLean interviewed by Armstrong.
127 Victoria SOS Newsletter, December 1966.
128 Sydney SOS Newsletter, December 1966.
129 Letter from Mrs Wharton to Sydney SOS, 16 December 1966. NLA: MS 3821-2.

Chapter 6: Gloves Off, 1967–69

1 Irene Miller interview, 31 July 2014.
2 Victoria SOS Newsletter, December 1966.
3 Sydney SOS Newsletter, February 1967.
4 WA SOS, 'Guest of Honour' [Leaflet], January 1967. NAA: A6122, 7008/54.
5 Sydney SOS Newsletter, February 1966.
6 Letter from Pert to NSW Police Commissioner, 10 February 1967. NLA: MS 3821-8.
7 Betty Harris, 'Letter to the Editor', *Newcastle Morning Herald*, 3 February 1967.
8 Grahame Garner, 'Vilma Ward and Norma Chalmers During Marshall Ky Demonstration' [photograph], January 1967. Fryer Research Mss F3400, Fryer Library, University of Queensland. http://espace.library.uq.edu.au/view/UQ:3786, accessed 29 June 2015.
9 Letter from V. Ward to A. Pert, 22 January 1967. NLA: MS 3821-5.
10 'Police Delinquency', *Brisbane Impact*, January 1967.
11 'Police Delinquency', *Brisbane Impact*, January 1967.

Notes

12   Sydney SOS Newsletter, February 1967.
13   Letter from A. Pert to Police Commissioner Bischof, 10 February 1967. NLA: MS 3821-5.
14   Paul Ham, *Vietnam: The Australian War* (Sydney: Harper Collins, 2008), 265.
15   Pam Young, *Daring to Take a Stand: The Story of the Union of Australian Women in Queensland* (Wavell Heights, Queensland: Pam Young, 1998), 94.
16   Sydney SOS Newsletter, March 1967.
17   'Placard Woman Defies Fine', *Australian*, 1 September 1967.
18   Letter from V. Ward to A. Pert, 15 March 1967. NLA: MS 3821-5.
19   Letter from A. Pert to Premier of Queensland, 14 March 1967. NLA: MS 3821-5.
20   Sydney SOS Newsletter, March 1967; Newcastle SOS, 'Annual General Meeting', 27 June 1967. NLA: MS 3821-1.
21   'Mrs Ward has Views on a Waste of Time', *Courier-Mail*, n.d. c. 1967. NLA: MS 3821-5.
22   Letter from V. Ward to A. Pert, n.d. c. 1967. NLA: MS 3821-5.
23   'The Rude Awakening of Vilma', *Sunday Truth*, 15 October 1967.
24   Young, *Daring to Take a Stand*, 101.
25   Victoria SOS Newsletter, May 1967.
26   Victoria SOS Newsletter, February 1968.
27   *Farrago*, Melbourne University's student newspaper, reported the SOS demonstration, supported by university students, had been a success with 'a large number' of conscripts accepting 'Form 7', the Application for Registration as a Conscientious Objector and several indicating they intended to use it. This was the first time the form had been handed out by protesters along with leaflets informing draftees of their rights under the law to register as conscientious objectors. 'Conscripts to Object', *Farrago*, 6 October 1967. NAA: A6122, 2621/6.
28   Victoria SOS Newsletter, March 1968.
29   Victoria SOS Newsletter, March 1968.
30   Victoria SOS Newsletter, March 1968.
31   'Wild Mobs Storm US Consulate, Police Headquarters', *Age*, 5 July 1968.
32   Victoria SOS Newsletter, July 1968.
33   Victoria SOS Newsletter, August 1968.
34   Victoria SOS Newsletter, August 1968.
35   Victoria SOS Newsletter, March 1969.
36   Jean McLean interview, 2 October 2014.
37   Victoria SOS Newsletter, November 1968.
38   'Protest Mother Won't Pay Fine', *Age*, 31 October 1968.
39   'By-Law Unjust – Students', *Age*, 13 February 1969.
40   McLean quoted in Greg Langley, *A Decade of Dissent: Vietnam and Conflict on the Australian Homefront* (Sydney: Allen & Unwin, 1992), 114.
41   'Editorial', *Age*, 5 February 1969.
42   Victoria SOS Newsletter, February 1969.
43   Victoria SOS Newsletter, February 1969.

44 Dick Shepherd, 'Unionists "Booked" at Viet. Protest', *Age*, 17 February 1969.
45 'Militant Women From the Save Our Sons', *Herald*, 27 February 1969.
46 Victoria SOS, 'You Will Not Be Fined For Reading This …' [Leaflet], early 1966. NLA: MS 9878-4.
47 'By-Law Cases All Adjourned', *Age*, 10 April 1969.
48 McLean quoted in Langley, *Decade of Dissent*, 114.
49 Corinne Kerby interviewed by P. Armstrong, 30 September 1990. NLA: MS 9878-3-3.
50 Rev. A.J. Lloyd, 'Letter to the Editor', *Herald*, 21 April 1969. NAA: A6122, 2621/119.
51 Victoria SOS Newsletter, March 1969.
52 McLean, 'Anti-Vietnam War Activist', in *Protesters*, ed. Gloria Frydman (Blackburn, Victoria: Collins Dove, 1987), 20.
53 Irene Miller interviewed by P. Armstrong, August 1990. NLA: MS 9878-3-2.
54 McLean interview.
55 Ceci Cairns interviewed by P. Armstrong, 24 August 1990. NLA: MS 9878-3-3.
56 Victoria SOS Newsletter, June 1968.
57 'Women Say a Word on War', *Tribune*, 29 November 1967.
58 McLean interview.
59 Ceci Cairns interviewed by Armstrong.
60 Maurie Mulheron interview, 20 October 2012.
61 Letter from A. Pert to Council for Civil Liberties, 30 March 1967. NLA: MS 3821-7.
62 Letter from A. Pert to the Premier of Queensland, 14 March 1967. NLA: MS 3821-5.
63 Sydney SOS Newsletter, June 1968.
64 Sydney SOS, 'A Woman's Declaration of Conscience' [Leaflet], June 1968. NLA: MS 3821-21.
65 Sydney SOS Newsletter, April 1969.
66 Sydney SOS Newsletter, August 1968.
67 Sydney SOS Newsletter, October 1969.
68 Sydney SOS Newsletter, March 1969.
69 'Leaflet Throwing Charge Dismissed', *Illawarra Mercury*, 3 September 1968. NLA: MS 3821-3.
70 Letter from R. Williams to A. Pert, n.d. c. March 1968. NLA: MS 3821-3.
71 Sydney SOS Newsletter, March 1969.
72 'Mother of Youth Gives Ultimatum', n.d. newspaper not identified. *Garber Collection*. Wollongong City Library: DMSS 225/2.
73 Mac Gudgeon interview, 17 November 2012.
74 Louis Christofides interview, 22 November 2012.
75 'Young Demonstrator a Pawn, Towns Says', *Illawarra Mercury*, 9 May 1968.
76 Sydney SOS Newsletter, May 1969; 'Protesters in Action', *Illawarra Mercury*, 9 May 1968.
77 'Report on Demonstration at Wollongong Office of Department of Labour and National Service', 22 May 1969. NAA: A6122, 2009/ 137.

78 Newcastle SOS, 'All Children Have the Right to Live' [Leaflet], 1967. NLA: MS 3821-1.
79 Victoria SOS, 'Save Our Sons Movement of Victoria Supports Draft Resistance' [Pamphlet], 1968. NAA: A6122, 2621.
80 Sydney SOS, 'Tony McFarland' [Leaflet], 1967. NAA: A6122, 1854/159.
81 Sydney SOS Newsletter, August 1967.
82 Mulheron interview.
83 Mulheron interview.
84 Jean McLean interviewed by P. Armstrong, 26 June 1990. NLA: MS 9878-3-2.
85 McLean interviewed by Armstrong.
86 Victoria SOS Newsletter, April 1969.
87 Brian Gill, 'Stayers Race in the Car Park, Too', *Herald*, 7 November 1967.
88 Cairns interviewed by Armstrong.
89 Cairns interviewed by Armstrong.
90 'Singer Holds Back Tax in Protest Over War', *Australian*, 18 November 1967.
91 'History of War Tax Resistance', *National War Tax Resistance Committee*. http://www.nwtrcc.org/history/history1960.php, accessed 17 March 2015.
92 'Singer Holds Back Tax in Protest Over War', *Australian*, 18 November 1967.
93 Letter from C. Tillet to A. Pert, 1 July 1967. NLA: MS 3821-8.
94 Joan Coxsedge, *Cold Tea for Brandy: A Tale of Protest, Painting and Politics* (Balwyn North, Victoria: Vulcan Press, 2007), 82.
95 Miller interviewed by Armstrong.
96 'Billy Graham Meeting', 17 March 1969. NAA: A6122, 2621/113.
97 Sydney SOS Newsletter, September 1968.
98 Ann Curthoys, *Freedom Ride: A Freedom Rider Remembers* (Crows Nest, NSW: Allen & Unwin, 2002), 30–31.
99 Sydney SOS Newsletter, August 1968.
100 Mulheron interview.
101 Dorothy Cora, *Noreen Hewett: Portrait of a Grassroots Activist* (Sydney: Older Women's Network of NSW, 2010), 26–27.
102 In a report to a superior, an ASIO field officer detailed how he or she had disrupted a 1965 speaking tour of North Queensland by Norma Chalmers, e.g. urging members of the National Civic Council and the local RSL to disrupt a meeting in Mackay, cancelling a hall booking and preventing Chalmers from meeting local abattoir workers. NAA: A6119, 2659/112.
103 Abolish Conscription Campaign, 'Caravan Against Conscription Report', 1968. NLA: MS 9152, 44.
104 Abolish Conscription Campaign, 'Caravan Against Conscription Report', 1968. NLA: MS 9152, 44.
105 Sydney SOS Newsletter, September 1968.
106 Abolish Conscription Campaign, 'Caravan Against Conscription Report', 1968. NLA: MS 9152-44.
107 Mulheron interview.
108 Sydney SOS Newsletter, September 1968.
109 Langley, *Decade of Dissent*, 111.

110 Sydney SOS Newsletter, July 1969.
111 'Housewife Prepares for Prison Term', *Illawarra Mercury*, 1969. *Garber Collection.* Wollongong City Library: DMSS 225/2.
112 Victoria SOS Newsletter, September 1969.
113 Sydney SOS Newsletter, June 1969.
114 Sydney SOS Newsletter, October 1969.
115 Hancock, 'Events and Issues that Made the News in 1969'.
116 Sydney SOS Newsletter, November 1969.
117 Victoria SOS Newsletter, November 1969.
118 Miller interview.
119 Joan Coxsedge interview, 3 April 2014.
120 Coxsedge interview.
121 Chris Cathie interviewed by P. Armstrong, 20 August 1990. NLA: MS 9878-3-2.
122 Coxsedge interview.
123 Victoria SOS Newsletter, September 1969.
124 Sydney SOS Newsletter, June 1969.
125 McLean interviewed by Armstrong.

Chapter 7: On the World Stage

1 'SOS Meeting', 22 May 1968. NAA: A6122, 2621/57.
2 Barbara Avedon, 'Primer Becomes a Peace Symbol', cited in Michelle Moravec, 'Another Mother for Peace: reconsidering maternalist peace rhetoric from an historical perspective, 1967–2007', *Journal of the Motherhood Initiative* 1, no.1 (2010): 13.
3 David Krieger, 'The Another Mother for Peace Consumer Campaign: a campaign that failed'. *Journal of Peace Research* 8, no.2 (1971): 163–166.
4 Moravec, 'Another Mother for Peace', 14.
5 Moravec, 'Another Mother for Peace', 12.
6 Catherine R. Stimpson, 'Forward' in Amy Swerdlow, *Women Strike for Peace: Traditional Motherhood and Radical Politics in the 1960s* (Chicago: The University of Chicago Press, 1993), xi.
7 Sydney SOS Newsletter, May 1968.
8 Sydney SOS Newsletter, May 1968.
9 Sydney SOS Newsletter, July 1969.
10 Maurie Mulheron interview, 20 October 2012.
11 Sydney SOS Newsletter, February 1968.
12 Victoria SOS Newsletter, April 1968.
13 Swerdlow, *Women Strike for Peace*, 220.
14 Swerdlow, *Women Strike for Peace*, 1, 160, 220.
15 'Mother Says We're Afraid', *Australian*, 6 May 1968.
16 Victoria SOS Newsletter, June 1968.
17 Corinne Kerby and Jean McLean interviewed by John Foster, *Australian Broadcasting Corporation* (Hobart), 25 July 1968. NAA: A6122, 2621/65.
18 Jean McLean interview, 2 October 2014.
19 'SOS Meeting', 22 May 1968. NAA: A6122, 2621/57.

20 Victoria SOS, 'SOS Movement of Victoria Supports Draft Resistance' [Pamphlet], c. 1968. NAA: MS 9878-4.
21 John Larkins, 'Bombshell Jean is Back from N. Viet', *Herald*, 11 July 1969.
22 Larkins, 'Bombshell Jean is Back from N. Viet', *Herald*, 11 July 1969.
23 Neil Jillette, 'Aust. Women Visit Hanoi', *Sydney Morning Herald*, 10 July 1969.
24 Larkins, 'Bombshell Jean is Back from N. Viet', *Herald*, 11 July 1969.
25 Jane Fonda, 'The Truth About My Trip to Hanoi', 11 July 2011, *Jane Fonda Official Website*. www.janefonda/the-truth-about-my-trip-to-Hanoi, accessed 1 April 2015.
26 Jack Darmody, 'She Refuses to Answer Police on Hanoi Visit', *Age*, 12 July 1969.
27 'DRV Taking No Risks On Bombings Says Woman Visitor', *Tribune*, 30 July 1969.
28 Larkins, 'Bombshell Jean is Back from N. Viet', *Herald*, 11 July 1969.

Chapter 8: 'Fan Mail'

1 Note from 'A Proud Mother of a Proud and Loyal Son' to Pert, n.d. NLA: MS 3821-10.
2 Greeting card from Melva Merletto to Helen Christofides, n.d. c. June 1970. Private Collection of Louis Christofides. Melva Merletto was a Communist Party of Australia candidate in the New South Wales Legislative Assembly elections for Kembla in 1968. She was one of the women who organised street meetings to support the coal miners on strike in 1949. *The Australian Women's Register*, http://www.womenaustralia.info/biogs/AWE1682b.htm, accessed 28 July 2015.
3 Letter from 'Anonymous' to Helen Christofides, 18 June 1970. Private Collection of Louis Christofides.
4 Dorothy Cora, *Noreen Hewett: Portrait of a Grassroots Activist* (Sydney: Older Women's Network of NSW, 2010), 24.
5 Joan Coxsedge interview, 3 April 2014.
6 Gordon Jamieson interview, 10 August 2013.
7 Margaret Reynolds interview, 2 November 2012.
8 Dorothy Dalton interviewed by P. Armstrong, 23 August 1990. NLA: MS 9878-3-2.
9 Thomas Hardy interview, 22 November 2012.
10 Hardy interview.
11 Hardy interview.
12 Irene Miller interviewed by P. Armstrong, August 1990. NLA: MS 9878-3-2.
13 Coxsedge interview.
14 Hardy interview.
15 Candy Cole interview, 11 November 2013.
16 Maurie Mulheron interview, 20 October 2012.
17 Coxsedge interview.
18 Sue Foster interview, 29 October 2013.
19 Letter to Pauline Armstrong, 7 December 1990. NLA: MS 9878-2.
20 Letter from J. Bonner to P. Ashcroft, 16 August 1965. NLA: MS 3821-3.
21 Letter from P. Ashcroft to J. Bonner, 23 August 1965. NLA: MS 3821-3.

22 Mac Gudgeon interview, 17 November 2012.
23 Letter to Armstrong, 7 December 1990. NLA: MS 9878-2.
24 Corinne Kerby interviewed by P. Armstrong, 30 September 1990. NLA: MS 9878-3-3.
25 Kerby interviewed by Armstrong.
26 Chris Cathie interviewed by P. Armstrong, 20 August 1990. NLA: MS 9878-3-2.
27 Coxsedge interview.
28 'Save Our Sons Meeting', 1 July 1965. NAA: A6126, 1338/49.
29 Email from Wendy Kendrick to author, 7 August 2014.
30 Letter from V. Ward to P. Ashcroft, 5 August 1965. NLA: MS 3821-2.
31 Mulheron interview.
32 Coxsedge interview.
33 Cathie interviewed by Armstrong.
34 'Fan Mail', n.d. NLA: MS 3821-10.
35 Sydney SOS, 'Memo Re: PMG', n.d. NLA: MS 3821-10.
36 Letter from A. Pert to Mrs Barnitt, 9 June 1970. NLA: MS 3821-6.
37 John Murphy, 'Breadwinning: accounts of work and family life in the 1950s', *Labour and Industry*, 12, no.3 (2002).
38 Susan Sheridan, *Who Was That Woman? The Australian Women's Weekly in the Postwar Years* (Sydney: UNSW Press, 2001).
39 Miller interviewed by Armstrong.
40 Candy Cole interview, 11 November 2013.
41 'The Australian Male', *Melbourne Observer*, 1 August 1971. NAA: A6122, 2622/156.
42 Margaret Reynolds, *Living Politics* (St Lucia, Queensland: University of Queensland Press, 2007), 55.
43 'Another SOS Committee' [Letter to the Editor], *The Armidale Express*, 7 July 1965.
44 Note from 'A Proud Mother of a Proud and Loyal Son' to Adele Pert, n.d. NLA: MS 3821-10.
45 Note from Anonymous to Adele Pert, n.d. NLA: MS 3821-10.
46 Dorothy Dalton interviewed by P. Armstrong, 23 August 1990. NLA: MS 9878-3-2.
47 John Murphy, *Imagining the Fifties: Private Sentiment and Political Culture in Menzies' Australia* (Sydney: UNSW Press, 2000), 26–29.
48 Victoria SOS Newsletter, 18 August 1965.
49 'Leaflet Throwing Charge Dismissed', *Illawarra Mercury*, 3 September 1968.
50 'Outburst by Mother', *The Mirror*, 19 September 1970.
51 Letter from P. Carlsen to A. Pert, n.d. NLA: MS 3821-10.
52 Letter from P. Carlsen to A. Pert, n.d.
53 Victoria SOS Minutes, 18 August 1965. NLA: MS 9878-4.
54 Letter from A. Pert to H. Philips, 5 October 1966. NLA: MS 3821-9.
55 Letter from N. Hewett to the Manager of *2UV*, 21 February 1968. NLA: MS 3821-8.
56 'Those Women with Banners', *Sun*, 14 December 1965.

57   Aubrey Collette, 'Australian Road Carnage' [Editorial Cartoon], *Australian*, 5 October 1971.
58   Letter from Sydney SOS to the Editor of the *Australian*, 5 October 1971. NLA: MS 3821-6.
59   'White Mouse Nancy Wake Dies', *Sydney Morning Herald*, 8 August 2011.
60   'War Heroine Says Australians Are Too Complacent', *Border Morning Mail*, 6 September 1966.
61   Letter from J. Golgerth to the Editor of the *Border Morning Mail*, n.d. NLA: MS 3821-7.
62   McLean, 'Anti-Vietnam War Activist', in *Protesters*, ed. Gloria Frydman (Blackburn, Victoria: Collins Dove, 1987), 25.
63   Cole interview.

Chapter 9: Moratoriums, Chain Gangs and 'Falsies'

1   'Women for Peace: why we chained ourselves', 1970 [Pamphlet]. *Garber Collection*. Wollongong City Library (WCL) DMSS 225/1.
2   Marian Sawyer, *Making Women Count: A History of the Women's Electoral Lobby in Australia* (Sydney: UNSW Press, 2008), 10–13.
3   Marilyn Lake, 'Women's Liberation', in *Australian Feminism: A Companion*, ed. Moira Gatens and Barbara Caine (Melbourne: Oxford University Press, 1998), 141.
4   Sydney SOS Newsletter, February 1970.
5   Sydney SOS Newsletter, February 1970.
6   Sydney SOS Newsletter, February 1970.
7   Victoria SOS Newsletter, February 1970.
8   Congress for International Cooperation and Disarmament, 'Newsletter: Vietnam moratorium campaign', 1970. *Reason in Revolt: Source Documents of Australian Radicalism*, https://www.reasoninrevolt.net.au/objects/images/image_viewer.html?a000729,1,1,S, accessed 11 May 2015.
9   'Newcastle Moratorium Campaign', 30 April 1970. NAA: A6122, 2009/152.
10 SA SOS, Annual Report, 1970. State Library of South Australia (henceforth SLSA): SRG 781/26/3.
11 SOS Sydney, 'Mothers in Mourning' [Leaflet], NLA: MS 3821-7.
12 'Celebrate Mother's Day in a Different Way' [Advertisement], *Advertiser*, 5 May 1970.
13 Victoria SOS Newsletter, March 1970.
14 'Anonymous Note on Returned SOS Leaflet', 1971. NLA: MS 3821-7.
15 Sydney SOS Newsletter, February 1970.
16 Letter from A. Pert to F. Garber, 26 March 1970. NLA: MS 3821-3.
17 Letter from S. Pritchard to J. Darling, 28 October 1970. SLSA: SRG 781/25/4.
18 Joan Coxsedge, *Cold Tea for Brandy: A Tale of Protest, Painting and Politics* (Balwyn North, Victoria: Vulcan Press, 2007), 77.
19 Bob Scates, *'Draftmen Go Free': A History of the Anti-Conscription Movement in Australia* (Richmond, Victoria: R. Scates, 1988), 57.
20 Joan Coxsedge interview, 3 April 2014.

21 Ralph Gibson, *One Woman's Life: A Memoir of Dorothy Gibson* (Sydney: Hale and Iremonger, 1980), 92.
22 Gibson, *One Woman's Life*, 92.
23 Paul Ormonde, *A Foolish Passionate Man: A Biography of Jim Cairns* (Melbourne: Penguin, 1981), 124.
24 'Helmeted Police Get Ready for Sit-Down', *Age*, 8 May 1970; Ormonde, *A Foolish Passionate Man*, 124.
25 'Govt. Bid to Bait Opposition Fails', *Age*, 8 May 1970.
26 Letter from D. Aujard to J. McLean, 13 June 1970, NLA: MS 9878-2.
27 Miller quoted in Greg Langley, *A Decade of Dissent: Vietnam and Conflict on the Australian Homefront* (Sydney: Allen & Unwin, 1992), 147.
28 Louise Oswald, 'Jean McLean Has a Look Back at the Moratorium', *Moorabbin Standard*, 19 May 1990.
29 Jean McLean interview, 2 October 2014.
30 Louise Oswald, 'Jean McLean Has a Look Back at the Moratorium', *Moorabbin Standard*, 19 May 1990.
31 Stephen Downes, 'The Moratorium Revisited', *Age*, 6 May 1980.
32 'Vietnam Moratorium Campaign', Brian Medlin Collection, Flinders University Library Special Collections.
33 Letter from A. Potticary to A. Pert, 27 May 1970. NLA: MS 3821-2.
34 Alma Scaysbrook, 'Speech to May 8 Moratorium Rally', in Sydney SOS Newsletter, May 1970.
35 Sydney SOS Newsletter, May 1970.
36 'Moratorium Goes Out With Music', *Age*, 11 May 1970.
37 'Newcastle Vietnam Moratorium Campaign', 27 April 1970. NAA: A6122, 2009/151.
38 Sydney SOS Newsletter, May 1970.
39 Scaysbrook, 'Speech to May 8 Moratorium Rally', in Sydney SOS Newsletter, May 1970.
40 Sydney SOS Newsletter, July 1970.
41 Coxsedge interview.
42 Ormonde, *A Foolish Passionate Man*, 123.
43 Jim Cairns interviewed by Robin Hughes, 22 May 1998. http://australianbiography.gov.au/subjects/cairns/interview5.html, accessed 1 July 2015.
44 McLean interview.
45 Sue McCulloch interviewed by P. Armstrong, 23 August 1990. NLA: MS 9878-3-2.
46 McLean interview; Sue McCulloch interviewed by Armstrong.
47 Jim Cairns, 'Some Results and Tasks of the Vietnam Moratorium', May 1970. *Reason in Revolt: Source Documents of Australian Radicalism*, http://www.reasoninrevolt.net.au/bib/PR0001738.htm, accessed 11 May 2015.
48 *Women for Peace* Pamphlet.
49 'South Coast Citizens Against Conscription Demonstrations', 23 June 1970. NAA: A6122/2009, 166.
50 'Women in Chains Protest', *Canberra Times*, 12 June 1970.

51 Dorothy Dalton quoted in Langley, *Decade of Dissent*, 88.
52 Victoria SOS Newsletter, May 1970.
53 McLean, 'Anti-Vietnam War Activist', in *Protesters*, 20.
54 Letter from Department of Labour and National Service to R. Miller, 2 November 1970. NLA: MS 9878-4.
55 'Fill-in-a-Falsie Instructions', 1970. NLA: MS 9878-4.
56 Victoria SOS Newsletter, May 1971.
57 Victoria SOS Newsletter, June 1970.
58 Victoria SOS Newsletter, June 1970.
59 Letter from D. Aujard to J. McLean, 13 June 1970. NLA: MS 9878-2.
60 Coxsedge interview.
61 Sydney SOS Newsletter, September 1970.
62 'SA Inquiry Will Seek Cause of Protest Violence', *Sydney Morning Herald*, 22 September 1970.
63 SA SOS, 'Secretary's Annual Report 1970–71'. SLSA: SRG 781/26/3.
64 Sydney SOS Newsletter, October 1970.
65 Sydney SOS Newsletter, October 1970.
66 Sydney SOS Newsletter, November 1970.
67 Letter from L. Heyde to J. Meng, 17 October 1970. NLA: MS 3821-6.
68 Letter from L. Heyde to J. Meng, 17 October 1970. NLA: MS 3821-6.
69 After 30 staff and students at Swinburne College in Melbourne were summonsed before the court on charges of incitement, SOS accused the government of 'acceding to the demands of the extreme conservative fringe'. Victoria SOS Newsletter, November 1970.

Chapter 10: The Fairlea Five and the 'Underground'

1 Sue McCulloch interviewed by P. Armstrong, 23 August 1990. NLA: MS 9878-3-2.
2 Victoria SOS Newsletter, February 1971.
3 Irene Miller interviewed by P. Armstrong, August 1990. NLA: MS 9878-3-2.
4 Victoria SOS Newsletter, February 1971.
5 Joan Coxsedge, *Cold Tea for Brandy: A Tale of Protest, Painting and Politics* (Balwyn North, Victoria: Vulcan Press, 2007), 83.
6 Jean McLean, 'Notes', 1973. NLA: MS 9878-4.
7 'Women Jailed for Trespass', *Canberra Times*, 9 April 1971.
8 Chris Cathie interviewed by P. Armstrong, 20 August 1990. NLA: MS 9878-3-2.
9 Joan Coxsedge interviewed by P. Armstrong, 31 August 1990. NLA: MS 9878-3-2.
10 Jean McLean, 'Notes', 1973. NLA: MS 9878-4.
11 William Miller interview, 30 July 2014.
12 P. Martin and S. Johnson, 'Statement: jail or justice', 9 April 1971. NAA: A6122/1853, 84.
13 'Cairns Calls for 200 to Break the Law', *Australian*, 13 April 1971; 'No Reprieve for Five Women Protesters', *Sydney Morning Herald*, 14 April 1971.
14 'Cairns Calls for 200 to Break the Law', *Australian*, 13 April 1971.

15 'March Planned in Support of Women in Gaol', *Australian*, 12 April 1971.
16 'Demonstration as Welcome for Jailed Women', *Canberra Times*, 17 April 1971; 'No Reprieve for Five Women Protesters', *Sydney Morning Herald*, 14 April 1971.
17 Letter from E. Tapp to P. Armstrong, date unknown. NLA: MS 9878-2.
18 SOS Sydney, 'Defend Civil Liberties' [Leaflet], 1971. NLA: MS 3821-24.
19 Sydney SOS Newsletter, May 1971.
20 'Mother is in Jail', *Sydney Morning Herald*, 10 April 1971.
21 'Gaoled Mothers Will Not Appeal', *Australian*, 10 April 1971.
22 '5 Mums Inside and 14 Children Wait', *Melbourne Observer*, 11 April 1971; 'Life Gets Tough When Mum's in Jail', *Sun*, 16 April 1971.
23 William Miller interview.
24 'Guarding Our Civil Liberties', *Australian*, 14 April 1971.
25 William Miller interview.
26 Cathie interviewed by Armstrong.
27 'Bubbly, Cheers as Five Leave Prison', *Australian*, 14 April 1971.
28 Jean McLean, 'A Personal Account', *Lot's Wife*, 6 May 1971; Jean McLean, 'My 11 Days in Archaic Fairlea Jail', *Sun*, 19 April 1971.
29 'A Chance to Run Fairlea', *Sun*, 12 May 1971.
30 Coxsedge, *Cold Tea for Brandy*, 86.
31 Sydney SOS Newsletter, May 1971.
32 Joan Coxsedge interview, 3 April 2014.
33 Jim Cairns interviewed by P. Armstrong, 5 August 1990. NLA: MS 9878-3-2.
34 Jean McLean, 'Notes', 1973. NLA: MS 9878-4.
35 'We Won: Cairns, no breach: Reid', *Age*, 20 April 1971.
36 'Anti-War Wife Goes to Gaol', *Illawarra Mercury*, 15 July 1971.
37 Sydney SOS Newsletter, August 1971.
38 'Defiant Mother', *Illawarra Mercury*, 16 July 1971.
39 Sydney SOS Newsletter, August 1971.
40 Sue McCulloch interviewed by P. Armstrong, 23 August 1990. NLA: MS 9878-3-2.
41 Greg Langley, *A Decade of Dissent: Vietnam and Conflict on the Australian Homefront* (Sydney: Allen & Unwin, 1992), 150.
42 Victoria SOS Newsletter, October 1970.
43 'Intercept: Brian Ross', 29/30 September 1969. NAA: A6122 2622/4.
44 'New Theatre', 26 November 1970. NAA: A6122 2622/70.
45 Michael Charles, 'Mercury Enters the Underground', *Illawarra Mercury*, 20 October 1969.
46 Jean McLean, 'The Safe House Project'. https://www.viclabor.com.au/jean-mclean/, accessed 2 January 2020.
47 Jean McLean, 'Notes', 1973. NLA: MS 9878-4.
48 McLean, 'Notes', 1973.
49 Letter from B. Ross to J. McLean, in Jean McLean, 'Notes', 1973. NLA: MS 9878-4.
50 'Brian Ross Set Free From Gaol', *Age*, 22 September 1970.
51 Jean McLean, 'This is Life for Brian Ross', *Sunday Observer*, 2 July 1970.

52   Bob Scates, 'Draftmen Go Free': A History of the Anti-Conscription Movement in Australia (Richmond, Victoria: R. Scates, 1988), 88.
53   Jean McLean interviewed by P. Armstrong, 26 June 1990. NLA: MS 9878-3-2.
54   Coxsedge interview.
55   Kevin Childs, 'The Anti-Draft Underground Looks After Its Own', *Age*, 19 November 1971.
56   McLean interviewed by Armstrong.
57   McLean interviewed by Armstrong.
58   Jean McLean, 'The Safe Houses Project', https://www.viclabor.com.au/jean-mclean/, accessed 2 January 2020.
59   Tony Dalton quoted in Langley, *Decade of Dissent*, 153.
60   Sydney SOS Newsletter, February 1971.
61   Mac Gudgeon interview, 17 November 2012.
62   Peter O'Brien interviewed by P. Armstrong, 16 June 1991. NLA: MS 9878-3-3.
63   McLean, 'Notes', 1973.
64   Ceci Cairns interviewed by P. Armstrong, 24 August 1990. NLA: MS 9878-3-3.
65   'Underground Fundraising Dinner' [Leaflet]. NLA: MS 9878-4.
66   Victoria SOS Newsletter, May 1971.
67   Cassandra Pybus, *The Devil and James McAuley* (St Lucia, Queensland: University of Queensland Press, 1999), 229.
68   'Few Incidents in Anti-War Marches', *Canberra Times*, 1 July 1971.
69   Sydney SOS Newsletter, September 1971.
70   Phillip Lynch, Extract from a Letter to Sydney SOS, reproduced in part in Sydney SOS Newsletter, April–May 1972.

Chapter 11: The Final Push

1   Sydney SOS Newsletter, June–July 1972.
2   Sydney SOS, Annual General Meeting, June 1972. NLA: MS 3821-23.
3   Sydney SOS Minutes, 11 March 1972. NLA: MS 3821.
4   Sydney SOS Newsletter, June–July 1972.
5   Sydney SOS Minutes, 11 March 1972.
6   Sydney SOS Minutes, 17 June 1972. NLA: MS 3821.
7   Sydney SOS, Annual General Meeting, June 1972. NLA: MS 3821-23.
8   Jean McLean interview, 2 October 2014.
9   McLean interview.
10   Sydney SOS Newsletter, August 1972.
11   Bob Scates, 'Draftmen Go Free': A History of the Anti-Conscription Movement in Australia (Richmond, Victoria: R. Scates, 1988), 101.
12   Joan Coxsedge interviewed by P. Armstrong, 31 August 1990. NLA: MS 9878-3-2.
13   Dorothy Dalton interviewed by P. Armstrong, 23 August 1990. NLA: MS 9878-3-2.
14   *CPD*, Senate, vol. 42, 18 October 1972, 1682.
15   *CPD*, Senate, vol. 42, 18 October 1972, 1682.
16   *CPD*, Senate, vol. 42, 18 October 1972, 1686.

17 Sydney SOS Newsletter, November 1972.
18 Sydney SOS Newsletter, September/October 1972.
19 'Gough's Generation', *Age*, 2 December 2002.
20 'Arrest of Candidate Ordered', *Sydney Morning Herald*, 8 February 1972.
21 'Draft Rebel Hits at Bungling', *Age*, 19 July 1972.
22 McLean interview.
23 'Draft Dodging No Crime', *Age*, 29 February 1972.
24 'Gough's Generation', *Age*, 2 December 2002.
25 'Whitlam Dared Over Poll', *Age*, 14 June 1972.
26 McLean interview.
27 Victoria SOS Newsletter, November/December 1972.
28 '1972 Legislative Election: House of Representatives', Adam Carr, Australian Election Archive, *Psephos*, http://psephos.adam-carr.net/countries/a/australia/1972/1972repsvic.txt, accessed 14 July 2015.
29 'Draft Resister', *Sydney Morning Herald*, 3 December 1972.
30 'Gough's Generation', *Age*, 2 December 2002.
31 David Williamson, 'Gough Whitlam: the mastermind of a revolution', *Australian*, 22 October 2014.
32 Scates, *Draftmen Go Free*, 102.
33 Jean McLean, 'The Safe House Project'. https://www.viclabor.com.au/jean-mclean/, accessed 2 January 2020.
34 Sydney SOS Newsletter, December 1972.
35 Sydney SOS Newsletter, December 1972.
36 Gary Brown, et al., 'Military Conscription: issues for Australia', *Current Issues Brief 7 1999–2000*. (Canberra: Foreign Affairs, Defence and Trade Group, 12 October 1999). http://www.aph.gov.au/About_Parliament/Parliamentary_Departments/Parliamentary_Library/Publications_Archive/, accessed 15 July 2015.
37 SOS Sydney Minutes, 14 April 1973. NLA: MS 3821.
38 Victoria SOS Newsletter, August 1973.

Chapter 12: Rolling up the Banners

1 Mac Gudgeon interview, 17 November 2012.
2 Sydney SOS Newsletter, December 1972.
3 Sydney SOS Newsletter, December 1972.
4 Sydney SOS Newsletter, December 1972.
5 Murray Goot and Rodney Tiffen, 'Public Opinion and the Politics of the Polls', in *Australia's Vietnam*, ed. Peter King (Sydney: Allen & Unwin, 1983), 164.
6 Peter Edwards, *A Nation at War: Australian Politics, Society and Diplomacy During the Vietnam War 1965–1975*. (Sydney: Allen & Unwin, 1997), 351.
7 Edwards, *Nation at War*, 351.
8 Between 1964 and 1972, 804,286 20-year-olds registered for National Service. Of these, 63,735 national servicemen served in the army, 567,238 were balloted out, 3563 were exempted (including 1242 conscientious objectors) and 35,548 received indefinite deferrals. Edwards, *Nation at War*, 369–370.
9 Email from Mac Gudgeon to the author, 16 November 2012.

10 Jean McLean interviewed by P. Armstrong, 26 June 1990. NLA: MS 9878-3-2.
11 McLean interviewed by Armstrong.
12 Letter from P. Ashcroft to V. Ward, 6 October 1965. NLA: MS 3821-5.
13 Ken Jack interview, 10 March 2013.
14 Jean McLean interview, 2 October 2014.
15 Sydney SOS Newsletter, December 1972.
16 Joan Coxsedge interview, 3 April 2014.
17 Jim Cairns interviewed by P. Armstrong, 5 August 1990. NLA: MS 9878-3-2.
18 Jean McLean interview, 2 October 2014.
19 McLean interview.
20 McLean interviewed by Armstrong.
21 Jim Cairns interviewed by Armstrong.
22 Peter O'Brien interviewed by P. Armstrong, 16 June 1991. NLA: MS 9878-3-3.
23 'By-Law Cases All Adjourned', *Age*, 10 April 1969; Rev A. J. Lloyd, 'Letter to the Editor', *Herald*, 21 April 1969. NAA: A6122, 2621/119.
24 McLean interviewed by Armstrong.
25 Nguyen, Thi Binh, *Family, Friends and Country: Autobiography*, trans. Lady Borton (Hanoi, Vietnam: Tri Thuc Publishing House, 2013), 10.
26 Nguyen, Thi Binh, *Family, Friends and Country*, 201.
27 Nguyen, Thi Binh, *Family, Friends and Country*, 103.
28 Joan Coxsedge, *Cold Tea for Brandy: A Tale of Protest, Painting and Politics* (Balwyn North, Victoria: Vulcan Press, 2007), 88.
29 Coxsedge, *Cold Tea for Brandy*, 88.
30 Coxsedge interview, 3 April 2014.
31 Sue McCulloch quoted in Greg Langley, *A Decade of Dissent: Vietnam and Conflict on the Australian Homefront* (Sydney: Allen & Unwin, 1992), 153.
32 Sue McCulloch interviewed by P. Armstrong, 23 August 1990. NLA: MS 9878-3-2.
33 Hugh Outhred interview, 28 November 2013.
34 Letter from B. York to P. Armstrong, 4 January 1991. NLA: MS 9878-2.
35 Letter from B. York to P. Armstrong, 4 January 1991.
36 Sam Goldbloom interviewed by P. Armstrong, 14 August 1990.
37 Goldbloom interviewed by Armstrong.
38 Louis Christofides quoted in Langley, *Decade of Dissent*, 223.
39 Gudgeon interview.
40 O'Brien interviewed by Armstrong.
41 Kev Gillett, 'It's Time Now Gough', 21 October 2014. *Kevgillett.net*, http://www.kevgillett.net/?p=8550, accessed 15 July 2015.
42 R. Steffan, 'Letter to the Editor', n.d., publication unknown, reproduced in Pam Young, *Daring to Take a Stand: The Story of the Union of Australian Women in Queensland* (Wavell Heights, Queensland: Pam Young, 1998), 93.
43 Noreen Hewett, 'The Anti-Vietnam War and Anti-Conscription Movements', in *A Turbulent Decade: Social Protest Movements and the Labour Movement, 1965–1975*, ed. Beverley Symons and Rowan Cahill (Newtown, NSW: Australian Society for the Study of Labour History (Sydney branch), 2005), 13.

44 Ann Curthoys, '"Shut Up, You Bourgeois Bitch": sexual identity and political action in the anti-Vietnam movement', in *Gender and War: Australians at War in the Twentieth Century*, ed. Joy Damousi and Marilyn Lake (Cambridge: Cambridge University Press, 1995), 338.
45 Curthoys, '"Shut Up, You Bourgeois Bitch"', 322, 338, 335.
46 Joan Coxsedge interview, 3 April 2014.
47 Corinne Kerby interviewed by P. Armstrong, 30 September 1990. NLA: MS 9878-3-3.
48 Sydney SOS Newsletter, December 1972.
49 Letter from P. Ashcroft to J. Golgerth, undated. NLA: MS 3821-9; Sydney SOS Minutes, 27 January 1966. NLA: MS 3821.
50 Coxsedge interview.
51 Jean McLean, 'Notes', 1973.
52 Gudgeon interview.
53 Golgerth interview.
54 Candy Cole interview, 11 November 2013.
55 Maurie Mulheron interview, 20 October 2012.
56 Letter from A. Scaysbrook and N. Mulheron to SOS members, April 1973. NLA: MS 3821-7.
57 Sydney SOS Minutes, 10 March 1973. NLA: MS 3821.
58 Victoria SOS Newsletter, August 1973.
59 A. Potticary, 'Save Our Sons', *Campaign for Peace in Vietnam Newsletter*, No.7, March 1973. NAA: A6122, 1813/169.
60 McLean interview.
61 On one occasion there was a violent demonstration outside McLean's home where the Vietnamese Ambassador was attending a luncheon. 'Vietnam Demonstration', NAA: A6119, 4035/105. In 1977, McLean returned to Vietnam at the invitation of the Vietnam Women's Union to lead a delegation of Australian women on a tour of South and North Vietnam. 'Australian Women's Visit to Vietnam'. NAA: A6119, 4035/88.
62 Irene Miller interview, 31 July 2014.
63 Ceci Cairns interviewed by Armstrong.
64 Sandra McLean, 'What Happened Next?' *Courier Mail*, 5 April 2003.
65 James Law, 'Cranky Granny Who Grilled PM Tony Abbott over the Federal Budget on Wake Up Not What She Seems', news.com.au, 14 May 2014.
66 'Spirited Activist Never Gave Up Fight', *Sydney Morning Herald*, 24 April 2012.
67 McLean interview.
68 Margaret Reynolds, *Living Politics* (St Lucia, Queensland: University of Queensland Press, 2007), 59.
69 Reynolds, *Living Politics*, 54.
70 Reynolds, *Living Politics*, 60.
71 Margaret Reynolds interview, 2 November 2012.
72 'Interview with Joan Coxsedge', *Women's Web*. http://www.womensweb.com.au/sources/Later Stories/Joan Coxsedge.htm, accessed 11 July 2015.

73 Coxsedge, *Cold Tea for Brandy*, 100; John Blaxland, *The Protest Years. Volume II: The Official History of ASIO 1963–1975* (Crows Nest, NSW: Allen & Unwin, 2015), 429–34.
74 Coxsedge, *Cold Tea for Brandy*, 107.
75 'Interview with Joan Coxsedge'. *Women's Web*. http://www.womensweb.com.au/sources/Later Stories/Joan Coxsedge.htm, accessed 11 July 2015.
76 *Victorian Parliamentary Debates*, Legislative Council, vol. 408, 12 August 1992, 81.
77 Coxsedge, *Cold Tea for Brandy*, 7–8.
78 Coxsedge interview.
79 McLean interview.
80 McLean interview.
81 Gary Brown, et al., 'Military Conscription: issues for Australia', Current Issues Brief 1999–2000, 12 October 1999. *Parliament of Australia*. http://www.aph.gov.au/About_Parliament/Parliamentary_Departments/Parliamentary_Library/Publications_Archive/CIB/cib9900/2000CIB07, accessed 7 July 2015.
82 Edwards, *Nation at War*, 371.
83 Brown, et al., 'Military Conscription: issues for Australia'.
84 Sydney SOS Newsletter, December 1972.

SELECT BIBLIOGRAPHY

Newspapers and Magazines

The Advertiser [SA]
The Age
The Armidale Express
The Australian
The Australian Women's Weekly
The Border Morning Mail
The Bulletin
The Canberra Times
The Courier-Mail [QLD]
The Daily Mirror [NSW]
The Daily News [WA]
The Daily Telegraph [NSW]
Farrago
Green Left Weekly
The Herald [VIC]
The Illawarra Express
Illawarra Mercury
Melbourne Observer
Moorabbin Standard
The Newcastle Morning Herald
The News [SA]
The Peacemaker
Queensland Guardian
South Coast Times
St George and Sutherland Shire Leader
The Sun [NSW]
The Sun-Herald [NSW]
The Sun News-Pictorial [VIC]
Sunday Observer [VIC]
The Sunday Times [WA]
Sunday Truth [QLD]
The Sydney Morning Herald
The Townsville Bulletin
The Tribune
The West Australian

Papers Held in Libraries and Private Collections

Abraham, Vivienne (MS 9152, National Library of Australia)
Armstrong, Pauline (MS 9878, National Library of Australia)
Australian War Memorial Leaflet Collection
Christofides, Louis (private collection)
Garber Collection (DMSS 225/1-2, Wollongong City Library)
Graham Garner Collection (Mss F3400, Fryer Library, University of Queensland)
Jamieson, Gordon (private collection)
Brian Medlin Collection (Flinders University Library Special Collections)
Outhred, Alan (private collection)
Papers of Hal and Sadie Pritchard (PRG 1561, State Library of South Australia)
Records of the Official Historian Peter Edwards – *A Nation at War* – Source Material.
    Working notes/research material. (AWM263, Australian War Memorial)
Save Our Sons (MS 3821, National Library of Australia)
Save Our Sons, South Australia (SRG 555, State Library of South Australia)
Union of Australian Women: Anti-Conscription Campaign (Save Our Sons) and
    related papers (SRG 781/26, State Library of South Australia)

SELECT BIBLIOGRAPHY

National Archives of Australia
Ashcroft, Doris Patricia (A6119, 5787)
Bendick, Dorothy (A6119, 6238, D4881)
Brown, Freda vol. 1–25 (A6119, 4905-4909; A6119, 4915; A6119, 4923-4926; A6119, 4932-4934; A6119, 4939-4942; A6119, 4958-4960; A6119, 4967-4968; A6119, 4973-4975)
Chalmers, Norma vol. 1–12 (A9626, 615; A6119, 1296-1297; A6119, 2657-2659; A6119, 2674; A6119, 2680; A6119, 2684-2685; A6119, 5790; A6119, 5853; A6119, 5850)
Committee for Defence of Bill White (A6122, 1824-1825)
Coxsedge, Joan vol. 1–7 (A9626, 176; A6119, 3988-3989; A6119, 4014-4016; A6119, 4093; A6119, 4094)
Curthoys, Barbara vol. 1–2 (A6119, 1556-1557)
Golgerth, Joyce (A6126, 1338)
Greenwood, Irene vol. 1–2 (A6119, 2250; A6119, 2750)
Gregory, Elizabeth Ann (A9626, 180; A6119, 4102)
Henderson, Marion vol. 1–4 (A9626, 554; A6119, 5702-5704)
Hewett, Noreen vol. 1–4 (A9626, 665; A6119, 6007-6010)
Holmes, Margaret vol. 1–2 (A6119, 3362-3363)
Lee, Margaret (nee Lennon) vol. 1–4 (A6119, 4568-4571)
Lee, Margaret Rae (A6119, 6149)
McDonald, Audrey vol. 1–7 (A6119, 2289; A6119, 5923-5924; A6119, 5655-5657; A6119, 5706)
McLean, Jean vol. 1–9 (A9626, 535; A6119, 3978-3979; A6119, 3995; A6119, 4032-4035)
Mulheron, Maurice vol. 1–3 (A6119, 3419-3421)
Mulheron, Nora vol. 1–2 (A6119, 3433-3433)
National Service Training Scheme General Representations 1962 (A463 1962/3685 PART I)
O'Sullivan, Ruby vol. 1–2 (A9626, 773; A6119, 6283-6284)
SOS NSW vol.1–6 (A6122/1665, A6122/1668, A6122/1853, A6122/1854, A6122/2009, A6122/2649)
SOS Queensland vol. 1–2 (A6122/1680, A6122/2010)
SOS SA (A6122/1813)
SOS Victoria vol. 1–3 (A6122/1678, A6122/2621, A6122/2622)
SOS WA vol. 1–2 (A6122 1682, A6122/2008)
Townsend, Simon vol. 1–3 (A6119, 2542-2543; A6119, 3191-3192)
Union of Australian Women (A6980, S250370; A12873, 15)
Women's International League for Peace and Freedom (A1533 1968/3078)

Interviews Conducted by the Author
Gil Chalmers (email), 30 August 2013
Louis Christofides, 22 November 2012
Candy Cole, 11 November 2013
Joan Coxsedge, 3 April 2014

Shelley Davies, 25 July 2013
Philip Decker, 2 December 2013
Sue Foster, 29 October 2013
Michael Golgerth, 21 October 2013
Mark Gregory, 6 November 2013
Mac Gudgeon, 17 November 2012
Elliot Hannay (email), 7 January 2013
Thomas Hardy, 22 November 2012
Ken Jack, 10 March 2013
Vern Jack, 12 February 2013
Gordon Jamieson, 10 August 2013
Wendy Kendrick (email), 7 August 2013
Jean McLean, 2 October 2014
Beryl Miller, 8 April 2014
Irene Miller, 31 July 2013
William Miller, 30 July 2013
Maurie Mulheron, 20 October 2012
Alan Outhred, 29 November 2013
Hugh Outhred, 28 November 2013
Robert Outhred, 20 January 2014
Lee Pinch, 6 November 2013
Vince Prasser, 4 March 2013
Margaret Reynolds, 2 November 2012
Joan Ross, 27 November 2013
Loma Thompson, 7 December 2012
Stuart Wearne, 14 May 2013

Interviews by Pauline Armstrong

(Pauline Armstrong Papers, National Library of Australia: MS 9878-3)
Ceci Cairns, 24 August 1990
Jim Cairns, 5 August 1990
Chris Cathie, 20 August 1990
Joan Coxsedge, 31 August 1990
George Crawford, 4 September 1990
Dorothy Dalton, 23 August 1990
Les Dalton, 23 August 1990
Sam Goldbloom, 14 August 1990
Corinne Kerby, 30 September 1990
Sue McCulloch, 23 August 1990
Jean McLean, 26 June 1990
Irene Miller, (day not recorded) August 1990
Frances Newell, 24 August 1990
Peter O'Brien, 16 June 1991

Other Interviews

Jim Cairns interviewed by Robin Hughes, 22 May 1998. *Australian Biography*. http://australianbiography.gov.au/subjects/cairns/interview5.html, accessed 1 July 2015.

Ray Collie interviewed by Stuart Reid, 1988. State Library of Western Australia: OH 2057.

'Interview with Joan Coxsedge', *Women's Web*. http://www.womensweb.com.au/sources/Later Stories/Joan Coxsedge.htm, accessed 11 July 2015.

'Jean McLean – My life in Photos', 19 February 2002. Australian Broadcasting Corporation (ABC). http://www.abc.net.au/dimensions_in_time/transcripts/s485125.htm, accessed 25 April 2012.

Peter O'Brien interviewed by Tim Bowden. 'Conversations with a Commonwealth Policeman I' ABC, 3 March 1991.

Peter O'Brien interviewed by Tim Bowden. 'Conversations with a Commonwealth Policeman II' ABC, 10 March 1991.

Secondary Sources

Alonso, Harriet Hyman. *Peace as a Women's Issue: A History of the US Movement for World Peace and Women's Rights*. Syracuse, NY: Syracuse University Press, 1993.

Andrews, Iris. *A History of the Newcastle / Central Coast Branch of the Union of Australian Women*. Newcastle, NSW: The Branch, 1997.

Appy, Christian. *Vietnam: The Definitive Oral History Told from All Sides*. London: Ebury Press, 2006.

Armstrong, Pauline. 'A History of the Save Our Sons Movement of Victoria: 1965–1973'. MA thesis, Monash University, 1991.

Ashbolt, Allan. *An Australian Experience: Words from the Vietnam Years*. Sydney: Australasian Book Society, 1974.

Barrett, John. *Falling In: Australians and 'Boy Conscription', 1911–1915*. Sydney: Hale and Iremonger, 1979.

Blaxland, John. *The Protest Years. Volume II: The Official History of ASIO, 1963–1975*. Crows Nest, NSW: Allen & Unwin, 2015.

Bolton, Geoffrey. *The Oxford History of Australia. Volume 5, 1942–1988: The Middle Way*. Melbourne: Oxford University Press, 1996.

Brown, Gary, Foreign Affairs Defence and Trade Group, 'Military Conscription: issues for Australia'. Current Issues Brief 1999–2000, 12 October 1999. *Parliament of Australia*. http://www.aph.gov.au/About_Parliament/Parliamentary_Departments/Parliamentary_Library/Publications_Archive/CIB/cib9900/2000CIB07, accessed 7 July 2015.

Burgmann, Meredith, ed. *Dirty Secrets: Our ASIO Files*. Sydney: NewSouth Publishing, 2014.

Burgmann, Verity. *Power and Protest: Movements for Change in Australian Society*. Sydney: Allen & Unwin, 1993.

Burgmann, Verity. *Power, Profit and Protest: Australian Social Movements and Globalisation*. Sydney: Allen & Unwin, 2003.

Bussey, Gertrude and Margaret Tims. *Women's International League for Peace and Freedom 1915–1965: A Record of Fifty Years' Work*. London: Allen & Unwin, 1965.
Cahill, Rowan. 'Vietnam Reading'. *Overland* 150 (1998): 11–15.
Cain, Frank. *ASIO: An Unofficial History*. Richmond, Victoria: Spectrum Publications, 1994.
Cairns, Jim. *Silence Kills: Events Leading Up to the Vietnam Moratorium on 8 May*. Melbourne: Vietnam Moratorium Committee, 1970.
Cairns, Jim. *Vietnam: Is It Truth We Want?* Melbourne: Victorian Branch of the Australian Labor Party, n.d. [1965].
Caulfield, Michael. *The Vietnam Years: From the Jungle to the Australian Suburbs*. Sydney: Hachette Australia, 2007.
Cavanagh, Michelle. *Margaret Holmes: The Life and Times of an Australian Peace Campaigner*. Sydney: New Holland, 2006.
Clutterbuck, Charlotte. 'Protests and Peace Marches: from Vietnam to Palm Sunday.' In *War, Australia and Vietnam*, edited by Kenneth Maddock and Barry Wright, 135–147. Sydney: Harper and Row, 1987.
Cochrane, Peter. 'At War At Home: Australian attitudes during the Vietnam Years.' In *Vietnam Remembered*, edited by Gregory Pemberton, 164–185. Sydney: New Holland Publishers, 2009.
Cora, Dorothy. *Noreen Hewett: Portrait of a Grassroots Activist*. Sydney: Older Women's Network of NSW, 2010.
Coxsedge, Joan. *Cold Tea for Brandy: A Tale of Protest, Painting and Politics*. Balwyn North, Victoria: Vulcan Press, 2007.
Coxsedge, Joan, Ken Coldicutt, and Gerry Harant. *Rooted in Secrecy: The Clandestine Element in Australian Politics*. Balwyn North, Victoria: Committee for the Abolition of Political Police, 1982.
Curthoys, Ann. *Freedom Ride: A Freedom Rider Remembers*. Crows Nest, NSW: Allen & Unwin, 2002.
Curthoys, Ann. 'History and Reminiscence: writing about the anti-Vietnam War movement'. *Australian Feminist Studies* 16 (Summer 1992): 116–136.
Curthoys, Ann. 'Mobilising Dissent: the later stages of protest'. In *Vietnam Remembered*, edited by Gregory Pemberton, 138–164. Sydney: New Holland Publishers, 2009.
Curthoys, Ann. '"Shut Up, You Bourgeois Bitch": sexual identity and political action in the anti-Vietnam War movement'. In *Gender and War*, edited by Joy Damousi and Marilyn Lake, 311–341. Cambridge: Cambridge University Press, 1995.
Curthoys, Ann. 'The Anti-War Movements'. In *Vietnam: War, Myth and Memory*, edited by Jeffrey Grey and Jeff Doyle, 81–107. Sydney: Allen & Unwin, 1992.
Curthoys, Ann. 'The Movement Against the War in Vietnam'. *Canberra Historical Journal* (September 2000): 29–33.
Curthoys, Ann, and John Merritt, eds. *Better Dead Than Red: Australia's First Cold War: 1945–1959*. Sydney: Allen & Unwin, 1986.
Curthoys, Barbara. 'The Union of Australian Women: a celebration'. *The Hummer* 2, no.7 (Summer 1996/97). http://asslh.org.au/hummer/vol-2-no-7/australian-women/, accessed 7 March 2015.

Select Bibliography

Curthoys, Barbara, and Audrey McDonald. *More Than a Hat and Glove Brigade: The Story of the Union of Australian Women*. Sydney: Bookpress, 1996.

Dalton, Dorothy, and Les Dalton. 'Anti-Uranium Activists'. In *Protesters*, edited by Gloria Frydman, 98–108. Blackburn, Victoria: Collins Dove, 1987.

Dalton, Les. 'Politics of the Australian Peace Movement: 1930s to 1960s'. *Centre for Dialogue Working Paper Series, No 2011/1*, Melbourne: La Trobe University, 2011.

Damousi, Joy. *Women Come Rally: Socialism, Communism and Gender in Australia 1890–1955*. Melbourne: Oxford University Press, 1994.

Damousi, Joy, and Marilyn Lake, eds. *Gender and War: Australians at War in the Twentieth Century*. Cambridge: Cambridge University Press, 1995.

Dane, Barbara, and Irwin Silber, eds. *The Vietnam Song Book*. New York: The Guardian, 1969.

Dapin, Mark. *The Nashos' War: Australia's National Servicemen and Vietnam*. Melbourne: Viking, 2014.

Darian-Smith, Kate, and Paula Hamilton, eds. *Memory and History in Twentieth Century Australia*. Melbourne: Oxford University Press, 1994.

Dumbrell, John, ed. *Vietnam and the Antiwar Movement: An International Perspective*. Aldershot, England: Avebury, 1989.

Edwards, Peter. *A Nation at War: Australian Politics, Society and Diplomacy During the Vietnam War 1965–1975*. Sydney: Allen & Unwin, 1997.

Edwards, Peter. *Australia and the Vietnam War*. Sydney: NewSouth Publishing, 2014.

Evans, Raymond. 'Conscription Riot.' In *Radical Brisbane: An Unruly History*, edited by Raymond Evans and Carole Ferrier, 156–160. Carlton North, Victoria: The Vulgar Press, 2004.

Evans, Raymond, and Carole Ferrier, eds. *Radical Brisbane: An Unruly History*. Carlton North, Victoria: The Vulgar Press, 2004.

Fabian, Suzane, and Morag Loh. *Left-Wing Ladies: The Union of Australian Women in Victoria, 1950–1998*. Flemington, Victoria: Hyland House Publishing, 2000.

Findlay, P. T. *Protest Politics and Psychological Warfare: The Communist Role in the Anti-Vietnam War and Anti-Conscription Movement in Australia*. Melbourne: The Hawthorn Press, 1968.

Fisher, Betty. *A Brief History of the Women's Electoral Lobby (SA) Inc*. Adelaide: Women's Electoral Lobby (SA), 1996.

Forward, Roy, and Bob Reece, eds. *Conscription in Australia*. St Lucia, Queensland: University of Queensland Press, 1968.

Francis, Rosemary. 'Women in Protest Movements: the Women's Peace Army and the Save Our Sons movement'. BA (Hons) thesis, University of Melbourne, 1984.

Frost, Frank. *Australia's War in Vietnam*. Sydney: Allen & Unwin, 1987.

Frydman, Gloria, ed. *Protesters*. Blackburn, Victoria: Collins Dove, 1987.

Gibson, Ralph. *One Woman's Life: A Memoir of Dorothy Gibson*. Sydney: Hale and Iremonger, 1980.

Gilbert, Alan D., and Ann-Mari Jordens. 'Traditions of Dissent'. In *Australia: Two Centuries of War and Peace*, edited by Michael McKernan and Margaret Browne, 338–365. Canberra: Australian War Memorial / Allen & Unwin, 1988.

Gilchrist, Roma Catherine. *Union of Australian Women: A History of the WA Branch*. Perth, WA: L.J. Fleay, n.d.
Gillett, Kevin. 'It's Time Now Gough', 21 October 2014. *Kevgillett.net*, http://www.kevgillett.net/?p=8550, accessed 15 July 2015.
Goot, Murray, and Rodney Tiffen. 'Public Opinion and the Politics of the Polls'. In *Australia's Vietnam*, edited by Peter King, 129–164. Sydney: Allen & Unwin, 1983.
Grey, Jeffrey. 'Getting Into the Books: Vietnam as history in Australia'. In *Vietnam: War, Myth and Memory*, edited by Jeffrey Grey and Jeff Doyle, 58–68. Sydney: Allen & Unwin, 1992.
Grey, Jeffrey. 'Memory and Public Myth'. In *Vietnam: War, Myth and Memory*, edited by Jeffrey Grey and Jeff Doyle, 137–154. Sydney: Allen & Unwin, 1992.
Grey, Jeffrey, and Jeff Doyle, eds. *Vietnam: War, Myth and Memory*. Sydney: Allen & Unwin, 1992.
Grieve, Norma, and Patricia Grimshaw, eds. *Australian Women: Feminist Perspectives*. Melbourne: Oxford University Press, 1981.
Guyatt, Chris. 'The Anti-Conscription Movement, 1964–1966'. In *Conscription in Australia*, edited by Roy Forward and Bob Reece, 178–190. St Lucia, Queensland: University of Queensland Press, 1968.
Hall, Simon. *Rethinking the American Anti-War Movement*. New York: Routledge, 2012.
Ham, Paul. *Vietnam: The Australian War*. Pymble, NSW: Harper Collins, 2008.
Hamel-Green, Michael. 'The Resisters: a history of the anti-conscription movement, 1964–1972.' In *Australia's Vietnam*, edited by Peter King, 100–128. Sydney: Allen & Unwin, 1983.
Heard, Barry. *Well Done, Those Men: Memoirs of a Vietnam Veteran*. Melbourne: Scribe, 2007.
Horne, Donald. *The Lucky Country: Australia in the Sixties*. Ringwood, Victoria: Penguin, 1964.
Horner, David. *The Spy Catchers. Volume I: The Official History of ASIO 1949–1963*. Crows Nest, NSW: Allen & Unwin, 2014.
Hyde, Michael. *All Along the Watchtower: Memoir of a Sixties Revolutionary*. Carlton North, Victoria: Vulgar Press, 2010.
Hyde, Michael. 'Getting Out of the Boat'. *Overland* 199 (June 2010): 10–17.
Hyde, Michael, ed. *It Is Right to Rebel*. Canberra: The Diplomat, 1972.
Inglis, K. S. 'Conscription in Peace and War, 1911–1945'. In *Conscription in Australia*, edited by Roy Forward and Bob Reece, 22–65. St Lucia, Queensland: University of Queensland Press, 1968.
Jauncey, Leslie C. *The Story of Conscription in Australia*. South Melbourne: Macmillan, 1968.
Jeffreys-Jones, Rhodri. *Peace Now! American Society and the Ending of the Vietnam War*. New Haven: Yale University Press, 1999.
Jordens, Ann-Mari. *Conscientious Objection and the Vietnam War*. Canberra: Peace Research Centre, Australian National University, 1989.
Jordens, Ann-Mari. 'Conscription and Dissent: the genesis of anti-war protest'. In *Vietnam Remembered*, edited by Gregory Pemberton, 60–81. Sydney: New Holland Publishers, 2009.

Kerby, Corinne. *Mainly Affirmative*. Melbourne: Georgian House, 1968.
King, Peter, ed. *Australia's Vietnam: Australia in the Second Indo-China War*. Sydney: Allen & Unwin, 1983.
Knopman, Debbie. *History of the Union of Australian Women, Eastern Suburbs Branch*. Sydney: UAW (NSW), 1995.
Krieger, David. 'The Another Mother for Peace Consumer Campaign: a campaign that failed'. *Journal of Peace Research* 8, no.2 (1971): 163–166.
Kruse, Darryn. 'The Vietnam Draft Registers in Victoria 1966–72'. BA (Hons) thesis, University of Melbourne, 1983.
Kuhn, Rick. 'The Australian Left, Nationalism and the Vietnam War'. *Labour History* 72 (May 1997): 163–84.
Lake, Marilyn. 'Women's Liberation', in *Australian Feminism: A Companion*, edited by Moira Gatens and Barbara Caine. Melbourne: Oxford University Press, 1998.
Lake, Marilyn, and Henry Reynolds, eds. *What's Wrong with ANZAC? The Militarisation of Australian History*. Sydney: University of New South Wales Press, 2010.
Landers, James. *The Weekly War: Newsmagazines and Vietnam*. Columbia: University of Missouri Press, 2004.
Lane, Don. *Trial and Error*. Brisbane: Boolarong Publications, 1993.
Laneyrie, Frances. 'Between Class and Gender: female activists in the Illawarra 1975–1980'. PhD thesis, Auckland University of Technology, 2010.
Langley, Greg. *A Decade of Dissent: Vietnam and the Conflict on the Australian Homefront*. Sydney: Allen & Unwin, 1992.
Lembcke, Jerry. *Hanoi Jane: War, Sex and Fantasies of Betrayal*. Amherst: University of Massachusetts Press, 2010.
Lembcke, Jerry. *The Spitting Image: Myth, Memory, and the Legacy of Vietnam*. New York: New York University Press, 1998.
Levi, Margaret. *Consent, Dissent, and Patriotism: Political Economy of Institutions and Decisions*. Cambridge: Cambridge University Press, 1997.
Levi, Margaret, and Stephen DeTray. *A Weapon Against War: Conscientious Objection in the US, Australia and France*. Canberra: Australian National University, 1992.
Lobl, Phyl. 'Tribute to a Rebel Girl'. *Australian Folk Songs*, http://folkstream.com/reviews/glen/, accessed 2 April 2015.
Lockhart, Greg. 'Into Battle: counter revolution'. In *Vietnam Remembered*, edited by Gregory Pemberton, 38–59. Sydney: New Holland Publishers, 2009.
Maddock, Kenneth. 'Opposing the War in Vietnam – the Australian Experience'. In *Vietnam and the Antiwar Movement: An International Perspective*, edited by John Dumbrell, 137–49. Aldershot, England: Avebury, 1989.
Maddock, Kenneth, and Barry Wright, eds. *War: Australia and Vietnam*. Sydney: Harper and Row, 1987.
Main, J. M., ed. *Conscription: The Australian Debate, 1901–1970*. Melbourne: Cassell, 1970.
McDonald, Audrey and Tom McDonald. *Intimate Union: Sharing a Revolutionary Life*. Annandale, NSW: Pluto Press, 1998.
McHugh, Siobhan. *Minefields and Miniskirts: Australian Women and the Vietnam War*. Sydney: Doubleday, 1993.

McIlroy, Jim. *The Red North: Queensland's History of Struggle*. Chippendale, NSW: Resistance Books, 2001.

McKernan, Michael, and Margaret Browne, eds. *Australia: Two Centuries of War and Peace*. Canberra: Australian War Memorial / Allen & Unwin, 1988.

McKnight, David. *Australia's Spies and their Secrets*. St Leonards, NSW: Allen & Unwin, 1994.

McLean, Jean. 'Anti-Vietnam War Activist'. In *Protesters*, edited by Gloria Frydman, 15–26. Blackburn, Victoria: Collins Dove, 1987.

McLean, Jean. 'My Life in a Distorting Mirror'. In *Dirty Secrets: Our ASIO File*, edited by Meredith Burgmann, 181–198. Sydney: NewSouth Publishing, 2014.

McLean, Rebecca. *S.O.S.* [documentary]. Canberra: Ronin Films, 1997.

Menghetti, Diane. *The Red North: The Popular Front in North Queensland*. Townsville: James Cook University, 1981.

Miller, Alan. *Fight Conscription*. Adelaide: Eureka Youth League, SA Section, n.d. [1950].

Miller, Beryl, and Susan Marsden. *Years of Struggle: Reminiscences of the Union of Australian Women in South Australia 1950–2005*. Adelaide: Union of Australian Women (SA), 2005.

Moore, Andrew. 'A Secret Policeman's Lot: the working life of Fred Longbottom and the New South Wales Police Special Branch'. In *All Our Labours: Oral Histories of Working Life in Twentieth Century Sydney*, edited by John Shields, 193–226. Sydney: University of New South Wales Press, 1992.

Moore, Eleanor. *The Quest for Peace As I have known It in Australia*. Melbourne: Wilke & Co., 1949.

Moravec, Michelle. 'Another Mother for Peace: reconsidering maternalistic peace rhetoric from an historical perspective, 1967–2007'. *Journal of the Motherhood Initiative* 1, no.1 (2010): 9–29.

Murphy, John. 'Breadwinning: accounts of work and family life in the 1950s'. *Labour and Industry*, 12, no.3 (2002): 59–75.

Murphy, John. *Harvest of Fear: A History of Australia's Vietnam War*. Sydney: Allen & Unwin, 1993.

Murphy, John. *Imagining the Fifties: Private Sentiment and Political Culture in Menzies' Australia*. Sydney: UNSW Press, 2000.

Murray, Suellen. 'Make Pies Not War: protests by the Women's Peace Movement of the 1980s'. *Australian Historical Studies* 37, no.127 (April 2006): 81–94.

Nathanson, Stephen. *Patriotism, Morality and Peace*. Lanham, MD: Rowman & Littlefield Publishers, 1993.

Nguyen, Thi Binh. *Family, Friends and Country: Autobiography*. Translated by Lady Borton. Hanoi, Vietnam: Tri Thuc Publishing House, 2013.

Nichols, David. 'Boiling in Anger: activist local newspapers of the 1960s and 1970s'. *History Australia* 2, no.2 (2005): 1–16.

Novak, Michael. 'Remembering 1968'. *National Review* 60, no.8 (5 May 2008): 50–54.

O'Brien, Phil. *Towards Peace – A Worker's Journey*. Brisbane: Social History of Australia Publishing Enterprise, 1992.

Ockenden, Julie. 'Anti-War Movement and the Student Revolt at Monash: an examination of contending ideologies 1967–70'. BA (Hons) thesis, Monash University, 1985.

Oliver, Bobbie. *The Perils of Ignoring History: 'Peace History' and Peace Research in Australia.* Canberra: Peace Research Centre, Australian National University, 1994.

Oppenheimer, Melanie. *Australian Women and War.* Woden, ACT: Dept. of Veterans' Affairs, 2008.

Oppenheimer, Melanie. *Volunteering: Why We Can't Live Without It.* Sydney: UNSW Press, 2008.

Ormonde, Paul. *A Foolish Passionate Man: A Biography of Jim Cairns.* Melbourne: Penguin, 1981.

Payne, Trish. *War and Words. The Australian Press and the Vietnam War.* Melbourne: Melbourne University Press, 2007.

Pemberton, Gregory. *All the Way: Australia's Road to Vietnam.* Sydney: Allen & Unwin, 1987.

Pemberton, Gregory, ed. *Vietnam Remembered.* Sydney: New Holland Publishers, 2009.

Pierce, Peter. '"Never Glad Confident Morning Again": Australia, the sixties and the Vietnam War'. In *Vietnam: War, Myth and Memory,* edited by Jeffrey Grey and Jeff Doyle, 69–80. Sydney: Allen & Unwin, 1992.

Pierce, Peter, Jeffery Grey and Jeff Doyle, eds. *Vietnam Days: Australia and the Impact of Vietnam.* Ringwood, Victoria: Penguin, 1991.

Prentice, James. 'Remembering the Brisbane Protests, 1965–72: the civil liberties movement'. *Queensland Review* 14, no.1 (2007): 25–37.

Prentice, James. 'The Brisbane Protests, 1965–72'. PhD thesis, Griffith University, 2005.

Pybus, Cassandra. *The Devil and James McAuley.* St Lucia, Queensland: University of Queensland Press, 1999.

Reynolds, Margaret. *Living Politics.* St Lucia, Queensland: University of Queensland Press, 2007.

Reynolds, Margaret. *The Last Bastion: Labor Women Working Towards Equality in the Parliaments of Australia.* Sydney: Business and Professional Publishing, 1995.

Ritchie, Donald A. *Doing Oral History: A Practical Guide.* Oxford: Oxford University Press, 2003.

Ruddick, Sara. *Maternal Thinking: Towards a Politics of Peace.* Boston: Beacon Press, 1989.

Russell, Lani. 'Today the Students, Tomorrow the Workers! Radical student politics and the Australian labour movement 1960–1972'. PhD thesis, University of Technology Sydney, 1999.

Saunders, Malcolm. 'Law and Order and the Anti-Vietnam War Movement: 1965–72'. *Australian Journal of Politics and History* 28, no.3 (1982): 367–379.

Saunders, Malcolm. 'Opposition to the Vietnam War in South Australia, 1965–73'. *Journal of the Historical Society of South Australia* 10 (1982): 61–71.

Saunders, Malcolm. *Quiet Dissenter: The Life and Thought of an Australian Pacifist, Eleanor May Moore 1875–1949.* Canberra: Peace Research Centre, Australian National University, 1993.

Saunders, Malcolm. 'The ALP's Response to the Anti-Vietnam War Movement: 1965–1973'. *Labour History* 44 (1983): 75–91.

Saunders, Malcolm. 'The Trade Unions in Australia and Opposition to Vietnam and Conscription: 1965–73'. *Labour History* 43 (November 1982): 64–82.

Saunders, Malcolm. 'Women On War'. *Peace Review* 5 (1993): 342–52.

Saunders, Malcolm. 'Youth and the Australian Peace Movement: a reply to Scott Poynting'. *Labour History* 57 (1989): 89–90.

Saunders, Malcolm and Ralph Summy. 'Odd Ones Out: the Australian section of the Women's International League for Peace and Freedom: 1919–41'. *Australian Journal of Politics and History* 40, no.1 (1994): 83–97.

Saunders, Malcolm, and Ralph Summy. *The Australian Peace Movement: A Short History*. Canberra: Peace Research Centre, Australian National University, 1986.

Sawer, Marian. *Making Women Count: A History of the Women's Electoral Lobby*. Sydney: University of New South Wales Press, 2008.

Scalmer, Sean. *Dissent Events: Protest, the Media and the Political Gimmick in Australia*. Sydney: University of New South Wales Press, 2002.

Scates, Bob. *'Draftmen Go Free': A History of the Anti-Conscription Movement in Australia*. Richmond, Victoria: R. Scates, 1988.

Sellars, Neal. *Fred Thompson, Communist, Union Organizer, Humanist: A Biography*. Townsville, Queensland: Neal Sellars, 2012.

Sheridan, Susan. *Who Was That Woman? The Australian Women's Weekly in the Postwar Years*. Sydney: University of New South Wales Press, 2002.

Shields, John. *All Our Labours: Oral Histories of Working Life in Twentieth Century Sydney*. Kensington, NSW: New South Wales University Press, 1992.

Shute, Carmel. 'Heroines and Heroes: sexual mythology in Australia 1914–18'. In *Gender and War*, edited by Joy Damousi and Marilyn Lake, 23–42. Cambridge: Cambridge University Press, 1995.

Simic, Zora. 'Butter Not Bombs: a short history of the Union of Australian Women'. *History Australia* 4, no.1 (2007): 1–15.

Siracusa, Joseph. *Through Thick and Thin: Anzus and the Origins of Australian and United States Involvement in Vietnam*. Armidale, NSW: University of New England, 2001.

Small, Melvin. 'Bring the Boys Home Now! Antiwar activism and withdrawal from Vietnam and Iraq'. *Diplomatic History* 34, no.3 (2010): 543–553.

Smith, F. B. *The Conscription Plebiscites in Australia, 1916–17*. North Melbourne: Victorian Historical Association, 1974.

Stevens, Rachel. 'Captured by Kindness: Australian press representations of the Vietnam War, 1965–1970'. *History Australia* 3, no.2 (2006): 1–17.

Stone, Gerald. *War Without Honour*. Brisbane: Jacaranda Press, 1966.

Stur, Heather Marie. *Beyond Combat: Women and Gender in the Vietnam War Era*. New York: Cambridge University Press, 2011.

Summers, Anne. *Damned Whores and God's Police*. Melbourne: Penguin, 1994.

Summy, Ralph. 'A Reply to Fred Wells'. In *Conscription in Australia*, edited by Roy Forward and Bob Reece, 200–222. St Lucia, Queensland: University of Queensland Press, 1968.

Select Bibliography

Summy, Ralph. 'Australian Peace Movement 1960–67: a study of dissent'. MA thesis, University of Sydney, 1971.

Summy, Ralph. 'Militancy and the Australian Peace Movement, 1960–67'. *Politics* 5, no.2 (1970): 148–162.

Swerdlow, Amy. *Women Strike For Peace: Traditional Motherhood and Radical Politics in the 1960s*. Chicago: University of Chicago Press, 1993.

Symons, Beverley, and Rowan Cahill, eds. *A Turbulent Decade: Social Protest Movements and the Labour Movement 1965–1975*. Newtown, NSW: Australian Society for the Study of Labour History (Sydney branch), 2005.

Teichmann, Max. 'The Cut-Lunch Commandos'. *Quadrant* 52, no.4 (2008): 72–74.

Thomas, Nick. 'Protests Against the Vietnam War in 1960s Britain: the relationship between protestors and the press'. *Contemporary British History* 22, no.3 (2008): 335–54.

Tiffen, Rodney. 'News Coverage of Vietnam'. In *Australia's Vietnam*, edited by Peter King, 165–187. Sydney: Allen & Unwin, 1983.

Tubbs, Michael. *ASIO: The Enemy Within*. Croyden Park, NSW: Michael Tubbs, 2008.

Vallentine, Jo, and Peter D. Jones. *Quakers in Politics: Pragmatism or Principle*. Alderley, Queensland: The Religious Society of Friends, 1990.

Walker, Bertha. *How to Defeat Conscription: A Story of the 1916 and 1917 Campaigns in Victoria*. Northcote, Victoria: Anti Conscription Jubilee Committee, 1968.

Wells, Fred. 'A Comment on Mr Guyatt's Chapter'. In *Conscription in Australia*, edited by Roy Forward and Bob Reece, 191–199. St Lucia, Queensland: University of Queensland Press, 1968.

Wells, Tom. *The War Within: America's Battle Over Vietnam*. Berkeley, CA: University of California Press, 1994.

Whitrod, Ray. *Before I Sleep: Memoirs of a Modern Police Commissioner*. St Lucia, Queensland: University of Queensland Press, 2001.

Wilson, Fiona. 'Women in the Anti-Vietnam War, Anti-Conscription Movement in Sydney 1964–1972'. BA (Hons) thesis, University of New South Wales, 1985.

Windschuttle, Elizabeth. *Women, Class and History: Feminist Perspectives on Australia, 1788–1978*. Sydney: Fontana/Collins, 1980.

York, Barry. 'Politics, Students and Dissent: Melbourne, 1966–1972'. *Journal of Australian Studies* 14 (1984): 58–76.

York, Barry. *Student Revolt: La Trobe University 1967–1973*. Campbell, ACT: Nicholas Press, 1989.

Young, Marilyn B., and Robert Buzzanco, eds. *A Companion to the Vietnam War*. Malden, MA: Blackwell Publishing, 2002.

Young, Pam. *Daring to Take a Stand: The Story of the Union of Australian Women in Queensland*. Wavell Heights, Queensland: Pam Young, 1998.

Zurbo, Sandra, ed. *Stories of Her Life: An Anthology of Short Stories by Australian Women*. Collingwood, Victoria: Outback Press, 1979.

INDEX

A

Abbott, Tony 272
Abolish Conscription Campaign 181
abortion 220, 275
Abraham, Shirley 31
Abraham, Vivienne 29, 30, 64, 69
Addams, Jane 10
Adelaide Airport protest 101
Agent Orange 265
Albury 149, 151, 182, 183, 214
Anderson, Joan 125
Anglican Church 38, 95, 237
Another Woman for Peace 271
Ames, Vilma 75, 76, 119, 121, 125, 126
arms race xx, 12, 32, 60, 61, 188, 192, 12
Armstrong, Pauline xiv, xxvi, 122, 266
Ashcroft, Patricia 49, 53, 56, 57, 63, 68, 69, 71, 73, 76, 84, 93, 97, 105, 110, 134, 141, 142, 143, 145, 205, 206, 260, 269
Askin, Robert 233, 237
Association for International Co-operation and Disarmament 32, 56, 57, 61, 62, 63, 96, 99, 271
Aston, William viii, x
Australia-Vietnam Association 271
Australian Broadcasting Corporation 41, 42, 43, 83, 151, 168, 195, 205, 229, 236, 242, 253
Australian Freedom League 3
Australian Labor Party (ALP) 14, 35-6, 39, 44, 51, 56, 59, 60, 64, 81, 82, 87, 89, 91, 93, 95, 99, 119, 120, 126, 148, 154, 156, 222, 236, 237, 251, 252, 254, 272, 273, 274
Australian National University 141
Australian Peace Council 15, 30
Australian Security Intelligence Organisation (ASIO)
  activities xvi, 81, 83, 86, 229
  agents and informants xxv, 55, 65, 68, 102, 110, 115

  on SOS groups 69, 96, 101, 109, 111, 112, 113, 114, 149
  on SOS members 47, 54, 56, 57, 58, 60, 62, 63, 67, 90, 97, 206, 207
  use of files xxvi, xxiv, xxv, 22, 53, 86
Australian Women's Weekly 41, 81, 209
Avendon, Barbara 191

B

Bacall, Lauren 191
Baez, Joan 179
Balch, Emily Greene 10
Bandler, Faith 51, 58
Barber, Nola 35, 119, 121, 212, 213
Barbour, Peter 274
Baxendell, Margaret 82, 83
Bendick, Dorothy 56, 57-9, 63, 136
Binh, Madame 193, 197, 264, 265
Bissett, Bob 246
Bloom, Isabel 15
Boardman, Beryl 109, 113
Boddy, Margaret 37
Bolte, Henry 225, 239
Bonner, Jean 23, 204
Bowen, Sally 99
'boy conscription' 2-3
Brisbane SOS (also known as Queensland SOS) xvii, xvi, xvii, 25, 29, 79-86, 131, 134, 135, 136, 145, 146, 147, 159, 160-3, 167, 247
Brown, Freda 66, 67, 69, 196
Brunker, Ethnee 90
Bryant, Gordon 148
Bury, Leslie 154
By-law 418 campaign 166-70, 195, 263, 266

C

Cairns, Ceci 171, 179, 246, 272
Cairns, Jim xix, xxv, 143, 168, 222, 224, 225, 226, 227, 228, 229, 237, 239, 249, 262, 263
Calwell, Arthur 51, 87, 138, 144, 156, 159

328

INDEX

Canada 117, 194, 195
Campaign for International Co-operation and Disarmament 169, 221, 224, 227, 266
Campaign for Peace in Vietnam 106, 107
Caravan Against Conscription 181-3
Cass, Moss 119
Cass, Shirley 119, 125, 126
Cathie, Chris 125, 188, 206, 207, 235, 238, 239, 271, 272
Catholic Church 32, 37, 38, 39, 40, 44, 89, 90, 202, 203, 237, 241
'chain gang' protest ix, 99, 189, 219, 228-9
Chalmers, Norma 80, 81, 83, 160, 182
Chifley government 12
child care 51, 220
China 43, 52, 59, 61, 63
Chipp, Don 148, 252, 254
Christian Women Concerned 38, 271
Christofides, Helen xiii, xxix, 33, 34, 199, 229
Christofides, Louis xiii, xxix, 34, 174, 175, 199, 229, 259, 267
civil disobedience xvi, 6, 9, 158, 163, 165, 166, 170, 172, 173, 187, 219, 229, 268
civil liberties 158, 160, 161, 167, 171, 237, 263
Clarke, William 109, 111, 114, 115, 116
Clements, Harold 109
Clift, Charmian 193
Coal miners' strike (of 1949) 51, 99
Cold War xv, xxiii, 2, 12, 30, 87, 192
Cole, Candy 45, 48, 67, 72, 73, 203, 209, 270
Collie, Elsie 109
Collie, Ray 109, 110, 113, 115, 140
Committee for the Abolition of Political Police 274
Committee in Defiance of the National Service Act 184
Commonwealth Defence Act 3, 11
Commonwealth Police xvi, 196, 229, 246, 253, 263, 267
Communist Party of Australia (CPA) xxv, 12, 32, 33, 36, 46, 50, 51, 52, 53, 56, 57, 58, 61, 63, 68, 69 81, 88, 89, 90, 91, 99, 108-9, 112-4

Connors, Rex 98
conscientious objectors
 individuals 33, 82, 98, 117, 181, 188
 SOS support for 82, 104, 106, 126, 146-7, 172, 177-8, 185, 188, 235, 245, 259, 261
 tactics 31, 61, 80, 83, 64, 138, 172, 177
 see also Brian King, Brian Ross, Bill White, John Zarb, court cases
Conscientious Objectors' Advisory Group 107
conscription see 'boy conscription', national service
conscription referenda WWI 7-10, 11, 96
Cook, Maureen 102
Cora, Dorothy 54
Cornell, Mollie 37
counselling services 132, 176, 259, 261, 270
court cases
 for conscientious objectors & draft resisters 175, 178, 245, 252-3, 155
 for SOS women 84, 100, 105, 138-40, 162, 163, 167, 174, 179-80, 212, 235-6, 240
 SOS support for 31, 80, 104, 123, 147, 178, 185, 261, 275
 see also High Court challenge
Coxsedge, Joan
 arrest 168, 235
 background 123
 Fairlea Five 235-6, 239, 262
 family 201, 203, 204, 207, 246
 moratorium role 222, 224, 227
 on SOS protests 180, 206
 on SOS radicalisation 187-8
 post SOS 270, 271, 274-5
 SOS Victoria committee 122, 124-135, 231, 251, 269, 244
 Vietnam visit 265
Crimes Act 159, 172, 173, 185, 234, 243, 250
Cuban missile crisis 13
Cullen, Edna 23, 93, 94, 95, 96, 222
Curthoys, Ann xiv, xxi, 269
Curtin, John 9, 11

329

D

Dalton, Dorothy 33, 202, 211, 222, 230, 245, 251, 272
Dalton, Les 33
Dalton, Tony 33, 241, 245
Davenport, Nancy 97, 98
Davies, Joan xviii, xxix, 114, 139-140, 222
Davies, Lloyd 114
Davies, Shelley 139, 140
Deakin, Elizabeth 25
Dean, David 25
Dean, Hazel 25-6
Decker, Joy 56, 58-9, 63
Decker, Philip 58, 59
Defence Forces Protection Act 197
Defence Legislation Amendment Act 276
Democratic Labor Party 148
demonstrations 30, 42, 62, 80, 82, 96, 114, 132, 136, 138, 140, 141, 147, 155, 161-2, 164, 171, 175, 186, 204, 220, 261, 263, 265, 267, 270
Department of Labour and National Service 229, 230, 235, 240
Doyle, Jan 90
Draft Resisters' Union 234, 241
Duncan, Peter 276
Dunstan, Don 232

E

East Timor 276
education 146, 155, 249
Edwards, Dot 102
Edwards, Peter 258
elections xviii, 17, 249
    1966 federal election 37, 115, 132, 153-7, 158
    1969 federal election 184-9
    1972 federal election 220, 243, 250, 252-6, 257, 262
environment movement xv, xxviii, 14, 250, 271
equal pay 14, 43
Eureka Youth League xxvi, 61
Evatt, H.V. 51

F

Fairlea Five x, 206, 234-40, 262, 265
Fairlea women's prison x, 235, 262
'falsies' 229-30
Federal Pacifist Council 13, 31, 37, 64, 271
feminism xix, 43, 212, 220, 263
Fisher, Lorna 152
Fitzgerald, Rose 76, 142, 143
Fonda, Jane 197
Forbes, Jim 46, 62, 140
Foster, Norm ix
Foster, Sue 48, 204
Fraser, Malcolm 221
Frazer, Margaret 15, 16
Freedom Ride 41, 181
fundraising xiii, xxviii, 87, 115, 123, 125, 127, 133, 170-1, 185, 193, 221, 233, 241, 246, 265

G

Garber, Flo x, xxix, 99, 100, 174, 175, 212, 219, 222, 228, 229, 240, 272
Garland, Winifred 56, 60, 63
gay rights xv, 220
Gerrard, Chris 174
Gibbs, Pearl 51
Gibson, Dorothy 29-30, 118, 125, 222, 224
Gibson, Ralph 30, 224
Gilchrist, Roma 108
Gillett, Kevin 267
Gilling, Jeremy 173
Goldbloom, Sam 227, 228, 266
Goldstein, Vida 6, 7, 9
Golgerth, Joyce
    ASIO 47, 55, 62, 65
    background 47-8, xxvi
    criticism 209, 216
    defence of SOS 49, 50, 72, 214
    family xi, xxvi, 45, 48, 204, 209, 260
    leadership xi, 46-9, 52-6, 63, 67-8, 269
    on conscription 45, 48, 63, 71
    post SOS 270
Golgerth, Michael xi, xxvi, 45, 47, 48, 204, 260, 270
Gorton, John ix, 184, 225
Gough, Hugh 38
Graham, Billy xiii, 180
Greenwood, Irene 111

INDEX

Greenwood, Ivor 251
Gregory, Ann 56, 60-2, 68
Gregory, Mark 61, 62
Gudgeon, Edna
  arrest 100, 174, 212,
  background 33, 34, 40, 99, 185, 222
  husband 99, 100, 205, 241
  post SOS 270
  SOS activities viii, x, xxix, 174-5, 188
Gudgeon, Mac 31, 101, 174, 245, 257, 259, 267, 270

H
Hamel-Green, Michael 246
Hammerly, Alice 125
Hardy, Esme 39, 40, 89, 90, 202, 203, 273
Hardy, Henry 39, 202
Hardy, Thomas 202, 203
Harris, Betty 160
Hasluck, Paul 16
Haylen, Les 51, 64
Haylen, Wayne 64, 138, 147
Helsinki 193
Henderson, Marion 29, 108, 109, 111, 112, 113, 115, 117, 193, 222
Hewett, Noreen
  background 33, 50-2, 50, 67
  defence of SOS 200, 213
  founding of SOS 50, 53-6, 69
  post SOS 273, 52
  son 33, 51, 52, 176, 181
  SOS activities 44, 57, 64, 68, 70, 73, 97, 98, 181, 182, 136, 268
  UAW 29, 5, 53
Heyde, Lilli 232, 233
High Court challenge 145-7
Hill, Joan 90
Hiroshima Day 93, 135
Hoare, Clair 101, 102
Hoare, Hazel 101, 104, 105
Hobson, Roy 95-6
Holding, Clyde 243
Holmes, Margaret 1, 13, 38
Holmgrem, Lavina 117
Holt, Harold xviii, 14, 37, 51, 83, 85, 110, 111, 139, 144, 145, 155, 156
Howard, John 276

Howe, Valerie 103
Hughes, William 3, 4

I
Indigenous issues 14, 31, 36, 40, 51, 181, 271, 273
International Women's Day 14
Iron Curtain 13, 18
  see also Cold War

J
Jack, Hazel 90
Jack, Ken 260
James, Albert 95
James, Merle 112
Jamieson, Gordon 82, 83, 86, 201
Jamieson, Shirley 82, 83, 201
Jensen, Nadine 139
John, Cecilia 6
Johnson, Les 144
Johnson, Lyndon B. 136, 138, 180
Johnston, Barry 252-4
Jones, Elizabeth 33, 212
Jones, Michael 173

K
Kane, Jim 109, 113, 116, 117
Keady, Edward 109
Keating government 276
Keeffe, Sheila 90
Kelly, Audrey 98
Kennedy, Graham 183
Kennedy, John F. xx, 192
Kent State University 225
Kerby, Corinne 41-2, 120, 151, 168, 169, 171, 205, 206, 269
Kirkpatrick, Daisy 176, 177
Ky, Ngyuen Cao 135, 159, 160, 161

L
Lake, Marilyn 220
Lane, Terry 168
Larsson, Stanley Gordon ix, x
Lee, Margaret 49, 56, 62, 64
legal aid 80, 132, 146, 176
Leslie, Bill 64
Liberal Party 14, 17, 21, 36, 37, 44, 105, 126, 142, 143, 148, 153, 154, 214, 230, 272

Little, Jack 148
Lloyd, A. J. 169
Lloyd, John 227
Lockwood, Terence 109, 115, 117
London Peace Society 4
Long Bay Gaol viii, 173
Longbottom, Fred 206
Lynch, Phillip 248

M

Macdonald, Molly 82
MacLaine-Cross, Jo 125, 143, 166, 167, 222, 235, 239
Marrickville Army Barracks xv, 46, 67, 134
Mason, Miriam 120
maternal peace activism 122, 220
May Day 135
McArthur, Isobel 25, 76, 93, 94, 95
McCormick, Edward 168
McCulloch, Sue 234, 241, 265
McCutcheon, Mary 125
McDonald, Noreen 38
McFarland, Tony 176
McGuinness, Shirley 109
McHugh, Siobhan xiv, 53
McLean, Jean
   arrest 251
   background xxvi, 120-1
   'Fairlea Five' 235-40, 262
   founding of Victorian SOS 76, 118-27
   leadership 100, 120, 125, 185, 215
   moratoriums 222-5, 266
   overseas visits 193-8
   post SOS 270-1, 273
   reflections on SOS 209, 263, 264, 276
   SOS protests 100, 44, 165, 180
   underground 242, 246, 259, 261
McMahon, William 255, 258, 262
media xvi, 13, 42, 43, 47, 54, 64, 67, 70, 83, 88, 92, 94, 119, 120, 137, 149, 155, 162, 168, 196, 198, 213, 230, 237, 241, 245, 253, 262, 265
Melbourne City Council 166, 168, 169, 264
Melbourne Cup xiii, 63, 178, 187

Menzies, Robert xi, xii, xvii, 1, 2, 10, 11, 12, 13, 16, 17, 23, 27, 45, 83, 104, 121, 141, 142, 143, 163, 211, 255
Methodists 37, 44, 95, 168, 237
Miller, Beryl 102
Miller, Bill 236, 238
Miller, Irene 28, 125, 131, 134, 135, 156, 158, 170, 180, 187, 203, 209, 225, 230, 234, 235, 236, 238, 271, 272
Monash University 122, 148, 165
Moore, Eleanor 5, 10
moratoriums 184, 188, 219, 221-33, 246-7, 258, 265, 266, 267, 275
Mother's Day 151, 191, 222, 223, 227
motherhood xx, 7, 9, 14, 210, 238, 263, 266
'Mothers in mourning' cartoon 223
Mulheron, Maurie xv, xxiv, 32, 70, 154, 156, 171, 177, 181, 182, 183, 193, 203, 207, 270
Mulheron, Nora xxiv, xxix, 29, 32, 100, 148, 177, 181, 192, 193, 203, 207, 260, 270, 271
music (anti-war music, folk songs) xii, 42-3, 122, 152-3, 144, 179
My Lai massacre 231

N

National Civic Council 39
National Council of Women 5, 8
National Front for the Liberation of South Vietnam 194, 196, 233, 264
National Service Act 37, 71, 145, 146, 173, 177, 184, 185, 188, 219, 222, 233, 241, 255, 256, 260
National Service Scheme 12, 16, 23
National Service Termination Bill 255
New Housewives' Association 14
New Zealand 192, 194, 241
Newcastle SOS 23, 78, 92-6, 141, 145, 150, 160, 175, 222, 233, 269
Nicklin government 161
Nixon, Richard 184
Noack, Errol 136
Noonuccal, Oodgeroo 51
Norris, Terry 168
North Vietnam 182, 193, 194, 195, 196, 197

INDEX

Northern Territory 76
nuclear disarmament *see* arms race

O

Oakleigh Moratorium Committee 224
O'Brien, Peter 246, 263, 267
opinion polls xv, 3, 12, 23, 118, 153, 156, 184, 258, 262
oral history xxiv, xxvi, xxvii, 258
Ormonde, Paul 227
O'Sullivan, Ruby 29, 45, 53, 56, 63-4, 69, 193
Outhred, Alan 181
Outhred, Ella 40-1, 146, 147, 176, 181, 183, 185, 222, 255, 260, 266
Outhred, Hugh 41, 176, 266
Outhred, Ken 40

P

pacifism 11, 13, 18, 22, 29, 31, 37, 64, 82, 90, 94, 147, 177, 213, 271
Pankhurst, Adela 6
Pankhurst, Emmeline 6
Paris 193, 194, 195, 196, 197, 264
Parkes 182, 184
Paterson, Fred 88
Paxton 82
Peacemaker 31, 58, 64
Peacock, Andrew ix
Pentridge prison 252, 255
Perkins, Charlie 41
Pert, Adele 85, 96, 139, 153, 162, 185, 208, 213, 227, 251
Perth Airport protest xviii, 139
petitions xii, 70, 80, 108, 132, 144,
Pettett, Richard 98
Pettigrew, Elsie 163
Petty, Bruce 223
Phillips, Nancy 89
poetry 9, 150-2,
Port Kembla 174, 246
Post, Lydia 28
Potticary, Audrey 102, 103, 104, 106, 107, 232
Prasser, Vince 90
Presbyterian church 121
Primmer, Cyril 251
propaganda 4, 9, 17, 223

Provisional Revolutionary Government 196, 264, 271
Pugh, Clifton 123, 171, 230

Q

Quakers 3, 13, 31, 37, 44, 79, 81, 82
    see also Religious Society of Friends
Queensland Peace Committee 80, 83, 84, 85, 86, 160
Queensland SOS *see* Brisbane SOS
Queensland Trades and Labour Council 82

R

Reed, Donna 191
Reid, Val 36, 38, 149, 150, 151,
religion 3, 68, 94, 108, 181
    see also Anglican, Catholic Church, Quakers
Religious Society of Friends 13, 81
    see also Quakers
Returned and Services League 26, 97, 135, 182, 201, 205, 232
Reynolds, Debbie 191
Reynolds, Henry 87, 210
Reynolds, Margaret xxv, 86-92, 144, 149, 201, 210, 270, 273
Richards, Jean 37,
Richmond Barracks 75
Robinson, Barry 64, 138
Rose, Peggy 24
Ross, Brian 242, 243
Ross, Joan 83, 147
Royal Commission (SA) 232
Rudd, Kevin 272

S

Santamaria, B.A 39, 120
Save Our Sons' delegations to Canberra 46, 62, 84, 122, 126, 140-44, 187
Save Our Sons' statement of aims xii, 70, 71, 79, 89, 94, 104, 112, 121, 127
Scates, Bob 243, 246, 255
Scaysbrook, Alma 40, 226, 227, 250, 255, 257, 258, 261, 269, 271
Send Our Sons Committee 210
Shute, Carmel 7

silent vigils 79, 80, 91, 96, 104, 132
Simes, D. J. 36, 37
Sisterhood of International Peace xx, 4-5, 10
Smale, Mary 100
Smith, Ian 239
Snedden, Billy 22,
socialism 15, 35, 113, 121, 164, 274
South African Rugby Union team tour 247
South Australia SOS xvii, 46, 76, 101-7, 136, 145, 157, 180, 222, 223, 226, 232, 233, 237, 249
South Coast Citizens Against Conscription 99, 175, 229, 250
South Coast Waterside Workers' Women's Committee 97, 99
South Vietnam 17, 135, 159, 194, 271
Southeast Asia Treaty Organization (SEATO) 192
Spanish Civil War 32
Spock, Benjamin 247
Sticklan, Mary 125
Stimpson, Catharine R. 192
strikes xiii, 36, 51, 90, 99, 158
Strong, Charles 5
student protests xii, xxi, xxiii, xxvi, 141, 161, 164, 166-70, 231
Summary Offences Act 235, 240
surveillance xvi, xxv, 113, 200, 206-7, 215, 246, 274
Swan Street army barracks 30, 75, 164
Sydney SOS
    activities 138, 139, 145-6, 160, 172, 180-4, 222, 226-7, 250, 252, 255
    criticism of 65, 69, 200, 210-12, 214-15
    end of 270-1, 276
    founding 4, 46-73
    links with other SOS groups 76, 77-86, 97-8, 112, 127-8, 152, 192, 240
    links with UAW xxi
    membership 23, 174, 249
    newsletters 161, 173, 223, 231, 247
    police 232, 245
    see also individual members including Patricia Ashcroft, Joyce Golgerth, Noreen Hewett, Nora Mulheron, Ella Outhred

T

Tapp, Eulalie 106
Tasmania xii, 14, 76, 77, 87, 88, 194, 241
tax xiii, 158, 179, 180
teach-ins 148
Teichmann, Max 148, 165
Thompson, Fred 36
Thompson, Loma 29, 36, 89, 90, 273
Thorp, Albert 109, 113
Thorp, Margaret 7, 109
Timms, Eleanor 90
Tomasetti, Glenys 41, 42-3, 92, 122, 125, 152, 153, 155, 179, 187
Tonkin, John 247
Townsend, Simon 181, 182
Townsend, Stephen 173
Townsville Peace Committee 87, 89, 91
Townsville Save Our Sons xii, xvii, xxiv, xxv, 29, 36, 39, 46, 76, 77, 78, 79, 86-92, 144, 149, 187, 201, 202, 210, 260, 273
Townsville Trades and Labor Council 91
trade unions 36, 59, 60, 63, 73, 79, 81, 88, 91, 94, 98, 99, 115, 162, 167, 169, 170, 171, 184, 200, 205, 222, 229, 236, 267
Traffic Act 161-3

U

Underground movement 100, 219, 234, 240-7, 252, 253, 254, 265
Union of Australian Women xx, xxiv, xxvi, 9, 13-15, 29, 35, 46, 49, 50, 53-9, 65-9, 73, 76, 80, 97, 102-4, 107-15, 136, 190, 196
United States xx, 37, 58, 194, 191, 194, 195, 222, 231, 247, 258, 264
United States Consulate 165, 234
University of Melbourne 43
University of Sydney 35, 62, 70, 181
University of Queensland 161

V

van Moorst, Harry 196
Victoria Barracks 166
Victoria SOS
    activities 222, 245, 260, 143-4, 158, 163-71
    elections 145, 154-5
    founding of 119-127
    leadership xvi, 124, 234
    membership 204
    newsletters 231, 256
    see also individual members including Joan Coxsedge, Jean Mclean, Irene Miller
Victorian Legislative Council 273, 275
Viet Cong 196, 233
Vietnam Action Committee 109, 114, 116
Vietnam Moratorium Campaign 117, 222
Vietnam Objectors' Campaign 116, 117
Vietnamese children 41, 140, 151, 171, 194
volunteering xxviii, 32, 36, 39, 48, 240, 275
Vroland, Anna 119

W

Wagga Wagga 182, 183
Wake, Nancy xxii, 214-15
Walsh, Nance 118, 125
War Precautions Act 6
war toys 58, 136-7
Ward, Vilma xvi, 29, 76, 79, 80, 83, 85, 86, 131, 137, 147, 160, 162, 187, 207, 272
Wearne, John 111, 113, 117
Wearne, Kathleen 109
Wearne, Stuart 113, 117
Webb, Shirley 90
Western Australia SOS xxv, xvii, xviii, 46, 77, 78, 107-117, 134, 139-40, 159, 149, 187, 222
Wharton, May 104, 105, 157
White, Bill 155-6
White, Isobel 156
Whitlam, Gough xii, xviii, 107, 184, 250, 253, 254, 255, 267, 276

Wilding, Gillian 44, 100
Williamson, David 255
Wilson, Dolores 113
Wollongong Moratorium Committee 28
Wollongong Railway Station 98, 175
Wollongong SOS 44, 97-101, 143, 151, 174, 187, 212, 228, 229
Woman Voter 6
Woman's Christian Temperance Union 3, 12, 104
Women Strike for Peace xx, 190-2
Women's Electoral Lobby 220
Women's International Democratic Federation 51, 52
Women's International League for Peace and Freedom xx, 2, 10-11, 12, 13, 16, 17, 18, 29, 31, 57, 79, 82, 101, 105, 111, 118, 119, 190, 223, 271
women's liberation xix, xxi, 210, 249, 269
Women's Peace Army xx, 4, 5-7, 9, 10, 12
Woodbury, Stan 229
Woodhams, Mary 109
Woodward, Joanne 191
World Congress of Women 193
World War I xix, xx, xxii, xxix, 2, 3-9, 10, 15, 17, 18, 26, 27, 29, 50, 152, 267
World War II xxii, 11-12, 13, 24, 25, 26, 27, 28, 31, 37, 42, 51, 62, 70, 82, 88, 90, 93, 95, 141, 205, 213, 214, 215, 223, 239

Y

York, Barry 266
Young Labor Association 164
Young Liberals 221
Young, Pam 161
Youth Campaign Against Conscription 59, 114, 138, 156, 164

Z

Zarb, John 178

ACKNOWLEDGEMENTS

Many people helped shape this project and I am indebted to those who generously gave their time to be interviewed or shared material over the years. I am especially grateful to Maurie Mulheron for giving me permission to examine the SOS collection at the National Library of Australia (NLA) and for sharing his memories of his amazing mother, Nora. I also sincerely thank Louis Christofides, Candy Cole, Joan Coxsedge, Shelley Davies, Sue Foster, Michael Golgerth, Mark Gregory, Mac Gudgeon, Tom Hardy, Ken Jack, Vern Jack, Gordon Jamieson, Jean McLean, Beryl Miller, Irene Miller, Bill Miller, Alan Outhred, Hugh Outhred, Robert Outhred, Lee Pinch, Vince Prasser, Margaret Reynolds, Joan Ross, Loma Thompson and Stuart Wearne for sharing their stories and archival material with me.

My heartfelt thanks go to Paul Sendziuk, who oversaw the first version of this project at the University of Adelaide and encouraged me to tell the wider story of 'those women with banners'. I am also grateful to Melanie Oppenheimer, Rob Foster, Claire Walker, Vesna Drapac, Christina Twomey, Al Thomson, Margaret Hosking, Skye Krichauff and Mike Harding for their feedback and support, and to all those who have provided assistance with accessing collections and photographs in libraries around Australia. Special thanks also to Joanne Mullins and Sam van der Plank at Monash University Press, and to Katie Connolly, for her keen eye and careful copyediting. I also gratefully acknowledge the support I have received in the form of an ECR publication grant from the International Australian Studies Association (InASA).

Acknowledgements

Everyone needs good friends in their corner. Thank you Lois Logan for housing and feeding me during research trips to Canberra and for brightening my days with your postcards; Murray and Anne Ness for coffee and generous technological support; and Annmarie Reid for keeping me laughing and company in 'Finland, Finland, Finland'. Finally, thank you Roy, Bronte and Jack for sharing me with this project for so many years; I could not have done it without your love and support.

ABOUT THE AUTHOR

Dr Carolyn Collins is a Research Fellow in the Department of History at the University of Adelaide where she completed an Arts degree, majoring in History and Classics, and, later, an Honours degree in US History. Her doctoral thesis was awarded the University Doctoral Research Medal. She has been a journalist for state and national newspapers, a magazine columnist and communications manager, and is the co-author (with Roy Eccleston) of *Trailblazers: 100 Inspiring South Australian Women*, and co-editor (with Paul Sendziuk) of *Foundational Fictions in South Australian History*.